This is a terrific book—smart, provocative, engaging, and clearly written. It offers a memorable set of readings for students and scholars alike. Each chapter is a gem of organization, integration, and argument. Trend's essays lead the reader through a maze of countervailing theories and positions leaving them with a much stronger sense of the complexity of our present time. Trend's book is less about critique (though the critique is powerful) and more about a kind of hope that is restrained yet feasible.

Richard A. Quantz, Professor, Miami University

Trend is a lucid writer able to unmask the internal contractions of the neoliberal order with theoretical and conceptual clarity, as he writes with urgency to make sense of a fractured America in a changing world economy.

Rodolfo D. Torres, Professor, University of California, Irvine, and former Adam Smith Fellow, University of Glasgow

Elsewhere in America offers a prescient, non-dialectical approach to alterity, deftly revealing the hidden paradoxes inherent to so-called positions of "center" and "margin" within current media-driven polemics. Skirting binary logic, Trend offers a series of daring new formulations for hybrid positionalities—neither utopian nor dystopian—that afford theory to be transposed effectively into practice. *Elsewhere in America* will sit on my bookshelf along side Chantal Mouffe and Henry A. Giroux as an invaluable go-to source for artists and writers rethinking democracy in this age of political extremism.

Juli Carson, Professor, Univesity of California, Irvine

ELSEWHERE IN AMERICA

Americans think of their country as a welcoming place where everyone has equal opportunity. Yet historical baggage and anxious times can restrain these possibilities. Newcomers often find that civic belonging comes with strings attached—riddled with limitations or legally punitive rites of passage. For those already here, new challenges to civic belonging emerge on the basis of belief, behavior, or heritage. This book uses the term "elsewhere" in describing conditions that exile so many citizens to "some other place" through prejudice, competition, or discordant belief. Yet in another way, "elsewhere" evokes an undefined "not yet" ripe with potential. In the face of America's daunting challenges, can "elsewhere" point to optimism, hope, and common purpose?

Through 12 detailed chapters, the book applies critical theory in the humanities and social sciences to examine recurring crises of social inclusion in the U.S. After two centuries of incremental "progress" in securing human dignity, today the U.S. finds itself torn by new conflicts over reproductive rights, immigration, health care, religious extremism, sexual orientation, mental illness, and fear of terrorists. Is there a way of explaining this recurring tendency of Americans to turn against each other? *Elsewhere in America* engages these questions, charting the ever-changing faces of difference (manifest in contested landscapes of sex and race to such areas as disability and mental health), their spectral and intersectional character (recent discourses on performativity, normativity, and queer theory), and the grounds on which categories are manifest in ideation and movement politics (metapolitics, cosmopolitanism, dismodernism).

David Trend is Chair of the Department of Art at the University of California, Irvine. He holds a PhD in Curriculum Theory and an MFA in Visual Studies. His books include *Worlding: Identity, Media, and Imagination in a Digital Age* (2013), *The End of Reading* (2010), *A Culture Divided* (2009), *Everyday Culture* (2008), and *The Myth of Media Violence* (2007), among others. Honored as a Getty Scholar, Trend is the author of over 200 essays and a former editor of the journals *Afterimage* and *Socialist Review*. He lives in Los Angeles, California.

CRITICAL INTERVENTIONS

Politics, Culture, and the Promise of Democracy

Edited by Henry A. Giroux, Susan Searls Giroux, and Kenneth J. Saltman

Twilight of the Social: Resurgent Publics in the Age of Disposability
By Henry A. Giroux (2011)

Youth in Revolt: Reclaiming a Democratic Future
By Henry A. Giroux (2012)

The Failure of Corporate School Reform
By Kenneth J. Saltman (2012)

Toward a New Common School Movement
By Noah De Lissovoy, Alexander J. Means, and Kenneth J. Saltman (2015)

The Great Inequality
By Michael D. Yates (2016)

Elsewhere in America: The Crisis of Belonging in Contemporary Culture
By David Trend (2016)

ELSEWHERE IN AMERICA

The Crisis of Belonging in Contemporary Culture

David Trend

Routledge
Taylor & Francis Group
NEW YORK AND LONDON

First published 2016
by Routledge
711 Third Avenue, New York, NY 10017

and by Routledge
2 Park Square, Milton Park, Abingdon, Oxon OX14 4RN

Routledge is an imprint of the Taylor & Francis Group, an informa business

Library of Congress Cataloging in Publication Data
Names: Trend, David.
Title: Elsewhere in America : the crisis of belonging in contemporary culture / David Trend.
Description: New York : Routledge- Taylor & Francis, 2016. | Series: Critical interventions
Identifiers: LCCN 2015042876| ISBN 9781138654433 (hardback) | ISBN 9781138654440 (pbk.) | ISBN 9781315623245 (ebook)
Subjects: LCSH: United States–Social conditions–1980- | Politics and culture–United States. | Neoliberalism–United States.
Classification: LCC HN65 .T73 1997 | DDC 306.0973–dc23
LC record available at http://lccn.loc.gov/2015042876

ISBN: 978-1-138-65443-3 (hbk)
ISBN: 978-1-138-65444-0 (pbk)
ISBN: 978-1-315-62324-5 (ebk)

Typeset in Bembo
by Taylor & Francis Books

Printed and bound in the United States of America by Publishers Graphics, LLC on sustainably sourced paper.

CONTENTS

BELONGING WHERE?

Introduction

Speaking at the 50th anniversary of the Selma to Montgomery marches, President Barack Obama described America as an incomplete project—a nation caught between ideals of a perfect union and the lingering realities of their failure. While citing advances in civil liberties since the bloody apex of the Voting Rights Movement, Obama also spoke of a federal report issued just days earlier documenting structural racism and misbehavior toward African Americans by police in Ferguson, MO, where some months previously law enforcement officers had killed an unarmed black teenager.[1] "We know the march is not yet over. We know the race is not yet won," the President stated, adding, "We know that reaching that blessed destination requires admitting as much, facing up to the truth."[2]

Elsewhere in America: The Crisis of Belonging in Contemporary Culture describes the nation's ongoing pursuit of that blessed destination. Like many utopian quests, this search says as much about current problems as it does about future aspirations. This book uses the term "elsewhere" to discuss these two Americas. In the first sense, elsewhere references existing conditions that exile so many citizens to "some other place" through prejudice, competition, or discordant belief. Even as "diversity" has become the official norm in American society, the country continues to fragment along new lines that pit citizens against their government, each other, and even themselves. Yet in another way, elsewhere evokes an undefined "not yet" that is ripe with potential. While the journey may be difficult, elsewhere can point to optimism, hope, and common purpose. It was in this latter spirit that Obama spoke of a nation eternally venturing into unfamiliar ground. "America is a constant work in progress," he said. "We were born of change."[3]

Obama's expansive rhetoric was hardly innocent in its appeal to "American" values. Modern nations define themselves through mythic ideals as much as through land or populations. Philosophically speaking, the problem with ideals lies in the very abstraction that gives them broad appeal. In a heterogeneous society like the U.S., familiar terms like "freedom" and "equality" are understood in radically different ways from region to region, and from group to group. America always has struggled with such contests of meaning, as grand ideals of unity and inclusion nearly always forget someone. Behind the country's mythic open door, newcomers often find that civic belonging comes with strings attached—riddled with conditions, limitations, and in some instances, punitive rites of passage. And for those already here, new rationales emerge to challenge civic belonging on the basis of belief, behavior, or heritage—as the idealized blessed destination is endlessly deferred.

Before the Beginning

In its original Latin, the word *Americus* described a kind of "elsewhere"—in denoting a *Mundus Novus* (New World). This idea soon assumed a magical meaning for explorers, synonymous with unknown territory and boundless possibilities–ideas that fit perfectly into a European view of the known world as something to be examined and cultivated. The very newness of the Americas seemed to offer unimagined potential, but its strange qualities also made settlers anxious. The unknown can have this effect, as the unfamiliar leaves one open to anticipation, speculation, and irrationality. Wonder can easily turn to fear, especially when it is undergirded by material need, habits of power, and religious rivalries. As *Elsewhere in America* explores this conflicted mindset, the larger question of the book concerns the way in which people fashion worlds relationally, and the difficulty of such "worlding" amid the push and pull of inherited oppositions. It looks at the way belonging locates between known and unknown, between recognized and invisible, between the friend and stranger in everyone—and in no one. *Elsewhere in America* is about finding ways through these perplexing paradoxes.

Contradictions were built into America from the start—most notably the tension between individual and community. And since the nation's founding, certain unresolved conflicts have animated debates in nearly every sector of society. Enlightenment ideals of autonomous agency invested "choice" and volition in American citizenship and national identity. It was thought that reason would modulate the marriage of democracy and capitalism in the new land, even in the face of cultural difference. But the colonists also brought with them histories of intergenerational rivalry, conflict, and trauma—which they soon began to replicate consciously or unconsciously. Hence the American self found itself burdened with epistemological baggage—manifest in the terms of subjectivity so often posed as familiar oppositions: one/many, inside/outside, them/us, etc.

It's no secret how this history unfolded—and that throughout its existence the United States has shown a strange tendency to turn against itself, dividing citizens against each other with a vehemence rivaling the most brutal regimes on earth. Some have rationalized the resulting crisis of "belonging" in America as an understandable consequence of cultural diversity, economic stress, and global threat. After all, haven't there always been "insiders" and "outsiders" in every culture? Aren't competition and aggression wired into human nature? Or is there something peculiar about the personality of the U.S.? Could it be that prejudice is the real legacy of the "American exceptionalism," in traditions dating to the genocide of indigenous populations, the subjugation of women, the rise of slavery, the scapegoating of immigrants, and the more recent assaults on the poor or anyone falling outside the realm of normalcy?

I discussed selected aspects of America's divisive pathology in my book *A Culture Divided: America's Struggle for Unity*, which was written in the closing years of the George W. Bush presidency.[4] Like many at the time, I had completely given up on the idea of "common ground" amid the residue of post-9/11 reactionary fervor and emerging economic recession. Media commentators were buzzing constantly about red/blue state polarization.[5] Opinions varied about the cause of the divide, attributing it to factors including regionalism, media sensationalism, partisan antipathy, or all of these combined. Also joining the fray were those asserting that the divide was fabricated, with evenly divided elections showing most people in the middle of the curve on most issues. My somewhat contrarian view was that the "problem" shouldn't be regarded as a problem at all. After all, America *always* had been divided—through war and peace, boom and bust. Division was the country's national brand. But as a book about politics, *A Culture Divided* didn't get to the roots or the lived experience of America's compulsive divisiveness.[6]

Elsewhere in America brings new specificity and depth to this issue, especially as cultural fragmentation finds fresh and unexpected form in a neoliberal landscape. While recognizing the benefits of nationalist belonging, *Elsewhere in America* charts the ever-changing faces of difference (manifest in topics ranging from sex and race to such areas as disability and mental health), their spectral and intersectional character (as seen in the new discourses on anti-normativity and cosmopolitanism), and the grounds on which categories are manifest in ideation and actions (seen in theories of performativity, post-identity, queer and dismodern theory). Through this range of conceptual approaches, *Elsewhere in America* attempts to mitigate the solipsism and appropriating tendencies of singular discourses or schools of thought—while also recognizing that complete escape is neither possible nor advisable.

Mapping Elsewhere

Elsewhere in America is arranged in three sections, each with a different conceptual orientation. Discussion mixes theory with concrete detail in exploring themes of opposition, fragmentation, and dissolution. A certain degree of historical counterpoint also informs discussion of the nation's continuing struggle to understand its ever-changing present moment. Part I ("Belonging There") describes historically grounded attitudes of certainty and apparent clarity in defining conventional American values and identities, even as these embody certain contradictions (such as the tension between individual and community). Part II ("Blurred Boundaries") looks at ways that such certainties have come unraveled as the diversity and multiplicities of American society have become more complex and contested (identity and "post" movements). Part III ("Belonging Elsewhere") then explores ways of moving forward through syntheses, new models of subjectivity (hybridities and singular-pluralities, for example), or yet-unknown possibilities.

Part I: "Belonging There: People like Us" looks at frequently contentious efforts to define (or redefine) America through the lenses of commerce, belief, conformity, and national security—recognizing the linkages of democratic capitalism with the enlightenment humanism of the founding era. The opening chapter, "Makers-and-Takers: When More Is Not Enough," examines the role of individualism and private property in notions of belonging, linking these to principles of the voluntary association and objective possession so central to American ideology, as well as the resulting exclusion, inequity, and paranoia they continue to generate. The following chapter, "True Believers: Spiritual Life in a Secular Age," extends this discussion with an examination of religion in the U.S., especially the remarkable dominance of Protestantism and its recurrent themes of persecution, redemption, and competitive proselytizing. Next, "Ordinary People: The Normal and the Pathological" looks at ideals of health and scientific rationalism, as well as practices of population management, which underlie utopian impulses to standardize bodies and behaviors of many kinds, but often betray long-standing power asymmetries in the process. Issues of power also inform the final chapter in this section, "Homeland Insecurities: Expecting the Worst," discussing perennial American worries about external threats and internal subversion. Many of these anxieties seem hard-wired in a nation with profound ambivalence about "belonging" to a global community.

Then discussion turns to ways that dividing lines have blurred in recent decades between such categories as public and private, fact and fiction, sameness and difference, wellness and disease. Key to this analysis are ways that distinctions between who belongs and who doesn't are shifting from visible differences to more subtle matters of mind, behavior, and identity. Hence, characteristics like national origin, sexual orientation, gender identity, and mental health are rising to a new prominence in debates over "mainstream values" or "common sense"— as long-standing patterns of exclusion, stigma, and discrimination find new expression. And while many of these are cultural issues or "matters of mind," their material consequences are very real indeed—resulting in legal decisions, institutional policies, and resource transfers—not to mention new antipathies of citizens toward one another.

Part II: "Belonging Somewhere: Blurred Boundaries" looks at the complexities of meaning and identity in an age of digital representation and cultural diversity. In the new millennium, America yearns for modernist ideals of certainty and security—even as it finds itself beset by a world of ambiguity and instability. The section's first chapter, "Reality Is Broken: Neoliberalism and the Virtual Economy," discusses the intersecting effects of Internet technology, simulated experience, financialized capital, and globalization in the ways that postmodern culture affects belonging. Next, "Mistaken Identities: From Color Blindness to Gender Bending" takes on issues of equality and equity in relation to identity, post-identity, and subsequent discussions. "No Body Is Perfect: Disability in a Posthuman Age" extends the discussions of normativity from Part I in considerations of the body, identity performance, ableism, and disability. And finally, the chapter "On the Spectrum: America's Mental Health Disorder" extends this topic further into topics of mental health and privacy rights.

From this, the question becomes what to do about it all. Is it ever possible to overcome America's seemingly "natural" patterns of conflict without getting lost in blurred meaning and indeterminacy? Would this even be desirable in a society that places so high a premium on personal autonomy, group identity, and democratic principles? In this spirit, *Elsewhere in America* reengages the paradox of oppositional thought, as well as emerging strategies to analyze its pernicious hold on U.S. society. Discussion in the book's next section focuses on such principles as irreconcilability, indivisibility, and hybridity—without recourse to either pessimism or optimism in their consideration.

Part III: "Belonging Elsewhere: The Subject of Utopia," reckons with the nondialectical as the ongoing challenge of the current moment, whether this involves holding simultaneous opposing ideas or struggling with the unconscious. To add specificity to the discussions, "Gaming the System: Competition and its Discontents" explores the collective "madness" of America's libidinous consumerism as a symptom of competitive desire. The next chapter, "To Affinity and Beyond: The Cyborg and the Cosmopolitan" also explores conciliatory belonging through models ranging from cyborg feminism to cosmopolitanism—referencing tensions between specific and general. "Medicating the Problem: The New American Pharmakon" addresses addiction and a medicated society in a literal sense, as well as the pharmakon as a metaphysical model. The book's closing chapter, "The One and the Many: The Ethics of Uncertainty" reengages the issue of American intersubjectivity in both reflective and speculative terms.

Living with contradictions certainly isn't easy, especially in difficult moments. But if there is such a thing as an ethics in conflicted times, it may well lie in a willingness to look beyond familiar guideposts. While it's commonplace to approach a problem with the tools one has at hand, the trickiest ones resist known methods—or more specifically, the methods one has at the time. In this sense, difficult problems require either help from someone else (relational knowledge) or a leap of faith (experimental knowledge). In either case, there is a moment of uncertainly or perhaps even failure, as one navigates the interval of "solving for an unknown."[7] The key lies in the willingness, courage, or humility to face this unknowing, and still proceed into the void—which is also the space of the possible.[8]

Notes

1 "Investigation of the Ferguson Police Department," U.S. Department of Justice Civil Rights Division (Mar. 4, 2015) http://www.justice.gov/sites/default/files/opa/press-releases/attachments/2015/03/04/ferguson_police_department_report.pdf (accessed Apr. 2, 2015).
2 Barack Obama, "Remarks by the President at the 50th Anniversary of the Selma to Montgomery Marches," (Mar. 7, 2015) https://www.whitehouse.gov/the-press-office/2015/03/07/remarks-president-50th-anniversary-selma-montgomery-marches (accessed Mar. 21, 2015).
3 Ibid.
4 David Trend, *A Culture Divided: America's Struggle for Unity* (Boulder, CO: Paradigm, 2009).
5 Ira Schor, *Culture Wars: School and Society in the Conservative Restoration, 1969–1985* (London and New York: Routledge, 1986); Geoffrey Hartman, *Minor Prophesies: The Literacy Essay in the Culture Wars* (Cambridge, MA: Harvard University Press, 1991); James Jefferson Hunter, *Culture Wars: The Struggle to Define America* (New York: Harper-Collins, 1991); Henry Louis Gates, *Loose Canons: Notes on the Culture Wars* (New York: Oxford University Press, 1992); Gerald Graff, *Beyond the Culture Wars: How Teaching the Conflicts Can Revitalize American Education* (New York: W.W. Norton, 1992); Margaret Heins, *Sex, Sin, and Blasphemy* (New York: The New Press, 1993); Fred Whitehead, *Culture Wars: Opposing Viewpoints* (San Diego, CA: Greenhaven Press, 1994); Russell Jacoby, *Dogmatic Wisdom: How the Culture Wars Divert Education and Distract America* (New York: Doubleday, 1994); Elaine Rapping, *Media-tions: Forays into the Culture and Gender Wars* (Boston, MA: South End Press, 1994).
6 See, for example, Montserrat Guibernau, *Belonging: Solidarity and Division in Modern Societies* (Cambridge: Polity, 2013); Natalie Masuoka and Jane Dunn, *The Politics of Belonging: Race, Public Opinion, and Immigration* (Chicago, IL: Chicago University Press, 2013); David Jacobson, *Place and Elsewhere in America* (Baltimore, MD: Johns Hopkins University Press, 2001); Constance Perin, *Elsewhere in America: Reading Between the Lines* (Madison, WI: Wisconsin University Press, 1988); Elizabeth Povinelli, *Economies of Abandonment: Social Belonging and Endurance in Late Liberalism* (Durham, NC: Duke University Press, 2011); Judith Butler and Athena Athanasiou, *Dispossession: The Performative in the Political* (Cambridge: Polity, 2013); Melissa Gregg and Gregory J. Seigworth, eds. *The Affect Theory Reader* (Durham, NC: Duke University Press, 2010); and Henry A. Giroux, *The Abandoned Generation: Democracy Beyond the Culture of Fear* (New York: Palgrave Macmillan, 2003).
7 Jacques Derrida, *Aporias,* trans. Thomas Dutiot (Stanford, CA: Stanford University Press, 1993) p. 15.
8 Trinh T. Minh-ha, *Elsewhere, Within Here: Immigration, Refugeeism, and the Boundary Event* (New York and London: Routledge, 2011).

PART I

Belonging There

People like Us

Nations are defined by the stories they tell about themselves, as well as the ways others see them. Part I: "Belonging There: People like Us" examines some of America's national stories, as their generalities often unravel in the contemporary United States. In principle, such broad narratives are seen as holding national societies together, giving them a sense of unity, common history, and singular purpose. But there is a problem. While the idea of a unifying story may have worked in some early tribal societies, the complexities of modern nation states frustrate narrative reduction (which itself has epistemological limitations), thus producing forms of civic tension in contemporary America. This section's title, "Belonging There," evokes the certainty with which some parties locate themselves with like-minded compatriots—"belonging" in neighborhoods, political parties, interest groups, or online communities.

Individual chapters in this section specify ways that broad categories of national belonging are undermined by discordant attitudes toward the economy, faith, normalcy, and security. Tensions between general and specific perspectives work against the ideal of perfect consensus in most modern nations, as does the self-limiting character of any single story. Conflicts inevitably result, as divergent opinions compete with nationalistic yearnings for wholeness and belonging. As Homi K. Bhabha wrote two decades ago in *Nation and Narration*, often these tensions become manifest in disagreements over the national "story" itself, which is doomed to an endless lack of closure. While these contests generate certain forms of discomfort, their dynamism also can produce moments of possibility. Bhabha writes that if the struggle for closure "questions the 'totalization' of national culture, then its positive value lies in displaying the wide dissemination through which we construct fields of meaning and symbols associated with national life."[1]

As a country with a relatively brief history, the United States hungers for a belonging mythology—with disparate interests vying for its authorship. Myths are more than simple stories. Whether representing tradition or ideology, mythology provides a connotative structure for social meanings manifest inside and outside of "language" per se. This is why certain myths are hard to contain, as Roland Barthes famously pointed out in his 1957 book *Mythologies*.[2] Myths of masculinity don't only come into use through classical tales of heroism, but also through the prosaic rituals of sports culture, militarism, and school bullying, for example. In common parlance today, a "myth" is widely understood to be a familiar belief that is false, such as the myth that money always brings happiness. As in advertising, such beliefs may not be true in a literal sense, but they often appeal to unconscious desires. This is what led Barthes to conclude that myths often function politically on some level, with this process unfolding in a most insidious way. On the surface myths appear to be transparent, "hiding nothing" even as they convey distortions. But at a deeper level, "myth transforms history into nature," Barthes observed, making its meanings seem as though they were always there. And of course many people do indeed subscribe to myths. This is where the obfuscations of myth become dangerous, with its ideations regarded "not as a motive, but as reason."[3] The naturalization of myth obscures its intentionality and ideology, creating the illusion that it is neutral and depoliticized.

Myth's sleight of hand can become especially potent when attached to notions of origins, authenticity, and other ideals of nationalist belonging. Keep in mind that America started out mired in contradictions—between public and private interests, between state and national governance—not to mention the divisions between separatists and loyalists, which persisted well past colonial times. The halcyon days of revolutionary unity always have been a convenient trope. In more practical terms, the term "United States of America" is better seen as a coalition of opposition, predicated upon a "new" egalitarian horizontality rather than an "old" aristocratic verticality. In this way, this purportedly "reasoned" revolutionary impulse in many ways replicated its "idealized" precursor in philosophical terms. Yet U.S. democracy always was more of a dream than a reality, even as particularized in constitutional and representative terms. This temporal slippage became glaringly obvious with the elision of the name United States of America to the nickname "America"—a term later recognized throughout the world as a synonym for U.S. imperialism.

Old habits die hard. If one looks at the current state of belonging and not belonging in the United States, there is plenty of repetition, denial, and repressed memory to inform the inquiry. Despite its enormous wealth and military might, the United States lumbers its way through the 21st century with a pervasive sense of insecurity—always worrying about external enemies or internal subversives. Some say this is a symptom of decline or a nagging fear of impending loss. Regardless of its origins, the U.S. counters its insecurities with grand assertions of power and ethical purpose—of the nation's unique role in history and global affairs. This is the mythology of "American exceptionalism", a tale of a heroic nation with a unique role in global affairs and human history. The problem is that any long view of civilization shows that this American mythology is far from exceptional. It's the same story great empires have told themselves throughout time. But as a relatively new empire the U.S. has less experience with historical memory, and if you haven't noticed, arguments over American history undergird many of the nation's recent cultural conflicts—with one side or another claiming a privileged access to the "truth" about founding principles, citizenship, marriage, and so on.

Behind this selective memory is a particular pathology that, while not unique to the U.S., assumes a certain potency given the nation's age and origins. If recent history teaches one anything, it shows a repeating cycle of unity and division, inclusion and exclusion, security and worry—in other words a continual return to certain narratives of desire and fear—from which the country seems unable to escape. The U.S. shares with other immigrant nations a longing for a sense of origins or home—a longing often twinged with nostalgic imaginings. But America still struggles with coming to terms with these yearnings. This may partly explain why a figure like Fox News commentator Bill O'Reilly chooses to look back only a decade or so to proclaim "the end of America as we know it" in his tirades about immigration and marriage equality.[4]

Another overarching conceit of these appeals to mythical idealism lies in their claim to exceed partisan politics or disputes over values. Presumably, it is argued, there is something "united" about the states of America. Like most mythic constructions, this story is instructive for its elisions and repressed elements. Settlers arriving in the U.S. from all parts of the world carried with them the residue of former ways of life (consciously or unconsciously). Prior hierarchical habits often proved very difficult to set aside. Perhaps most significantly, transition to the new world was often marked by trauma. Remember that huge numbers of early immigrants left their homelands under duress, with many dying in transit or entering lives of servitude upon arrival. Then the brutality of settling the new land began—with a genocidal program to exterminate indigenous populations. Next came a violent revolution, decades of internal conflict, a massive slave trade, battles over borders and land, the Civil War, and the horrific military conflagrations of the 20th century.

Much more is understood today than ever before about the intergenerational character of suffering and loss. But little has been written into common accounts of American history of the grief, depression, confusion, distrust, denial, guilt, anger, and revenge impulses buried in the collective American psyche. Again and again, the U.S. seems to relive such repressed memory as contemporary experience. Images from the past resurface into the present, attaching themselves to a changing array of heroes and villains at home and abroad. This failure to find closure means that the object is always deferred—and never actually found. What remains is a continual search for truth, manifest in an anxious struggle for meaning.

Notes

1 Homi K. Bhabha, "Introduction: Narrating the Nation," *Nation and Narration* (London and New York: Routledge, 1990) p. 3.
2 Roland Barthes, *Mythologies* (1957), trans. Annette Lavers (London: Paladin, 1972).
3 *Mythologies*, p. 128
4 Bill O'Reilly, "Fox News Election Coverage," (Nov. 6, 2012) http://www.youtube.com/watch?v=peiANkiO1qQ (accessed May 5, 2014).

1

MAKERS-AND-TAKERS

When More Is Not Enough

To most middle-class Americans, a yearly income of $400,000 probably sounds like pretty good money. It's nearly eight times the average family income and surely a fantasy for the 50 million Americans living in poverty. But hold on a minute. According to the *Wall Street Journal*, it's practically impossible to scrape by with such a six-figure income. "You're just breaking even," explained *WSJ* Wealth Advisor Veronica Dagher in a video segment on the journal's website. What with vacations, the country club, and the mortgage on that $1.2 million house—not to mention those pesky taxes on income, property, and purchases—high earners "feel like they are just nearly getting by."[1] Under such financial duress, is it any wonder that publications like the *WSJ* report that the nation's upper class increasingly feels under assault?

Obviously these sentiments are striking at a number of levels, and illustrative of America's twisted thinking about wealth and poverty. In historical terms, the country has promoted itself as a land of freedom and opportunity, where people rise and fall on their own merits. Yet within this thinking a certain normative logic has tended to hold sway, with too much or too little money seen as undesirable. The mythical figure of the "Average American" persists in the country's infatuation with its celebrated middle class. But now these once-balanced sentiments are getting more ideologically charged. Despite the banking scandals of the early 2000s, conservatives again insist that wealth should be seen as virtue in its own right in a "post-civil rights" era. Even liberals are beginning to reconsider previous approaches to income redistribution and government assistance. Ironically these shifts are paralleling a shrinkage of the American middle class in every state in America.[2] While the gap between the haves and the have-nots is no secret, statisticians see such stratification intensifying even as the recession of the early 2000s winds down.

Still, it's the attitudinal hardening that is so striking—a growing disregard for those left behind in a winner-takes-all America. Explanations abound for this shift: lingering bias and structural inequality; rising tides of competitive individualism; a loss of connection and community concern; and a decline in faith and altruism are often cited. Sociologists have long written of commodity fetishism, conspicuous consumption, and other performances of class status in societies that place high premiums on upward mobility. But in more immediate terms, the recent recession brought money worries to most American families, even wealthy ones. Beset by feelings of insecurity, many yearn for reason and certainty as they anticipate the future. And so has returned the Darwinian figure of the "undeserving poor" as a concept that justifies affluence while obfuscating more difficult questions.[3] Some even say that the wealthy assuage their guilt with beliefs that poor people bring hardship on themselves.

In this context, the expression "makers-and-takers" has entered popular discourse as a form of shorthand for conflicting economic philosophies. Famously revealed in billionaire Mitt Romney's quip about America's "47 percent," makers and takers describes a nation divided into two classes: one of producers, the other of parasites. As the U.S. still struggles with recessionary aftereffects, this dichotomy continues to resonate with voters, rhetorically drawing a line between a class of autonomous "job creators, entrepreneurs, and innovators" and others "dependent on government, who believe they are victims."[4] Romney's divisive populism played well in conservative circles, as it collapsed a swath of issues into familiar tropes of success and failure. Hinging on the premise that values emerge from economic relationships, a similar ontology (somewhat ironically) defined Marx's dialectical materialism.[5]

Credit for the capitalist version of this philosophy often goes to Ayn Rand, specifically as espoused in her 1957 novel, *Atlas Shrugged*. The book depicts a dystopian America in which the titans of industry have their successes crushed by government regulators—and consequently "shrug" off their ambitions and dreams. Rand termed her metaphoric anticommunism "moral objectivism"—setting forth an absolutist agenda of "rational self-interest" and acquisitive impulses as sacred values. These ideas played well in the Cold War era by pitting individual "freedom" against collectivist "tyranny." As she put it, "No rights can exist without the right to translate one's rights into reality—to think, to work and to keep the results—which means: the right of property."[6] Rand disciples would argue that society should be seen as a collection of individuals in constant competition—with the virtuous wealthy (makers) naturally prevailing over the undeserving poor (takers).

Ironically Rand herself never framed making and taking in such simplistic terms. Instead she saw both forces coalescing against the real enemy: big government. In this view, producing and consuming are not opposed to each other, but instead represent the highest of personal values. Rand's free market vision attached no guilt in the honest making/taking of goods or maximization of wealth. Thus, when society's individualized maker/takers run into trouble they are completely justified in finding new ways of operating: fresh territories to tame, markets to occupy, or populations to dispossess. Dispossession can assume many forms—ranging from the material belongings or resources of the vulnerable, to the very sense of belonging associated with membership in the acquisitive economy. In this view, dispossession has both physical and metaphysical dimensions—unified by certain principles: the disposability of individuals and groups, the privatization and commodification of what is public, and the moral righteousness of neoliberal modernity.

The Wealth of Nations

The makers-and-takers debate has deep roots in the American psyche. Democracy may not require a market economy, but capitalism inheres in democracy's Euro-American history. A tension between private and public interest was built into the U.S. economic system from the beginning, owing to 18th-century beliefs that this balance would self-regulate—much as it was thought that gun ownership required no oversight. As initially conceived by Adam Smith, the "invisible hand" of the private marketplace required little more than modest taxation for the public good. Somewhat forgotten today, Smith fully advocated the appropriate role of government in such things as the funding of schools, the building of bridges and roads, and of course the maintenance of the national military. Smith's *The Wealth of Nations* set forth a philosophy of economic principles based on newly recognized Enlightenment ideals of individualism. Set against the backdrop of oligarchical tyranny, Smith and others saw a collective benefit in the unleashing of self-interest—with the broader society enjoying the fruits of personal agency and innovation as a new land was being settled and a new nation built. This was termed at the time a "liberal" approach to governance and economics. Smith truly believed that personal interest indirectly promotes the public good when he wrote that the individual "intends only his own gain, and he is in this, as in many other cases, led by an invisible hand to promote an end which was no part of his intention. Nor is it always the worse for the society that it was no part of it. By pursuing his own interest he frequently promotes that of the society more effectually than when he really intends to promote it."[7]

There is no understating the role of property in early American formulations of democracy, capitalism, and citizenship itself. While Western society didn't invent the idea of private property, it would refine this principle into ideals of free market competition and the liberal state, allowing many "makers" to innovate and build while also collecting more than their fair share of benefit. Unfortunately this free market utopia couldn't keep the makers happy for very long. It seems that for all the property and privilege they accumulated, more was never enough, even in the good times. Shortly before America's founding, John Locke had written of the individual as "the proprietor of his own person," giving a materialist inflection to prior notions of self-mastery. Philosophers of the time had been wrestling with the ponderous questions of being and self-consciousness. But the idea of self-ownership had a particular appeal to populations arriving in the Americas. "Subjects" in the new land could *own* themselves, as well as other goods. And just as importantly, they could possess land and homes: private domains. Let's not overlook the noteworthy contradictions in this new scheme—that voting citizenship was linked to land ownership, that citizens also could own other people as indentured servants or slaves, and that most of the population (notably, women and indigenous people) also fell outside the bounds of self-ownership. Nor should one forget the linguistic embeddedness of owning in expressing autonomy, affiliation, or relationship: *myself, my country, my friends, I-take-thee,* and so on. All of this suggests a level of abstraction in ownership as it links to personal identity.[8]

The appeal of individualism isn't exactly rocket science, owing to widely held beliefs that a "self" set apart from others is a crucial building block of subjectivity. This lonely soul often receives credit for the gifts of reason, literacy, scientific empiricism—and ultimately, the concepts of democracy and capitalism. Even this idea was suppressed by religious determinism until the 1700s. In pre-Enlightenment days the idea of an autonomous subject was largely discounted in favor of supernatural beliefs in predestination. Remember that in political terms, Western secular democracy emerged as a novel expression of human agency. Decision-making became vested in the reasoning abilities of individual agents, presumably able to assess truth claims. But the emerging concept of the American "citizen" had two sides: private and public. *Private citizenship* entailed the freedom to serve one's own interests, acquire benefits, and advocate one's views without undo interference. *Public citizenship* entailed similar freedoms to vote, participate in governance, and to join others for collective benefit.

From the beginning, America's founders envisioned a productive tension between public and private interests. Benjamin Franklin and Thomas Jefferson saw discord and disagreement as healthy antidotes to prior political systems based on uniform beliefs or brute authoritarianism. Private motivation was a vital force in this formulation, but it was only half of the equation. Without public interest the system would lose both its purpose and its dynamism. Faith in the rational abilities of ordinary people defined a novel form of politics based on the "consent of the governed." The so-called Age of Reason and its recognition of a distinctly "human" mind said that people could find their own way in the world. Democracy constituted the crowning achievement of this fresh way of thinking.

The emerging democratic impulse famously advanced a novel paradigm in human affairs: that an informed citizenry could be the sovereign power of the land. For the first time in history, faith was vested in the ability of common citizens to use their own knowledge as a source of power. Not that everybody thought it would work. People inside and outside the American colonies worried that such an arrangement would end in chaos and anarchy. After all, for centuries people around the world had accepted the premise that leadership came from some higher intelligence. They weren't entirely wrong. The American Revolution took a long time to garner consensus, with colonists and loyalists deeply divided in the decades leading up to 1776. Nor did the cessation of fighting settle the matter for good. Unrest continued for decades to follow, setting in place a legacy of political division within the United States that persists even to this day. While it is commonplace in contemporary U.S. political discourse to lament the fraying of national unity and a purported lack of common purpose, the notion of a contentious polity was anticipated from the start. The founders recognized this in embracing a political philosophy in which disagreement was not suppressed—as in oligarchic or despotic regimes—but instead was celebrated in the continual testing and revaluation of ideas. This is why the nation's founders took great pains to protect the open marketplace of ideas through freedoms of speech, assembly, and the press.

Fundamental to these values was the interplay of knowledge and opinion—an exchange famously advanced during the Enlightenment era by new forms of communication, among other factors. Undoubtedly, the European development of the printing press contributed to expanding literacy rates, along with a growing mercantile culture and a burgeoning Protestant movement. Most importantly, the proliferation of printed texts enabled a broad-based expansion of reading, which in turn further escalated the demand for printed materials. The literacy boom gave "ordinary" people unprecedented access to knowledge of all sorts. Both *The Wealth of Nations* and America's Declaration of Independence described a citizenry capable of rational decisions—whether in the marketplace or the polling place. The two founding documents were predicated on the existence of the public sphere animated by reasoned exchange.

Expressed in the language of democracy, American capitalism is a system in which citizens literally vote with their money. A patron walks into a store selling various kinds of shoes, and discerns one kind to be better than the others. The purchase of one brand of shoes discourages the making of others. And as this pattern is replicated, the market's "invisible hand" raises the quality of footwear. Many people still believe this quaint theory. Unfortunately, Smith and his contemporaries were unable to foresee the way in which modern corporations would later aggregate consumers and optimize profit making. Smith couldn't predict how a mechanized shoe factory could multiply the reward system in geometric terms. But by the next century G.W.F. Hegel would begin to figure things out, noting in *The Philosophy of Right* the tendencies of bourgeois societies to generate an over-accumulation of wealth, a concomitant class of paupers, and means of advancing their interests through trade and colonization.[9]

A student of Hegel, Karl Marx later would excoriate the "surplus" profits generated by industrialization, not to mention its effects on workers and consumers.[10] And so in the mid-1800s the critique of capitalistic excess would begin. As today, advocates for businesses would claim that profits translated into more jobs, wages, and spending—in an endlessly upward spiral. Of course the problem was that factory owners weren't satisfied with simply selling more goods and hiring more workers. With growing numbers of urban job seekers, factory owners applied competitive market principles in the hiring and retention of employees. Marx called this the commodification of labor—as the activity of work became abstracted as a mere cost of industrial production. Class-consciousness was born as laborers came to understand and communicate about their collective exploitation.

Strikes occurred, unions were formed, and collective bargaining emerged—eventually prompting the government to step in. Over time regulatory measures would contain the labor market, as well as the not-so-invisible hands of monopolies. Just as representative democracy organized collective decision making on a large scale, liberal economic principles sought to rein in expansive capitalism. And before long, new communications technologies would change democracy and capitalism. Exponential increases in the quality and quantity of information would magnify differentials between private and public interests. As the pace of media innovation accelerated, the government's ability to modulate its influence could not keep pace—especially in countries where historically free speech was politicized. Private interest would come to trump public concern nearly everywhere in the American mediascape.

The Great Depression of the 1930s disproved the invisible hand theory. When markets are left to their own devices extreme profits and losses get out of control, excessively rewarding and punishing people as a consequence. During the Depression years, John Maynard Keynes proposed that governments could keep economies from melting down again.[11] Without advocating absolute federal management of the economy (as in European socialist and communist nations of the time) Keynes proposed correcting market problems with regulations, taxes, and incentives. Herein lies a basic tension between current conservative and liberal economic thinking. Proponents of Smith's principles argue a laissez-faire approach in the belief that a generalized free market is a self-correcting mechanism on all levels of scale. Keynes differentiated between small "microeconomic" matters like consumer decisions and larger "macroeconomic" ones like monetary policy, with the government playing an appropriate role in the latter. Hence, to Keynes matters like federal control of interest rates, tax policy, and infrastructure spending could be used to correct market excesses in what again would be termed a "liberal" economic philosophy.

The premise of liberal economic mediation makes sense in theoretical terms, although to this day staunch free market advocates will argue that any interference with the invisible hand mucks up the system. The devastation of the Great Depression was widespread enough to generate popular support for government intervention in macroeconomic matters. It worked during the 1930s as the globe was lumbering toward World War II, during which the role of federal spending, employment, and economic intervention largely went unquestioned. But the American industrial war machine also blurred the lines between government and private industry, creating what President Eisenhower in the 1950s would name "the military-industrial complex."

During this period Chicago economist Milton Friedman alternately would use the terms "neoliberalism" and "laissez-faire capitalism" in proposing a third way philosophy bent on sustaining private sector interests in this heated environment. Friedman's arguments easily found traction in an era of Cold War anti-communist paranoia, especially as Friedman would characterize growing government as the enemy of freedom and democracy. Of course Friedman would never acknowledge that the booming postwar economy had benefited enormously from a previous decade of massive government war spending followed by heavy federal infrastructure expenditures on education, interstate highways, and an array of other programs. Nor perhaps could Friedman foresee the way business interests would be able to insinuate themselves into electoral politics, influence voting outcomes, lobby for legislation, and otherwise compromise government. Neither did many free market apologists like Friedman fully account for world economic systems, instead tending to view the United States as an isolated and "exceptional" engine of boundless expansion.

But of course the postwar period of American economic expansion didn't last forever. Industrial production and consumer demand fell, tax revenues dwindled, infrastructure spending shrank, and trade deficits followed—even as the U.S. was spending wildly on a nuclear arms race and military adventures in Korea, Vietnam, and elsewhere. Eventually a comprehensive oil embargo by OPEC members would force America to recognize its vulnerability in the global economy, while reawakening attention to Middle East politics. Critics of neoliberalism began framing the situation in global terms. Their logic was simple. Like the great colonial powers of the past, American foreign policy was driven largely to compensate for dwindling resources at home. In this sense, noble ideals touting the expansion of democracy and freedom (and capitalism) around the globe served two purposes: one political, the other economic. The first was aimed at containing the expansionist impulses of the Soviet Union and China—and this was how public debate was framed regarding U.S. military deployments. The second had to do with securing American interests in the developing world, where natural resources and new consumer markets could serve to replenish the U.S. economy. In a sense, the world's two postwar industrial giants functioned as makers/takers on a global scale.

As the binary balance of power has shifted since then, the U.S. has emerged as the world's dominant "taker" even as its role as the largest "maker" has been eclipsed by other nations. Some would even argue that declines in U.S. exports and trade put further pressure on America's need to continue its foreign plunder. For instance, it's no secret that as tobacco consumption has dropped by 50 percent in the U.S., cigarette sales in Eastern Europe, Africa, Asia, and Latin America are growing at astronomical rates—with American companies like Philip Morris leading the way. Nations that receive American foreign policy attention frequently become consumers of U.S. goods.[12] These premises were outlined by David Harvey in his frequently cited article entitled "The New Imperialism: Accumulation by Dispossession," in which he linked America's declining economic hegemony to its increasingly imperialist and militarized adventures around the globe. Harvey wrote that "the inability to accumulate through expanded reproduction on a sustained basis has been paralleled by a rise in attempts to accumulate by dispossession. This, I conclude, is the hallmark of what some like to call 'the new imperialism.'"[13]

My mention of Philip Morris is hardly incidental in this discussion. Naturally, the United States sees its own citizens as worthy of good health, consumer safety, and government intervention on their behalf. The same rules do not apply to those living in nations that are perceived to be disposable—where life literally is regarded as having less value. There is a variety of theories about how such attitudes of disposability arise. In general terms, people who aren't known, seen regularly, or brought to public attention in a coherent fashion easily become reduced to abstractions. Decades of social theory have taught that such abstraction—or objectification—is the first step in licensing harm or violence against someone. Hundreds may die in a distant disaster or as the result of American military action, but these casualties lose their humanity as they are reduced to statistical reports or journalistic sound bites. In a similar way, the rising tide of cancer diagnoses, of families losing loved ones to illness, and other forms of human suffering resulting from American tobacco sales abroad are hardly even known to U.S. media consumers. In a recent article entitled "Are Some Lives Disposable?" Adrian Parr and Brad Evans expand this discussion by asking "What about all the species that have gone extinct as the climate changes and habitats disappear, and yet greenhouse gas emissions persistently rise? What might we say about the malnourished and starving living with crippling hunger pains and thirst on a daily basis while millions of tons of food waste enter landfills each year?" They add, "Or for that matter the victim of psychological abuse who learns to live with the torment such that the eventual physical blow becomes a relief from what is imagined?"[14] Parr and Evans link these issues to structural conditions enabling a neoliberal economy to feed on the disposable while bureaucratically obfuscating its operations.

Just as objectification enables epistemic violence, disposability similarly licenses the kind of structural dispossession visited on populations at home and abroad. People rendered unimportant or invisible easily get labeled as parasitic "takers"—and deserving of disregard and exploitation, as competing concerns or claims are relegated to the realm of scattered noise.[15] As Elizabeth A. Povinelli has recently observed, contradictions to this logic are rarely directly discernable—and are often intentionally hidden, as in workplace discrimination, police brutality, or military drone attacks. These operations do not register "as things in the ordinary sense of the term but rather as actions like a sighting or citing. They exist insofar as they are evoked to conjure, shape, aggregate, and evaluate a variety of social worlds, and each of these conjurings, shapings, aggregations, and evaluations disperse liberalism as a global terrain."[16]

This is the insidious nature of elite neoliberalism—rarely inflicting harm with the overt brutality or explicit violence that finds its way into the headlines, but instead manifest in less visible shifts in resources, attitudes, policies, and behaviors that allow its consequences to become woven into the "ordinary" fabric of everyday life. An eroding minimum wage makes life increasingly difficult, but in tiny increments. Government agencies and programs are not eliminated, but they are gradually defunded. Colleges admit disadvantaged students, but offer little to help them to graduate. Because these operations work in the background of everyday life, those who are victimized frequently remain unable even to recognize what is wrong. Something is getting in the way, holding them back, making life more difficult. But what is it? To many such "abandoned" people the answer is to blame themselves.

Other People's Money

It's worth restating that the U.S. was still digging its way out of recession when makers-and-takers popped into the popular zeitgeist. Many of the nation's so-called makers were finding themselves with less, and they understandably looked for someone to blame. But one couldn't count on cable news to remind these maker/takers that the bogeyman of American government collects fewer taxes than practically any other industrialized nation on earth, and that as a consequence America's social welfare system is one of the most stingy and punitive. Nor would Fox & Co. want to acknowledge the productive character of low-income workers, disability recipients, stay-at-home parents, the young, the elderly, and the other parasitic takers. Forget that these disparaged populations consume goods, provide wage labor, pay sales tax, and enrich society in innumerable ways, whether they are acquiring resources or not.

Philosophically speaking, it's hard to avoid the familiar "self/other" paradigm in this discussion. This fundamental opposition operates in the Western philosophical mind as a primary engine of inclusion and exclusion. The so-called constitutive other denotes an entity that is outside the self or that is in some way not the same. Dozens of models have been used to explain this basic idea or to reflect critically on the processes of selfhood. In popular usage, the term "subjectivity" denotes the organization of information within a person. Subjectivity implies the existence of a self—or "subject"—that produces the experience of being. Classical philosophy has long debated whether the subject is a stable or changing entity. But there is no debate over the mutability of subjectivity, since so many factors (individuation, maturation, socialization, life experience) influence the subject over time.

All this weighs heavily on the subject's interactions with the world of people and things around it—defined as external "objects." Subjects and objects exist relationally and react to each other, and as a consequence, subjectivity is continually confirmed, challenged, and otherwise updated through the interplay with objects. Or put another way, the subject exists in relationship to what is "other" than the self. Hegel was among the first to put the matter this starkly—that people come to know themselves in comparison to what they are not.[17] He proposed that when two people meet, an essential tension is created as they recognize that they are not the same. To resolve this tension, they incorporate aspects of each other into themselves through a process he called "sublation." In other words, they learn from each other. But Hegel also shrewdly noted that sublation is rarely shared equally in a world of difference and power. Hence, otherness becomes the basis for attitudes of superiority and inferiority.

The self/other formulation is useful as far as it goes. But it has a number of obvious flaws, not the least of which is its categorical reductionism. Things get even messier when one looks harder at the notion of the self. Martin Heidegger more or less demolished the notion of a definitive self by saying that "being" was largely an open question—that the subject is always transient.[18] So where does this leave an America (or any modern nation) premised on a presumption of consensus values? The answer is somewhere in between the stable and transient self, between the closure of certainty and the instability of uncertainty. This becomes manifest in public policy and political discourse through a continually contested definition of otherness. The makers-and-takers debate restages the constitutive other opposition in economic terms—although one also sees this shifting figure in various objects of public derision and fear—as the terrorist replaces the communist, the immigrant supplants the welfare recipient, and the mental patient becomes more worrisome than the criminal.

But a lot more is involved, obviously. Animating makers-and-takers discussions are the deep divisions over the nature of citizenship and collectivity, autonomy and interdependence—divisions that favor some over others, with a "traditional America" pitted against "changing demographics."[19] There is a regrettable history of this kind of thinking in American dreams of upward mobility, divine purpose, manifest destiny, exceptionalism, and world domination. This terminology bespeaks an increasingly rigid demarcation in American ideological debate. Conservatives argue that the U.S. government redistributes excessive amounts of money from a diminishing pool of hard-working makers to a quickly expanding population of loafers. Liberals contend that the government doesn't redistribute enough because the tax system is skewed in favor of the wealthy. According to a recent article in *The Economist* magazine, neither of these positions is accurate.[20] Wealthy people are supposed to pay more in a progressive tax system, but most of them find ways to minimize these costs. Some low earners pay no federal income tax, but most pay payroll tax, sales tax and sometimes property tax. In a study analyzing all forms of taxation, tax credits, and subsidies for America's poor, it turns out that the United States is one of the least redistributive economies in the world.[21]

America's income disparities are so widely acknowledged that they are a global cliché. Yet only a few years ago conservatives were railing against the "class warfare" of liberals who raised the issue. CBS News recently said that America's top 1 percent control 36 percent of wealth, which is shocking enough in its own right.

Meanwhile, social mobility declines, the workforce becomes less educated, innovation slows—as the U.S. becomes less and less able to compete in the global marketplace. Poverty statistics are equally disturbing, with one in six Americans living below the national poverty line (approximately $22,000 for a family of four)—the highest rate in 50 years. But beyond this, the federally designated "low income" category now includes an alarming 33 percent of working families. Unemployment numbers may move up and down by fractional percentage points, but massive numbers of people who do work simply don't earn enough to get by.[22]

Systems that produce winners must also generate losers. The Italian economist Vilfredo Pareto famously proposed this zero-sum game paradigm. In a world of monetary and material limits, one person's gain always occurs at the expense of another.[23] In today's economy, this notion of limits informs policies ranging from redistributive taxation to energy cap-and-trade rules. Pareto applied his thinking about systemic economies to both material wealth and human capital.[24] It's a recognized economic fact that low-income workers put most of their earnings back into the economy. People paying lower taxes, no taxes, or receiving some form of assistance are hardly the segment of the population who park their money in real estate, futures options, gold investments, or offshore accounts. Then one needs to consider the surplus value of work itself and the economic reality that employees rarely receive the full value of their labor. The working poor (and almost everyone else) lose a little in both the production and the consumption ends of life. And this doesn't begin to account for the economics of unpaid labor.

The Virtues of Selfishness

Unilateral taking goes by another name, of course. It's called *theft*. In the critical discourse of neoliberalism and class politics (i.e., "making and taking") people are rarely so blunt as to categorize predatory capitalism as stealing. It is now widely known that corrupt corporate CEOs, greedy investment bankers, and even financiers who commit outright fraud, rarely go to jail. And those who profit through exploiting the daily needs of poor and working-class families never get accused of anything. The owners of payday loan services, overpriced supermarkets in bombed-out neighborhoods, or fast food chains catering to overburdened working parents—who questions their entrepreneurial energy? Meanwhile, rich kids caught shoplifting never see a minute in jail, while America's prison population swells with African-American and Latino youth committing such inconsequential offenses as talking back to a teacher or walking outside late at night. Crime does happen. People do indeed "take" things illegally. But the number of such offenses has dropped every year for the past two decades.[25] There are fewer burglaries and stolen cars, for example. But what has increased—and is difficult to track sometimes in numerical terms—are illegal monetary transactions and investment fraud. What has grown and continues to expand are the forms of theft sanctioned in an economy in which concepts of making and taking become interchangeable.

Part of the problem lies in the mystification of monetary value itself, with the transition from "industrial capital" to "financial capital." In an age of credit cards, one-click buying, online banking, and computer-driven stock market investments—money has become abstracted as never before. Years ago it was hard to imagine leaving one's house without carrying at least a little cash. Nowadays many people go days or weeks at a time without even handling actual currency. Needless to say, as money has become invisible some people have seen this as an opportunity. Let's bring this discussion down to a personal level. For some Americans, completing yearly income tax forms is a simple matter of reporting income, checking off deductions boxes, and either writing a check or getting a refund. But it's no secret that for many individuals—especially wealthy ones—tax filing is an elaborate cat-and-mouse game to fend off government efforts to "take" what they "make." Lots of people end up in a moral quandary in this annual showdown between personal and collective interests. Tax filing is a perfect example of how ethics become fuzzy in an age of monetary abstraction. It's no grand logical leap to see how self-interest can interfere with moral reasoning in the ethereal universe of options and credit swaps. As a largely imaginary substance, exchange value is a product of the mind.

Sociologists have looked at making and taking through the lenses of normativity, social control, and deviance. These days almost everyone agrees that normality is a social construct, varying across space and time, and contingent on changing values. And as will be detailed later in this book, it's long been recognized that statistical "deviation" is more frequently found in nature than actual midpoints or average values. Nevertheless, some behavioral norms are undeniable. This is why societies establish broad rules of conduct that are held in place by behavioral habits, legal constraints, or other forms of social control. In the 1890s French sociologist Émile Durkheim found that an insatiable demand for "more" drove people's ambitions and consumer behavior. This libidinous "anomie," as Durkheim termed it, had to be kept in check by conventions of normality and moral institutions like the family and religion.

In the 1930s American sociologist Robert K. Merton applied the idea of anomie in explaining impulses of upward mobility and class envy in the U.S. Perhaps more importantly, Merton looked at ways that norms and well-meaning public policies could negatively affect individuals and groups via "unintended consequences."[26] In other words, many people were not merely constrained by moral ideals, but often by "anomie strain" created by structures within society itself. Pushing back against the causes of selective poverty and discrimination might be considered "deviant" in a technical sense, but such opposition also was necessary to advance the greater good. Following Merton, the field of sociology began to chart deviance in a more open-ended way, noting its many pathways and inflections. Terms like "positive deviance" and "resistant deviance" began to enter the picture, as sociologists also began to look more closely at crime. Might it be possible that some of America's most venerated values support criminal attitudes as well? Arguments are mounting that mythical beliefs in limitless opportunity are now coming in conflict with everyday reality. As Chris Hedges writes in *Days of Destruction, Days of Revolt*:

> The vaunted American dream, the idea that life will get better, that progress is inevitable if we obey the rules and work hard, that material prosperity is assured, has been replaced by a hard and bitter truth. The American dream, we now know, is a lie. We will all be sacrificed. The virus of corporate abuse—the perverted belief that only corporate profit matters—has spread to outsource our jobs, cut the budgets of our schools, close our libraries, and plague our communities with foreclosures and unemployment.[27]

As individuals increasingly see their wages diminished and their futures put in doubt, antisocial attitudes are making a Darwinian comeback. Criminality and theft are valorized in movies like *American Hustle* (2013), *Now You See Me* (2013), and *American Heist* (2015)—all of which celebrate hyperbolic theft on a large scale. These attitudes have no clearly articulated politics.

The Tea Party and Occupy Wall Street movements enflamed members with visions of property theft or takeover. Not unlike the 1960s, the new millennium has brought with it a populist licensing of the "civil disobedience" valorized by Henry David Thoreau against an authoritarian "machine." Thoreau never told people to steal things. But as the title of the book, *Crime and the American Dream* implies, authors Steven F. Messner and Richard Rosenfield find that dishonest "taking" comes surprisingly naturally in the land of the free. From their perspective, most crime in the U.S. does not arise from the "sickness" of individual pathology or the "evil" of moral failing—or even such conditions as poverty and discrimination, ineffective law enforcement, or the lax punishment of criminals.

"Crime in America derives, in significant measure, from highly prized cultural conditions," Messner and Rosenfield write, explaining that "the American dream itself and the normal social conditions engendered by it are deeply implicated in the problem of crime."[28] Specifically, they point to America's preoccupation with success "at any cost," with little thought about how goals are pursued. This "creates and sustains social structures incapable of restraining criminogenic cultural pressures."[29] The costs to American society are devastating. Even though violent crime in the U.S. has decreased steadily in recent decades, the nation still locks up plenty of people at a cost of $74 billion per year.[30] Crime economists measure costs of criminality in terms of the offense itself (damage/loss, law enforcement, insurance, prosecution, and incarceration costs) and secondary impacts (long-term damage to victims, decline in the quality of life, lowered property values, population migrations). An estimated $1.7 trillon per year was lost to crime in the U.S. in the early 2000s, amounting to $1,686 for every individual.[31] With the rise of Internet crimes like identity scams and intellectual property theft, an additional $400 billion has been added to these numbers.[32]

Cultures of Unreason

Maybe America is losing its mind. Predatory profiteering, out-of-control consumerism, and nonsensical debates like makers-and-takers all seem to suggest that there is something wrong with America's collective thought processes. In a nation that finds itself evenly divided on almost every major issue of the day, citizens and scholars are pondering America's social fragmentation. Is this simply a function of the massive scale and diversity of the U.S.? Or too much media influence? Worries about an America in decline also seem to be everywhere these days, as do popular explanations for the nation's diminished status. How is it that this great country seems to be coming unglued? More than one observer believes that the U.S. simply has lost its grip on reality in a culture of fleeting images and short attention spans. A postmodern failure of "reason" is a familiar theme in recent books ranging from Susan Jacoby's *The Age of American Unreason* (2007) and Dick Tavern's *The March of Unreason* (2007) to more recent works like *Constructions of Neoliberal Reason* by Jamie Peck (2010) and Dale Jamieson's *Reason in a Dark Time* (2015).[33] A lot of these works use the concept of reason to bludgeon someone else's position or thought processes, while others simply impugn the intelligence of the American public. One of the most widely read of these books was *The Assault on Reason* (2007) by former Vice President Al Gore, which ranked number one on the *New York Times* bestseller list for its first month in print.

"Why do reason, logic, and truth seem to play a sharply diminished role in the way America now makes important decisions? How has a persistent preference for falsehoods come to prevail even in the face of massive and well understood evidence to the contrary?" Gore asks.[34] How could the world's most powerful military power plunge itself into a massive war with a country like Iraq, which had not attacked us or threatened U.S. national interests? Why was the country so willing so quickly to reverse its three-century prohibition against torturing prisoners? Or more widely stated, how could America allow post-9/11 despair to be so cynically manipulated? To Gore the answer is clear. An image-saturated society has lost the ability to reason—largely because it has lost the knack of reading. Joining a long line of media reactionaries, Gore decries what he sees as an atrophy in public literacy—leaving Americans vulnerable to advertisers and political hucksters promising money, protection, or both. Gore argues that a weird kind of "unreason" has begun to take over, largely driven by the ways people now get their information about vital issues. *The Assault on Reason* cites recent statistics about how movies, cell phones, iPods, instant messaging, and video games all compete for people's attention. Meanwhile, the average American *still* watches 2.8 hours of television every day, despite the rise of online diversions.[35] And by a three-to-one margin, Americans still turn to Fox News, CNN, MSNBC, and the major networks for news—with print and radio accounting for 9 percent and 6 percent, respectively.[36]

The Assault on Reason and similar books share certain common themes, not the least of which is their uncritical media formalism. Privileging one form of communication (reading) over another (television) neatly dodges issues of meaning and politics that infuse any text. While some kinds of media certainly may be more immediate and ubiquitous than others, their content is always written by someone—and those writers, producers, and their sponsors are what really matters. But more to the point is the very paradigm of "reason" itself, whose presumed supremacy has pushed alternative views to the side for centuries. The Age of Reason replaced hierarchies based on superstition or inherited privilege with forms of authority based on knowledge. Hence, the idea was born that reason separated humanity from other species, that some humans had more reason than others, and that "reasonable" people could always find their way to what is true.

History has shown how terribly wrong societies can go in the pursuit of reasonable objectives—whether this entails the "reasonable" use of slave labor to build the U.S., to the "reasonable" laws regulating women's reproductive rights, to the "reasonable" pursuit of Al Qaeda into the nation of Iraq. Not that any of this is news. Kant and Hegel both saw problems in classical reason—although they reached different conclusions—in debates dating to America's founding decades. If the contemporary era has shown anything, it is that few purportedly "reasonable" ideas hold true for all people and for all time. Ontologically, proposals for a return to reason share much with the makers-and-takers debate—as concepts including everyone and no one. Ideals of reason often have functioned as devices for naturalizing social hierarchies and particular regimes. And in a U.S. political context, they now replicate age-old phantasms of "real Americans" freely exercising rational choice in the voting booth and the marketplace. Naturally, this appeal to a national "common sense" would exclude the non-reasonable and nonproductive takers discussed above, and in doing so resurrects the same exclusionary logic that has defined the U.S. since its earliest days.

But the popular discourse on reason makes one important point—that *culture* matters, especially as normative values find their ways into people's minds. Louis Althusser wrote about this in the 1970s, using the term "ideology" to discuss the "imaginary relationship of individuals to the real conditions of existence."[37] In saying this, Althusser was following Jacques Lacan's proposition that what is truly "real" can never be fully known, but at best approximated in the imaginary realms of the mind (ideals) and their representations in language. This is why people interpret events differently and develop discordant opinions. But while ideology may reside in people's heads, Althusser was quick to point out that it is acquired through day-to-day experiences in the material world. This occurs on conscious and on unconscious levels. Hence, even as one might deliberately choose a particular set of beliefs (like being a "Republican," for example), these conscious decisions often rest on unexamined or preexisting assumptions (like being born a U.S. citizen). The point is that people's belief systems are but partially traceable and often are influenced by ideological "apparatuses" they don't fully apprehend. Families, nations, religions, legal systems, and communication networks are some examples of these apparatuses. Needless to say, Althusser argued that people's behaviors and beliefs were too complicated to be explained by the principles of "reason" that America's founders so valued.

Following the work of Althusser and others, the how and why of ideology has received considerable attention from academics, especially as it affects such fundamental activities as working and spending money. Emerging from 20th-century Marxism, "cultural studies" were part of a broader movement to turn the lens of intellectual analysis on the fabric of everyday life. Beginning with a post–World War II interest in the British working class, writers like Raymond Williams, Stuart Hall, Angela McRobbie, and Judith Williamson began to look at how capitalism played out in the things people found important, the ways that media affected them, and the manner in which material possessions gave meaning to their lives. Among others, Paul Willis would assert the centrality of consumer culture in giving people a sense of personal identity and agency in the world.[38] Willis even went so far as to suggest that people could see through the ideological manipulation of politicians and advertisers—accepting whatever pitches they found credible and tossing the rest aside.

If only things were that simple. The process of ideology described by Althusser turns out to be highly variable according to time and circumstance. Cultural messaging isn't something that can be turned on or off like a light switch. And certainly it doesn't affect all demographic groups the same way. Ideology works in the foreground and background, in the present moment and over time, in one's conscious mind and in the deep recesses of one's senses, perceptions, and affective responses. Its effects can be momentary, cumulative, partial, overlapping as people accept, reject, negotiate, or unconsciously receive messages. Michel de Certeau wrote about the indeterminacy of consumerism and spectatorship, noting that individuals at best exercise partial control over what they see and the way that they interpret it.[39] As de Certeau adds, any conversation about the way viewers receive "the images broadcast by television (representation) and the time spent watching television (behavior) should be complimented by a study of what the consumer 'makes' or 'does' during this time and with these images."[40]

It would seem that this leads back into the epistemological rabbit hole of subjectivity—about the self and its relationship to what lies outside. Do audiences have agency in voting or consuming, or does the process work in reverse? The obvious answer is that both processes operate simultaneously, as reader response theorists pointed out some time ago. Citizens certainly express a sense of "self" through their purchasing and voting decisions, but much of the thinking attached to their preferences comes from the public sphere. Might one conclude that the very image of a "self" that many feel they express derives largely from images coming from elsewhere? Is this image-constructed self really an illusion? Should one conclude that what gets called the self actually derives from external fabrications?

The answer is both and neither. On the one hand, the sense of freedom experienced in selecting a purchase often is little more than a cruel illusion of choice. The marketplace has already preselected the range of items available.

Consumers get pleasure from the belief that they "choose" from Amazon's inventory, much like they vote for a candidate preselected by a mainstream political party. On the other hand, it's worth pondering that all life is a similar set of choices from what is offered. Much of the time the line between actual and virtual isn't always clear. This isn't always a bad thing. While one can argue that many people construct their worlds from received images, the process still retains generative and creative aspects. Philosophers of language have asserted that the idea of an "authentic" self is more of a fantasy than a reality. Nevertheless, a hunger persists for an anchor. Hence, choosing among images or commodities can be just as personal an act as naïvely believing one truly experiences reality.

All of this wreaks havoc on the makers-and-takers discussion. Remember that the original premise of capitalism hinged on the presumed rationality of consumers to vote with their money. This followed from the belief that a literate and informed citizenry was capable of making decisions at the ballot box. But everyone knows that both buying and voting are heavily influenced by *irrationality* of all kinds—and the apparatus of ideology is always working in the background. Old-school social theory used to argue that unwitting masses were duped into "false consciousness" by the chicanery of capitalist ideology. No doubt this is true to a certain extent. But this model never gave people much credit for independent thinking. And it also assumed that people's only real desires were those they got tricked into having. More recent theories of culture look at things somewhat differently, suggesting that ideology doesn't so much give people new ideas about what they want, but instead attaches to what they *really* value—like interpersonal relationships, feelings of security, and optimism about the future. And in turn, these valued substances link to deeper needs, desires, and drives, which many people may not even recognize in themselves. Advertising and other forms of media convince viewers that they can only get these things by behaving in certain ways or buying the right things.[41] This bait-and-switch game is the real genius of modern capitalism. It convinces people that happiness and security lie in material possessions and superficial signs of success. Through this process consuming is deeply linked to identity. A person needs to have the right car or the right clothes to be admired, desired, or successful. And who doesn't aspire to such things?

None of this would be quite so bad if the messaging of advertising and media conveyed a modicum of cultural neutrality. But American capitalism seems to foster persistent worry about impending loss, even in the absence of credible threat. This chapter's discussion of the makers-and-takers debate has detailed how these nagging anxieties fuel the distrust and selfishness so common in today's America, as well as some of the ways that symbols and slogans can animate conflicts with historic roots in the American imagination. Nations and other groups define themselves through symbolic economies of belonging, which bear a tentative relationship to material participation, contribution, or benefit. In this sense, citizenship in any nation always entails a degree of contradiction. Such ontological tensions are especially likely in a nation such as the U.S., where the opposition of the individual to the community is built into the very fabric of personal subjectivity and collective consciousness.

Notes

1 Veronica Dagher, "Do You Make $400,000 a Year but Feel Broke?" WSJ Video (Sept. 4, 2014) http://www.wsj.com/video/do-you-make-400000-a-year-but-feel-broke/387CA8E8-2C0F-449B-8F8F-7BBCF70EE954.html (accessed June 1, 2015).

2 Alicia Parlapiano, Robert Gebeloff, and Shan Carter, "The Shrinking American Middle Class," *New York Times* (Jan. 26, 2015) www.nytimes.com/interactive/2015/01/25/upshot/shrinking-middle-class.html?_r=0&abt=0002&abg=0 (accessed June 7, 2015).

3 Michael B. Katz, *The Undeserving Poor: America's Enduring Confrontation with Poverty* (Oxford and New York: Oxford University Press, 1989).

4 MoJo News Team, "Full Transcript of the Mitt Romney Secret Video," Mother Jones (Sept. 19, 2012) www.motherjones.com/politics/2012/09/full-transcript-mitt-romney-secret-video#47percent (accessed Nov. 2, 2014).

5 "Society does not consist of individuals, but expresses the sum of interrelations, the relations within which these individuals stand." Karl Marx, *Grundrisse: Foundations for the Critique of Political Economy* (1858) (Moscow: Progress Publishers, 1977) p. 265.

6 Ayn Rand, *Atlas Shrugged*, 35th Anniversary Edition (New York: Dutton, 1992) p. 1062.

7 Adam Smith, *The Wealth of Nations* (1776) (New York: Penguin Books, 1982) p. 456.

8 Étienne Balibar, "My *Self* and My *Own*," in Bill Maurer and Gabrielle Schwab, eds. *Accelerating Possession: Global Futures of Property and Personhood* (New York: Columbia University Press, 2006) p. 27.

9 Georg Wilhelm Friedrich Hegel, *The Philosophy of Right* (1821), trans. Alan White, (New York: Hackett, 2015).

10 Karl Marx, *Capital: A Critique of Political Economy*, Vol. 1 (1867), trans. Samuel Moore and Edward Aveling (Moscow: Progress Publishers, 1887).

11 John Maynard Keynes, *A Treatise on Money* (New York: Harcourt, Brace & Co., 1930).

12 "Tobacco Industry: Market Research Reports, Statistics and Analysis," Report Linker (October 2013) http://www.reportlinker.com/ci02053/Tobacco.html (accessed May 18, 2014).

13 David Harvey, "The New Imperialism: Accumulation by Dispossession," *Socialist Register*, 40 (2004) p. 69.

14 Adrian Parr and Brad Evans, "Are Some Lives Disposable?" *Al Jazeera* (Feb. 14, 2014) http://www.aljazeera.com/indepth/opinion/2014/02/are-some-lives-disposable-201421255735775353.html (accessed May 18, 2015).

15 Jacques Rancière, *Disagreement: Politics and Philosophy* (Minneapolis: University of Minnesota Press, 1998).

16 Elizabeth A. Povinelli, *Economies of Abandonment: Social Belonging and Endurance in Late Liberalism* (Durham, NC and London: Duke University Press, 2011) p. 18.

17 Georg Wilhelm Friedrich Hegel, *The Phenomenology of the Spirit* (1807), trans. A.V. Miller (Oxford and New York: Oxford University Press, 1977).

18 Martin Heidegger, *Being and Time* (New York: Harper Perennial Modern Classics, 2008).

19 Bill O'Reilly, "Is Traditional America Gone for Good?" *Fox News* (Nov. 12, 2102) http://www.foxnews.com/transcript/2012/11/13/bill-oreilly-traditional-america-gone-good/ (accessed Nov. 1, 2014).

20 "Makers and Takers: America's Government Redistributes, but Not Well," *The Economist* (Oct. 12, 2012) http://www.economist.com/node/21564407 (accessed May 5, 2014).

21 Ibid.
22 Brandon Roberts, Deborah Povitch, and Mark Mather, "Low-Income Working Families: The Growing Economic Gap," The Working Poor Families Project (Winter 2012–2013) http://www.workingpoorfamilies.org/wp-content/uploads/2013/01/Winter-2012_2013-WPFP-Data-Brief.pdf (accessed Aug. 9, 2014).
23 Vilfredo Pareto, *Manual of Political Economy,* trans. Alfred N. Page (New York: A.M. Kelley, 1971).
24 Kathleen Miles, "Next Time Someone Argues for 'Trickle-Down' Economics, Show Them This," *Huffington Post* (Feb. 17, 2014) http://www.huffingtonpost.com/2014/02/06/rich-richer_n_4731408.html (accessed Nov. 1 2014).
25 "Violent and Property Crime in the US—Crime in America," Crime in America (2014) http://www.crimeinamerica.net/crime-rates-united-states/ (accessed Aug 9, 2015).
26 Robert K. Merton, "The Unanticipated Consequences of Purposive Social Action," *American Sociological Review,* 1, no. 6 (Dec. 1936) pp. 894–904. http://www.d.umn.edu/cla/faculty/jhamlin/4111/2111-home/CD/TheoryClass/Readings/MertonSocialAction.pdf (accessed Aug. 14, 2015).
27 Chris Hedges and Joe Sacco, *Days of Destruction, Days of Revolt* (New York: Nation Books, 2012) pp. 226–227.
28 Mark Twain, as quoted in Steven F. Messner and Richard Rosenfield, *Crime and the American Dream,* 5th ed. (Belmont, CA: Wadsworth, 2011) p. 1.
29 *Crime and the American Dream,* p. 11
30 Robert J. Shapiro and Kevin A. Hassett, "The Economic Benefits of Reducing Violent Crime" (June 19, 2012) Center for American Progress, http://www.americanprogress.org/issues/economy/report/2012/06/19/11755/the-economic-benefits-of-reducing-violent-crime/ (accessed Aug. 14, 2014).
31 David. A. Anderson, "The Cost of Crime," *Foundations and Trends in Microeconomics* 7, no. 3 (Sept. 2012) http://ideas.repec.org/a/now/fntmic/0700000047.html (accessed Aug. 14, 2014).
32 "The Economic Impact of Cybercrime and Cyber Espionage," Center for Strategic International Studies (2013) http://www.mcafee.com/us/resources/reports/rp-economic-impact-cybercrime.pdf (accessed Aug. 14, 2014).
33 Susan Jacoby, *The Age of American Unreason* (New York: Pantheon, 2007); Dick Tavern, *The March of Unreason: Science, Democracy, and the New Fundamentalism* (New York and Oxford: Oxford University Press, 2007); Jamie Peck, *Constructions of Neoliberal Reason* (New York and Oxford: Oxford University Press, 2010); Dale Jamieson, *Reason in a Dark Time: Why the Struggle for Climate Change Failed—and What It Means for Our Future* (New York and Oxford: Oxford University Press, 2015).
34 Al Gore, *The Assault on Reason* (New York: Penguin 2008) p. 1.
35 "American Time Use Survey," U.S. Department of Labor: Bureau of Labor Statistics (2013) http://www.bls.gov/news.release/atus.nr0.htm (accessed July 18, 2013).
36 Lydia Saad, "TV Is Americans' Main Source of News," Gallup Politics (July 8, 2013) http://www.gallup.com/poll/163412/americans-main-source-news.aspx (accessed July 18, 2013).
37 Louis Althusser, *Lenin and Philosophy and Other Essays,* trans. Ben Brewster (New York: Monthly Review Press, 1971) p. 109.
38 Paul Willis, *Common Culture: Symbolic Work at Play in the Everyday Culture of the Young* (Boulder, CO: Westview Press, 1990).
39 Michel de Certeau, *The Practice of Everyday Life,* trans. Steven Randall (Berkeley: University of California Press, 1984).
40 *The Practice of Everyday Life,* p. xii.
41 Hans Magnus Enzenberger, *Critical Essays* (New York: Continuum, 1982).

2

TRUE BELIEVERS

Spiritual Life in a Secular Age

When I first walked into Hobby Lobby more than a decade ago, the place didn't seem especially religious. I'd been traveling in the American South and the store's dorky name had made me curious. While the craft superstore didn't seem particularly remarkable, it felt strangely dislocated in time and place—a shrine to the gendered character of domestic handiwork in certain pockets of American society, even in contemporary times. With areas labeled "Floral," "Fabric," "Jewelry," "Needle Work," and "Wedding Goods" the store's promotional materials featured cheery female advisors offering helpful tips. As Hobby Lobby's upbeat web site put it: "From knitting, crocheting, sewing and bow making to floral designs and seasonal decorations, our project guides and videos will take your projects from drab to fab!"[1] Seen in these terms, the $3.3 billion Hobby Lobby franchise makes a lot (or most) of its money from women—a fact that adds a bitter irony to the company's recent success in convincing the Supreme Court that the religious beliefs of its male CEO were more important than contraceptive insurance provisions for its female employees.[2]

The putative crux of the Hobby Lobby case was the separation of church and state, but with a slightly paranoid constitutional twist. The company asserted that the Affordable Care Act had violated its religious "freedom" (and that contraceptive coverage also would cost it millions). While the case enraged feminists and women's health advocates, it also left most Americans scratching their heads over how such an antiquated view of reproductive rights could prevail in the nation's highest court. More generally, the decision raised troubling questions about the rising political influence of faith in America at a time when religious practice is declining statistically. While most in the U.S. still report that they "belong" to a church or other place of worship, in growing numbers they no longer attend services.[3]

Beliefs and behaviors don't always align in the contemporary U.S., as personal assertions of faith become detached from collective practices of worship. Yet a residual sense of religious affiliation persists, especially among those who see the U.S. as a land of unrestricted worship—a nation founded by people who in many instances had been persecuted on the basis of belief. Hence, many regard religious liberty as one of the country's foundational values. But even a casual look at American history reveals a peculiar tendency of newly arriving groups establishing barriers against other faiths, even as religious "tolerance" was being written into law. Of course competing belief systems are as old as humanity itself, often intersecting with tribal and ethnic rivalries reinforced by geography or national boundaries. Persecution and exile narratives have always been central in Abrahamic, Hindu, and Buddhist traditions. And Christian faiths (to which 77 percent of Americans subscribe) have had a particularly contentious past, often manifest in intergroup antagonism and violence, not to mention campaigns to conquer or convert non-Christians.[4]

Today's most pressing political concern among religious Americans is the decline of faith itself, with nearly three-quarters of believers expressing worry about an increasingly secular society.[5] As tensions rise between "believers and nonbelievers," many feel that the government is to blame, leaving the nation evenly divided over whether politicians should be judged by religious criteria. Aside from this broad concern, reproductive choice remains a hot-button issue, especially as it is affected by health-care legislation. And in the second decade since 9/11, anti-Muslim bigotry seems to be increasing rather than slowing down. Perhaps the most visible site of the religious culture war was the battle over marriage equality, and the presumed affront to sacred tenants posed by the unions of same-sex couples. But while fundamentalist and evangelical Christian groups have been most vocal in this argument, it would be inaccurate to pit marriage equality and Christianity against each other.

In a predominantly "Christian" nation, most Americans have favored marriage equality since 2010. In surveys leading up to the U.S. Supreme Court's 2015 ruling validating the constitutionality of same-sex unions, the Pew Research Center, Gallup Poll, and Bloomberg National Poll all reported aggregate support for same-sex marriage at 55 percent, with a Washington Post/ABC Poll putting the number at 59 percent.[6] Religious groups had lined up on both sides of the issue, with white mainline Protestants (62 percent), white Catholics (58 percent), and Latino/Chicano Catholics (56 percent) all favoring same-sex unions. Marriage equality was favored by 83 percent of Jewish Americans. Opposing same-sex marriage were white evangelical Protestants (69 percent), African-American Protestants (59 percent), and Latino/Chicano Protestants (49 percent).[7]

The marriage equality debates illustrate an important point about the relationship between politics and faith in American life. As a matter of philosophical idealism, religion translates variously and often unpredictably into voter behavior and public policy. Vocal extremists often grab headlines, skewing public perceptions of their numbers and impact. And opinions shift over time, as traditional beliefs are confronted with changing realities. Although issues of marriage and family have attracted a lot of attention in the 2000s, the weird discontinuities between faith and government have played out in all sorts of ways since the founding of the U.S.—and even before. While the separation of church and state has remained a dictum of official policy, the slippery relationship between idealism and realism has been an ongoing problem, creeping into debates over national security, immigration, free speech, tax law, employment equity, reproductive rights, race and ethnicity, and many other matters.

In most accounts, the separation of church and state premise dates to Thomas Jefferson's 1802 letter to a Baptist Church in Danbury, Connecticut, in which Jefferson wrote that "Religion is a matter which lies solely between man and his God," and that "the legislative powers of government reach actions only, and not opinions"—famously adding that the "legislature should make no law respecting an establishment of religion, or prohibiting the free exercise thereof, thus building a wall of separation between church and state."[8] While these phrases are cited often by religious groups as proof of the Christian intentions of the nation's founders, a close reading of the Constitution finds no such provisions whatsoever. The document contains no references to Jesus, Christianity, or God. And when religion is mentioned in the original text (there is only one reference), it is cast negatively—as something to be kept at a distance from the government. Article 6 states that "No religious test shall ever be required as a qualification to any office or public trust under the United States." Of course these days it is commonplace for judges and elected officials to be sworn into office with their hands on Bibles. But this is a convention rather than a legal requirement. As David Niose points out in his book, *Nonbeliever Nation*, the secular character of elected office is evidenced in the careful wording of the oaths that public officials take. As signed into law by George Washington and the federal legislature in 1789, the Congressional oath reads "I do solemnly swear that I will support the Constitution of the United States" and does not include "so help me God" or any similar statement.[9]

But the U.S. is a famously religious country, nevertheless. To many people faith provides a handy philosophical system for explaining some of the most sobering questions of values and mortality. A recent Harris Poll shows that a strong majority (74 percent) of U.S. adults say that they believe in God, although this number was higher (82 percent) five years ago. The majority currently also believe in miracles (72 percent), heaven (68 percent), the survival of the soul after death (64 percent), and the devil (58 percent).[10] It's worth noting that America's level of religiosity sets it apart from other industrialized nations. The WIN-Gallup Global Index on Religion, which scores nations on levels of belief and nonbelief, gives a significantly higher rating on religiosity to the U.S. (60) than countries like Australia (37), Canada (46), France (47), and Germany (51).[11] Opinions vary over why Americans seem so bent on faith. Possible explanations include the relative youth of the U.S. as a nation, the history of religious persecution experienced by the nation's settlers, and the ongoing competition among U.S. religious organizations.[12] One theory even suggests that America's economic growth has been powered by a fear of hell.[13]

Despite America's pronounced religiosity, the numbers of the faithful are on the decline. One-fifth of U.S. adults—and more than one-third of those under 30—now say they don't subscribe to any religion at all. These numbers include more than 13 million self-described agnostics and atheists, along with 33 million individuals identified as "nones" (who simply decline from identifying a faith). There is an age correlation in the "nones" population, with younger people the most non-religious. Nones make up 32 percent of 18–19-year-olds, 21 percent in the 30–49 cohort, 15 percent of people aged 50–64, and 9 percent of those over 65.[14] But something else is going on as well. According to the Pew Research Religion & Public Life Project, three-quarters of nones were raised with a religious affiliation that they now have abandoned. Many people reported feeling put off by religious institutions, which they said were too concerned with "money and power." The character of belief is shifting as well. In the past 30 years the number of people who say that religious texts should be interpreted "literally" has dropped by 20 percent.

Surprised by Sin

Part of the problem has to do with differences in what God means to people. While faith often is practiced collectively, it is also a highly personal matter for many Americans. This creates all kinds of variations in the way people understand their religions—and even the ways they interpret doctrinal texts. Since the invention of the printing press, sacred writings and legal compacts have served as kind of social glue—enabling forms of education, politics, and collective understanding, which were unimaginable in times of oral storytelling. People look to certain books and documents as evidence of prior wisdom and consensus, often overlooking the temporal context of such earlier writings. In public policy, amendments get written into documents like the U.S. Constitution to adjust to a changing world. But when it comes to works presumably written by God, such revisions are hard for some to contemplate. To make matters worse, religious texts often contradict themselves.

Recently former President Jimmy Carter observed that the expansive character of the Christian Bible, with its 36,000 verses of anecdotes and parables, allows readers to find justifications for just about any belief they want. In particular, Carter pointed out how biblical texts have been twisted by religious leaders to promote the subordination of women to men. Discussing his book *A Call to Action: Women, Religion, Violence, and Power,* Carter drew clear connections between Christian scriptural teaching and misogyny: "The most serious and unaddressed worldwide challenge is the deprivation and abuse of women and girls", which he says is "largely caused by a false interpretation of carefully selected religious texts."[15]

Although matters of the body figure prominently in many religious doctrines, in recent years they have become a major preoccupation of the American Christian right. Carter's deconstruction of biblical interpretation echoes what Stanley Fish said in his 1967 book, *Surprised by Sin: The Role of the Reader in* Paradise Lost.[16] In that work, Fish advanced what would later be termed "reader-response" or "reception theory". Simply put, *Surprised by Sin* proposed that readers play a collaborative role with authors in creating the meanings that arise from written texts. Perhaps it's no coincidence that Fish's book largely addressed the "original sin" of Adam and Eve as depicted in Milton's *Paradise Lost.* Not unlike Carter, Fish advanced the thesis that readers express their own interests in whatever truths or inferences they draw from books, often finding what they were already looking for. Notably, *Surprised by Sin* brokered a resolution in an ongoing debate over whether Milton's poem favored Satan or God—with Fish proposing that interpretation varied among readers, and that the true hero of the book was, in fact, its audience.

None of this sat well with literary scholars or Christian moralists of the time, especially those committed to ideals of authorial intent. While in many ways *Surprised by Sin* simply extended ongoing critiques of philosophical absolutism, some felt that Fish's arguments favored reader autonomy over ethical principle. Much of this discontent echoed ongoing worries about postmodernism. Could the questioning of meaning foreclose the possibility of moral grounding? Or did it mean, as one cynic put it, that "Nothing is true everywhere, and everything is true somewhere"? Of course Fish wasn't alone in challenging established hierarchies of knowledge. Roland Barthes's essay "The Death of the Author," also published in 1967, similarly had pointed out that books often took on lives of their own.[17] And Barthes made no bones about directly taking on what he termed the "author-God" in an obvious assault on biblical absolutism. All of this led to assertions that postmodernism promoted an empty relativism, which would open the door to evil and depravity. While postmodernism was being misrepresented as a reactionary denial of textuality and authorship, few of its proponents were ever so extreme in their views. Questioning how meaning is made is not the same as denying the possibility of meaning altogether. Such totalizing dogma was exactly what most postmodernism was trying to avoid. The point was to create an atmosphere in which questions were possible—and alternatives viable.[18]

Behind these controversies was a bigger question about how people make sense of their lives—about the ways they understand themselves, other people, and the larger universe. In this sense, it's no surprise that debates over meaning and signification so often circle back to the topic of God. Without suggesting that one can *never* tell truth from falsehood, it's also worth remembering that no one has all the answers—and that people are always learning from each other. The lesson is that reason is relative, contextually driven, and subject to changing standards and definitions. Unfortunately this relative view of reason is the last thing many Americans want in times of uncertainty. Relative thinking doesn't provide such solace in the face of a faltering economy or a threatening world. This results in pressure to find answers, to locate unifying truths.

True Believers?

Religion takes many forms, serves many purposes, and remains one of the most heavily debated topics in the world. Most American children are exposed to organized belief systems before they can read—and later get taught religion in school. Religion not only infuses individual subjectivity, but also serves important social and cultural functions—as a foundation for community, a conduit of tradition, a guide to behavior, or a set of philosophical laws. Many adults equate religion with their families, homelands, or native communities. Anthropologists draw connections between religion and magical thinking, especially among early societies. As Clifford Geertz observed in 1973, religion provides a link between phenomena people can't understand and the reality of their daily experience. To Geertz, organized belief systems were part of "a system of inherited conceptions expressed in symbolic forms by means of which men communicate, perpetuate, and develop their knowledge about and attitudes toward life."[19] As such, Geertz joined many of his era in viewing religion as a social construction—a system of invented meanings that people make up and pass along to subsequent generations.

Not surprisingly, the idea of religion as fiction has proven divisive—evidenced in the continuing opposition between believers and nonbelievers. One way of viewing this divide is through an "orthodox/progressive" dichotomy. In this shorthand for Western philosophical thinking, orthodox views favor universal, timeless, and transcendent values.[20] A progressive perspective tends toward specificity, contemporaneity, and concreteness. But this model leaves out those falling between or outside its polarities. Even though most recent studies of American religiosity record a large number of people classified as "nones," the question of uncertainty about faith has been more difficult to measure. Less than 1 percent of people will actually call themselves "agnostics," as evidenced in the American Religious Identification Survey.[21]

A searching discussion of faith occurred in a famous exchange between Sigmund Freud and C.S. Lewis.[22] Rather than a face-to-face conversation, the "debate" took the form of essays written by Lewis in the decades following Freud's death in 1939. Freud had addressed the topic of religion in many of his writings, openly expressing his atheistic views. But as a psychoanalyst, Freud sought not only to explain the irrationality of religion, but also the *source* of this irrationality. In his essay "The Future of an Illusion" Freud had pondered the human propensity for magical thinking, noting the attributions of gender and power often associated with faith. Freud saw "God the father" as the perfect object of childhood insecurity and desire, as well as a suitable edifice for social rituals and "laws" of conduct. In other words, faith is pure transference. Human anxiety and wanting become attached to the figure of God, who, not so coincidentally, is absent until one dies. As Freud wrote, "man's helplessness remains and along with it his longing for his father, and the gods."[23] Hence, the concept of God has a threefold purpose: to "exorcise the terrors of nature," "reconcile men to the cruelty of Fate," and "compensate them for the sufferings and privations which a civilized life in common has imposed on them."[24] As would be expected, Freud had plenty to say about guilt—or superego—a concept that many religions literalize in the notion of sin. In this sense, it might be said that Christianity's notion of "original sin" has a psychoanalytic dimension in ascribing guilt to human existence itself. The human subject's innate proclivity for moral failure creates a perpetual double bind, generating a shame that is only escapable through death and spiritual transcendence.

For his part in the debate, Lewis had the advantage of hindsight. Lewis's predilection for magical thinking already had appeared in his Christian parable book series *The Chronicles of Narnia*.[25] But Lewis tried to engage Freud's own work, even as he wrote off the entire psychoanalytic project to a misguided materialism. To Lewis, theories of drives, complexes, and the unconscious were useful—but only up to a certain point. Lewis rejected Freud's contention that an eternal soul was rooted in an unconscious denial of death, for example. Was this simply Lewis's unconscious talking? In this sense, one might say that Freud and Lewis were not so much discussing religion as they were debating different philosophical systems. They literally didn't "believe" in the same things. Lewis posited the mutually exclusive terms of the argument at one point, stating: "Here is a door behind which, according to some people, the secret of the universe is waiting for you. Either that's true or it isn't. If it isn't, then what the door simply conceals is the greatest fraud."[26] This statement could apply either to religion or science, although one must doubt that was what Lewis had in mind. In the end, the debate between Freud and Lewis ended just about where it began—in an epistemological standoff, elliptically phrased by Lewis: "If the whole universe had no meaning, we should never have found out that it had no meaning."[27]

The Freud/Lewis debate had many unacknowledged shortcomings, among them its assumptions about gender roles and Western cultural specificity. While Carl Jung would replicate similar patriarchal thinking, his interdisciplinary engagement with anthropology, art, Eastern philosophy, and mental health yielded a unique perspective for his day on matters of faith. Despite its universalizing tendencies, Jung's "psychologization of religion" proposed a model of the human psyche bent on the pursuit of "wholeness" rather than an ultimate reunion with God per se. For a time, Jungian thought became a more palatable alternative to the binary "believer/nonbeliever" dichotomy. Ideas of interdependence and oneness with the universe inspired forms of quasi-secular spiritualism and humanism. But these ideas had their own problems.

The term "humanism" sometimes carries religious inflections, even as it has been contested in its overly broad applications. In common parlance, a humanist is seen as someone who cares about people or studies a humanistic discipline like history or philosophy. This dual interpretation dates to Latin scholars in the second century. Almost from the beginning, European definitions of human and humanity seemed colored by cultural implications, especially as colonization assessed non-Western "others" as primitive, savage, or otherwise less than human. This generated etiologies of ethnocentrism, tribalism, racism, and related forms of aggression, exploitation, discrimination, and, ultimately, slavery itself. Throughout all of this, humanism continued to bear the dual inflection of ethical belief and informed reason. Both of these views supported ideals of subjective autonomy—including the ability to choose between good and evil. By the 1800s Europeans had begun using the term "human" to distinguish mortals from God. For example, the English would say that Christ was not "merely human," but was born of a "divine nature." During this period this same humanism also was used to suggest a common ground between antagonistic Catholic and Protestant camps (i.e., they both worshipped the same God). This egalitarian impulse would broaden in the 20th century, as technology brought the world closer, while justifying new kinds of global conflict. Utopian humanism would soon attach to a downplaying of human difference and an erasure of cultural specificity. Along the way, humanism shifted to its current nonreligious connotation, with distinctions sometimes made between "spiritual humanist" and "secular humanist" practices. Some secular humanists argue a distinction between moral philosophy and a belief in God, while others insist upon an ethics of pure reason.

While the literal definition of the term "atheist" is a person who believes that God does not exist, a fair number of American atheists equivocate on the matter somewhat. Of the 2.4 percent of people in the U.S. who identify with atheism, one in seven say that they believe in God or universal spirit.[28] And 26 percent reported to the Pew Research Center that they see themselves as spiritual people, with 82 percent also adding that they feel "a deep connection with nature and the earth." But atheists have acquired a bad name in today's Christian mind, although the negative impact of this bad image often goes unnoticed.[29] Nothing has been made of the ban on atheists still upheld by the Boy Scouts of America, for example. The silent sanctioning of this kind of exclusion is but one indication of the continuing outsider status of atheists. Secular humanists rarely organize politically, except in local skirmishes over the teaching of creationism in schools. Part of the anti-atheist dilemma in American culture stems from inherited prejudices from World War II, when the uber-secular program of the Nazi regime reignited religious fervor in the U.S. and around the world. As recently as 2010, Pope Benedict blamed the Holocaust on the same "atheist extremism" and "aggressive secularism" that sanctioned the atrocities of the Third Reich.[30]

And then there is love—a religious concept if ever there was one. Love spills all over spiritual doctrines of many kinds. God gives love, receives love, inspires love, or represents the notion of love itself. Most of the time, the exact meaning of love goes undefined in texts like the Christian Bible, the Koran, or the Torah. Etymologists might point out that the ancient Greeks defined four kinds of love:

kinship, friendship, romance, and divine. Christian theologians distinguish between *eros* (romantic bonding) and *agape* (love of others). Both the Bible and the Torah have "love thy neighbor" passages, much as Islamic texts speak of compassion, kindness, and "brotherhood." Buddhism and Hinduism also speak of both interpersonal love and broader forms of loving other beings. With both psychological and biological dimensions, love resists reduction to a single set of theories or principles. But as is no secret, love has become a contentious topic in contemporary America, as divergent beliefs have come into conflict with public policy.

Barthes might have predicted such disagreements when he wrote in *A Lover's Discourse* about the failure of language to adequate describe the "hallucination" that love constitutes.[31] Focusing on interpersonal love, Barthes noted the subjective experience of love, as directed toward an identified object, even when mutually experienced. This yields simultaneous similarities and differences in love, as with other affective states. Following his other writings on language and meaning, Barthes cast love as an incredibly "wild" substance contingent on what people see and don't see, hear and don't hear, know and don't know—all influenced by their varied histories, cultures, and feelings as these shift from circumstance to circumstance.

Like other powerful emotions (such as hope, fear, trust, and guilt), love easily gets called into service to make certain kinds of arguments. Inasmuch as American marriage laws are considered matters for each state to decide, it is no surprise that President Obama searched for general principles as his views on marriage equality "evolved." In making his first pro-marriage equality statements, Obama invoked principles of Christian theology (the ethic of reciprocity) and U.S. foundational doctrine (inalienable rights of citizenship). "I want everyone treated fairly in this country. We have never gone wrong when we've extended rights and responsibilities to everybody," Obama said, later adding: "Freedom is the ability to go into a store or a restaurant without the fear that you'd be refused service because of who you are or who you love."[32]

As an affective state, love correlates with empathy in many religious doctrines. Psychologist Silvan Tomkins spoke of love in empathic terms in stating that "Christianity became a powerful universal religion in part because of its more general solution to the problem of anger, violence, and suffering versus love, enjoyment, and peace."[33] As a term, "empathy" came into common usage in the 1800s from the earlier word "sympathy." Empathy took on its contemporary meaning in the 20th century, when sociologist Herbert Mead wrote about it as a process of identifying with the experience of another person—essentially a means of seeing the other in oneself. As the field of psychology grew in the post–World War II era, researchers like Tompkins would begin to link empathy to infantile negotiations of needs and desire. Sometimes refuting Freudian principles, child development psychologists looked at "object" loss in theorizing children's abilities to think relationally, develop socially, and build capacities to "read" other people. This interpretive capability was seen in the prelinguistic communication between infant and caregiver as, for example, when one mimics the smile or gesture of another. More recent research has studied the way this "mimetic" function occurs in "mirror neurons" of the brains of animals and humans.[34] The neurons in the brain of the observer fire in the same way as those of the creature observed, replicating a sensation of performing the same action.

Many of the cues one picks up from facial expressions or bodily gestures do not register in the cognitive mind. As mentioned above, the mimesis of the primate and human infant cannot be categorized as language per se. Empathy is loosely categorized as an affective state of the kind described in critical theory as subjective, sensuous, prereflexive, symbolic, relational, inbetween, or alongside. As such, empathy and love are perfectly set up as religious ideals, inasmuch as these states name what is otherwise unnameable. Among adults, empathy is associated most commonly as the ability to recognize someone else's loss or misfortune—famously remembered in Bill Clinton's "I can feel your pain" statements. American Christian denominations often reference the generosity and self-sacrifice modeled by Jesus—as churches link their proselytizing to avowed altruism. But make no mistake about it, organized religion in the U.S. is big business—often linked to finely articulated political agendas. The commodification of religious conversion—most starkly dramatized by televangelists—is part of the marketing agenda that drives so many people away.

Selective Memories

Just as memory is essential to subjectivity, the organization of memory as "history" weighs heavily on belonging and non-belonging. Actions in the present moment are always predicated on past experience about what helps or hinders. Animals may be driven largely by genetic instincts, which partly explain the evolutionary processes of adaptation, mutation, and survival. But within human species, the process is complicated by the vast diversity and the complexity of society. For this reason there is a certain inevitably to arguments over history—and a fallacy to the commonly held view that history is simply a set of natural facts or a public record. History derives from choices made about what to remember. And histories always are written by people with a point of view, whether or not they admit it or are conscious of their biases. This is neither good nor bad. But it means that people often arrive at different ideas about what has taken place in the past and how this experience should guide them in the future. This dilemma has been pondered by anthropologists, humanists, scientists, psychologists—in short, practically everyone who has spent time thinking about the nature of history in this world. Individuals carry different ideas about the world and its past, and in groups they seek to confirm these ideas. Hence, groups will disagree in their memories of the past, as well as how those views might guide the present moment. This wouldn't be such a problem if everyone acknowledged what was going on. After all, our democracy is all about the value of competing perspectives in the marketplace of ideas. The problem occurs when an individual or group begins to claim that its version of history trumps all others.

In his classical work, *The Foundations of Historical Knowledge*, scholar Morton White went to great lengths to point out that the key job of an historian has to do with "explanation and selection." People who write about history must choose the things they will and will not talk about as a matter of mere practicality. By necessity this means making judgments, formulating generalizations, and invariably calling upon certain values in the process. As White put it, the historian employs a set of criteria and "because he records certain events rather than others, he may depend upon value judgments that guide the selection."[35] This means that while historical events take place in the past, the writing of history occurs in the present. Historians bring to the writing of history their understandings, philosophies, and biases. They also bring the insights of the contemporary moment. In the words of Eric Foner, historians "view the constant search for new perspectives as the lifeblood of historical understanding."[36] In recent years, history has figured prominently in political debates as both parties have appealed to the past. How many times has one heard politicians quoting snippets from the Declaration of Independence, the U.S. Constitution, or the writings of patriots who've been dead for hundreds of years? This appeal to "origins" and the founding principles of the nation often accompanies arguments that the United States has somehow lost its way or fallen from grace—and that steps need to be taken to reclaim the country's glorious past.

Obvious parallels can be seen between this line of historicism and religious fundamentalism. The human impulse to look to great texts or books from the past has been studied endlessly. In theoretical terms, the two general categories for the interpretation of texts like the Constitution and the Bible are *exegesis* and *hermeneutics*. Exegesis focuses on a thorough analysis of the content of the text, asking what the work was trying to say. In this sense, exegesis would address the "original intent" of America's founders or the specific messages God sought to transmit through a religious writing. Much of contemporary political discourse, especially that set forth by Tea Party groups, tends to fall into the category of exegesis, as passages are quoted to back up specific arguments. The problem is that a careful analysis of the Constitution and the Declaration of Independence shows that these documents say many (and many different) things, and sometimes contradict themselves. As in religious texts like the Bible, the Koran, or the Talmud, selective quotations can prove just about any point.

Hermeneutics puts the "readings" of exegesis in a broader context, asking how different people understand the meanings of texts in different eras and for varying purposes. A hermeneutic analysis of the Constitution or the Bible would point out that the times have changed since these documents were written. For example, could the framers of the Constitution have anticipated a time when people no longer needed guns to protect their property or to ward off the armies of the British Crown? Could the writers of the Declaration of Independence have foreseen the abolition of slavery or the enfranchisement of women voters? The term "hermeneutic distance" refers to the gap separating different interpretations of a given text—between past and present, for example.

What people do about hermeneutic distance varies according to personal philosophy. Does one invest faith completely in a single historic document because it sets forth "universal" values that hold true for all people through all of time? Or should people recognize that the text was a product of its moment and at best laid out guidelines that applied in certain circumstances? These questions lie at the heart of political divisions that have dogged the U.S. for over two centuries. Perhaps nowhere is the conflict between exegesis and hermeneutics more apparent than in divisions within today's Supreme Court. Conservative justices Antonin Scalia and Clarence Thomas root their opinions in "originalist" interpretations of law. They treat America's founders as a unique breed, capable of rising above their own circumstances or interests in crafting lasting documents for generations to come. In contrast, liberal justices like Ruth Bader Ginsburg and Stephen Breyer take a more pragmatic approach in applying the nation's founding documents to a world that has changed since the 1700s.

Appeals to an idealized past—and debates about the meaning of that history—are nothing new. The U.S. was formed in a radical break from past traditions. This explains why groups from across the political spectrum reach for revolutionary-era philosophy to justify their political agendas—in an endless cycle of insider/outsider posturing. Within decades of the nation's founding, Andrew Jackson positioned himself as "a guardian of a threatened Republican tradition" in seeking to curtail the "tyranny and despotism" of the banking industry.[37] Running for president in 1860, Abraham Lincoln asserted that the nation's founding "fathers" had favored the abolition of slavery, even as his opponents were claiming that the nation's "founders" supported slavery. Franklin D. Roosevelt was fond of quoting Thomas Jefferson in seeking to reconcile individual property rights and government interests. Later Martin Luther King would argue in his "I have a dream" speech that the civil rights struggles of the 1960s were extensions of the principles of the Emancipation Proclamation written a century earlier, which itself reflected founding principles. "When the architects of our republic wrote the magnificent words of the Constitution and Declaration of Independence," King stated, "they were signing a promissory note to which every American was to fall heir. This note was a promise that all men … would be guaranteed the unalienable rights of 'Life, Liberty, and the Pursuit of Happiness.'"[38]

Today's Tea Party movement extends this venerable tradition of contentious historicism. As stated on TeaParty.org, "The true founders of the Tea Party are the brave patriots who dared to challenge the status quo in 1773. We are merely their beneficiaries."[39] Emerging one year into the Obama presidency, the Tea Party hardly had a long-standing "status quo" to fight against. But it certainly had another beef. The Democratic Party had successfully wrestled control of the federal government after eight years of Republican rule, only to find the nation in economic free-fall. The Obama administration and a Democratic Congress moved quickly to rein in the reckless habits of the banking industry and to bail out homeowners. New policies were set in place, which upset many conservatives, especially the 2009 Homeowners Affordability and Stability Plan to help nine million families to avoid foreclosure. Labeling those with mortgage troubles "losers," an outraged CNBC business commentator and former hedge-fund manager named Rick Santelli used the term "Tea Party" in calling for opposition. The name quickly caught on among conservatives as a way to unify against the new liberal majority in power. Evoking metaphors of colonial rule, the conservative Tea Party movement would oppose "big government" plans to regulate corporations, strengthen the social safety net, crack down on gun sales, or increase taxes. Yet at the same time the Tea Party encouraged an expanded role for the government through increased military spending, enhanced immigration controls, and the enforcement of English as the national language. Most recent statistics put membership in various Tea Party political groups at approximately 22 percent of the voting population, a figure roughly equivalent to the number of Americans who identify as "liberal." A Bloomberg National Poll showed that 40 percent of Tea Party supporters are 55 years of age or older, 79 percent are white, 61 percent are men and 44 percent identify as born-again Christians.[40] While the Tea Party hardly can be called a majority movement, its unifying capabilities among both wealthy and disaffected conservatives had sufficient strength to hand Republicans majority control of the House of Representatives in 2010 and the Senate in 2014.

The success of the Tea Party illustrates how a carefully scripted version of past history can be used to motivate populist fervor, even when the script is inaccurate. From Michelle Bachman placing the Battle of Lexington in the wrong state, to Sarah Palin praising Paul Revere for a pro-gun gallop through the streets of Boston—facts, it seems, are far less important than emotional appeals to "liberty" or the Second Amendment. Advertisers and psychologists have recognized for quite some time that fear of loss can be more powerful than desire. This strategy has been time tested. In 1892 the People's Reform Party came up with an agenda with remarkable similarities to that of today's Tea Party. "We meet in the midst of the nation brought to the verge of moral, political, and material ruin," the Reform Party platform stated. The U.S. was said to be "rapidly degenerating into European conditions. The fruits of the toil of millions are badly stolen to build up colossal fortunes for a few." To remedy the situation the Reform Party aspired to "restore the government of the Republic to the hands of the plain people, with which class that originated."[41] Similar revolutionary movements would emerge in the 1930s and again in the 1950s, appealing to populist conservativism in times of economic or political uncertainty.

An idealized unity consistently has animated these populist accounts of U.S. history, a belief that in the past Americans were one people. Perhaps this is the nation's most enduring fiction. Any account of America's past reveals that the country always has been divided—usually in a more or less equal liberal/conservative split.

The nation's political ancestors argued vehemently among themselves in writing the Declaration of Independence and the Constitution. Indeed, their tendencies to disagree informed the very contents of those documents, the "checks and balances" structure of our tripartite government, and the distribution of power along local, state, and federal lines. As a consequence, disagreement and dissent remain protected in constitutional freedoms of speech, assembly, and the press.

Most contentious in recent Tea Party revisionism is the selective way that founding documents have been interpreted on issues of individual and community interests. Contrary to what one hears today, the nation's founders seemed interested in finding a balance. They recognized the reciprocal relationship between citizens and the state, with one enabling the other. "A citizen," wrote Samuel Adams, "owes everything to the commonwealth."[42] Or as Benjamin Rush put it, "every man in a Republic is public property. His time and talents, his youth, his manhood, his old age—all belong to his country."[43] These men were making a simple point: that in those early revolutionary days the *interdependence* of people was perfectly clear. Capitalism might provide incentives for achievement, but social structure was needed to organize people's efforts. Democracy would enable shared decision making, but a government was needed to operationalize the decisions. If subsequent history has shown anything, it is that while everyone can agree that ideals like "freedom," "liberty," and "equality" are enviable goals, agreement seems to fracture over how to achieve those ends.

Certainly America's founding documents provide guidance on how to think about these issues. But they raise as many questions as they settle. As former Supreme Court Justice David Souder put it, the problem and the brilliance of the Constitution is that it resists a single interpretation because it is rooted in "a pantheon of values" rather than a solitary dogma. "Not even in its most uncompromising and unconditional language" does the Constitution resolve its own internal contradictions. "The Constitution's framers left much to be resolved another day, and another day after that, for our cases can give no answers that fit all conflicts, and no resolutions immune to rethinking when the significance of old fact may have changed in the changing world."[44]

History of Religious Outsiders

Religion has polarized American society long before the nation's founding. While some settlers came to the new land because of religious persecution, many others brought deeply entrenched religious antagonism along with them. This is one reason why efforts were made to establish the U.S. as a secular country with no official faith. But before recounting this history, it's important to note the extent to which narratives of antagonism, vengeance, punishment, persecution, and martyrdom inhere in Western faith itself. Without stating the obvious, one can say that America's dominant religious belief system—Christianity—is premised as much on fear and suffering as it is on hope and joy. In storytelling terms, these elements are essential to the dramatization of good-versus-evil narratives, not to mention the soul's ultimate assignment to heaven or hell. While many of today's most pious Christian organizations will rally against violence or eroticism in movies and computer games, they see no problem whatsoever in biblical tales of vengeance, murder, or sexual servitude. Most Christian children get these messages before they have learned to read, as in the iconic New Testament story of the ritual torture and execution of Jesus. When the crucifixion narrative was cinematically dramatized in Mel Gibson's *The Passion of the Christ,* critic Roger Ebert called the film "the most violent movie I have ever seen."[45]

In his book, *Things Hidden Since the Foundation of the World*, René Girard writes of the origins of sacrificial violence in the Christian mind.[46] Famous for his theories of mimesis, Girard begins by looking at the original Christian myth of the god-victim executed by an anonymous crowd. This myth would later form the basis of ritual reenactments in religious ceremonies (the Holy Eucharist) perpetuating the idea of violence. Against this psychic background, that stage would be set for the displacement of anguish and violence onto other objects. Girard's insight lay in recognizing that that structure of the myth itself (and God's underlying sanctioning of violent behavior) was more potent than any laments over Christ's innocence. Murder would be ritualized, copied, and translated into new forms against others in an endless chain of traumatic repetition.

An outsider mentality is crucial to the Christian mindset, inasmuch as Jesus is depicted as a renegade within the Jewish population of a then Roman-occupied Palestine. The growth of early Christianity is partly attributed to the continued resistance of Jewish leaders to the new faith. But martyrdom proved remarkably potent as an organizing tool, as early Christians shrewdly publicized Roman atrocities against congregation members. Both Christianity and Islam spread as resistance movements throughout the Mediterranean Basin, until the Edict of Rome relaxed policies against Christians in AD 313 and officially adopted the "Catholic" (literally meaning "all-encompassing") faith for the empire shortly thereafter. From the very beginning two distinct pressures dogged the Christian faith: a continuing impulse to innovate and change, manifest in new sects and splinter groups; and an ongoing antagonism against rival faiths, most notably manifest in violent conflicts with Byzantine Muslims. Efforts to maintain a centralized Christianity governed by Rome began to falter as the faith reached more distant regions in Europe. By the 1000s popes had begun cracking down within Europe with Inquisitions and launching militarized Crusades into the Middle East. Christianity effectively split soon thereafter along Western Catholic and Eastern Orthodox lines, as new sects also began popping up despite violent church efforts to suppress them. Calvinist, Lutheran, and Episcopal branches emerged in the Protestant Reformation of the 1500s, as Rome was dispatching missionary expeditions to Africa, Asia, and North and South America. Protestant and Catholic faiths were quite literally warring against each other in a Europe in which secular states had yet to be invented—leaving both sides with something to gain from territory in the New World. But it would take nearly 300 more years for the idea of a nonreligious republic to be born.

Needless to say, this violent religious history was well known to early settlers. Hardly anyone living in Europe had been untouched by intergenerational religious conflict and its resultant trauma. The church-sponsored colonization of the U.S. began with Christopher Columbus in his second expedition in 1493, which launched nearly 200 years of Spanish exploration and settlements in the American South and Southwest. French Catholics had made similar inroads in the Deep South, Midwest and Quebec Province. Meanwhile, Protestant brigades had begun landing along the North and Central Atlantic coasts. As the Church of England moved into Virginia, its various dissident sects settled Massachusetts (Pilgrims and Puritans), Pennsylvania (Quakers and Amish). Catholics initially settled Maryland as Germans and Dutch (Quakers and Lutherans) also arrived. These groups brought their religious antagonisms with them, manifest in exclusionary practices that varied from locale to locale. All of this was taking place in an unstructured land of outposts and settlements in which a hostile natural environment was the biggest initial challenge facing everyone. Add to this the harsh fact that over half of those embarking from Europe died on voyages across the Atlantic.

Given these hardships, it is not surprising that early Americans clung to faith and formed communities around it. Religious solidarity was more than a philosophical ideal, since church-based society also was the basis of material survival. Beyond this, religious mythology also informed attitudes toward the land itself, as well as the purpose of the new settlements. These attitudes are described at length in Richard Slotkin's *Regeneration through Violence: The Mythology of the American Frontier, 1600–1800.*[47] In general terms, Christian settlers saw themselves on a divine mission of wilderness conquest and personal salvation informed by biblical narratives and legends derived from European literature. In the minds of many, the land that would become the United States embodied the search for the Heavenly City, Jerusalem, the New Canaan, the Holy Grail, *The Pilgrim's Progress*, or the recovery of the Golden Age. The Exodus of the Israelites from Egypt was a popular theme in which "the New World was seen primarily, not in the physical terms of chivalric romance, but in terms of psychological and spiritual Quest, the quest for salvation in the wilderness of the human mind and soul."[48] In a more secular interpretation, Slotkin also describes the sexualized narrative in Roman mythology of the union between the hero king and the goddess of nature—a psychic reconciliation of what he terms a "reasoning, cold, masculine consciousness" with "feminine principles of passivity, passion, and acceptance" in the interest of a unified subjectivity.[49]

It's important to point out that these wilderness myths and conquest rationalizations varied greatly among settler groups. But one thing they shared was a common antipathy for indigenous peoples. In the Puritan mind, for example, native populations would come to embody antithetical images of Christian moral theories, beliefs, and rituals—thus forming a clearly racialized good-versus-evil divide. This is the common opposition shown in every cowboy movie or other depiction of the American West. But as Slotkin points out, the construction of the "Indian" as *other* was also crucial to the consolidation of divergent European cultures into a unified white American identity. Keep in mind the centuries of religious conflict the settlers had brought with them, not to mention economic and social class differences. In this context, native "devils" provided the perfect displacement. It didn't take long for these differences to form justifications for violence in the name of divine will. Fanned by paranoia spread in print media, settlers would become unified in direct fears of native atrocities or captivity in "heathen" hands. This alone could rationalize aggression in the name of a biblical "Holy War." Many texts of the era also equated conflicts with indigenous people to more recent Protestant–Catholic wars in Europe. Nathaniel Saltonstall's *The Present State of New-England with Respect of the Indian War* (1675) explicitly makes this analogy.[50] The book also describes divisions among settlers over whether to befriend or subjugate native peoples. All sorts of disagreements broke out during the 1600s over "discipline" versus "tolerance" in regard to the indigenous population, reflecting schisms within settler groups between strictly orthodox and relaxed progressive religious practices. One prevailing narrative described the colonial adventure as a "test of faith" by which settlers would be judged for all eternity.

Religious differences among settler groups often produced their own bloody consequences, although popular accounts of American history usually leave this out. Catholic Spanish settlers in St. Augustine, Florida seized a largely French colony in 1565 in nearby Fort Caroline, with the Spanish commander writing to King Phillip II that he "hanged all those we found" because "they were scattering the odious Lutheran doctrine in these Provinces."[51] The Puritan settlement of Massachusetts Bay kept itself "pure" by banning all competing faiths, especially Catholic "Papists." John Tracy Ellis wrote that a "universal anti-Catholic bias was brought to Jamestown in 1607 and vigorously cultivated in all the thirteen colonies from Massachusetts to Georgia."[52] Virginia passed a Catholic exclusion law in 1642. In Puritan Boston, four Quakers were hanged in public between 1659 and 1561 for refusing to denounce their faith. In New Amsterdam, Peter Stuyvesant expelled all Jews for fear they would "infect the colony." Maryland similarly denied civil rights to Jews. Throughout the 1700s Georgia, New York, and Rhode Island banned Catholics from holding public office. And Delaware required all citizens to swear an oath of allegiance to the Holy Trinity.

Thomas Jefferson recognized the problems to national unity that religiosity was causing, but failed in his first effort to legislate religious equality in Virginia. James Madison would later take up Jefferson's cause, but only after being outraged by the arrest of Baptist ministers in Virginia. In a document entitled "Memorial and Remonstrance against Religious Assessments," Madison asked: "Who does not see that the same authority which can establish Christianity, in exclusion of all other religions, may establish with the same ease any particular sect of Christians, in exclusion of all other sects?"[53] As late as 1784 efforts continued to include religious provisions in the U.S. Constitution, with Patrick Henry trying to mandate Christian instruction as a matter of law. But the final document ratified in 1787 eliminated all such language. As Kenneth C. Davis observed in a recent essay entitled "America's True History of Religious Tolerance," the nation's founders "may have thanked Providence and attended church regularly—or not. But they also fought a war against a country in which the head of state was the head of the church. Knowing well the history of religious warfare that led to America's settlement, they clearly understood both the dangers of that system and of sectarian conflict."[54]

Despite these efforts to neutralize religiosity, American Protestant Christianity has maintained its hegemonic hold on U.S. culture. The peculiar confluence of unregulated faith, competition among sects, and the Western cult of the individual has produced a plethora of contradictions. Christian biblical doctrines of charity and "brotherly love" conflict with practices of exclusion and prejudice toward other faiths. In some cases, the separation of church and state is valued only to the extent it allows Christian groups to flaunt tax laws and civil rights provisions. Some churches also aggressively fundraise and organize to influence legislation. One sees in these inconsistencies a conflict between principles of internal doctrine and church outreach. Keep in mind that an expansionist program was at the core of Christianity from the very start—from accounts of the life of Jesus to the rapid growth of the early Christian Church. Missionary and conversion impulses motivate Christianity perhaps more so than any other faith. Often these efforts are rationalized as a charitable enterprise, thereby wrapping any expansionist motivations in the more palatable guise of goodwill and even self-sacrifice.

While one can say that most American Christians conduct themselves within the bounds of propriety, extremist groups continue to appear in the headlines. The legacies of ancient Holy Wars reemerge in conflicts over gender and reproductive rights (the "War on Women"), reasoned inquiry (the "War on Science"), and the Muslim world (Islamophobia linked to the "War on Terror"). At the fundamentalist fringes of Christianity are those promoting hate and violence against anyone they deem immoral. Political candidates for offices at every level of government feel obliged to broadcast their Christian credentials. Protestants always have held the majority of seats in the U.S. Congress. The 113th Congress was 57 percent Protestant, 30 percent Catholic, 8 percent Jewish, and the remaining 5 percent Quaker, Buddhist, or undisclosed.

The negative history of American Christianity had been widely documented, but rarely discussed as a systemic problem. As with other formulations of American mythology, "faith" remains an ambivalent value. Freedom "from" religion easily slides into freedom "to" practice religion. The U.S. may have no national religion according to law, but history has shown that legal prohibitions alone cannot reform deeply held cultural values. Anti-Catholicism has a long history in America—some of it originating from long-standing biases among British settlers against both the Papacy and Church of England. Despite the secular pronouncements of the U.S. Constitution, so-called nativist Protestant movements in the early 1800s asserted that Catholicism was both theologically problematic and politically destabilizing. These sentiments gained strength as the U.S. saw increased immigration during this period from Ireland and Germany, resulting in calls to contain Catholic populations and limit their westward movement into the new frontier. From 1854 to 1856 the Know Nothing Party would gain popularity in the U.S. based in part on the idea of restricting Catholic immigration. Catholic schools became targets following the success of New York City's Tammany Hall in securing state money. Before long anti-parochial "Blaine Amendment" school bills (named after Maine senator James G. Blaine) would be passed in 34 states. Anti-Catholicism was a central tenant of the Ku Klux Klan movement of the 1920s—as well as the career of Supreme Court Justice Hugo Black, who was a KKK supporter. In 1928 Catholic presidential candidate Al Smith lost the Democratic nomination to Franklin D. Roosevelt. The election of John F. Kennedy as president in 1960 showed an evolution in mainstream attitudes toward Catholicism. Subsequent scandals over long-hidden sexual abuses by Catholic priests tarnished the church's image in the 2000s, as favorable views of U.S. Catholics dropped to 45 percent in a study by Gallup.[55]

Anti-Semitism has been a persistent problem for Jewish Americans, dating back to long before the nation's founding. Some historical accounts date the origins of Anti-Jewish thinking to ancient Greece and Egypt. But the roots of American anti-Jewish bigotry have roots in European Christian faith, dating to the First Crusade (1096), the expulsion of Jews from England (1296), the Spanish massacres (1391), the Inquisition, Cossack massacres in Ukraine (1648), pogroms of Imperial Russia (1821 and 1906), and the French Dreyfus affair (1896–1906). Once a term referring to a family of languages spoken in West Asia, the word "Semitic" acquired its Jewish specificity in Germany during the 1800s. In 1843 Karl Marx commented on then-ongoing anti-Semitic debates in his essay "On the Jewish Question", in which he posited the incompatibility of Christianity and Judaism in the secular capitalistic state.[56] But Marx could not foresee the confluence of fascism and eugenics that would lead Nazi Germany to its genocidal "ultimate solution" in the World War II era. In the decade following the Holocaust, Hannah Arendt would focus more directly on racism as an organizing principle of anti-Semitism within the broader context of colonialism. Focusing on the totalitarian regimes of Nazi Germany and communist Russia, Arendt noted ways that ethnocentrism could support autocracy in suppressing opinion, especially when minority opinion was rendered illegal or kept in check by state-authorized violence.[57] Though it may come as a surprise to many Americans, Anti-Jewish sentiments still persist in the U.S. and around the world. As recently as 2013, surveys by the Anti-Defamation League have shown that close to 19 percent of Americans hold anti-Jewish views—numbers that are worse in Western Europe (24 percent), Eastern Europe (34 percent), Asia (22 percent), and the Middle East and North Africa (74 percent).[58]

Islamophobia has become the 21st century's licensed form of bigotry, owing to the close association of Muslim religion and terrorism in the Western mind. But such attitudes have much earlier origins. In many accounts, prejudice toward Islam can be dated to the Age of Exploration, especially the colonial expansion of the British Empire. In his 1978 book *Orientalism*, Edward Said noted the beginnings of this in the 1500s, when Westerners cast Asian populations in general and Middle Easterners in particular as "exotic" others.[59] Influenced by post-structuralism, Said proposed that Western colonizers projected their own desires and anxieties onto the inexplicable signifier of the East—easily constructing an inverted image of the Western self so ingrained in European literature and media that it became naturalized for centuries. Writing in the 25th anniversary edition of *Orientalism*, Said would specify his original premises further, noting growing tendencies to reduce populations into "unifying rubrics like 'America,' 'The West,' or 'Islam' and invent collective identities for individuals who are actually quite diverse."[60] Additional stereotypes narrowly associate the Islamic religion with Middle East oil-producing countries. (In fact, OPEC nations comprise but a small fraction of a large constellation of predominately Muslim nations as diverse as Afghanistan, Algeria, Egypt, Indonesia, Malaysia, Saudi Arabia, and Turkey). With 1.57 billion followers, Islam accounts for 23 percent of the world population. In comparison, Christianity's 2.1 billion adherents account for 29 percent of the world.[61]

While the existence of Muslim extremism in isolated regions is undeniable, the long history of terrorism within the U.S. by other groups, including Christian extremists, remains ignored or forgotten. Following 9/11, U.S. law enforcement found itself with often-conflicting definitions of what constituted a terrorist act, with the FBI eventually differentiating between crimes committed inside and outside the U.S. and between those committed by American citizens and others. Within these expanded definitions, "domestic terrorism" has come to include violence by mass killers, anti-abortion extremists, and organized hate groups, among others.[62] In recent years the FBI has also become increasing vigilant in monitoring animal rights and environmental groups.

While attacks by Islamic groups account for a small portion of terrorist violence in the U.S., they still get most of the attention. In 2014 journalist Nathan Lean pointed to what he termed an "Islamophobia industry" in the U.S. as a "multi-million dollar network with deep pockets and extensive political connections" consisting of "right-wing bloggers, politicians, academics and terrorism 'experts,' all of whom are committed to telling us the truth, the whole truth, and nothing but the truth of Islam."[63] Those who fund and encourage this industry often accuse anyone who calls attention to anti-Muslim hate speech or discrimination of engaging in "political correctness." It seems that within certain communities in the U.S., sentiments persist that "sensitivity to the feelings of Muslims has run amok and that it is time to stand up to the global threat posed by the global Muslim population to Western values."[64]

Issues of gender, sexuality, and family have informed the beliefs of many faiths—with the patriarchal underpinnings of Islamic traditions often held to exemplify its archaic orientation. But certain U.S. Christian groups continue to reveal comparable tendencies. American Christian fundamentalists have stood at the forefront of the so-called War on Women during the 2000s—witnessed in legislative and rhetorical attacks on women's rights across the nation. Issues include a wide variety of policy efforts designed to place restrictions on women's health care and erode protections for women and their families. According to the American Civil Liberties Union, examples "at the state and federal level have included restricting contraception; cutting off funding for Planned Parenthood; state-mandated, medically unnecessary ultrasounds; abortion taxes; abortion waiting periods; forcing women to tell their employers why they want birth control, and prohibiting insurance companies from including abortion coverage in their policies."[65]

Perhaps no issue in the new millennium had proven more divisive among American Christians than that of marriage equality. As discussed at the beginning of this chapter, six out of ten U.S. Protestants seem to favor same-sex unions, with opposition most strongly held among evangelical groups. Evangelicalism equates to literalist interpretations of biblical gospels, and dates specifically to the British American "pietism" of the 1800s. In simple terms, evangelicals believe that the liberalizing trends of mainline Protestantism went too far. Hence, invocations of a nostalgic return to origins are frequently heard in evangelical rhetoric, which are often contrasted to perceived declines in morality and laments over the loss of what is "truly" American. Peculiar to evangelical groups from the 1700s to today is an aggressive entrepreneurialism, manifest in energetic outreach. This partly explains why evangelical church membership (now at just under 40 million) accounts for 60 percent of American Protestantism.[66] Little analysis of this phenomenon has taken place. Some observers believe that the confluence of post-9/11 anxiety and economic recession produced a fertile climate for evangelical beliefs, which also easily accommodate latent xenophobic tendencies. In a recent essay in the *American Scholar* about the famed "Crystal Cathedral," journalist Jim Hinch noted that the once-commanding ministry of Rev. Robert Schuler had fallen into bankruptcy.[67] Perhaps a bellwether of things to come for evangelicalism more generally, Hinch cited changing demographics in Southern California, in which rising immigrant populations from Latin America and Southeast Asia had displaced the once-dominant white majority. An article in the *New York Times* similarly cited recent declines in evangelical numbers, noting a survey finding concerns over evangelical extremism among 53 percent of Americans.[68]

This wavering of support has not been lost on evangelicals themselves, with one prominent figure lamenting a possible future of "religion without the Holy Ghost, Christianity without Christ, forgiveness without repentance, salvation without regeneration, politics without God, and heaven without hell."[69] These comments reveal not only a yearning for fundamentalism and a politicization of religion, they also point toward intolerance of moderate views. Specifically worrisome to evangelicals are the growing numbers of those described above as "nones"—people who might identify as spiritual, but who reject organized faith or hard-line dogma. As Kevin Shrum writes in the *Christian Post*:

> How does one live as a Christian in an era where same-sex marriage is now the norm, where homosexuality is openly celebrated, where hypocrisy in the church is consistently exposed, where atheism is not just an alternative intellectual option, but a hostile enemy, where Christianity is viewed as the enemy and not the founder and friend of America, and where the "spiritual shallowness" of many Christians, especially evangelical Christians, is being exposed for what it is—an Americanized version of cultural Christianity that is not authentic, genuine, or biblically orthodox? The answer is that we learn from our brothers and sisters in other nations who have lived "behind enemy lines."[70]

Clearly battle lines are being drawn and redrawn in a continuing struggle over religion in America. Given the long-standing predilection of the U.S. population toward Christian faith and ideology, the terms of this struggle are essential to understanding the premise of *Elsewhere in America*. Yet perhaps most troubling in the contentious opposition between believers and nonbelievers in America is the growing perception of a widening divide. Christians of every denomination report what they sense to be a growing hostility toward their beliefs—especially in popular culture and government—even as the absolute numbers of self-described Christians in America holds steady.[71] Spurred perhaps by worries of vocal born-again evangelical minorities, deeply entrenched fears of persecution seem to be rising, even among mainstream Christian groups. Writing in the *American Conservative*, Donald Devine recently wrote of this rising anxiety in an article entitled "Are American Christians Paranoid?" While confirming the worries of his fellow believers in a litany of antigovernment complaints, Devine closed his essay with an appropriate message: "Danger comes from those who claim the whole truth and are determined to force it for the other person's good."[72]

Notes

1 "Projects and Videos," Hobbylobby.com (n.d.) http://www.hobbylobby.com/projects (accessed June 11, 2015).
2 Adam Liptak, "Supreme Court Rejects Contraceptives Mandate for Some Corporations," *New York Times* (June 30, 2014) http://www.nytimes.com/2014/07/01/us/hobby-lobby-case-supreme-court-contraception.html?_r=0 (accessed June 11, 2015).
3 "Public Sees Religion's Influence Waning," Pew Research Religion & Public Life Project (Sept. 22, 2014) http://www.pewforum.org/2014/09/22/public-sees-religions-influence-waning-2/ (accessed Nov. 3, 2014).
4 "In U.S. 77% Identify as Christian," Gallup Politics (Dec. 24, 2012) http://www.gallup.com/poll/159548/identify-christian.aspx (accessed June 22, 2014).

5 "Public Sees Religion's Influence Waning."
6 "Polling Data and the Marriage Equality Movement," Marriage Equality USA, http://www.marriageequality.org/polls-and-studies (accessed May 26, 2015). See Adam Liptak, "Gay Marriage Backers Win Supreme Court Victory," *New York Times* (June 26, 2015) http://www.nytimes.com/2015/06/27/us/supreme-court-same-sex-marriage.html (accessed June 26, 2015).
7 "A Shifting Landscape: A Decade of Change in American Attitudes about Same-Sex Marriage and LGBT Issues," Public Religion Research Institute (Feb. 26, 2014) http://publicreligion.org/research/2014/02/2014-lgbt-survey/ (accessed May 24, 2014).
8 Thomas Jefferson, as quoted in David Niose, *Nonbeliever Nation: The Rise of Secular American* (New York: Palgrave, 2014) p. 51.
9 *Nonbeliever Nation*, p. 54.
10 "Americans' Belief in God, Miracles and Heaven Declines," Harris Interactive (Dec. 13, 2013) http://www.harrisinteractive.com/ (accessed May 27, 2014).
11 "Global Index of Religiosity and Atheism—2012," WIN-Gallup International, http://www.wingia.com/web/files/news/14/file/14.pdf (accessed May 28, 2015).
12 E. Brooks Holifield, "Why Do Americans Seem So Religious?" *Sacred Matters*, https://scholarblogs.emory.edu/sacredmatters/2014/01/21/why-do-americans-seem-so-religious/ (accessed May 28, 2014).
13 Michael Fitzgerald, "Satan, The Great Motivator," Boston.Com (Nov. 15, 2009) http://www.boston.com/bostonglobe/ideas/articles/2009/11/15/the_curious_economic_effects_of_religion/ (accessed May 28, 2014).
14 "'Nones' on the Rise," Pew Research Religion & Public Life Project (Oct. 9, 2012) http://www.pewforum.org/2012/10/09/nones-on-the-rise/ (accessed June 1, 2014).
15 President Jimmy Carter, as quoted in Allison Flood, "Jimmy Carter Rails against World-wide 'Abuse of Women and Girls' in New Book," *The Guardian* (Mar. 24, 2014) http://www.theguardian.com/books/2014/mar/24/jimmy-carter-call-to-action-women-girls-abuse (accessed May 24, 2014). See, Jimmy Carter, *A Call to Action: Women, Religion, Violence and Power* (New York: Simon & Schuster, 2014).
16 Stanley Fish: *Surprised by Sin: The Role of the Reader in* Paradise Lost (Cambridge, MA; Harvard University Press, 1967).
17 Roland Barthes, "The Death of the Author," *Aspen*, nos. 5–6 (1967).
18 Craig Owens, "The Allegorical Impulse: Toward a Theory of Postmodernism", reprinted in Brian Wallis, ed., *Art after Modernism: Rethinking Representation* (New York: New Museum, 1984) pp. 203–205.
19 Clifford Geertz, *The Interpretation of Cultures* (New York: Basic Books, 1973) p. 89.
20 James Jefferson Hunter, *Culture Wars: The Struggle to Define America* (New York: Basic Books, 1991).
21 "American Religious Identification Survey," ARIS (2008) http://b27.cc.trincoll.edu/weblogs/AmericanReligionSurvey-ARIS/reports/ARIS_Report_2008.pdf (accessed June 1, 2014).
22 Armand M. Nicholi, Jr. *The Question of God: C.S. Lewis and Sigmund Freud Debate God, Love, Sex and the Meaning of Life* (New York: Free Press, 2002).
23 Sigmund Freud, *The Future of an Illusion*, (1927) reprint edition (New York: Martino Fine Books, 2011) p. 17.
24 Ibid.
25 C.S. Lewis, *The Chronicles of Narnia* book series (New York: Macmillan: 1950–1956).
26 Armand M. Nicholi, Jr. "Why Freud & Lewis?" PBS.org http://www.pbs.org/wgbh/questionofgod/why/index.html (accessed June 1, 2015).
27 C.S. Lewis, *Mere Christianity* (New York: HarperOne, 2001) pp. 45–46.
28 "5 Facts About Atheists," Pew Research Center (Oct. 23, 2012) http://www.pewresearch.org/fact-tank/2013/10/23/5-facts-about-atheists/ (accessed June 3, 2014).
29 *Nonbeliever Nation*, p. viii.

30 *Nonbeliever Nation*, p. 77.
31 Roland Barthes, *A Lover's Discourse: Fragments,* trans. Richard Howard (New York: Hill and Wang, 1978).
32 "Obama Backs Gay Marriage," *Huffington Post* (May 9, 2012) http://www.huffingtonpost.com/2012/05/09/obama-gay-marriage_n_1503245.html (accessed June 3, 2014); "Obama Redefines Freedom in Recent Speech," Western Journalism (Mar. 14, 2014) http://www.westernjournalism.com/obama-redefines-freedom-recent-speech/#vb3kyCrWV7xbx B6U.99 (accessed June 3, 2014).
33 Silvan Tompkins, *Affect Imagery Consciousness: Anger and Fear*, Vol. 3 (New York: Springer, 1991) p. 29.
34 Marco Iacoboni, "Grasping the Intentions of Others with One's Own Mirror Neuron System," *PLOS Biology* (Feb. 22, 2005) http://journals.plos.org/plosbiology/article?id=10.1371/journal.pbio.0030079 (accessed May 12, 2015).
35 Morton White, *The Foundations of Historical Knowledge* (New York: Harper & Row, 1965) p. 3. For a thorough discussion, see: E.J. Dionne, Jr., *Our Divided American Heart: The Battle for the American Idea in an Age of Discontent* (New York: Bloomsbury, 2012).
36 Eric Foner, *Who Owns History? Rethinking the Past in a Changing World* (New York: Hill and Wang, 2002) p. xvi.
37 Andrew Jackson, as quoted in *Our Divided American Heart*, p. 54.
38 Martin Luther King, Jr., *I Have a Dream Speech* (Aug. 28. 1963) http://www.americanrhetoric.com/speeches/mlkihaveadream.htm (accessed May 11, 2015).
39 Rick Santelli, "About Us," *TeaParty.org*, http://www.teaparty.org/about-us/ (accessed June 28, 2014).
40 "The Tea Party, by the Numbers" (Oct. 18, 2013) *Bloomberg View*, www.bloombergview.com/articles/2013-10-18/the-tea-party-by-the-numbers (accessed June 28, 2014).
41 *Our Divided American Heart*, p. 194
42 Jonathan N. Neen, *Creating a Nation of Joiners: Democracy and Civil Society in Early National Massachusetts* (Cambridge, MA: Harvard University Press, 2008) p. 14.
43 Steven Watts, *A Republic Reborn: War and the Making of Liberal America, 1790–1820.* (Baltimore, MD: Johns Hopkins University Press, 1987) p. 132.
44 *Our Divided American Heart*, p. 133.
45 Roger Ebert, "*The Passion of the Christ*," (Feb. 24, 2004) http://www.rogerebert.com/reviews/the-passion-of-the-christ-2004 (accessed June 19, 2014).
46 René Girard, *Things Hidden since the Foundation of the World* (Stanford, CA: Stanford University Press, 1987).
47 Richard Slotkin, *Regeneration through Violence: The Mythology of the American Frontier, 1600–1800.* (Norman: University of Oklahoma Press, 1973).
48 *Regeneration through Violence*, p. 39.
49 *Regeneration through Violence*, p. 29.
50 Nathaniel Saltonstall, as cited in *Regeneration through Violence*, pp. 81–83.
51 Kenneth C. Davis, "America's True History of Religious Tolerance," *Smithsonian Magazine* (Oct. 2010) http://www.smithsonianmag.com/ist/?next=/history/americas-true-history-of-religious-tolerance-61312684/ (accessed June 20, 2014).
52 John Tracy Ellis, *American Catholicism* (Chicago, IL: University of Chicago Press, 1956) p. 101.
53 James Madison, as quoted in "America's True History of Religious Tolerance."
54 "America's True History of Religious Tolerance."
55 Jeffrey M. Jones, "Americans Have Net-Positive View of U.S. Catholic Church" (April 15, 2008) http://www.gallup.com/poll/106516/americans-netpositive-view-us-catholics.aspx (accessed June 21, 2014).
56 Karl Marx, "*On the Jewish Question*" (1843) (New York: CreateSpace Independent Publishing Platform, 2012).

57 Hannah Arendt, *The Origins of Totalitarianism* (New York: Schocken, 1951).
58 "The Largest Survey Ever of Anti-Semitic Attitudes," Anti-Defamation League (2013) http://global100.adl.org/ (accessed June 22, 2014).
59 Edward Said, *Orientalism*, 25th Anniversary Edition (1978) (New York: Vintage, 2003).
60 *Orientalism*, p. xxiii.
61 "Global Christianity: A Report on the Size and Distribution of the World's Christian Population," Pew Research Religion & Public Life Project (Dec. 19, 2012) http://www.pewforum.org/2011/12/19/global-christianity-exec/ (accessed June 22, 2014).
62 "Definitions of Terrorism in the U.S. Code," Federal Bureau of Investigation http://www.fbi.gov/about-us/investigate/terrorism/terrorism-definition (accessed Nov. 6. 2014).
63 Todd Green, "Fighting Islamophobia with 'Political Correctness,'" *Huffington Post* (June 19, 2014) http://www.huffingtonpost.com/todd-green-phd/fighting-islamophobia-by-_b_5508761.html (accessed June 23, 2014).
64 Ibid.
65 "The War on Women," American Civil Liberties Union, https://www.aclu.org/blog/tag/war-women (accessed June 22, 2014).
66 "The Rise of Evangelicals," *Christianity Today* (June 9, 2005) http://www.christianitytoday.com/ct/2005/juneweb-only/42.0a.html?paging=off (accessed June 22, 2015).
67 Jim Hinch, "Where Are the People?" *American Scholar* (Winter 2014) https://theamericanscholar.org/where-are-the-people/#.VVFEvVztixo (accessed May 10, 2015).
68 John S. Dickerson, "The Decline of Evangelical America," *New York Times* (Dec. 15, 2012) http://www.nytimes.com/2012/12/16/opinion/sunday/the-decline-of-evangelical-america.html?pagewanted=all (accessed June 22, 2014).
69 Bert M. Farias, "In the American Christian Church the New Mission Field," *Flaming Herald* (June 19, 2014) http://www.charismanews.com/opinion/the-flaming-herald/44351-is-the-american-church-the-new-mission-field-redefining-american-christianity (accessed June 22, 2014).
70 Kevin Shrum, "The Truth about Post-Christian America" *Christian Post* (May 27, 2014) http://www.christianpost.com/news/the-truth-about-post-christian-america-120233/ (accessed June 22, 2014).
71 "Public Sees Religion's Influence Waning."
72 Donald Devine, "Are American Conservatives Paranoid?" *American Conservative* (Oct. 29, 2013) http://www.theamericanconservative.com/articles/are-american-christians-paranoid/ (accessed Nov. 7, 2014).

3

ORDINARY PEOPLE

The Normal and the Pathological

Every day Americans are confronted by norms. And in different ways they negotiate the often complicated idea of achieving normality—by striving to achieve some standard, rejecting such measures altogether, or finding a place somewhere in between. From early childhood people are conditioned to internalize certain norms of intelligence, income, success, happiness, and even longevity itself. Newborn babies are "scored" within minutes of birth according to vital signs and appearance. Pediatricians chart the growth of youngsters with precise metrics of growth and development. Then standardized testing starts in school—as a precursor to workplace performance evaluations. Many people balance their diets based on normative calorie allotments as they compare their earnings to that of the "Average American."

It's hard to imagine any aspect of contemporary life that has not been subject to the calculation of some norm, median, or average. All of this produces a profound ambivalence toward the concept of the normal. On one level, it's common to accept normality in some form or another, simply as a matter of practicality. At the same time, it is obvious how often most people fall outside standard measurements. And one gets mixed messages these days, as variation has become a point of pride in the new millennium. All Americans are unique and individualized—like the proverbial snowflake—with giant corporations extolling them to "Think Different" or "Have It Your Way."

The normal increasingly shows up in popular culture, as seen in movies like *The Search for Normal* (2014), *Finding Normal* (2013), *This Is Normal* (2013), *Leaving Normal* (2011), *Next to Normal* (2011) *Profoundly Normal* (2011), and *My Normal* (2010). Themes of normativity always have figured prominently in stories about growing up and assimilation. It's also worth observing that marketing demands of the media industry dictate that almost every media product reflects the normative interest of some audience cohort. Television is notorious for this, given the huge financial investments and program competition involved. The short-lived series *The New Normal* (2012), which explored themes of gay parenting, failed to gain the audience of producer Ryan Murphy's hugely successful *Glee* series—although Murphy's subsequent film adaptation of the Larry Kramer play *The Normal Heart* (2014) gained considerable critical praise.

In recent years, the terms "normality" and "normativity" have appeared often in academic discourse as though they were interchangeable. Technically speaking, normal refers to an identified standard (normal height, for example), while normative carries an injunctive connotation (normal height is desirable). This points to the relative interpretation of norms, and how "new" normativities can replicate the very structures they presumably would subvert. Publishing on normativity has been huge, with Amazon listing over 40,000 titles that include the term "normal." Keep in mind that normal remains an important topic in statistics, medicine, and mental health (more on this later). But popular interest and academic scrutiny to the topic has been robust nevertheless. Self-help books abound for those struggling to fit in or resisting pressures to do so, as well as a plethora of coming-of-age fiction works covering the same ground. Titles say a lot for such works as *Be Normal* (2014), *Attempting Normal* (2014), *Next to Normal* (2010), *Something like Normal* (2013), *Is This Normal?* (2009), *Not Exactly Normal* (2006), *Faking Normal* (2014), *Normal Is Broken* (2014), and *Normal Gets You Nowhere* (2011). Not surprisingly, many of these books either directly or indirectly address normality as a form of identity performance.[1] This theme was explicitly taken up in Jeanette Winterson's memoir *Why Be Happy When You Could Be Normal?* (2014), Lennard J. Davis's *The End of Normal: Identity in a Biocultural Era* (2013), and J. Jack Halberstam's *Gaga Feminism: Sex, Gender and the End of Normal* (2012).[2] Other academics currently working on the topic of normativity include Georgio Agamben, Lisa Duggan, Bruno Latour, Jasbir Puar, Ellen Samuels, Dean Spade, Maria do Mar Castro Varela, Michael Warner, and Robyn Weigman—to name but a few. In one way or another, the topic of normality infuses contemporary intellectual and political movements in feminism, multiculturalism, queer theory, postcolonialism, and disability studies.

Might it be possible that in the 2000s "diversity" has become the new normal? Has the outsider mythology of earlier decades become the new insider conceit? Can a person have it both ways? In what follows I will describe the origins of the normality as a conformist ideology, emerging from European scientific reasoning in the 18th and 19th centuries. Troubles with normality began in the anti-authoritarian era of the 1960s, which also witnessed the civil rights era, the contemporary feminist movement, antiwar activism, advocacy for the disabled, and the visibility of LGBT communities. Despite conservative resistance and political setbacks, changes in U.S. public opinion and population demographics have decentered a once-universal preoccupation with normality. But like American Christianity, the appeal of normative standards continues to influence society in many ways. In part this results from the impracticality of completely abandoning normality, especially regarding such issues as health and inequality in statistical terms. While uniform standards can be problematic, normality also provides an important reference point for America's collective existence. Normative ideals provide the basis for law and public policy—and for this reason are subject to continual debate and revision. Like many conceits of "belonging," the etiology of "normal" as a conformist ideology is deeply rooted in ways people understand themselves and others.

Inventing Normal

Historically speaking, the concept of a "normal" person is a relatively recent idea, first emerging in the 1800s with the establishment of school grading standards in France. Before that, normal had a more practical denotation dating to 1650 in the Latin *normalis,* meaning "made according to a carpenter's square." To understand the force of the "normal," it's important to consider the idea that preceded it: the "ideal." Before the scientific revolution and its accompanying understandings of genetics and evolution, human traits were often attributed to supernatural causes. In an age in which people's bodies were often subject to frailty and illness, ideas of divine purpose held an enhanced potency. "Ideal" bodies were rarely found in the "real" world and so became the stuff of fantasy, manifest in artworks or religious texts. This magical view of ideal bodies would be swept away with the rise of medical science and empirical measurement in the 17th and 18th centuries. With new understandings of nutrition, sanitation, and disease transmission, governments began to take a more active role in maintaining the health of populations. Statistical standards began to emerge against which people could be measured. Before long, definitions of what constituted a "healthy" body (and mind) made their way into public policy, as governments sought ways to ward off epidemics, bolster worker productivity, and build stronger societies. This led to vaccination drives, systematic quarantines, and institutions to house the chronically ill—all in the interest of promoting "normal" health in the greatest possible number of people.

Various scientists played roles in this story. Perhaps most notably, Charles Darwin's theories about the "evolution" of natural species led to beliefs that human populations could be improved with proper management—although Darwin himself never made this logical leap. As Darwin's ideas about natural selection became increasingly accepted, strategies would emerge to nurture desirable (normal) demographic outcomes, and weed out undesirable (abnormal) traits. Shortly after his death, Darwin's principles of natural selection would become translated into campaigns advocating the improvement of populations through higher reproduction among people with desired characteristics. With the new scientific approaches to the human body came presumed insights into the individual mind and the collective psyche—from phrenology and reflexology to theories of genetic inferiority, class distinction, and human nature. Along the way mathematicians developed ways of representing data to make patterns more observable.

During this time the new "science" of sociology was emerging in the work of French philosopher Auguste Comte, who named the new discipline in 1838. Comte used the term "sociology" to describe a novel way of looking at society, which would bring history, psychology, and economics together in a scientific approach to collective behavior. In the decades following the French Revolution, Comte proposed a rational approach to social problems in a field he termed "positivism." Rejecting then-dominant philosophical traditions governed by introspection and intuition, Comte broke new ground in proposing that sensory experience could be charted by using positivist logical analysis and mathematics. One of Comte's lasting insights lay in recognizing the circular interplay of observation and theory in science. Combine all of this with the ever-present desire for public well-being—and thus began the statistical mapping of public health, notably in the work of Belgian statistician Aldolphe Quetelet in the early 1800s. Quetelet adapted methods used by astronomers to quantify celestial abnormalities to his charting of people's heights and weights, arriving at what he termed *l'homme moyen*—or the "average man." And Quetelet took matters one step further in being the first to write of "deviations more or less great from the mean" constitutive of what he deemed "ugliness in the body as well as vice in morals."[3]

Britain's Sir Francis Galton probably did more to promote the episteme of the "normal" than anyone in the 19th century. A half cousin of Darwin, Galton charted human normalcy and deviance with righteous zeal. Like many scholars of his era, Galton believed that general principles governed human nature and society—and that these could be understood and mastered. Like his contemporaries Nietzsche and Marx, Galton was a philosophical materialist and a firm believer in social engineering. Within a decade of Quetelet's writing on deviation, Galton would be strategizing methods in the 1830s for the systematic elimination of "defectives" from England, a population that included the physically disabled, the "feebleminded," the deaf, the blind, and so on. This thinking would later evolve into the eugenics movements of the 1900s and would inspire subsequent genocide and ethnic cleansing movements. Here again appear the 19th-century tendencies to link empirical measurement and observation of the body with an assessment of identity and worth. In a related innovation, Galton developed the contemporary science of fingerprinting—from which he drew two notable conclusions: first, that the uniqueness of the fingerprint matched the uniqueness of the individual person; and second, that fingerprints could reveal otherwise "invisible" aspects of a person's heredity and character.

Galton's work would have profound implications in "scientifically" validating latent prejudices against certain groups. This is empiricism at its worst: the belief that observable variations from "normal," as Galton termed it, constituted markers of characteristics that could and should be eliminated from a given society. Keep in mind that this was also a time when the novel idea of the "individual" citizen was driving democratic political ideology. Perhaps it is understandable that the delicate balance between personal subjectivity and collective interest was not fully recognized, as nations like the U.S. maintained simultaneous systems of individual rights and group inequality. Yet this same slippage between scientific reason and social formation has remained in play ever since in understandings of norms, humanity, cultural values, and social management.

At the core of the normal/deviant divide lies the tendency to conceive all manner of things in terms of pairings. Commonly associated with the 17th-century writings of European René Descartes (i.e., Cartesian Dualism), the binary paradigm can be dated to earlier epochs and other continents. The ancient societies of China, Egypt, Greece, India, and Persia all had dualistic models of thought, as did Native American and Australian cultures, as well as some in Africa and Asia. Often this thinking had religious roots, although not always. It seems so obvious to divide the world into opposed pairings. But as understandings of linguistic signification have shown, things really are not that simple. At best, binary models provide a convenient shorthand for reducing complex ideas to an easily communicated form. Today most people are hardly so naïve as to presume a simple dichotomy between right and wrong. And they know that two-party political systems often fail to account for the vast array of opinions that don't fit into their overarching categories.

But dualistic thinking structures the ways most Americans conceive the world and see themselves—in habits of mind held in place by philosophical traditions, ethical convictions, narrative conventions, legal precedents, and a sound-bite culture predicated on expediency at any cost. Not only does this rule out gray areas of morality or middle-of-the-road political ideas (which actually account for most people's positions in those areas), the imposition of black-and-white thinking on a technicolor world imposes a filter on such concepts as mind/body, health/illness, knowledge/ignorance, natural/artificial, self/other, male/female, friend/enemy, good/evil, majority/minority, and so on. All of this leaves begging the obvious question of why anyone would want to obfuscate the spectral diversity of existence in favor of a narrow view. Is it merely the comfort of a presumed certainty? Or can one infer more in the compulsive repetition of binary models across such a wide expanse of discourses and practices? Let's get right to the point: none of the oppositions I've just mentioned are neutral designations. Every single pairing comes loaded with associations and values for its stakeholders, raising epistemological questions of who stands where, how they got there, and in what manner such positions are identified or hidden.

But this is only part of the story. The distinctions people make among each other have cognitive, affective, political, and historical roots; they are influenced by biology and neurochemistry; they can be inherited and acquired via socialization; they are influenced by environment and culture; they are subject to such vicissitudes of individual experience as luck or trauma; they can result from both predictable cause and chance; they can be contested, corrected, unlearned, forgotten, or ignored. Contemporary social sciences don't give much credence to animalistic survival theories per se, especially when the topic turns to the adult mind. But a fair amount of attention has been given to the prevalence of fear in today's world. One theory holds that human brains have a certain propensity for what is termed "continuity monitoring."[4] In essence, people tend to feel more comfortable in situations of stability or coherence, and uncomfortable when such continuity is broken. A discordant noise or unfamiliar design may seem jarring or merely unpleasant. But when the topic turns to unfamiliar people, the story becomes highly context dependent. Social psychologists sometimes speak of stereotypes in neutral terms—that is, as cognitive templates for sorting people into recognizable categories. Obviously, these categories tend to acquire values. And here again enters the role of vision and observation. What someone looks like is often one's first line of assessment. And like it or not, for many of people a form of normative logic guides continuity monitoring.

More than one theorist has pointed out how the norms of language can limit what gets said or thought—without one even noticing it. Not only does language change over time, but the very conventions of intelligibility tend to pull people back to familiar phrasing and the arsenal of shared references in common usage. Even the term *difference*, so fondly used by linguists, raises the same issue. Difference may on first blush seem to imply a balanced comparison or equivalence, but turn to any specific object and one finds oneself asking, "Different from what?" Even such simple comparisons need to be seen within relational fields or conceptual systems—they are *never* truly neutral. Even if one imagines two perfectly identical objects, there is no guarantee that anyone would see them in equivalent terms, as Immanuel Kant pointed out. Then add the element of time to such perspectival variation, as Gottfried Leibnitz did, and the matter gets even more complicated. Fast-forward to 20th-century thinking and poststructuralists would go even further in remarking on the instability of language, pointing out the endless ways that meanings mutate in every new context or moment.

Georges Canguilhem presciently addressed these issues in his landmark 1943 book *The Normal and the Pathological*, in which he pointed out that in any set of items the norm is simply an average or middle number. As such, normative items are neither superior nor more common than others, even though they can become socially constructed as such. Canguilhem cogently observed that like many concepts, normality is defined reflexively (in terms of what it is not). "Every value must be earned against an anti-value," Canguilhem wrote, adding that norms often accrue degrees of authority and autonomy in disproportion to their empirical derivation. He pointed out how this can cause problems, since "The normal is not a static or peaceful, but a dynamic and polemical concept."[5] But this very dynamism also can open possibilities: "The norm, by devaluing everything that the reference to it prohibits from being considered normal, creates on its own the possibility of an inversion of terms. The norm offers itself as a possible mode of unifying diversity, resolving difference, settling in this agreement."[6] In pointing out such conceptual slippage, Canguilhem argued that "The logical norm in which the truth prevails over the false can be inverted into a norm where the false prevails over the true."[7] Even more radically, Canguilhem pointed out that in nature, numbers, and society non-normative elements are often more common than normative ones: "Without a doubt there's one way to consider the pathological normal, and that is by defining normal and abnormal in terms of relative statistical frequency."[8]

This principle can be illustrated by thinking about what a normal person is not. In most people's minds, "normal" wouldn't mean somebody wealthy or poor. It wouldn't be anyone from outside the country or newly arrived. Nor would it include anyone especially old or young. Cross out people too large or too small. Then exclude those with illnesses or disabilities. Many people might leave out racial or ethnic minorities, as well as anyone gay or gender variant. And of course normal doesn't mean anyone too brilliant, intellectually challenged, or with a psychiatric diagnosis. Nor would people qualify who have been in trouble with the law. Atheists and overly religious types wouldn't fit the average mold either. People in specialized lines of work aren't typical either, nor are those who have little or a great deal of education. Add all of these excluded groups together and you reach a number at least double the size of the population. The point is that in one way or another, the myth of normality excludes everyone. It is a cultural construction with one fundamental purpose: to support social hierarchies. Variously deployed, the concept of the norm can be used to exclude and devalue just about anyone. Everyone is deviant in someone's register. As Audre Lorde wrote, "Somewhere, on the edge of consciousness, there is what I call the mythical norm, which each one of us within our heart knows 'that is not me.'"[9]

Laws of Averages

Conflict can consolidate group identity—and war does this on a national scale as nothing else can. In 1950s America, all sorts of public worries lingered over insiders/outsiders. As the U.S. sought to expand its brand of democracy around the globe, its internal democratic failures also became more evident. Not unlike today, contests emerged over who counted as a "true American." Was it simply a patriot or a veteran, or a productive worker? What about women, immigrants, people of color, LGBT groups, the disabled, student activists, and native peoples? With these questions, the U.S. moved from a postwar posture of social conformity to a painful process of ameliorating difference. Much of this would unfold in arguments about normality. But part of the problem was that the concept of normality was relatively new—and easily confused with supervening nationalistic ideals. In the decades following World War II, conformist ideology struggled against entrenched patterns of bias and discrimination in America. While antifascism and anticommunism would generate international antagonism, the trauma of war also had fostered within many countries yearnings for group solidarity and common purpose. Throughout the U.S. and around the world a desire grew for a return to equilibrium, deceptive as the notion might have been. This meant a return to "normal" life: status quo social values, business practices, and power relations—but with a fresh emphasis on economic growth and global relationships.

These desires for normalcy could not fully erase the trauma of war in the Western mind. Something terrible had gone wrong with the modernist program of continued progress and endless expansion. Not only had millions died in a spiraling conflict that ultimately involved most of the world's nations, but human "technology" had revealed two new weapons. The first, as detailed above, was the scope of scientifically orchestrated genocide in the name of the Nazi Holocaust. The second was the unleashing by the U.S. of thermonuclear weaponry on the cities of Hiroshima and Nagasaki. While one cannot extrapolate or apply principles of individual psychology to entire populations, notions of collective trauma provided at least a useful metaphor for explaining the public experience of wars, national tragedies, terrorist attacks—and the way such events often alter political opinion and other terms of collective consciousness. Suffice to say that as the U.S. was groping for utopian beliefs in the postwar years, many citizens were still mourning their dead and worrying about the future. This caused many to question the thought processes that had brought the nation to that moment, and for some this meant taking pause over the values and even the leaders responsible. Questions would soon emerge over the overarching premises of capitalism and socialism, and obviously of fascism and totalitarianism. In America, long-standing patterns of inequity would soon need addressing.

History is rarely as simple as it appears, shifting as it fragments with each new reading in a changing present. Nor is history linear or cyclical in any eminent sense. The understanding of it subjectively resides between a contingent past and a continually shifting present. The best one can do is to pick at threads of meaning or attempt to see the folds of time. Americans commonly associate the 1960s as a period of rupture and turmoil in public memory. The year 1963 is especially noteworthy, remembered by many for President John F. Kennedy's assassination. That event shook public consciousness much like 9/11 would do. But 1963 also was a banner year in the expression of rising oppositional sentiment toward the ethos of normalcy.

Standard Deviations

In 1963 Martin Luther King gave a now-famous speech originally titled "Normalcy, never again" to an audience of 250,000 gathered for the March on Washington for Jobs and Freedom. Toward the end of the address, as the story goes, gospel singer Mahalia Jackson shouted to King to improvise on his prepared remarks, calling out: "Tell them about the dream, Martin!" after which King's iconic "I have a dream" refrain was heard. The "Normalcy, never again" speech occurred nearly a decade after the U.S. Supreme Court's *Brown v. Board of Education* decision banning school segregation—resulting in protests, marches, and eventually violence uprisings across the U.S. The year 1963 also marked the publication of Betty Friedan's *The Feminine Mystique*, criticizing what she termed "normal femininity" in postwar America. In her book, Friedan critiqued the then-ascendant practice of psychiatry as one of several elements of what she termed "a problem that knows no name" becoming apparent in the postwar years when women married young, moved to the suburbs, and abandoned their ambitions. In her chapter on Freud, Friedan wrote that "'Normal' femininity is achieved, however, only in so far as the woman finally renounces all active goals of her own, all her own 'originality,' to identify and fulfill herself through the activities and goals of husband, or son."[10]

Such is the discontinuity among political movements. Certainly there had been plenty of activism around issues of race and gender before this period, not to mention afterwards. But power, resistance, and alternative formulations can elude conveniently mapped patterns, if they can be recognized at all. In retrospect, the 1950s are commonly seen as a period of economic expansion and deferred population growth domestically—as the nation became deadlocked in a bipolar geopolitical power struggle and nuclear arms race with the Soviet Union. Social conformity and public fear went hand in hand as middle-class Americans hunkered down in an increasingly privatized consumerism. As the nation was clamoring to master the new commodity known as the Hula-Hoop, a rising discontent was emerging. Anyone complaining about continuing structural poverty was quickly branded a communist—including King, for example. Hence, many factors converged to consolidate the ideology of the normal for which the 1950s are so well known and against which so much activism in the 1960s would react. Both King and John F. Kennedy would die in 1963, ironically shortly before many of the most important pieces of civil rights legislation they advocated would be adopted—the Equal Pay Act (1963), the Civil Rights Act, (1964), and the Voting Rights Act (1964).

Writing in 1963 on behalf of Students for a Democratic Society (SDS), Tom Hayden presciently proposed a polymorphous coalition of what he termed "outlaws" from the normative "establishment."[11] Presaging contemporary "Occupy" movements, Hayden proposed a coalition largely based on economic deprivation and inspired by what were termed at the time "Negro" civil rights movements. While Hayden's formulation would rely on a vanguardist leadership of university students and intellectuals, his thinking is notable for its vision of a coalition of groups defined by their common estrangement from power: African Americans, Latinos, working- and middle-class whites (including the "employed but economically insecure"), women, both young and aged populations, and others he grouped into what he termed the "visible and invisible poor."[12] Also worth mentioning is the care Hayden took in *not* specifying exactly how this new radical movement would unfold—although he had no difficulty in naming the opposition: "business interests, certain sectors of the military establishment, Southern racists and their political representatives, and large portions of the small-town and suburban middle classes."[13] In geopolitical terms, Hayden could point to already-failing U.S. "counter-insurgency" efforts in Vietnam, where the Viet Cong won its first major victory in the 1963 Battle of Ap Bac.[14]

The year 1963 also saw the publication of two important sociological works on the topic of normality: Howard S. Becker's *Outsiders: Studies in the Sociology of Deviance* and Erving Goffman's *Stigma: Notes on the Management of Spoiled Identity*.[15] Together these two books expressed growing interest in Émile Durkheim's concept of *anomie*—or "normlessness"—discussed in Chapter 1 of this book. Durkheim devised his concept of anomie to explain suicides in French Catholic and Protestant populations, concluding that the distancing of individuals from groups could be understood through the new science of social behavior. Initially Durkheim's sociology was viewed with suspicion in the U.S., due in part to its associations with European-style social planning, as well as its then-strange mix of science and humanities. But by mid-century, sociology would find an unlikely ally in the emerging practices of market research and advertising. As Frankfurt School scholars were theorizing the manipulation of the masses in Europe, Madison Avenue would make use of the same principles to expand American consumer society. Media played a key role at this moment, as war-era propaganda techniques were turned to commercial ends. Before long, patriotism and consumerism became conjoined in the concept of the "Average American." What happened next requires little explanation, as contradictions became increasingly visible between democratic idealism and the day-to-day experience of so many inside the U.S. and in nations around the world.

Suffice to say that Becker's *Outsiders* and Goffman's *Stigma* had much to say about norms. Sociologists and criminologists frequently cite *Outsiders* for its use of "labeling theory" in analyzing deviance as a socially constructed category. Becker made the then-radical argument that social deviance had less to do with people identified as deviant than it did with the groups identifying them. "Social groups create deviance by making the rules whose infraction constitutes deviance," Becker wrote, adding that "deviance is not a quality of the act a person commits, but rather a consequence of the application by others of rules and sanctions."[16] Becker's relativism flew in the face of the empiricist social science doctrine of the time, inherently arguing for approaches that were more interdisciplinary and qualitative. Even as sociology was struggling to establish its own legitimacy, Becker pushed for intensified fieldwork and new methodologies. Becker would apply these ideas in later research on artists, musicians, political activists, drug users and others who "stand outside the circle of 'normal.'"[17]

As Becker pushed for a more relational and phenomenological understanding of labeling, Goffman looked closely at perceptions of difference and their consequences. Goffman wrote of what he termed "actual social identities" and "virtual social identities," noting that slippages often occur in the arbitrary assignment of stigma to difference.[18] Goffman identified those making the assignments as "the normals," who transform "a whole and usual person to a tainted, discount coupon." Such an attribute is a *stigma*, Goffman wrote. "An attribute that stigmatizes one type of possessor can confirm the usualness of another, and therefore is neither credible or discreditable as a thing in itself."[19] The subtitle of Goffman's *Stigma* was *Notes on a Spoiled Identity*. Mounting a broad-based critique of normativity, Goffman identified three domains of stigma: "abominations of the body" (physical impairments and deformities); "blemishes of character" (mental illness, homosexuality, criminality); and "tribal stigmas" (race, nationality, and religious belief). Even Goffman recognized the crudeness of these categories, and he apologized for his overgeneralizations as he searched for an overarching theory. Like Canguilhem, Goffman noted the reciprocal definitional relationship of normality and deviance, also pointing out that any person may be labeled variously by different groups over time, and that people could traverse the normal/deviant divide voluntarily and involuntarily. Characteristic of the civil rights thinking of the time, Goffman also said that a "spoiled identity" could mean "not quite human." Written over half a century ago, Goffman's writing has both an antiquated tone and an eerie prescience in describing the workings of prejudice and bigotry:

> On this assumption we exercise varieties of discrimination, through which we effectively, if often unthinkingly, reduce his life chances. We construct a stigma-theory, an ideology to explain his inferiority and account for the danger he represents, sometimes rationalizing an animosity based on other differences such as those of social class. We use specific stigma terms such as the cripple, bastard, moron in our daily discourse as a source of metaphor and imagery, typically without giving thought to the original meaning. We tend to include a wide range of imperfections on the basis of the original.[20]

Stigma marks a specific historic moment within the field of sociology in mapping the social construction of bias and a host of related issues. In both intellectual and political terms, *Stigma* was responding to a sociological positivism, which viewed most forms of difference as empirical facts, often verified by scientific or medical reasoning. Most of the public saw race and gender as aspects of nature rather than artifacts of human consciousness. And the so-called cultural turn that swept through academic disciplines in the 1970s had yet to occur (postmodernism and poststructuralism had not yet taken hold). The enduring relevance of *Stigma* as both a work and conceptual model lies in Goffman's efforts to make a constructionist argument while also acknowledging the material underpinnings of bias.

One sees in Goffman's *Stigma* a work emerging in the context of these broader movements to acknowledge and rectify inequality. Always a politically informed discipline, sociology was struggling to identify patterns of collective thought and behavior, especially as manifest in organizations, institutions, and the interests supporting them. The final pages of *Stigma* declare the need to examine in depth each form of stigma, as well as to investigate the social motivations behind negative labeling and the consequences it produces. Contemporary thinking on identity has done just this—in addressing differences in three ways: as *material facts*;

as *socially constructed categories*; and as *everyday experiences* experienced by those affected. Here again, the prescience of *Stigma* becomes apparent in Goffman's efforts to delineate the subjective experience of the stigmatized individual within the matrix of an externally produced material and socially constructed identity. Later scholarship would explicate the ways that "expert" discourse often overlooked the phenomenology of the "spoiled" identity. But Goffman didn't miss this key element, writing, for example, that "The stigmatized individual tends to hold the same beliefs about identity that we do; this is a pivotal fact. His deepest feelings about what he is may be the sense of being a 'normal person,' a human being like anybody else, a person, therefore, who deserves a fair chance and a fair break."[21]

No discussion of normativity would be complete without the figure of Michel Foucault, who analyzed the arbitrary ways that normative reasoning (and its materialist critiques) sometimes had operated, often outside the conscious understanding of those involved. Largely unknown at the time to American readers, Foucault launched this analysis in his 1963 doctoral dissertation entitled *The Birth of the Clinic*.[22] In that work, Foucault mapped out his initial critique of 18th-century scientism, and particularly the way that medical knowledge had dehumanized the sick by separating their bodily conditions from their identities. This transformed anyone falling outside normative parameters of "health" into little more than a collection of symptoms, often with pejorative associations. Always attendant to issues of social power, Foucault's *The Birth of the Clinic* identified the "medical gaze" of the god-like physician as an emergent form of authority. Not surprisingly, Foucault would zero in on the representational slippage implicit between symptom-*signifiers* and diagnosis-*signifieds*—as he pointed out how doctors' opinions often varied even as they insisted on their absolute certainty. Later Foucault would apply his thinking about medical authority more broadly in a critique of institutionalized power throughout society. Such power percolated through the language, attitudes, and available knowledge of any time or place—creating a kind of envelope that both enabled and limited certain kinds of ideas. In his book, *The Order of Things*, Foucault called this envelope the *episteme*.[23] Foucault's episteme provided a term for the way notions such as the ideal or the normal could take over a society—not simply by separating "good" from "bad," or truth from falsehood, but also by determining the very parameters of discussing such things.

Much as Thomas S. Kuhn in his book, *The Structure of Scientific Revolutions*, had questioned linear views of "normal science," Foucault would say that "in any given culture and at any given moment, there is always one episteme that defines the conditions of possibility of all knowledge, whether expressed in a theory or silently invested in practice."[24] Adding nuance to Max Weber's sociological critiques of objectivism and rationalization, Foucault would apply his idea of the episteme to analyses of social control, population management, and systems of authority and power—especially in modern societies—in his formulation of the term "biopower."[25] Yet even in Foucault's descriptions of biopower as a "relation" as well as a thing, a micro as well as a macro force, and an omnipresent as well as identifiable phenomenon—there still lingered in his writing the sense of a possibility of stepping outside the normative.

In the following decades, many sectors of American society would challenge normative conventions. But perhaps no population advanced this issue more than the LGBT community. Rampant Reagan-era homophobia and government inaction in addressing HIV-AIDS politicized sexual orientation the 1980s and early 1990s. A rich academic literature began to grow around the issue of "heteronormativity" and its attendant social conventions, especially as critiqued in the then-emergent scholarly field of queer theory, which is discussed at length in Chapter 10. Writing about this activity in a 2015 issue of the journal *Differences*, Robyn Wiegman and Elizabeth A. Wilson explain that "If these theorists share little else, what they do share is a conviction that norms are conceptually and politically limiting. For these theorists, norms have a readily identifiable outside, are univocally on the side of privilege and conventionality, and should be avoided."[26] While underscoring the importance of an *oppositional* "antinormativity" as an historical and conceptual framework, Wiegman and Wilson also note the inescapability of norms in certain *structural* contexts, given their relative position as components of larger totalities. They point out that critiques of normative positions can imply—or actually establish—their own norms, as Canguilhem suggested above in discussing normative inversion. Hence, Wiegman and Wilson conclude: "Our hypothesis is this: antinormative stances project stability and immobility onto normativity. In so doing, they generate much of the political tyranny they claim belongs (over there) to regimes of normativity."[27] Recognition of this has led in recent years to a more cautious approach to antinormativity, and in some instances, a rejection of the strategy, owing to its capacity to replicate structures it wants to undo.

Common Denominators

Issues of normativity and antinormativity are more than theoretical pursuits. As discussed at the beginning of this chapter, norms are so ubiquitous in contemporary culture that many Americans take them for granted—even as they feel ambivalent about normative standards or pressures to "fit in." Normativity has driven mass marketing and entertainment ever since media technologies first made such communication possible. Until the emergence of the Internet, it appeared that corporate consolidation would aggregate ever larger media networks into a single global marketplace with its own normative logic. And of course writers from Marshall McLuhan to Thomas Friedman had predicted this. Yet here again one encounters the problem of confusing appearances with fact. Large populations or global audiences do not in themselves make for homogeneity. Logically speaking, the opposite is more likely even in Darwinist terms. The more creatures there are, the greater the possibility of variability. This leads to two inescapable conclusions. Normality is a myth. Deviation is the reality.

But this is hardly the message people get in the media they consume every day, much as one might believe that times change. Particular kinds of images bombard Americans everywhere they look: billboards, magazines, movies, television, and the Internet. These images of people, their bodies, and pursuits are not chosen on the basis of accurately representing the diversity of the audiences receiving them. Instead they are chosen to conform to commonly held stereotypes held out as ideals. By now almost everyone is well aware that advertising and movies present images of impossibly "perfect" faces and bodies. While viewers may (or may not) fully recognize the "unreality" of these idealized images, the relentless repetition of the same kind of imagery has a norming effect on desire itself. This is a function of the way that ideology works in the foreground and background of the mind.

For many years I have routinely shown my undergraduate classes the now classic *Killing Us Softly* videos by gender educator Jean Kilbourne. In one often-quoted passage, Kilbourne remarks that "from a very early age we must spend enormous amounts of time, energy, and above all money, striving to achieve this look, and feeling ashamed and guilty when we fail. And failure is inevitable because the ideal is based on absolute flawlessness. The most important aspect of this flawlessness is that it cannot be achieved."[28] Any look at history or global culture reveals that the definition of this flawlessness varies across time and space. But especially in Western society, certain heavily gendered and power-laden extremes continue to hold sway. Kilbourne's observation that idealized yearnings begin in childhood square with psychoanalytic principles of object relations. At an early age youngsters learn to see themselves as images depicting both the self and its representation to others. This imaginary "me" is subject to all kind of influence from inside and outside, especially as wants and desires enter the picture.

Following his work on labeling theory, Goffman proposed that this influence often operates through what he termed "codes of gender."[29] Goffman noted how these codes become internalized (consciously and unconsciously), manifest in behaviors, and called forth in advertising and entertainment media. More recently the hegemonic internalization and behavioral enforcement of these binary codes has been examined in greater detail, notably in the work of R.W. Connell and Judith Butler, among others.[30] The expression "gender policing" is now used in recognition of the ways people are punished or rewarded according to the degrees to which they are able to achieve these unachievable ideals. Again, this is a system in which everybody loses, except the advertisers and merchandisers who sell remedies for people's presumed failures. While gender policing presents many adults with a series of choices over normativity, antinormativity, or negotiating the spacing between, the stress of the gender binary can be especially trying to teenagers in the process of finding themselves in a developmental stage that psychologists term differentiation. And let's face it, kids can be mean to each other.

Everyone knows what a bully is, but before the last decade the widespread prevalence of bullying and its sometimes deadly consequences were largely ignored. Over 85 percent of K–12 students report that they have been bullied or have participated in the bullying of someone else. Boys may be bullied more often than girls, but it seems that bullying frequently is an equal opportunity problem. While it is impossible to attribute a single cause to bullying, all evidence shows that gender nonconformity and presumed homosexuality are key factors. In her book, *The Bully Society*, Jessie Klein noted that eight in ten young adults see themselves as falling outside the coded ideals of "hypermasculinity" and "hyperfemininity," but that our culture seems much more nervous about gender variance in men than in women.[31] Largely owing to the contemporary women's movement, girls today have much more access to both the traditionally considered masculine and feminine aspects of their personalities. But for the most part, boys seem to be told that they can express only a narrow range of themselves. How strange that American society would worry about men who are insufficiently muscular, tough, or aggressive in a nation where men commit 90 percent of all violent crime and 98 percent of sexual assaults.[32]

Bullying numbers vary widely because the definition of the term remains vague. Schoolyard beatings and hurtful online postings can both be called forms of bullying. Klein reports that 95 percent of bullying incidents are never reported as such, given that bullying can be physical, verbal, incidental, subtle, systematic, and of course brutally violent.[33] To make her case most emphatically, Klein analyzes one of the most talked about categories of violence in America today: the phenomenon of school shootings and bombings. She reports that in the past three decades 166 young people have committed such crimes, 147 of whom were boys—most of whom "struggled for recognition and status among their peers." As Klein explains, "The majority of them languished at the bottom of the social hierarchy. They tended not to be athletic. They were also described in the media as skinny, scrawny, short, lanky, or pudgy. They were teased for looking feminine or gay."[34]

Obviously few ostracized kids turn out to be killers. But the scourge of bullying has broader effects, as young people try to compensate or act out in different ways. While assailants sometimes speak of their crimes as "retribution" against those who ignored then, many less extreme forms of victimization play out against women and men on a daily basis.[35] Hazing, rumoring, verbal abuse, and cyberbullying fall within this category. All of this feeds a larger culture of exclusion in which bullying is practiced, sanctioned, and most of all, *normalized*—not only by kids, but also modeled by parents, coaches, and administrators in schools and colleges. Adults bully each other all the time in the workplace or in social contexts.

What can one unambiguously state about norms? Logically speaking, the most obvious problem with norms lies in the very empiricism they seem to imply. In mathematical terms, norms are statistical values generated by finite sets of data. One can measure the size of a dozen apples and arrive at a normative figure for that particular group, but this may not be the norm for all apples. This same discontinuity applies in correlating one norm to another. The normative apple from the dozen may be sweet, while the norm from another group may not be. The problem is that the brain is wired to correlate observations of things that appear similar through what psychologists term "heuristics," which constitute one of the primary building blocks of learning (i.e., "once burned, twice shy").[36] Making matters worse, heuristics often operate unconsciously—meaning that continual vigilance is necessary to confirm or invalidate any given one. Heuristics offer one explanation, among many, for historical and contemporary habits of mind deriving from norms.

But on a deeper level, normative principles presume a totalizing inclusiveness—and herein lies a greater concern. As this chapter has detailed, concepts of norms and deviance play a central role in belonging and not-belonging in America. In part, normality pervades contemporary culture in the U.S. because it resonates so strongly with egalitarian values inherent in terms like the "average citizen" and "common man." Yet scratch the surface of the these noble sentiments—and one finds persistent anxieties over concerns ranging from public health to economic productivity, as well as a nagging fear of difference. By posturing themselves as benign and universal, these concepts obfuscate the tyranny they exert. Statistical norms become calculable only in relation to a recognized set of data. This may sound harmless enough until one finds oneself on the outside the solipsism of either concept. Unfortunately this outsider status is inevitable—so much so that it indeed affects everyone within reach. For all their apparent inclusiveness, norms imply a knowable and finite definition of inclusion within a greater totality. And even today, the associations of norms with heath, achievement, and appropriate conduct give the idea a patina of fairness and neutrality—even norms hold prejudice and bigotry in place.[37] This is much more than a philosophical dilemma in today's world or in past history. Through language and representation all people get rendered as objects to some extent, and as such become vulnerable to diminished status.[38]

Notes

1 Judith Butler, *Gender Trouble* (New York and London: Routledge, 2006). Performativity is the well-known concept Judith Butler used to describe both conscious and unconscious patterns of behavior toward others.
2 Lennard J. Davis, *The End of Normal: Identity in a Biocultural Era* (Ann Arbor: University of Michigan Press, 2014); Jeanette Winterson, *Why Be Happy When You Could Be Normal?* (New York: Grove Press, 2013); J. Jack Halberstam, *Gaga Feminism: Sex, Gender, and the End of Normal* (Boston, MA: Beacon, 2012).
3 Adolphe Quetelet, quoted in Lennard J. Davis, "Introduction: Normality, Power, and Culture," in Lennard J. Davis, ed. *The Disabilities Studies Reader*, 4th ed. (New York and London: Routledge, 2013) p. 2.
4 E.H. Gombrich, *The Sense of Order: A Study in the Psychology of Decorative Art* (New York: Phaidon, 1994).
5 Georges Canguilhem, *The Normal and the Pathological* (1966), trans. Carolyn R. Fawcett (Brooklyn, NY: Zone Books, 1989) p. 239.
6 *The Normal and the Pathological*, p. 240.
7 Ibid.
8 *The Normal and the Pathological*, p. 137.

9 Audre Lorde, *Sister Outsider* (Berkeley, CA: Crossings Press, 1984), p. 116.
10 Betty Friedan, "The Sexual Solipsism of Sigmund Freud," in *The Feminine Mystique* (New York: W.W. Norton, 1963) p. 188.
11 Tom Hayden and Carl Wittman, "An Interracial Movement of the Poor?" See also, Tom Hayden, "America and the New Era," unpublished manuscripts, http://www.sds-1960s.org/documents.htm (accessed May 4, 2013).
12 "An Interracial Movement of the Poor?" p. 12.
13 "America and the New Era," p. 4.
14 "America and the New Era," p. 7.
15 Howard S. Becker, *Outsiders: Studies in the Sociology of Deviance*, (New York: The Free Press, 1963); Erving Goffman, *Stigma: Notes on the Management of Spoiled Identity* (New York: Simon & Schuster, 1963).
16 *Outsiders*, p. 9.
17 *Outsiders*, p. 15.
18 *Stigma*, p. 2.
19 *Stigma*, p. 3.
20 *Stigma*, p. 4.
21 *Stigma*, p. 7.
22 Michel Foucault, *The Birth of the Clinic: An Archaeology of Medical Perception* (1963) (New York and London: Routledge Classics, 2003).
23 Michel Foucault, *The Order of Things: An Archaeology of the Human Sciences* (1966) (New York: Pantheon, 1970).
24 Thomas S. Kuhn, *The Structure of Scientific Revolutions* (Chicago, IL: University of Chicago Press, 1962); Michel Foucault, *The Order of Things: An Archeology of the Human Sciences* (New York: Pantheon, 1970) p. 168.
25 Michel Foucault, *Discipline and Punish: The Birth of the Prison* (New York: Random House, 1975).
26 Robyn Wiegman and Elizabeth A. Wilson, "Introduction: Antinormativity's Queer Conventions," *Differences*, 26, no. 1 (2015) p. 12.
27 "Antinormativity's Queer Conventions," p. 13.
28 Jean Kilbourne, *Killing Us Softly 4: Advertising's Image of Women*, directed by Sut Jhally (Northampton, MA: Educational Video Foundation, 2010).
29 Erving Goffman, *Gender Advertisements* (New York: Harper and Row, 1979).
30 R.W. Connell, *Masculinities* (Berkeley: University of California Press, 2005); Judith Butler, *Gender Trouble: Feminism and the Subversion of identity* (New York and London: Routledge, 1990).
31 Jessie Klein, *The Bully Society: School Shootings and the Crisis of Bullying in America's Schools* (New York: New York University Press, 2012) p. 40.
32 "Violent Crime," U.S. Bureau of Justice Statistics (2012) http://www.bjs.gov/index.cfm?ty=tp&tid=31 (accessed Aug. 3, 2014).
33 *The Bully Society*, p. 76.
34 *The Bully Society*, p. 17.
35 Scott Jaschik, "Deadly Rampage," *Inside Higher Ed* (May 27, 2014) https://www.insidehighered.com/news/2014/05/27/uc-santa-barbara-students-killed-shooting-rampage (accessed Nov. 10, 2014).
36 Paul Rozin and Carol Nemeroff, "Sympathetic Magical Thinking: The Contagion and Similarity 'Heuristics,'" in Thomas Gilovich, Dale Griffin, Daniel Kahneman, eds, *Heuristics and Biases: The Psychology of Intuitive Judgment* (New York: Cambridge University Press, 2007).
37 Judith Butler, *Giving an Account of Oneself* (New York: Fordham, 2005).
38 N. Katherine Hayles, *How We Became Posthuman: Virtual Bodies in Cybernetics, Literature, and Informatics* (Chicago, IL: University of Chicago, 2008).

4

HOMELAND INSECURITIES

Expecting the Worst

National security, airport security, border security, bank security, home security, school security, cyber security. In post-9/11 America, worries over threat and vulnerability haunt the public mind and animate public policy as perhaps never before. A dangerous world calls for constant vigilance, tougher laws, and higher fences, or so many argue. But how real are these threats? Could it be that the nation's apprehensions and suspicions have deeper roots and a more complex etiology? What drives America's apparent need to divide the world, other people, and even its own citizenry into categories of friend and enemy?

Mostly associated today with the invisible specter of terrorism and a few highly publicized tragedies, security can be a fragile state of mind or an aggressive response to perceived risk. In either case, "feeling secure" is contingent on time, place, and identity. This creates a paradox of sorts. If one provisionally can define the feeling of security as a kind of anticipatory projection, security becomes a mixture of acquired experience and a sense of what may or may not happen in the future—both tempered by perceptions of present circumstance.[1] In psychological terms, a sense of security is based on the expectation of consistency in the provision of what one wants or needs. In other words, absence and loss are held in abeyance in the "secure" state—which remains a boundary event.

Owing to security's abstract character, it becomes intensely vulnerable to suggestion and the vagaries of social construction. In many instances, what counts as security gets defined by its opposites, discussed by sociologists in recent decades as a "culture of fear" and "the risk society."[2] Scapegoating often figures prominently in campaigns to quell public anxiety, as security searches consciously or unconsciously for an object to vanquish. And the media often plays a big role in defining such "moral panics," as Stanley Cohen termed them in the 1970s.[3] In what follows, this chapter will outline some of the disconnections between empirically documented harm and the quite disparate ways that risk is publically conceived. Then I will examine the experience of these contradictions, as they play out in lives affected by security policies, institutional practices, the politics of threat in everyday life, and the violence of organized hate.

Americans live in a world of invisible menace—or so it seems. Warnings fill the mediascape about ways that citizens could be harmed individually or collectively. While it's not always in the forefront of people's thinking, a lot of what Americans believe and do is conditioned by worry that something might go wrong. So people organize their behaviors to remain safe—especially those with the resources to do so. Some gravitate to certain neighborhoods to live. Others think about the safety of cars and other products. Many try to avoid junk food and harmful chemicals in consumables. And in the back of many people's minds are worries about their jobs, the economy, crime rates, and threats to the nation's security. Advertisers, politicians, and other special interests offer ways to protect public safety, as religion promises a world free of worry in the life to come. But exactly why the country is afraid is rarely addressed. It's not that the answers aren't being offered. Critics point to media sensationalism, political manipulation, public apathy, and alienation. But in all the talk about "a dangerous world," precious little attention is given to exactly who is feared and why. America needs to take a hard look at its anxious feelings and attitudes, as well as those who gain and lose from popular disquiet. Because often the nation seems to get it wrong.[4]

The term "Homeland Security" now has become a fixture in public life, resplendent with autochthonic associations of refuge, protectionism, and romantic nationalism. To a country overwhelmed with grief and confusion after 9/11, any fascistic connotations of the term "homeland" were papered over in the name of patriot solidarity—often cast in terms of a mythological return to origins. Like many protective measures, Homeland Security soon would create barriers of both defense and containment. It wasn't initially recognized that while "secure" facilities may keep outsiders away, they also tend to imprison those inside.

America's millennial military adventures—including those initially supported by popular majorities—clearly fostered forms of enmity and its characteristic retribution impulses. While much can be said about the confusion following the World Trade Center and Pentagon attacks, the misrecognition of the enemy caused immediate problems. The U.S. and its leaders were unfamiliar with multinational, stateless opponents—and hence embarked on a new form of global warfare, eventually focusing on a country that had never itself launched a single attack on America. In true scapegoat fashion, fictional rationales soon became accepted as fact—with a well-organized program of public fear mongering and revenge motivating the invasion of Iraq and later campaigns in Afghanistan. More problematically, the subsequent realization that the enemy indeed was not a clearly identifiable nation licensed a secondary displacement of Al Qaeda terrorism onto Muslim and Arabic people in general—or anyone who might be mistaken as such.

In recent years, sadly the world has become familiar with the unintended consequences and outright failures of America's security apparatus. Homeland Security may have begun with airport baggage checks and enhanced counter-espionage measures, but the U.S. Department of Homeland Security, with a budget exceeding $47 billion, quickly expanded its reach into 187 federal agencies—from the National Security Agency (NSA), the Secret Service, the FBI, and the CIA to Health and Human Services, Transportation Safety, and Citizenship and Immigration. Most notoriously, the use of ubiquitous surveillance technology by the NSA to monitor Internet activity, telephone calls, and personal mail created public outrage and worry, notably following the release of hundreds of thousands of secret government files by WikiLeaks and Edward Snowden. All of this reached Orwellian proportions with revelations that high-level government offices had secured cooperation from some of American's largest communications companies (AT&T, Verizon, Google, Apple) in spying on citizens. With groups like the ACLU and other government watchdogs entering the fray, concerns over privacy made headlines around the globe, as other nations began to recognize the international reach of the U.S. security machine.

Within the U.S., a jittery population remains sanguine about such intrusions. With the rise of what are now termed "domestic terrorist" incidents, a recent Pew Research Center poll shows that 62 percent of Americans express willingness to sacrifice privacy to allow the federal government to investigate potential terrorist attacks, even at the expense of their civil rights. And a majority (56 percent) say that the NSA's tracking of millions of phone records is similarly acceptable. According to Pew, "While the public is more evenly divided over the government's monitoring of email and other online activities to prevent possible terrorism, these views are largely unchanged since 2002."[5] This raises important questions about how worry and apprehensions of threat affect daily life, erode citizens' trust in each other, undermine their sense of community and common purpose, and ultimately contribute to prejudice and even violence. Understanding perceptions of a dangerous world is no simple matter, although singular explanations abound. Sensationalized news reporting, political polarization, class warfare, and social alienation lead the list—and these are hardly trifling concerns. But then add declines in education and public literacy, the marketing of fear in selling products, religious extremism, changing population demographics, and the social consequences of new technologies—and the discussion quickly gets more complicated.

A Dangerous World?

So let's start with a few basics. Security and danger are arguably two of the most fundamental human feelings. Like it or not, they motivate a lot of what people think and do. Danger can trigger primitive drives and feelings, yet it also activates regions of the brain that process cognition and reasoning. For prehistoric human beings, sensations of danger provided important warnings about predators and threats of many kinds. And even today the sight of a snake on the front lawn provokes a visceral reaction in almost anyone. This is one reason places of refuge like homes remain so emotionally laden. It's also why Americans collectively lavish so many resources on "defense." Let's try to calculate for a minute just how much gets spent on protection of one kind or another. One doesn't normally lump sunscreen, car alarms, health insurance, and organic foods in a single category, but many of these expenditures originate from the same self-protective source. Then it has to be pointed out, though it's rarely expressed this way, that half of every dollar one pays in federal taxes goes to protecting the nation from foreign enemies.[6]

As the foregoing discussion highlights, public worries about risk often conflict with practical thinking. Irrational fears abound about unlikely harm, even as more common dangers often are ignored. In the wake of several highly publicized school shootings and terrorist bombings, students and parents began worrying about the safety of educational institutions. The perceptions of "danger" in schools, or more emotionally, *to children*, is now part of a public "common sense." Little mention is made that scarcely half a dozen such attacks take place each year in the U.S.—a rate that has remained relatively constant for 30 years. Tragic as any such incidents are, the broad-based perception of an "epidemic of violence" in schools belies evidence that the chances of a young person being harmed in this way fall somewhere in the range of one in two million.[7] I often point this out to my undergraduate students, then mention the comparatively high rates of school-related injuries, fatalities among young drivers, bullying-related harm, or the largely underreported number of gun deaths that take place in places other than schools. While six young people lost their lives in such school shootings during the past year, over 25,000 people died in alcohol-related car fatalities, with 42 percent aged between 16 and 24.[8]

But even this example doesn't go far enough. While some will argue that a "hard-wired" animalistic fear animates a person's core sense of being, the role of instinct remains a matter of scientific disagreement. The social conditioning behind fear has been studied extensively, with an entire literature discussing the relationship between security and anxiety in the field of infant attachment. In an earlier age of parenting, psychiatrist John Bowlby wrote in his classic work *A Secure Base* (1988) of how a mother "immediately after her infant is born, picks him up and begins to stroke his face with her finger tips. At this the baby quietens."[9] In this instant a pattern of behavior begins, a relationship of comfort and security between caregiver and child. A baby (and later a toddler) receiving consistent attention and nurturance feels safe—and from this experience begins to formulate a worldview in which human communication operates effectively, needs are recognized and met, and people can be trusted. This emerges from consistent engagement and support at an early age. In contrast, youngsters who receive variable, truncated, or repeatedly interrupted care, or who experience mistreatment, neglect, or abuse, fall prey to what is termed "insecure attachment." Here the worldview is characterized by failed communication, unsatisfied needs, and an understandable view that others may not automatically be trustworthy. This sounds a little bit like America's culture of fear, doesn't it?

But not all fear is irrational. Feeling anxious about the unknown derives from its unpredictability. Experiential learning often results from trial and error, which necessarily entails an occasional bad outcome. Even as interest and curiosity encourage new exploration, logic guides a person toward what is known and safe. Here again, a sense of security derives from perceptions of constancy and certainty. And conversely, this is how strangers can seem more likely to pose threats. Psychologists also link this to "familiarity heuristics"— assumptions that pre-experienced patterns will replicate in the future. In their classic 1977 essay "Judgment under Uncertainty," Daniel Kahneman and Amos Tversky outlined how these underlying thought processes can be activated, exaggerated, or pushed in irrational directions in conditions of stress or during conflicts (over limited resources, for example).[10]

Unfortunately, calculated degrees of stress and conflict are built into American society—and have been since its beginnings. Indeed, U.S. parliamentary capitalism was designed to encourage certain tensions as a source of democratic dynamism. Fueled by values of competition and personal gain, U.S. society tends to view life as a series of contests in which aggression is the name of the game. And as everyone knows, this quickly can get ugly—turning competitors into enemies. As National Football League (NFL) coach Vince Lombardi once spoke of American competitiveness: "Winning isn't everything; it's the only thing."[11] Inevitably this means that someone has to be defeated, pushed down, or otherwise forced to accept a lesser share of points, money, or winnings. This puts all Americans at odds with the collective ethos so necessary in balancing personal interests with the common good. Philosophically speaking, it's the self/other paradigm yet again. Throughout American history the nation has struggled with this tired dualism—manifest in the implicit contradiction between private liberty and public interest.

There is no avoiding the role of popular culture in this discussion. American entertainment and athletic culture relentlessly valorize competition and conflict: movies and television shows about crime, war, or predatory capitalism; sporting contests described as "showdowns" or "battles." Almost no aspect of social existence escapes reduction to a confrontation between real or imagined friends and enemies. Rising viewer appetites for violent representations have only increased these tendencies. Apocalyptic movie spectacles, graphic news reports, and hyper-realistic simulation games extend a growing spiral of conflict-based entertainment. Alarmed parents, educators, and mental health experts have battled to regulate and contain the seemingly unstoppable flow of such material—as free speech advocates and the news/entertainment industry have pushed back. But regulation efforts have never got very far—for a very simple reason. Conflict always has been a key ingredient in dramatic storytelling, a driver of narrative engagement throughout time in art, literature, religion, and entertainment. But in a media-saturated culture—where the line between fact and fiction can blur—ubiquitous media violence encourages the widely held belief that real-life danger is everywhere.

Adding to concerns about the media are growing frustrations over the increasingly polarized character of politics in the U.S., the crudeness of partisan debates, and the rise of polemic "news" masquerading as objective reporting. Not that any of this is much of a secret. After all, poking fun at journalistic bias has become one of the most popular forms of television comedy, thanks to the success of long-running programs like *Saturday Night Live* and *The Daily Show*. But at a deeper level, these popular satires reveal that there is something behind their humor. Psychoanalysts would argue that jokes are a way of negotiating uncomfortable topics or covering over unconscious distress. After all, the irony beneath much humor functions by inverting a recognized meaning, displacing the original into the realm of the absurd. In the case of extremist political "news" lampooned by comedians, the parody replicates its object even in its critique. This is the tricky aspect of ideology. Even when consciously named or joked about, its underlying structure remains in place—and is sometimes even enhanced.

Barbarians at the Gate

Public insecurities exploded in the postwar television age of nuclear fears and Cold War paranoia. As children were hiding from bombs under school desks, J. Edgar Hoover's FBI was trampling privacy in its hunt for spies. This intersection of media visuality and fear took many forms—most notably in suspicions that the entertainment industry itself was a front for communist propagandists. And not unlike today, public appetites were strong for stories of intrigue and deception. Postwar Hollywood flooded the mediascape with movies and television programs about hidden threats, malevolent enemies, and spies depicted in espionage stories—*Betrayed* (1954), *The Man Who Never Was* (1956), *The 39 Steps* (1959)—or tales of metaphoric invasion by aliens from outer space—*The Day the Earth Stood Still* (1951), *They Came from Outer Space* (1953), *Invaders from Mars* (1953), *Invasion of the Body Snatchers* (1956). Meanwhile, television was serving up suspense and crime programs, not to mention military combat shows. Also in this paranoid atmosphere, television's "investigation" format emerged in programs like *Confession*, featuring an interviewer questioning presumed drug users, sex offenders, and other stereotypical deviants.[12]

Again and again, the tension between security and threat would find visual representation in American mass media—although these motifs have a much longer history in Euro-American culture. For three centuries, vision and observation have been crucial elements in colonizing Western premises of "knowing" the world, reducing its unpredictability, and otherwise taming its "nature." The science-inspired empiricism of seeing, documenting, and analyzing observed facts provided (and still provides) a sense of control, certainty, and with these perceptions, a degree of security—as discussed in recent years in books like Nicholas Mirzoeff's *The Right to Look: A Counterhistory of Visuality.*[13] Mirzoeff picks up his story with the panoptic power of the gaze, noting that "the right to look" implies a privilege of some to do the looking. This gazing may be reciprocal in some instances, but often is not. The observer may be unseen, invisible, or even internalized in the consciousness of the one observed. In the latter sense, the observer need not even be looking for the gaze to operate.

Common to all of these scenarios is a structural asymmetry—an advantage (exercised, unexercised, recognized, or unrecognized)—of the seer over the seen. Given the ubiquity of visual culture in modern society, nearly everyone is complicit with such conventions of gazing—whether toward advertisements, commodities, other people, or themselves. Following this premise, visuality activates scenarios constructing the external other as an object, perhaps generating anxiety, but often requiring organization or domination.[14] In this sense, looking is all about interpretation—and the potential of power to enter the equation—from bodily objectification, to surveillance, to the deployment of vision-based programs of globalization and their continuing neoliberal adaptations. Mirzoeff goes so far as to historicize visuality in geopolitical terms: "visualized dominance" via the mechanisms of surveillance implemented in the slave era; "imperialist visuality" manifest in representations of global empire building; and the visual rhetoric of "the military-industrial complex." Is it any wonder that today questions of media representation seem to figure so prominently in security debates?

America's insecurity culture also links to a broader crisis of modernity. In *Civilization and Its Discontents*, Sigmund Freud wrote of security as a benefit of what he regarded an organized and modern society. In Freud's view, civilization had tamed the forces of nature and the irrationality of human impulse—with government, medicine, law, and education providing forms of protection and predictability. In other words: security. So what is the problem now? How is it that the "civilization" Freud talked about seems to be fraying at the seams? The answer would seem to lie in the conceptual vagaries of secure feelings. Social institutions can never provide the absolute assurances that Freud theorized. And as recent experiences have shown, security also often takes a toll on personal freedom. So in a postmodern age, when reminders of security failures greet Americans every day, the inadequacies of civilized security give way to a generalized ethos of anxiety. Zygmunt Bauman discussed this in his rejoinder to Freud, *Postmodernity and Its Discontents*, observing declines in public self-assurance, confidence about the future, and trust in other people.[15] With an eerie prescience, Bauman pointed to three emergent categories of anxiety: *uncertainty* (worries over an unpredictable future), *insecurity* (fears of impending loss or decline), and *unsafety* (apprehensions of danger or harm).[16] It should go without saying that such perceptions are held in varying degrees, contingent on social location, and not necessarily unique to the current moment. But a generalized anxiety hangs in the air nevertheless, even with the world's most powerful military power.

This partly explains the scapegoat culture now permeating American society—most notably around the issue of immigration—even as antipathies toward newcomers collide with U.S. values of inclusion. Anti-immigrant sentiments rarely get expressed in uniform terms—revealing deep contradictions in the nation's views of outsiders, as well as America's tendencies to squeeze the vulnerable. In some instances the economic value of cheap labor seems impossible to reconcile with workers' needs for public services like hospital care and education. Elsewhere, high-tech centers like Silicon Valley actively recruit non-U.S. citizens from throughout the world to drive innovation. And at many American universities, scientific research benefits from the massive influx of international faculty and students. All of this wreaks havoc on simple definitions of the "immigrant," the "illegal," and so on.

Conflicted opinions over immigration have thrown American politics into chaos, causing conflicts within both Republican and Democratic camps. Looming large in these discussions are worries over presumed terrorist threats posed by "insecure" borders and lingering suspicions about unfamiliar newcomers. These stereotypes are applied most aggressively toward those coming to the U.S. from its southern neighbors. Yet even a casual analysis of trade statistics shows that trade imbalances between the U.S. and Mexico may have favored the latter slightly, even as immigration to the U.S. from Mexico has slowed to a standstill. Moreover, the American economy benefits greatly from Mexico as a customer. In fact, Mexico today stands as the world's second-largest importer of U.S. goods after China.[17]

The immigration issue is a classic example of how public opinion becomes confused—and as a consequence cultural divisions get reinforced or created anew.[18] While federal and local governments have struggled in recent years to enforce laws of all kinds—including those having to do with border control—no one who pays even minimal attention to current events would conclude that the decline in the U.S. economy can be attributed to something as simple as undocumented border crossing. The question of immigration drifts easily into the nexus of fear, security, individualism, and national interest—demonstrating how America's collective psyche can be warped and its instincts diverted toward punitive ends.

The security culture resulting from this misrepresentation of threats does more than simply put people on edge. Opportunistic politicians gain support from anxious voters by promising to hire more police or make the army stronger. There is nothing new about this. Politicians throughout history have used public worries about crime or immigration to convince voters that they were right for their jobs. This propagation of misinformation has even more profound effects for foreign policy and defense. These are areas considerably more removed from people's lived experience than crime and hence even more contingent on media representation. Regardless of one's opinion about the "War on Terror," there is little doubt that public knowledge about the campaign is limited to what

Washington releases. This is done because war is the ultimate example of rationalized state aggression. To gain public consent for war its stakes must be raised to the level of myth and history.

While rogue nations and terrorist states continue to evoke fears of external threats to the U.S., worries about enemies lurking at home continue to fester. Network TV shows like *The Black List, Homeland, Scandal, State of Affairs, Madam Secretary, Nikita,* and *The Americans* suggest that popular appetites for such xenophobia have never been higher—especially when government secrecy adds spice to the mix. Just as many of these recent offerings animate a thinly veiled animus against vaguely defined "anti-American" villains, the new spy thrillers also capitalize on worries about enemies in the workplace, the neighborhood, or even one's bedroom. It goes without saying that media depictions of sleeper cell villains or covert assailants reinvigorate old racial stereotypes. Adding to such visual markers as skin color and clothing, spoken language always has featured in movies and television as a way of othering certain characters in the mind of a presumed English-speaking audience. Ironically this practice continues even as the U.S. becomes increasingly linguistically diverse and as international markets for U.S. media products become essential to the successes of movie and television products.

Whether in the form of an accent or another language itself, the way words are spoken now resonates more than ever with difference and potential threat. Thus, the matter of "foreign" languages and their media depiction becomes another articulation of tensions between cultural diversity and a latent yearning for national unity and wholeness. Many people are unaware that America does not have an "official" language, even as roughly 80 percent of the population indeed does speak English.[19] According to recent Census Bureau figures, more than 381 languages are used today within the United States.[20] Spanish ranks second among languages spoken in the U.S., and is spoken by approximately 13 percent of residents. In fact, the U.S. has the fifth-largest Spanish-speaking population in the world, surpassed only by Mexico, Argentina, Colombia, and Spain itself.

Still, an intolerance persists within the U.S. for languages other than standard written English—despite the nation's uniqueness in the world as the only major power comprised almost entirely of immigrant peoples. All of this gets more complicated as the issue of literacy becomes politicized. While many languages are spoken, written, signed, and read in the U.S., the issue becomes not so much a problem of "illiteracy," but rather a compulsive push for a universal competence in written and spoken English. Every day one hears complaints about the character or intelligence of immigrants lacking English proficiency but possessing quite competent literacy in other languages. The truth is that most non-English speakers and not-yet-citizens are completely "literate" if one defines this trait as the capacity to function in a society. Certainly, corporate America has no problem responding in this regard with bilingual product packaging and advertising. And government has stepped in with multilingual education, tax materials, and health-care information.

In historical terms, panics over English seem to parallel moments of national expansion or crisis. Efforts to agree on a single language in the U.S. date back to the early 1800s. With the purchase of the Louisiana Territory in 1803, America found itself owning a huge French-speaking territory. Following the turmoil of the American Civil War, French language rights of the region were eliminated. With the cessation of the Mexican-American War in 1848, the U.S. possessed a Spanish-speaking region. Three decades later, the California constitution was amended to permit only English for "official writings, and executive, legislative, and judicial proceedings."[21] In 1868 The Indian Peace Commission of 1868 recommended English-only schooling for First Nation Peoples. In the early 1900s Theodore Roosevelt used the bully pulpit of the White House to declare that "We have room for but one language in this country, and that is the English language." Then came World War I, and with it a popular campaign against the use of German, including removing German-language books from libraries. More recent English Only movements assert that a coherent society requires a common language. This idea appeals to anti-immigrant groups who believe that "foreigners" are fraying the fabric of American society with their different customs, beliefs, and languages.[22]

Debates over national security, border enforcement, and a "common language" for the U.S. leave begging the question of what it's like to be considered a threat, an "illegal," or an illiterate within this framework. The inability of American politicians to agree on what frequently is termed "commonsense reform immigration policy" has meant that millions of newcomers are forced to live in hiding.[23] This often includes the children of immigrants born in the United States. The concept of living "invisibly" is nothing new; it can be applied to numerous groups throughout American history, including those obliged by virtue of immigration status, nationality, religion, racial or ethnic identity, sexual orientation, gender identification, intellectual disability, or mental health status to feign various normative standards or otherwise "pass" as a matter of necessity or convenience. As the most obvious examples of this phenomenon, undocumented workers are often described in the press as "hiding in plain sight," along with such other social pariahs as terrorists and Internet predators. All of this reflects beliefs prevalent in popular culture about the nature of visibility and invisibility, the structure and stability of identity, as well as where threat does and does not exist in daily life. Little attention is ever given to the subjective experience of invisible existence or the fact that in many cases people have little choice but to live as such.

Privacy Rights and Wrongs

Concepts of privacy often lie behind debates about security, secrecy, public safety, and invisibility—not to mention principles of private property and personal space. Derived from the Latin term *privatus*, privacy literally means to be "separated from the rest" in an antithetical relationship to what is commonly held or "public." There are psychological dimensions of privacy, which link to notions of sensitivity, intimacy, individuality, and the personal. To many people, privacy correlates to concealment or remaining out of sight from others. Intention is implied even in this most simple definition, although simplicity quickly disappears with even a little consideration. Privacy can imply protection or secrecy. For many reasons, this separateness is seen as an important privilege in democratic societies. The "right to privacy" implies something fundamental in keeping one's business to oneself—in maintaining a distance between the personal and the public, the individual and the collective.

In many ways, America's preoccupation with privacy dates to the origins of the country itself, with concerns regularly emerging on several fronts. While the original U.S. Constitution did not explicitly address privacy, subsequent addenda were written to protect religious practice, speech, and assembly, and perhaps most significantly, the privacy of the homes and property from "unreasonable" search. First, and most obviously, privacy attaches to ideals of "self-ownership" discussed earlier. Political debates beginning at the nation's founding have reoccurred with startling regularity over public and private space—built into America's founding documents, which often referenced the sanctity of personal dwellings. Closely linked to individual personhood is the concept of private land, similarly designed as a counterpart to territory held for common benefit. Again, the inherent tension between individual and community has produced repeated arguments over the methods of maintaining equilibrium in the economic system. New forms of media communication always seem to be greeted with excitement and anxiety in their apparent ability to destabilize personal privacy and public interest. Here again, tensions between privacy and government policy have produced heated arguments for over two centuries. Finally, widely publicized threats to national security or public safety frequently have triggered heightened surveillance, paranoia, and both legitimate and reactionary concerns about privacy and the potential of government overreach.

Immigration to pre-revolutionary America was largely driven by economic desperation—perhaps more so than by political or religious conflict. While much is made in contemporary times of the foundational intentions of the nation's "fathers," demands over privacy are largely absent from the Declaration of Independence and the U.S. Constitution. Both are primarily political documents, with the former codifying complaints against British taxation and the latter the blueprint for a new government. While the Constitution avoided the word "privacy," it had plenty to say about the stationing of soldiers and the issuance of general warrants—which indirectly addressed privacy of the home and of people's papers and documents. By 1789 the Bill of Rights would directly discuss privacy of individuals and groups in mapping out the separation of church and state, freedom of expression, and protections against "unreasonable" search and seizure.

While espionage in America dates to the age of Benedict Arnold, ideals of privacy became contentious in national security worries of the early 20th century.

Shortly after the U.S. entered World War I, the National Security Act (1917) and the Sedition Act (1918) were written to prosecute spies and to limit anti-American speech. Emma Goldman was among those convicted in the early years of these statutes, although these same laws were used in later cases against Eugene Debs, Father Charles Coughlin, Alger Hiss, Julius and Ethel Rosenberg, Daniel Ellsberg, and Bradley Manning. In the pre-9/11 era, worries about communism motivated nearly all such cases, most famously those occurring during the Cold War period. In what remains the darkest chapter in the history of American privacy debates, the House Un-American Activities Committee (HUAC) operated from 1938 to 1969. Charged with rooting out alleged communists, the HUAC publicly, and sometimes secretly, investigated tens of thousands of citizens involved in campus activism, the civil rights movement, and, most notoriously, the Hollywood film industry. Supporting the HUAC, the FBI under J. Edgar Hoover conducted covert surveillance of hundreds of prominent public figures, politicians, professors, and activists—and not only concerning their threats to national security. Retrospective investigations into Hoover's files revealed that the FBI uncovered an extramarital affair involving Martin Luther King, Jr. and attempted to blackmail King with the evidence.

While running for the presidentcy, former HUAC member Richard Nixon would later make a further mark in the history of American secrecy in authorizing a burglary of the Democratic National Committee Headquarters at its Watergate offices in Washington, DC. After a botched cover-up of the plan, it was later revealed the Nixon had ordered wiretaps and covertly recorded years of his own office meetings and phone calls. The Watergate scandal triggered widespread calls for privacy protection. Shortly following Nixon's resignation from the presidency, Congress enacted the Privacy Act of 1974, establishing for the first time in the nation's history a "Code of Fair Information Practice" limiting the authority of the federal government to collect or use personal information attributable to individuals.

The following two decades saw both expansions and restrictions of personal privacy rights, largely pertaining to employment records and consumer information. Arguably, the most important privacy issue of the period involved health care. In the early 1980s a then-unnamed cluster of fatal illnesses began appearing among gay men in some of America's largest cities, and by 1985 closeted actor Rock Hudson died from complications of HIV-AIDS. Soon it would be discovered that the illness also affected the heterosexual population, and was spreading among injection drug users and recipients of blood transfusions. Under pressure from religious conservatives, the government initially declined to react to the epidemic as thousands died. These tragic circumstances led to formation in 1987 of the AIDS Coalition to Unleash Power (ACT-UP) to raise public awareness of the need for legislation, medical research, and treatment protocols for the disease. Famously using the slogan "Silence=Death," ACT-UP brought a degree of unity and visibility to LGBT communities at both a local and national level, while also fostering broader coalitions. These efforts resulted in the Comprehensive AIDS Resource Emergency (CARE) Act in 1990, which remains the largest federally funded program for people living with HIV-AIDS. Another landmark piece of health-care privacy legislation was the 1996 Health Insurance Portability and Accountability Act (HIPAA), the first national law to protect people's medical records—vesting control of such information in the hands of care recipients. HIPAA remains today a vital privacy control point governing physicians, hospitals, researchers, and insurance providers.

Medical privacy resonates with fundamental precepts of individual autonomy and civil liberty. In turn, these intersect with care management, medical ethics, data collection, recording keeping, and epidemiological research, among other issues. Certainly there is hardly anything more personal than one's own body. And perhaps nowhere else have the interests of individuals and societies become more contentious than over issues of illness and health—especially when matters of rights and faith conflict. Matters of sex and sexuality would generate further tensions and anxieties. As recent history has shown, what is repressed tends to resurface, as manifest in recurrent debates over laws governing reproduction, marriage, and the family. A persistent question in all of these debates has centered on the relationship of public policy to personal life—strangely inflected in the United States by religious ideology, which most feel should play no role in government policy.

With the rise of personal computing and network technology, a fresh wave of privacy legislation began to emerge to protect groups ranging from children to drivers. The infamous attempt by Bill Clinton to deny his affair with a White House intern again reminded Americans that presidents often have things to hide. Then came the election of George W. Bush, the events of September 11, 2001, and the subsequent USA PATRIOT Act of 2001. The acronym for the law stands for "Uniting and Strengthening America by Providing Appropriate Tools Required to Intercept and Obstruct Terrorism." The deleterious effects on privacy of the Patriot Act are now well known, especially as the reach of law enforcement has expanded in recent years, and includes within its scope: ubiquitous monitoring and data collection on individuals and business, enhanced criminal prosecutorial powers, extralegal arrests and imprisonment, travel security measures, trade restrictions, heightened border controls and security, and immigration restrictions and deportations, assassinations and military interventions in foreign nations.

While public fears about the government's ability to monitor Internet activity are nothing new, no one could have predicted the heights to which surveillance has risen as domestic terrorism incidents have continued, notably the Boston Marathon bombing and later incidents. It is now commonly known that virtually all Internet communications and telephone calls are subject to inspection by law enforcement. Complicating the issue of privacy in the Internet age is the issue of self-disclosure. Employers and college admissions offices now have the ability to view applicants' Facebook or Twitter activity, not to mention their blogs or postings across the infoverse. Elementary and middle schools now counsel young people on the importance of remaining cognizant about the permanence of their online footprints. All of this underscores the fuzziness of concepts like "public" and "private."

Something to Hide

Taken literally, something that is hidden is concealed or kept out of sight. Intention is implied even in this most simple definition, although simplicity quickly disappears with even a little consideration. Hiding can imply either deceit or protection, not to mention "hide-and-seek" kinds of play. But hiding is also seen as an important privilege in democratic societies. The "right to privacy" (as discussed above) implies something fundamental in keeping one's business to oneself—in maintaining a separation of the personal from the public, the individual from the collective. In most people's minds, hiding alternately can refer to concealing and preserving, and of course an animal's hide is what envelops and protects the body inside. So the impulse and act of hiding can carry varied meanings and motivations. But always there is the suggestion of a relationship—of something or someone being hidden from the observing intelligence of another sentient being, whether animal or machine.

In ontological terms, questions can be posed about the demarcation between what is concealed and what is revealed. Hiding attaches itself to structures of subjectivity itself, which has been variously described in terms of interiority and exteriority, as well as the impossibility of such a distinction. In American concepts of autonomous personhood, the idealized distinction between self and other is reinforced in the act of hiding—as well as other familiar binary oppositions: individual/group, normal/abnormal, safety/risk, citizen/government. Like many of the dualisms discussed throughout this book, discussions of privacy have much to do with demarcations between the invisible and the visible. The act of hiding often carries an intention in response to a perceived threat or objective, although not always so. Necessarily this discussion must begin with a return to the problematic of interiority and exteriority as it pertains to performances of obfuscation and disclosure. Again, the neat separation of these categories must be undone, even as one relies upon dualistic heuristics as a point of departure in discussing ingrained and seemingly naturalized constructions. Wary of the dangers of claiming equivalences or even correspondence among the myriad identities possessed within and among individuals, it nevertheless can be said that almost everyone has at some point in their lives felt they have something to hide.

The premise of hiding carries an implicit assumption about the possibility of being hidden, raising immediate questions about who is hiding what from whom, as well as why and how this is being done, where and when, and of course, how effective the hiding is. Such granular questions play out in specific acts of hiding and what provisionally one might call *objectivist* and *subjectivist* interpretations of these acts. That is to say, from an objectivist perspective an entity is hidden as an empirical fact or "actuality." In a subjectivist view, an entity is unseen in conceptual or "virtual" terms. Needless to say, these two domains only begin to explain how hiding—or any experiential phenomena—actually work. Objectivism and subjectivism intersect, overlap, duplicate, contradict, and otherwise inform each other in myriad ways. Hence, if one wants to use these concepts at all, they are better seen as components of an integrated system—which also has other parts.

One of these parts would necessarily reside in the experience of the parties involved. What is it like to be hidden, secretive, fugitive, lost, or forgotten? The overdetermined ontologies of objectivism and subjectivism—especially as debated in the social sciences—often leave little room for the phenomenological experience of those they analyze. Take the well-known story of Anne Frank and her family, who were objectively hiding from capture and likely execution. They were subjective fugitives of a hateful ideology. But Frank herself came to experience her "Secret Annex" in a tiny attic space as a secure refuge. The apparent naïvety of Frank's perceptions is part of what gives her diaries their enduring emotional resonance, as readers are well aware of the end of the story. As Frank poignantly writes, "The Annex is an ideal place to hide. It may be damp and lopsided, but there's probably not a more comfortable hiding place in all of Amsterdam. No, in all of Holland."[24] Aside from its value as personal testimony, the diary of Anne Frank holds significance in the context of the "hidden."

Things and people are hidden for many reasons. The absence of something hidden can give it a presence. If someone steals your car, you don't forget about the car—at least not right away. But in a deeper sense, absence creates a void or negative space in time. If you've never owned an automobile, the lack of a car shapes your relationship to transportation, to convenience, to daily life in general. Part of what made *Anne Frank: The Dairy of a Young Girl* so important was the way it helped to give a voice to the millions lost during the Nazi Holocaust. No one needed to tell the families of the dead that they were gone. But the stories of loss—and of literal "hiding"—needed to be known more broadly. While Frank herself did not survive the war, the small red-and-white journal she received for her 13th birthday became an actant for an absent archive. At the time of her death in the Auschwitz concentration camp, Frank's diary was unknown by anyone beyond her surviving family members. It was a silent and invisible chronicle—one among the millions of anonymous stories erased by Nazi genocide. Inasmuch as the adolescent Frank had imagined a public audience for the book, her writing, her telling, had failed.

But the subsequent journey of Frank's little book illustrates an enormously important point about silence, apparent failure, and historical processes. Events occur in time and space, as well as human subjectivity. A failure today does not negate the action that took place. A statement consigned to silence was still made somewhere in time. Contained within every failure or silence is both the negative space of absence, but also the perpetual possibility of presence. As Frank's story further illustrates, the accretion of past utterances into the history of the present is frequently discontinuous and invariably mediated. As such, *The Diary of a Young Girl* problematizes neat categorizations of invisibility/visibility or silence/voice.

One sees in the archive of *Anne Frank: The Diary of a Young Girl* a repeated doubling of visibility and invisibility, each side echoing the other and establishing a space in between. Seen today as a text of historical significance and broad-based moral appeal, Frank's book nevertheless required government intervention decades after its initial publication to appear in unexpurgated form. The diaries still remain suppressed in selected localities. In this sense, Frank's thoughts rendered into text have remained both hidden and revealed. Also residing in that space between presence and absence is the translucent presence of the author herself. Between the objective actuality of published texts and the subjective ideations of their various editors and agents, Anne Frank remains a ghost. It is a mistake to think of objective and subjective analysis, or visibility and invisibility, as anything more than virtual constructions. Yet these habits of mind can have life-or-death consequences, as the Anne Frank story so dramatically documents.

These protracted mediations of the Anne Frank story illustrate the function of literature described at a contemporaneous historical moment by Simone de Beauvoir in her memoir of pre-liberation Europe, *La force de l'âge*.[25] Not unlike Frank and others who lived through that traumatic period, Beauvoir saw herself as a "witness" to a world undeserving of trust. For Beauvoir, written texts carried the potential—but not the guarantee—of conveying experience from one person to another. She coined the expression "detotalized totality" to describe this contingency. Worlds described in written works remain partially hidden, existing in a realm of constant becoming; these worlds can never be grasped as "totalized" entities in the Heideggerian sense of an already-present truth.[26] Written works constitute gestures toward totality bound within the limits of the text. In this sense, a distance inheres between writer and reader, as the world within the written work struggles to be revealed.

While the etiology of the Nazi program is complex and historically specific, the Holocaust nevertheless motivated international efforts following World War II to define genocide and protect against its recurrence. In 1946 the first session of the newly established United Nations General Assembly would agree to classify genocide as a violation of international law, but was unable to formulate a precise definition of the crime. Recognition of the unique history of Jewish persecution would lead to the establishment of the nation of Israel in 1948, even as some argued that the Nazi Holocaust had broader origins. A consensus would emerge within a few years that genocide constituted "the intent to destroy, in whole or in part, a national, ethnical, racial or religious group," although disagreements persisted over considerations of politics, ideology, and social status, in defining victimized groups.

It shouldn't be forgotten that World War II also affected populations within the U.S. As conflicts began overseas, suspicions became widespread about anyone of German or Japanese heritage. While Germans could pass as part of a Euro-American "mainstream," Japanese were immediately persecuted. Within two months of the declaration of war, Franklin D. Roosevelt ordered the mass incarceration of 117,000 Japanese Americans, largely from western states, many of whose families had been citizens for generations. It was thought that people of Japanese heritage were prone to sabotage, and that the success of the Pearl Harbor attack partly resulted from espionage by Japanese Americans in Hawaii and California. The hastily built detainment camps in remote uninhabitable areas were notoriously crowded, unsanitary, and inhumane—with barbed wire fences and other security measures. Most detainees in the camps lost their jobs, homes, businesses, and often their health. The Pearl Harbor surprise attack seemed to confirm a constellation of extant prejudices and racist attitudes, many of which were later discussed by Edward Said in his book, *Orientalism*. While broadly applicable in discussions of racial prejudice and hate, Said historicizes the "Orient" as a European cultural construction of the self/other character in which specific unfamiliar or "exotic" traits would become simultaneously cast as enticing and dangerous.[27] Mirroring this dualism was a similar construction of Western culture as evolving and progressive in contrast to unchanging and barbaric Eastern sensibilities.

Even in contemporary times Asian Americans are frequently regarded as "perpetual foreigners," unlike any other ethnic group. Media stereotypes of stealth and duplicity had been present in American popular culture for decades prior to World War II in characters including Fu Manchu, Madame Butterfly, and the Dragon Lady. As in these latter examples, an impulse to sexualize Asian people, especially women, as simultaneously seductive and submissive would pervade American culture through the Vietnam era and beyond. Some date the "feminization" of Asian men to the mid-1800s, when restrictive labor laws banned such immigrants from male-intensive factory jobs and obliged many to work as household domestics, cooks, and launderers. More importantly, from the mid-19th century, mainstream America had already begun to see immigrants from Asia as an economic threat. Impulses of hard work and family solidarity characteristic of every immigrant group would nevertheless be mythicized as unique ethnic traits, providing yet more evidence of an Asian threat. All of these myths and stereotypes found a consolidating rationale in World War II.

Following World War II, efforts to account for its atrocities began in earnest. Hannah Arendt is well known for discussing colonial and totalitarian ideologies as governing factors in the rise of the Nazi regime and the subsequent ascendance of the Soviet Union.[28] In Arendt's view, such larger systems of thought and bureaucracy could better explain the political success of the Nazi program than the racist beliefs of a minority of the German people. The broad-based ethical slippage that permitted the Holocaust resulted from a more generalized replacement of faith with secularism (not to be confused with atheism), which Arendt and others viewed as an important, albeit dangerous, antidote to religious determinism. None of this made Arendt very popular in the postwar years, despite her imprisonment by the Nazis and lifelong commitment to the study of anti-Semitism. Always a Heideggerian (in every sense of the term), Arendt later would draw an important distinction between violence and power, pertinent to this discussion of security and hiding. To Arendt, power does not require the visible exercise of violence, although power is often the goal of violence. Power itself is a structural relationship with no inherent requirement of brute force. When a power relationship is unstable (as when it is formed, threatened, or otherwise reorganized), violence can become a utilitarian means to an end. And as Arendt was quick to point out, bureaucratic violence can render both the subjects and objects of violence as anonymous in their collectivity.[29] Government actions are carried only by faceless functionaries against groups similarly lacking individual specificity.

Organized Hate

It is tempting to consign the genocidal programs of the Third Reich to an archive of historical anomalies—that "never again" might such a thing happen. Although the enormity and intergenerational consequences of the Holocaust still haunt the world, subsequent genocidal campaigns—both large and small—have been documented in numerous countries: Argentina, Armenia, Bangladesh, Bosnia, Brazil, Burundi, Cambodia, Darfur, East Timor, Guatemala, Ethiopia, Iraq, Laos, Lebanon, North Korea, Rwanda, Sri Lanka, Tibet, West New Guinea, and Zanzibar, among others. But this listing of genocide by country is misleading, inasmuch as it suggests a phenomenon identifiable in national terms—as though such factors as region, nation, religion, or ethnicity might in themselves explain raw fact of organized hatred. The simple reality is that hate exists and reproduces itself in every nation and locality. It lives in workplaces, schools, and families; among wealthy and poor, educated and uneducated, believers and unbelievers. And while the consequences of hate sometimes rise to public consciousness in news accounts, all data suggest that most hate-related victimization remains unreported. In the U.S. alone, the Southern Poverty Law Center estimates that only 5,000 hate crimes are reported of the 250,000 that occur each year.[30]

Hate can take many forms: as mental process, material practice, state policy, and political tool. As such hate can't be easily wiped away by legal means. Hate can be as invisible as what drives some into hiding. Organized hate generally entails three key ingredients: existing intergenerational prejudice; an economic crisis in search of a scapegoat; and a fear-mongering political party. Like violence, hate sometimes gets attributed to hard-wired fear responses or instincts for self-preservation. No serious scientific evidence exists to support these links to interpersonal behavior per se, although the cultural propagation of fear and competitive attitudes has been widely documented and analyzed. In their book *Why We Hate*, Jack Levin and Gordana Rabrenovic have engaged the evolutionary rationale for hate in noting that a "wariness of outsiders became, in the Darwinian sense, a strength of those who were able to survive and pass on their legacy to future generations. But what began likely as genetic was soon learned behavior in each successive generation."[31] The authors note that "white supremacists were not born loathing blacks and Latinos. Muslims were not born hating Jews and Christians. Americans were not born despising Arabs."[32] While many people "have a predisposition to view outsiders with a degree of skepticism, hating outsiders, or those from specific groups, is taught. Haters learn such ideas either early in life from their parents or later in life from their friends, classmates, teachers, religious leaders, and the mass media."[33]

The reciprocal character of hate also bears underscoring. Much as violence can beget further violence, hate also often propagates itself in a mirroring response from its object. This can manifest in either a logical cause/effect fashion, or an emotional response. Beyond any cognitive dimensions of intergenerational hate often lies an important affective dimension: hate as revenge. Levin and Rabrenovic cite statists revealing that as many as 8 percent of hate crimes result simply from retaliatory impulses. Offenders often don't know their victims, but assault those they associate with prior wrongdoing. The Florida shooting of teenager Trayvon Martin by neighborhood vigilante George Zimmerman is one notable case of this. Taken a step further, widespread calls for the execution of Zimmerman can be seen as another dimension of revenge-driven feelings. Levin and Rabrenovic point to the ongoing Israeli-Palestinian conflict as a broader example of this phenomenon.

Hate crimes and genocide are often characterized as "crimes against humanity," especially when such victimization has perceived ethnic, racial, or otherwise biological origins. Elsewhere in this book I have discussed problems associated with the terms "human" and "humanity" resulting from their generalizing implications. One can perhaps speak of the human species as a biological designation, but as soon as discussions turn to humanity, human values, religious humanism, or even human rights—implications of universality are invariably colored by the perspectives of the speaker. Suffice to say that whether one is discussing crimes against humanity, hate, capital punishment, or declarations of war—distance seems an enabler of antipathy. Revenge or proactive violence becomes conscionable when the identity of a person or group can be abstracted into a single offending element or trait. George Zimmerman had never murdered anyone before Trayvon Martin. But Martin became in Zimmerman's mind a powerful surrogate for past offences, which evidence suggests Zimmerman associated with African-American men in general. This simple act of mental slippage provides a tragic logic to certain strains of hate and prejudice in the displacement of one set of prior behaviors onto an unrelated third party.

Statistically speaking, there has been some good news recently about hate—at least in terms of crime. According to FBI Uniform Crime Reports, overall numbers of hate-motivated assaults have declined continually since 1995, although Islamic-identified people continue to be disproportionately victimized.[34] Underlying these declines is a disturbing trend, however. Hate has gone underground. Overt public expressions of racism and homophobia may have lost the public sanction they once had, but bigotry is finding new life on the Internet—where people with fringe views on just about any matter can find like-minded spirits and support. This makes it almost impossible to track the number of people in hate groups with any reliability. Not only does the Internet allow hate to spread anonymously, but it also globalizes such ideologies. This encourages the relatively new "lone wolf" phenomenon of individuals who privately perseverate on their ideas, find encouragement online, and devise means to execute violent attacks in ways that are completely unpredictable. While the frequency of domestic terrorist bombings and mass shootings remains relatively small in statistical terms, interventions against such assaults are increasingly difficult to put in place.

Is there anything to do about this? Philosophers, criminologists, and sociologists have pondered the nature of hate for quite some time. Most commonly, hate is attributed to an anger or injury that becomes projected onto another person or group. The scapegoating of immigrants and ethnic minorities makes sense to those worried about unemployment or the changing face of their neighborhoods. Anger against women and LGBT populations comes easily to groups concerned about changing "family values" and the rising secularization of society. In other words, hatred often manifests as an attitude about a problem, which is then projected onto something (or someone) else. Some psychoanalysts link this to early subject/object experiences, notably the relationship of infant and (m)other. As the maturing child emerges from this early pairing, vulnerability and worry often occur in the anticipation of separation. In her book, *Hatred and Forgiveness*, Julia Kristeva associates hateful thinking with the abjection produced in this moment, as the hating person relives this primal memory and connects it to a person, group, or thing in the present.[35]

While analytic insight is one way of correcting this hateful misrecognition, Kristeva notes how religion and love historically have served similar ends. But in any of these corrective scenarios, the key seems to lie in "forgiving" the original source of pain. By necessity this involves some kind of engagement with the hated object in literal or symbolic terms. Put another way, hatred is enabled by fear of psychic loss. Overcoming hatred toward another comes from moving through internalized injuries, generally in an engagement with the source of abjection. In elemental terms, this means bridging the gap between subject and object. Obviously this is easier said than done. And sometimes it requires participation from both sides of the exchange. Hence, overcoming hatred becomes a continual work in progress. How this might be accomplished will be discussed in Parts II and III of this book.

Notes

1 Brian Massumi, *The Politics of Everyday Fear* (Minneapolis: University of Minnesota Press, 1993).
2 Stuart Hall et al., *Policing the Crisis: Mugging, the State and Law and Order* (London: Macmillan, 1978); Barry Glassner, *The Culture of Fear: Why Americans Are Afraid of the Wrong Things* (New York: Basic Books, 2000).

3 Stanley Cohen, *Moral Panics and Folk Devils* (London and New York: Routledge, 1972).
4 *The Culture of Fear.*
5 "Majority Views NSA Phone Tracking as Acceptable Anti-terror Tactic," Pew Research Center for the People and the Press (June 13, 2013) http://www.people-press.org/2013/06/10/majority-views-nsa-phone-tracking-as-acceptable-anti-terror-tactic/ (accessed July 15, 2013).
6 Brad Pulmer, "America's Staggering Defense Budget, in Charts," *Washington Post* (Jan. 7, 2013) www.washingtonpost.com/blogs/wonkblog/wp/2013/01/07/everything-chuck-hagel-needs-to-know-about-the-defense-budget-in-charts/ (accessed Nov. 15, 2014).
7 "School Shooting Statistics" (April 19, 2013) http://www.statisticbrain.com/school-shooting-statistics/ (accessed July 20, 2013).
8 See "Alcohol Impaired Driving," Traffic Safety Facts, U.S. Department of Transportation, National Highway Safety Administration http://www-nrd.nhtsa.dot.gov/Pubs/811606.pdf (accessed July 20, 2013). Taking a comparative view of terrorism, while 9/11 and subsequent attacks have resulted in roughly 3,000 U.S. fatalities, CDC statistics show that 364,000 Americans have been killed since 9/11 as a result of non-terrorist gun violence. See Conor Friedersdorf, "The Irrationality of Giving Up This Much Liberty to Fight Terror," *The Atlantic* (June 10, 2013) http://www.theatlantic.com/politics/ archive/2013/06/the-irrationality-of-giving-up-this-much-liberty-to-fight-terror/276695/ (accessed July 20, 2013).
9 John Bowlby, *A Secure Base: Parent-Child Attachment and Healthy Human Development* (New York and London: Routledge, 1988) p. 6.
10 Daniel Kahneman and Amos Tversky, "Judgement under Uncertainty: Heuristics and Biases," *Science*, 27 (Sept. 1974) 1124–1131.
11 Alfie Kohn, *No Contest: The Case against Competition* (New York: Houghton Mifflin, 1988) p. 3.
12 See Andrew Ross, *No Respect: Intellectuals and Popular Culture* (London and New York: Routledge, 1989) p. 104.
13 Nicholas Mirzoeff, *The Right to Look: A Counterhistory of Visuality* (Durham, NC: Duke University Press, 2011).
14 Jacques Derrida, *Right of Inspection*, trans. David Wills (New York: Monacelli, 1999) p. xxvi.
15 Zygmunt Bauman, *Postmodernity and Its Discontents* (London: Polity, 1997).
16 Zygmunt Bauman, *In Search of Politics* (Palo Alto, CA: Stanford University Press, 1999) p. 17.
17 See "Lost in the Shadow of the Fence," Immigration Policy Center (July 2013) http://www.immigrationpolicy.org/just-facts/lost-shadow-fence (assessed July 17, 2013).
18 "Sealing the U.S. Border Would Cost an Additional $28 Billion a Year," *Business Week* (Mar. 13, 2013) http://www.businessweek.com/articles/2013-03-13/the-price-tag-for-sealing-the-u-dot-s-dot-border-isnt-pretty (accessed July 16, 2013).
19 "Language Use in the United States: 2011," *The United States Census Bureau* (Washington, DC: U.S. Census Bureau, 2001). https://www.census.gov/hhes/socdemo/language/ (accessed April 19, 2015).
20 Ibid.
21 United States Indian Peace Commission, *Proceedings of the Great Peace Commission of 1867–1868* (Washington, DC: Institute for the Development of Indian Law, 1975).
22 See Geoff Nunberg, *Resolution: English Only, Linguistic Society of America.* Internet reference (Dec. 28, 1986) http://www.linguisticsociety.org/resource/resolution-english-only (accessed May 12, 2015).
23 "Creating an Immigration System for the 21st Century," Whitehouse.gov (2014) http://www.whitehouse.gov/issues/immigration (accessed Nov. 15, 2014).

24 Anne Frank, *Anne Frank: The Diary of a Young Girl,* trans. B.M. Mooyaart (New York: Bantam Reprint, 2003).
25 Simon de Beauvoir, *La force de l'âge* (Paris: Galliard, 1960).
26 Toril Moi, "What Can Literature Do? Simone de Beauvoir as a Literary Theorist," *PMLA* 124:1 (Jan. 2009) p. 192.
27 Edward Said, *Orientalism* (New York: Vintage, 1979).
28 Hannah Arendt, *The Origins of Totalitarianism* (New York: Harcourt, Brace, Jovanovich, 1973).
29 Hannah Arendt, *On Violence* (New York: Important Books, 2014).
30 "DOJ Study: More than 250,000 Hate Crimes a Year, Most Unreported" SPLC Hatewatch http://www.splcenter.org/blog/2013/03/26/doj-study-more-than-250000-hate-crimes-a-year-a-third-never-reported/ (accessed June 25, 2013).
31 Jack Levin and Gordana Rabrenovic, *Why We Hate* (New York: Prometheus Books, 2004).
32 *Why We Hate*, p. 63.
33 Ibid.
34 Mike Brunker, Monica Alba, and Bill Dedman, "Snapshot: Hate Crime in America, by the Numbers," NBC News (April 26, 2014) http://www.nbcnews.com/storyline/jewish-center-shootings/snapshot-hate-crime-america-numbers-n81521 (accessed June 29, 2014).
35 Julia Kristeva, *Hatred and Forgiveness* (New York: Columbia University Press, 2010).

PART II

Belonging Somewhere

Blurred Boundaries

It's said that America has moved from "solid" to "liquid" times, as communication technologies, a global economy, and changing social attitudes have blurred familiar boundaries of all kinds.[1] Part II: "Belonging Somewhere: Blurred Boundaries" describes a time in which long-standing ideals of certainty and security have melted—undermining familiar underpinnings of national belonging while also bringing others forward. Some date this liquid era to the decades after World War II, when the unifying narratives of modernist "progress" had given the world genocide, nuclear weaponry, and destruction—only to be followed by environmental damage on a global scale. Civil rights and feminist movements in the United States soon would raise further questions about the nation's traditions and their legitimacy. Shortly after the celebrations of the new millennium, America was greeted by an unsettling presidential election, the attacks of 9/11, and global economic collapse. As a divided Congress found itself unable to fix the nation's problems, divisions grew between rich and poor while public distrust of authority rose on many registers. Everywhere people seem to hungering for answers.

Societies react to collapse and disasters in certain patterns. While opinions vary on whether these jolts result in continuity or change, it is hard to deny the temporary destabilization that major events cause in the lives of individuals and groups. The common conclusion is that a moment of potentiality occurs, influenced by what existed before and colored by expectations of what is to follow. Regardless of where one stands on debates over "shock doctrines," the disruptions of the 2000s brought heightened levels of disorientation, suspicion, and worry—manifest in massive levels of resentment toward government, business, and institutional authority on many levels. As faith in leadership declined amid revelations of corruption and greed, the individualized consumption of goods became a more popular expression of "choice" than going to the polls. To make matters worse, centrist politics left national government teetering on vital issues, with massive infusions of capital able to exert influence in unprecedented ways.

These changes raise deeper philosophical questions about the ways that societies understand their place in the world, conditioned as they are by apparent and unapparent factors. Decades of deconstruction theory have pointed out the contingency of meaning, noting ways that ideas can be interpreted quite differently in varying contexts. Put simply, anything like a "common sense" needs to be approached with caution in a society in which difference is continually in play.[2] When applied to identity, these notions challenge principles of hierarchy, heritage, purity, and destiny, among others. And following this thinking, knowledge itself is not always what it seems, organized as it often is through rules and structures that enable and limit potential ideation.[3] Grand axioms of human progress become suspect (postmodernism) as universal truths lose stability (poststructuralism). But this isn't simply a matter of philosophy. Global population migrations change demographics inside the U.S. and around the globe. Old economic models also have come undone (postindustrialism) in an age of financialized capital and flexible accumulation (post-Fordism). As the global empires falter (postcolonialism) the dominance of the U.S. itself has declined (post-Americanism).

"Belonging Somewhere" examines an age in which "diversity" has become the new order of the day. What remains when traditional categories of belonging and non-belonging yield to a new recognition of particularity and difference? Beginning in the 1990s, cautionary voices began to warn that the abandonment of categorical ideals—such as class consciousness, for example—might yield a dangerous atomization of the kind Marx warned against more than a century ago. Is it possible that as difference becomes the new status quo, the American balance between individual and community is shifting? Certainly the balance is changing in both visible and invisible ways. The dematerialization of labor and commerce unhinges these important parts of life in space and time, resulting in new forms of abstraction. Old ways of social gathering are giving way to new forms of disembodied interaction as well as electronic community. Media decentralization allows viewers to reinforce their personal preferences and opinions. All of these yield a social moment in which we are "alone together" in new and unexpected ways. With public apathy rising to unprecedented highs, America's most common family unit is now a single person living alone.

As America increasingly becomes a society of atomized individuals, other kinds of dislocation are occurring. Distinctions are disappearing between private and public. While surveillance technologies allow authorities to track the most intimate habits of individuals, the Supreme Court has afforded businesses previously sanctified "free speech" rights of citizens. As online technology has allowed anyone to become a media personality, reductions in government programs push many into the marketplace for life's basics. Meanwhile, the new phenomenon of transmedia creates immersive informational envelopes in which people are bombarded by simultaneous messages in various forms (advertising, entertainment, and news reporting), often coordinated to support specific brands, products, or opinions.[4] Increasingly the population feels powerless to combat the neoliberal agenda, even as the nation's overall economic status continues to decline in the global economy.[5]

The chapters in "Belonging Somewhere" seek to ground these often perplexing experiences of boundary blurring by addressing four interrelated themes: the rise of virtual experience; the transition to post-identity; the social construction of disability; and increasing attention to matters of mental health. If the U.S. is indeed becoming a society of solitary individuals, some attention to personal subjectivity may be warranted. For decades communications professionals have known that audiences exercise a fair amount of agency—as failed politicians and merchandisers can attest. In what would later be termed reception theory, media scholars would observe that viewers sometimes believe and other times don't believe what they see. Audiences also interpret media messages differently from one another, inferring varied meanings and drawing different conclusions. All of this creates certain instabilities in the transmission of ideas from sender to receiver in both cognitive and emotional terms. This means that people make choices deciding what to believe, what to buy, and even more importantly, where to place their ideological and affective investments—even as the lines around all of these things become fuzzy and confused.

Negotiations of meaning can be seen in those who resist, confront, or find ways of ameliorating the spaces between commonly accepted views of margin and mainstream.[6] In other words, boundary blurring is taking place across identities and material practices in ways that many people don't realize. Gender-bending teenagers are showing the world that traditional definitions of "male" and "female" are losing relevance. Grassroots entrepreneurs are making goods and selling them on the Internet, thereby finding their way around mainstream retailers or online giants like Amazon.com.[7] This blurring of boundaries has both positive and negative implications, with plenty of room in between. As long-standing social structures weaken or melt, moments of instability present both possibilities and risks. As reactionary voices proclaim the "end of America as we know it," others argue that change is the only constant that defines a revolutionary people. Is it possible or even desirable for singular values to define a country of such complexity?

Notes

1 Marshall Berman, *All That Is Solid Melts into Air: The Experience of Modernity* (New York: Penguin, 1988); Zygmunt Bauman, *Liquid Times: Living in an Age of Uncertainty* (London and New York: Polity, 2007); Bill Nichols, *Blurred Boundaries: Questions of Meaning in Contemporary Culture* (Bloomington: Indiana University Press, 1995).

2 Jacques Derrida, *Writing and Difference*, trans. Alan Bass (London and New York: Routledge, 1978)

3 Michel Foucault, *The Archaeology of Knowledge and the Discourse on Language*, trans. A.M. Sheridan Smith (New York: Pantheon, 1972).

4 Henry Jenkins, *Convergence Culture: Where Old and New Media Collide* (New York: NYU Press, 2008).
5 Elizabeth A. Povinelli, *Economies of Abandonment: Social Belonging and Endurance in Late Liberalism* (Durham, NC, and London: Duke University Press, 2011).
6 Alyssa Quart, *Republic of Outsiders: The Power of Amateurs, Dreamers, and Rebels* (New York: The New Press, 2013).
7 *Republic of Outsiders*, p. xv.

5

REALITY IS BROKEN

Neoliberalism and the Virtual Economy

Lines are blurring in the new millennium as never before: between public and private, local and global, high and low culture. In the new America, corporations are afforded the rights of people, as the privacy of citizens becomes little more than a joke. And forget about those categories of what nostalgically were called "imagination" and "reality." Entertainment has merged with journalism, and vice versa, in an age when people get their news from TV comedy shows. Gender roles and family values are up for grabs as the Internet reinvents social life. And even as corporations grow larger and more powerful, technology offers ever-expanding avenues of consumer choice and self-expression. Some describe this as a postmodern moment: when past rules, conventions, and beliefs simply no longer apply. And all the evidence seems to confirm this, as subjectivity itself becomes a montage of images. Hence, diversity has become the new order of the day. Everyone is different, "special," and free to dwell in the postmodern American dream.

But something haunts this forest of signs. Liberation from the past fosters anxiety about the future, especially as material reality keeps rearing its head. Language is the devil of postmodern thinking—following the basic proposition that linguistic meaning shifts with context and interpretation. People use words, stories, and images in trying to explain the world, but often don't get things completely right. In creating a narrative version of reality, language rarely yields a faithful representation of what "is," although it sometimes points to what "might be." None of this is especially new. Stories have always created fantasy worlds in the minds of individual listeners and readers, much as Aristotle once described.[1] But this challenge of meaning seems ever more complicated in a virtual age infused with media imagery, online communities, and immersive game environments.

Solitary journeys into narrative worlds can have a distancing effect, reinforcing a sense of isolation. It may seem counterintuitive to think that the very language through which people communicate with others also pulls them into themselves. But this often-unexamined sense of "self" is critical in considering who does and who does not seem to "belong" in America. In U.S. culture, the latent sense of alienation via language is encouraged by an ethos of self-reliance, personal achievement, and privacy. Unfortunately this heightened emphasis on individualism and being oneself also provides a distraction from realities like the widening gap between rich and poor in the United States—that 10 percent of the people take home 50 percent of the nation's wealth.[2] While many find themselves working harder to get less (or not having jobs at all), few of them are able to name the reason for their difficulties. Prevailing American myths of freedom and opportunity tell people that success or failure is a personal matter. But can this really be true when nearly everyone is struggling? Part of the problem lies in exactly the postmodern state of affairs described above. The blurring of lines between public and private, between the real and imaginary—these aren't simply matters of perception. Formerly separate operations of government and business are becoming intricately intertwined—sometimes supporting each other, but also occasionally coming into conflict. Fictionalized news reports and exaggerated advertising claims actually do become reality when they change citizens' voting preferences and consumer choices. And matters get worse when people blame themselves for failures rather than recognizing broader forces working against them.

And things *have* gotten worse. As the wealth gap continues to benefit a small minority of Americans, nearly everyone else suffers. This was the message of the Occupy Wall Street slogan: "We are the 99%." In broader social terms, individual differences also manifest themselves in disparities in education, employment, health care, and housing—all of which continue to worsen. It turns out that postmodern culture hasn't put a dent in school inequities, workplace bias, homelessness, and the lower life expectancy among certain groups.[3] All of this was exacerbated by the global recession of the early 2000s, as economic hardship and human difference began to intersect in both familiar and unfamiliar ways. Earlier in this book I described the philosophical and historical etiology of this problem in entrenched attitudes toward private property and competition. Throughout the history of the United States, "us versus them" thinking has exerted a powerful hold on American culture. But this simple dichotomy doesn't fully explain how disparities now play themselves out in an age of blurring boundaries. In some ways this chapter is a bad news/good news story; but it will also examine the space in between. The blurring of boundaries may have made critical consciousness more elusive, but it has also opened up new possibilities.

Neoliberalism Revisited

In recent decades, the blurring of fact and fiction has led philosophers to rethink notions of conceptual boundaries, how to find them, and whether or not this is feasible or advisable. Opinion often divides between the separatist impulses of Kantian real/ideal modeling and the integrative principles of Hegelian sublation/synthesis. Beginning in the 1990s, theorists began considering the role of language in this problem through what would be termed "discursive materialism."[4] Integrating principles of historical materialism with broader analyses of ideological reproduction, a new form of "cultural Marxism" would emerge to address ways that the perceived "internal" spaces of consciousness are organized by "external" factors like language and authority. Around this time, Gilles Deleuze and Félix Guattari described a "new materialism" driven by a self-aware consciousness.[5] Bruno Latour noted that such self-awareness was driven by intention and agency, even as Jacques Lacan would chart the limits of introspection.[6] More radically, the "speculative realism" of Quentin Meillassoux would question the entire premise of "correlational" models of "thinking" and "being"—proposing that the two can be seen independently.[7] And more recently, Alan Badiou and Slavoj Žižek, among others, have argued that a revision of Marx's "dialectical materialism" might be the best way forward, even as others have argued for "materialism without materialism."[8]

Notably, in recent years many discussions about materialism have resurrected an old term from economics: *neoliberalism*. Initially coined in the 1960s by "Chicago School" pro-business moderates such as Friedrich von Hayek, the term later acquired negative connotations as it became synonymous with a more radically expansive agenda—driven by the doctrine that market exchange represents an ethic in itself, suitable as a guide for all human endeavors. In his book, *A Brief History of Neoliberalism*, David Harvey described this doctrine as "a theory of political economic practices that proposes that human wellbeing can best be advanced by liberating individual entrepreneurial freedoms and skills within an institutional framework characterized by strong private property rights, free market, and free trade. The role of the state is to create and preserve an institutional framework appropriate to such practices."[9] Harvey and others have been quick to point out the dubious logic of a doctrine premised on uniform definitions of "human wellbeing," equal abilities of individuals to compete, and the immanent transparency of state actions. Hence, neoliberalism is now commonly used by progressives as an all-purpose referent for capitalistic excesses.[10] Admittedly, this sounds a little bit vague—and initial uses of the concept in the early 2000s did indeed lack specificity, especially when they boiled down to convenient pro-neoliberal (right) versus anti-neoliberal (left) opposition.

The origins of classical liberalism and their evolution into neoliberalism during the 1960s were discussed earlier in this book. Part of what differentiates the current moment is the transition of the global economy from industrial to financial capitalism.[11] In this new arena, financial instruments have taken the place of material goods as money itself becomes the prime object of exchange. But this "monetizing" function of neoliberalism is hardly an abstraction. The worldwide recession of the early 2000s may have resulted from massive trading miscalculations on the part of major banks, but huge numbers of those investments were tied to sub-prime mortgage instruments that put millions of people out of their homes—and would later leave them without jobs as well. As everyone knows, little punitive action was taken against the bankers—as the 99 percent found itself faced with increasingly precarious employment and an ever-shrinking social safety net. Corporations grew bigger and more complex through mergers, global partnerships, and outsourcing—as jobs became increasingly temporary, contingent, intermittent, or otherwise transformed into what is euphemistically termed "casual" labor. For many American workers, such amenities as retirement benefits, paid sick leave, childcare, and vacations have become little more than nostalgic memories of a past era. And largely kept from public view are the manufacturing jobs once located in the United States, now held by workers in poor countries that often lack the protection of labor laws.

The new neoliberal American marriage of democracy and capitalism is pushed ever onward through the evolution of new communication technologies. Sitting alone at their keyboards, Americans increasingly define themselves through their online profiles, browsing preferences, and consumer habits—even as this data is collected, analyzed, and sold. Government snooping may get most of the headlines, but the bigger story lies in the way new circuits of subjectivity now exist to reify identity within the logic of consumption. It's no secret that voting increasingly is seen as simply another consumer choice, as most people feel their ballots have no effect. In a culture of political amnesia and instant gratification, clicking away on the Amazon website has become the dominant way that American citizens express their opinions. Meanwhile, moral relativism abounds—for better or for worse. Adherence toward social conventions is softening, as progressive attitudes toward race and gender are softening in a post-identity moment. Yet at the same time, concerns about a loss of values—so often attributed solely to conservatives—may indeed have some merit. Recent studies have shown that the average American young adult has difficulty identifying a significant "ethical" issue, and that many say that morality is simply a matter of "personal choice" akin to buying a song on iTunes. "I don't really deal with right and wrong," one teenager replied to a researcher. "It's up to the individual. Who am I to say?" [12] While this may be interpreted as a refreshing "tolerance" of diverse values, such attitudes are worrisome nevertheless in a nation in which prejudice continues to fester and the gap between wealth and poverty continues to widen.

Citizenship, Inc.

Long ago Marx coined the term "commodification" to describe the sleight of hand through which noneconomic items and ideas get transformed into saleable goods. Initially Marx was thinking about human labor, but he quickly adopted his notion of commodification to human consciousness itself. Marx talked about the way capital alienated individuals from their work products, from each other, and indeed from their own subjectivity—as the marketplace treated individuals as objects of exchange rather than people. Most presciently, Marx described the psychic manipulation through which individuals come to blame themselves for their failures. After all, the American dream tells us citizens that this is a land of boundless opportunity, where all are "free" to achieve their highest aspirations. It couldn't be the system itself that is making people work harder and harder for less and less. There must be something wrong with each and every person. The radical reversal proposed by Marx was for people to see themselves collectively: not alone, but sharing common difficulties and achievements. It was a vision of sociality rather than individualism—and for that reason was rabidly opposed by corporate America throughout the 20th century. Global antagonism and the Cold War arms race may have been the public face of this confrontation, but the real site of struggle was over the nature of human subjectivity itself.

For obvious reasons, commodification is especially potent in the United States, given American culture's romantic beliefs in individual autonomy and "freedom." Considerable debate surrounds the question of whether the Internet does anything to change the conversation—echoing long-standing worries that novel communication technologies open new doors for duping an unsuspecting public. Keep in mind that a major theme of 20th-century Marxism focused on the role of new communications media, especially as those industries were consolidating in the hands of huge corporations. As previously discussed in this book, opinion continues to divide over views of the human subject and the tricky question of self-consciousness. To put the matter simply, in popular discourse it is often difficult to convince people that they may not be aware of why they want what they want—whether their desires originate in unexamined impulses or in a catchy advertising pitch.

In recent years, much has been made of the 2010 "Citizens United" ruling of the U.S. Supreme Court, which conferred on corporations the same rights as individual citizens in making political campaign contributions. As it turns out, the principle of "corporate personhood" has a 200-year history in American law. In the early 1800s the Supreme Court ruled in favor of Dartmouth College when the state of New Hampshire attempted to interfere with its operations—on the grounds that Dartmouth's "corporate" rights were equivalent to "individual" property rights. In the 1920s Congress passed the first version of the "Code of Laws of the United States" (U.S.C.), listing 51 items of legislation that apply to the entire nation. From that point forward, the U.S.C. has held that the term "person" includes "corporations, companies, associations, firms, partnerships, societies, and joint stock companies, as well as individuals."[13]

Aside from historical precedents or legal correctness, the Citizens United matter has significantly altered both the financing and transparency of American politics. More than money alone, this has worried those now trying to reverse the ruling. Keep in mind that prior campaign funding laws both *limited* and *identified* contributions in an effort to level the economic playing field, especially in terms of outside advocacy groups like Citizens United. The court decision enabled both *electoral influence* and the *obfuscation of financing*. As such, Citizens United evoked the ire of many as one of the most brazen incursions of "private" power into the most sacred "public" space of democracy: the free election. It bears reiterating here that this new arrangement makes perfect sense within the logic of neoliberalism—defined as a *rational* restoration of private interests necessary to contain the excesses of the liberal state. Here as elsewhere, views of capitalism as a "natural" system of individualized values are pitted against the "artificial" constraints of collective regulatory processes or Keynesian macroeconomics.

If only things were that simple. As the Citizens United case makes clear, perhaps the biggest problem with neoliberalism lies in the obscurity of the concept itself. Even as academics increasingly adopt the term "neoliberal" as a way of describing the blurred boundaries between public and private, most American citizens see only the tired choice of "liberal" or "conservative" in their political decisions and in matters that affect their daily lives. Few people recognize that such distinctions have largely lost their meaning in an age in which the marketplace and the state have become so deeply intertwined. Most importantly, the false two-party dichotomy offered to the American electorate simultaneously excludes other options and extinguishes citizen agency in the face of what is seen as a closed system.

Given these limited political choices, many people may feel the effects of neoliberalism, but don't know what it is. In academic circles the new neoliberalism has prompted a resurgent interest in the writings of Michel Foucault, who relentlessly analyzed the ways that seemingly invisible forces work on individuals and societies. Drawing on history, philosophy, and psychoanalysis, Foucault's concepts of "governmentality" mapped a theory of the political mind that went beyond the materialist leanings of his predecessors and the linguistic preoccupations of his contemporaries.[14] Unsatisfied with the neat dogma of Marxist objectification, Foucault argued that disciplines of power went deeper and emerged earlier in human subjectivity and history itself.

Anxiety was a necessary element of neoliberal governmentality, according to Foucault—especially manifest in worries about loss of "freedom." Foucault was among the first to elaborate on the merger of government and business functions. After all, what could be more central in modern subjectivity than the roles of citizen and consumer? Foucault zeroed in on the ways that worry, fear, normativity, and health concerns motivated people. But perhaps most importantly, he pointed to the role of technology in the process—not in the sense of "new technology" alone, but instead in the way that technology had assumed an organizing function throughout human history. Like any good poststructuralist, Foucault refrained from placing a positive or negative value on technology per se. But he did note the ongoing lure of technology as a synonym for progress. So powerful is this lure, Foucault said, that technological thinking comes to inhere in human consciousness. Often without realizing it, people internalize systems of thinking that place limits on what they think and who they imagine themselves to be. Foucault termed these "technologies of the self." And as a consequence of this, many people also come to see external "technologies of power" as somehow natural and ever present. Trickier still, parts of these technological operations work outside conscious awareness—in the background workings of desire and yearning, for example.

Such contradictions abound in a citizen's experience of neoliberal governmentality. When freedom hinges on submission to power, how is resistance even conceivable? Foucault frustrated this conundrum even further in noting that many of people's attitudes toward power are formulated a priori (before conscious thought). In other words, one never can step outside of technologies of power (or technologies of the self). This led to the assertions by Jürgen Habermas that Foucault had become lost in linguistic theory—and had cast aside the potentials of modernist rationality.[15] In many ways this debate restaged long-standing philosophical disputes dating back to Plato over the accessibility or inaccessibility of reality to the human mind. The new twist to the discussion added in the late 20th century was that the entire argument was itself a product of Western thinking. Keep in mind that the Foucault/Habermas debate had its own historical specificity, emerging in what one might call the "early" postmodern days of the 1980s and early 1990s. At the time, postmodernism was offering important insights about the nature of representation, media, and politics, as the powerful hold of governmentality had yet to be fully recognized.

Things are very different today as the "invisible" effects of neoliberalism are now especially palpable in the unhappiness of so many people—caught, as they are, between conflicting beliefs in the potential of individual ambition tempered by worries that loss lurks around every corner. Is it any wonder that the population is now even divided on whether governmentality is their friend or enemy? Then add other factors. When Foucault wrote about technologies of power he had no idea that such a thing as the Internet would both connect and isolate citizens on such a massive scale. This is problematic enough in its own right. But what if the thing one calls the "self" is displaced or obscured from view? Overwhelmingly, contemporary culture is predicated on consumption, ownership, and possession of one form or another—so much so that the human subject becomes lost in a field of objects. When the celebrated American individual is reduced to a set of purchasing decisions, how much agency and "citizenship" remains?

The Politics of Culture

Postmodernism is often characterized as a critique of "modern" orthodoxies, a rejection of inherited traditions and aesthetics in favor of an unbounded relativism. Of course this working definition assumes that rules and tradition can be named and refuted in the first place. One can generalize about fatiguing Western epistemology as a kind of backdrop for broader crises of meaning and faith. But is it even possible to grasp the matter so easily? As Fredric Jameson cogently asked in the early 1980s, "What if the 'idea' of progress was not an idea at all, but rather the symptom of something else?" Writing in his essay "Progress versus Utopia: Can We Imagine the Future?" Jameson put his finger on the matter of a "political unconscious," which by itself laid bare the premises of a "reason" to which anyone might have access.[16] Jameson said that the best one can do is to find traces of this unconsciousness in narratives, practices, and institutions. Literature, popular media, and artworks are some of the places to locate these traces. Jameson would characterize postmodernist ideologies as a symptom of late capitalist "modes of experience" (i.e., neoliberalism). Today these lines of thinking are resurfacing in a profusion of new theory responding to neoliberalism by underscoring the dialectical character of late capitalism—as simultaneously virtual and real. While online shopping may further abstract the idea of money, the bill always falls due at some point. And although movies may be registers of a political unconsciousness, someone has to pay for them to be made or watched.

Much of this thinking can be construed in terms of "culture," broadly defined as shared patterns of belief, communication, and behavior—often manifest in artifacts and discourses. Marx's dialectical materialism said that mystification was built into capitalist culture from the beginning, although it would take Antonio Gramsci to explain more fully how culture plays into the market scheme. Gramsci took a constructionist view of ideology, asserting the "learned" quality of social power dynamics. As he put it, "Every relationship of hegemony is necessarily an educational relationship."[17] In this Gramsci was not simply talking about formal education. He was referring to the more subtle processes through which people are socialized to recognize and validate authority, especially state power. These processes infuse all sites of the social apparatus: the workplace, the church, the theater, as well as the school. In the 1960s Louis Althusser described capitalism as a sophisticated system that operated not by coercion, but by seductively "calling out" to people with promises of a better life. While Althusser saw such "interpellation" as an almost irresistible force, later theorists gave human subjects a bit more credit. All of this has led to a more complicated view of commodification—operating variously for different people and shifting in the way it works across space and time.

Such "negative" cultural critiques certainly made a lot of sense on one level—focusing as they did on the way human desire gets linked to money, achievement, and systems that promise upward mobility. In the 1970s Hans Magnus Enzenberger refined Marx's theories of mystification further in saying that the culture of capitalism didn't exactly deceive the masses into "false" desires (for products or services). Instead it found ways of satisfying "real" desires (for such values as happiness or security) via substitution. For example, Coca-Cola ads don't so much convey the flavor of the drink, as they show groups of people having fun. Leftist scholars today speak often of this operation of culture in socializing citizens into roles of subservience—their desires for political engagement or personal fulfillment transformed into consumer choices. "Public pedagogy" is the term used by the educational theorist Henry A. Giroux to describe this new terrain.[18] Giroux writes that neoliberalism "construes profit making as the essence of democracy, consuming as the only operable form of citizenship, and upholds the irrational belief that the market can not only solve all problems but serve as a model for structuring all social relations. It is steeped in the language of self-help, individual responsibility and is purposely blind to inequalities in power, wealth and income and how they bear down on the fate of individuals and groups."[19]

A more "positive" view of culture flourished for a time during the 1980s and 1990s—partially in response to the perceived pessimism of Marxist critique. Upstart groups of scholars in the 1980s began to celebrate the "creative" potentials of consuming—attributing to individuals the ability to resist or collaborate with commodification.[20] Proponents of what was termed the "cultural studies" movement argued that intellectuals had ignored the empowering potentials implicit in entertainment, and even in consuming. By viewing ordinary people as "cultural dopes," Marxist scholars had inadvertently reinforced the very social hierarchies they claimed to be contesting. Originating from studies of working-class youth in Great Britain, cultural studies soon became an academic fad in the U.S., asserting that serious study was merited in examining the mundane activities that actually fill most people's days. My book *Cultural Pedagogy* was one of many works in this genre.[21] Like others, I noted that TV, games, and shopping consumed 80 percent of most people's leisure time.[22] Rather than "bad" habits or a waste of time, might it be possible that these activities could affirm subjective agency—even in the face of a manipulative system?

Unifying these negative and positive views of culture was the figure of desire—the force that seems to bring together subjects and objects of want. Consciously or unconsciously, everyone *desires* something—and most people feel unsatisfied much of the time. Plato was among the first to speak about the mutability of desire, urging the suspension or postponement of human appetites in the interest of ideal virtues. Hegel later would describe desire as a primary relationship between self and other—saying that the human subject identifies the external other via its dissimilarity to the "self" or its possession of some unfamiliar attribute. To Hegel the human "ego" tries to fix this by copying, merging, or battling over the difference. In this sense, dictionary definitions of desire as a "want or wish for (something)" are not far off the mark.[23] Hegel pointed out the importance of examining desires, whatever forms they take. But this is a tricky process since so many desires lurk beneath the radar of conscious thought. Hegel proposed a kind of thought-experiment in which people could step out of themselves and look back on their thinking in a critical way. Calling this "self-consciousness," Hegel argued that such analysis of the desiring self/other dialectic was part of what kept humanity moving forward toward an ultimate freedom.

All of this has a bearing on the blurred state of virtual living. If desire lies behind both negative and positive functions of self/other relationships, how does one form an effective opposition to a force as ubiquitous as global capitalism? Is it possible to resist the exploitation of desires that are so deeply embedded that one may not recognize them? The answer is yes and no. Across a wide range of theoretical fields, cultural scholars and activists have worked to dismantle notions of inside and outside. Jacques Rancière was one of many criticizing absolutist models that framed ideology as either reproduction or resistance. Looking to aesthetic and affective processes, for example, Rancière described a push-and-pull process of commodification, as it sometimes wins and other times loses its grip over people.[24]

Recently, the philosopher Bernard Stiegler has written about the ways this machine operates in relation to consumer desires and the voracious demand for quick profits in some quarters. On the one hand, Stiegler sees the relentless forces of capitalist ownership and production churning out a seemingly endless array of goods—driven, to put it bluntly, by insatiable greed. In supply-and-demand terms this production is met by the hunger of consumers, driven by libidinous desires for objects of possession. As noted earlier, this process is relatively transparent when one thinks of the way advertising works to substitute products like telephone rate plans, for example, for more deeply held things people want like "Friends and Family."

"The *American way of life* invented the figure of the consumer whose libido is systematically put to work on the problem of excess production," Stiegler states.[25] Unfortunately there is a problem with this relationship, inasmuch as libidinous consumer drives are but momentarily satisfied by purchases. This leads to the kind of short-term thinking seen in so much marketing and buying behavior: the constant array of "new and improved" commodities, version upgrades, as well as the supply of ever more specific products derived from market segmentation. These quickening cycles generate bursts of profit for individual companies, as similar cycling occurs in the computerized investment arenas of stocks, derivatives, and credit swaps.

All of this takes place within a finite set of limits, as Pareto pointed out so long ago.[26] Even in the abstract worlds of financialized capital, constraints on monetary supplies hold economics in place. Add to this the finitudes of natural resources and the constraints of environmental concern. These limits auger against exclusive forms of short-term thinking—because an actual end point always lurks in the background. Seen in such a systemic analysis, capitalism becomes a kind of pharmakon—which partly explains why people on differing sides of the political aisle see it so differently. The tricky question put forward by Stiegler and others is how to get people to see capitalism as the integrated system it is—neither a blessing nor a curse, but instead a dynamic system for accommodating society's underlying material and psychic economies.

All of this has led to a certain amount of hand-wringing among academics about how to be an activist in contemporary culture. With the economic demise of the publishing industry, it is nearly impossible for writers or scholars to make a living without some kind of appointment at a college or university. While some get by driving cabs and waiting on tables, most of today's most well-known thinkers find themselves in the double-blind of writing from within the enclave of higher education. This can create problems as academics come to depend on the approval of their peers in order to keep their jobs or advance in the system. What counts as "new knowledge" in a rarefied academic discipline may look like gibberish to people living in the "real" world, just as "best sellers" often fail to address serious matters with depth or sophistication.

Such inside/outside debates are especially pronounced in the art world. It should go without saying that the idea of art as ideology and social critique is as old as history itself—either in a direct sense or in the way art presents symbolic values. Images often have depicted power relations among people, whether one is discussing idealized representations of the body, scenes of battle and conquest, or depictions of pastoral estates owned by the gentry. And this isn't counting religious iconography cherished by so many. Plato and Socrates spoke often about the political uses of art in instilling citizenship, even sanctioning censorship to help buttress state authority. Tensions between wealth and poverty would inform centuries of political artworks. Richard Wagner's 1848 essay "Art and Revolution" romanticized philosophical disputes in ancient Greece as a metaphor for class uprisings in Europe at the time—ideas that proved influential in the Russian Revolution six decades later. Anti-capitalist avant-garde movements of the 20th century include Dadaism, surrealism, situationism, and lettrism, among others. And of course art was deployed in the interest of state propaganda throughout the world. Indeed, it is commonly known that the U.S. government promoted American abstract expressionism around the world during the Cold War era as evidence of the nation's values of freedom and individual expression—conveniently downplaying the socialist leanings of many of the artists themselves.

Aesthetic Contradictions

Psychologists have long recognized the value of symbolic representation in working though questions or problems. Works of art or music often allow the expression of thoughts that are otherwise hard to articulate. In the 1950s the anthropologist Gregory Bateson proposed a way of addressing the conundrum of holding competing values in one's mind. One way is to name the paradox for what it is. Gregory Bateson used the term "double bind" in the 1950s to describe the dilemma of thinking through mutual contradictions.[27] Bateson was concerned with the ways that double binds often paralyze people in the proverbial "no-win" situation. Capitalism creates a particular kind of double bind, as a system that constrains as it liberates. Obviously all of this can get confusing. At the store you can choose cash or credit, but you still end up paying one way or another. This kind of contradiction replicates itself everywhere. Bateson proposed a particular way of getting around the problem: the imaginary space of play.[28] Beginning with observations of children and primates, Bateson saw play as a meta-environment in which oppositions can be played out hypothetically or alternatively. Roles can be invented and reinvented. Games can have rational or irrational rules. Bateson even went as far as to assert that the imaginary "worlding" of play modeled the psychic space of communication itself. As might be expected, Bateson's work on play became fertile ground for educational theorists, especially those studying the question of why grown-ups abandon play in their transition to normative adulthood. The mentally ill seem to play in certain delusional states, Bateson observed. But for the most part such impulses are repressed in the interest of adult reason, or in many cases, religious faith.

By some definitions, aesthetics can be a form of play—a gateway out of the double bind. Admittedly aesthetics is yet another vague term, subject to exactly the sort of "individual" interpretation exploited by neoliberalism. But one can also think about aesthetics as an open terrain in which the pressures of ideology can be accepted, opposed, or at least negotiated—especially when considering aesthetics in terms of adult play. This might seem a romantic idea in the current era, especially in this chapter's sober discussion of neoliberalism. What role do aesthetics or play have in matters of economics, consumer culture, and creeping authoritarianism? The answer is that these two realms of experience—aesthetics and play—have become so ubiquitous in contemporary culture that they become invisible in most people's conscious awareness. People live their daily lives immersed in media images, as communications scholar George Gerbner once put it, "like fish in water."[29] Advertisements surround everyone on the streets, screens, and what people hear and read, as movies, television, YouTube videos, Twitter, Vine, Facebook, and Instagram create a "transmedia" envelope of constant media stimuli—all of it operating through a language of aesthetics. As for play and games, not only do sports provide templates for many children to learn about the world of social interaction, but they also comprise a gigantic (and critically underexamined) realm of entertainment. And then there is the phenomenon of computer games. According to the most current statistics, two out of every three American households have a cache of electronic games, with one in three people playing games on their cell phones.[30] Globally, people now spend twice as much on games as they do on movies.

Aesthetics and play are never innocent categories. While one can talk about images, art, or games as abstract categories or items that produce pleasure, aesthetics and play nearly always carry the baggage of preexisting meaning and contextual significance. Decades ago, the field of art history moved from the premise of "appreciating" artworks to the more critical task of figuring out why certain objects held significance in their times. Gayatri Spivak describes her recent book *An Aesthetic Education* as an effort toward "productively undoing another legacy of the European Enlightenment—the aesthetic. Productive undoing is a difficult task. It must look carefully at the fault lines of the doing, without accusation, without excuse, with a view to use."[31] Spivak notes that the concept of "aesthetic play" originated in the work of 18th-century German poet and philosopher Johann Christoph Friedrich von Schiller, who sought to reconcile then-emerging principles of reason with those of emotionality. In an updating of Kant's equation of "beauty" with "the good," Schiller wrote that beauty was not merely an aesthetic ideal, but also an aspect of morality. While Schiller contrasted the pleasure of aesthetic play to the toil of physical work, he insisted that both were driven by an overarching set of "laws." In Schiller's thinking, these laws were not so much constraints as they were the very source of human "freedom." Such was the solipsism of the Western Enlightenment in constructing a world according to its own terms.

Western aesthetics later would be linked to class privilege and power, notably in works like Terry Eagleton's *The Ideology of the Aesthetic* and Pierre Bourdieu's *Distinction: A Social Critique of the Judgement of Taste.*[32] While these works pointed to the aesthetic as a tool of bourgeois capitalism, both Nazi Germany and the Soviet Union showed how cultural propaganda could be deployed by the state in the interests of fascism and communism, respectively. All of this made clear the workings of aesthetics of on public consciousness—a process initially conceived to operate in uniform terms. Twentieth-century "Frankfurt School" cultural theorists railed against the operations of a "consciousness industry" that duped people into lives of mindless consumerism. More nuanced understandings of media reception followed in the latter half of the 20th century, informed by linguistic theory and empirical studies of audiences—both of which revealed a certain messiness in mass communications. Generalized sales pitches could reach people, but they often did so incompletely or with unanticipated effects. By the late 1900s interdisciplinary movements in media and cultural studies began looking at these variances with growing interest, noting diverse forms of aesthetic reception in specific demographic cohorts, notably among the young. In some instances, distinctions between "high" and "low" culture were pondered and debated—usually by intellectuals and artists threatened in this changing landscape. Much of this was rendered irrelevant with the rise of the Internet in the 1990s, as relationships between makers and consumers began to blur. Media empires collapsed and symphonies lost their audiences, as individuals began posting home-made images, music, and movies online—and new microeconomies emerged around these emerging cultural forms.

Today aesthetics stands alongside concepts like democracy and faith—as an idea that is widely supported but rarely defined. There are dozens of theories about how aesthetics do their job—as messages are encoded by their makers, decoded by recipients, and organized through media forms, institutions, markets, and the subjectivities of everyone along the way. Academic disciplines have linked "art" to almost every debate about race, class, gender, faith, fantasy, hope, fear, money, politics, science, history, and of course utopia. Groups have waged tribal wars over the disciplinary integrity of aesthetics versus their "relational" contingency to other aspects of life. Scholars have debated the phenomenon of "art worlds" as meta-structures attempting to segregate or legitimize selected definitions of culture over others. All of this is symptomatic of a growing confusion about what "art" is in an age when everyone can become a creative producer.

As recently as a decade ago, less than 5 percent of respondents to national surveys said that they did anything "artistic" or "creative" in their daily lives.[33] Few visited art museums or went to concerts, with younger people showing the least interest. Some analysts attribute this to the growing influence of mass culture as an autonomous force. Others examining consumer culture have blamed art institutions for not meeting audience demand. Data collected by the National Endowment for the Arts (NEA) between 1982 and 2002 revealed overall declines in attendance for classical music (−12 percent), musical theater (−10 percent), ballet (−7 percent), art fairs (−22 percent), and historical sites (−26 percent)—although museum attendance remained relatively constant.[34] These patterns would continue in the following decade, as documented in NEA studies released in 2013.[35]

Outside the museum, the concept of "creativity" moved from margin to mainstream. Once a term associated with artists or hobbyists, creativity has acquired a special value in the new millennium, owing to its associations with inventiveness, novelty, and flexibility. Richard Florida's 2002 book *The Rise of the Creative Class* broadened the definition of "creative professional" to include scientists and engineers, university professors, poets and novelists, artists, entertainers, actors, designers, and architects. To Florida, such people comprised "a fast-growing, highly educated, and well-paid segment of the workforce on whose efforts corporate profits and economic growth increasingly depend."[36] Before long the term creativity began popping up everywhere, as the creative class became associated with "creative industries," "creative entrepreneurship," "creative zones" in cities, and such aphorisms as "creative problem solving" and "creative management."

Before long social theorists began to note how neatly creativity mapped onto the logic of neoliberalism. Creativity workers tended to be self-employed, transient, adaptable, and otherwise perfectly suited to the needs of the modern corporation. At the same time, companies throughout America began promoting creativity as an antidote for everything from stalled careers and troubled relationships to boredom and depression. A 2015 *New York Times* article entitled "We're All Artists Now" spoke of the new face of creativity "as a model of self-fulfillment and a way to get ahead," asserting, that "the possibility for creative self-expression is everywhere."[37] Not everyone has been thrilled by this apparent cooptation of artistic sensibilities. Does the widespread embrace (and commodification) of creativity rob it of any subversive potential? Writing in *October* magazine, Isabelle Graw noted parallels between the growth of creativity as a cultural value and the astronomical rise of art auction prices driven by America's wealthy. "If I declare something to be 'art,' I have already passed a value judgment," Graw observed, noting the extraordinary intersection of aesthetic and economic meaning in the present moment.[38] This raises the question of where artistic impulses of social critique will next emerge.

Virtual Rebels

Then there is the blurring inherent in digital culture and networked society. Considering these aspects of "virtual" subjectivity, psychologist Sherry Turkle has described the double bind that technology creates in neoliberal culture. As Turkle wrote, "Technology is seductive when what it offers meets our human vulnerabilities.[39] Unlike many writing of the Internet age as either an era of utopian connection or radical alienation, Turkle delved into the paradoxical tensions between individual and community. "We are lonely but fearful of intimacy," she wrote, adding that, "networked life allows us to hide from each other, even as we are tethered to each other."[40] Without a doubt, these are confusing times. As discussed above, once familiar lines continue to blur between public and private, truth and deception, free will and determinism.

Aesthetics can be both value laden and malleable, and culture both confining and emancipating. Amid a sea of forces that seem so large, it sometimes appears that one has little choice but to capitulate. Yet as strange as this might sound, it doesn't seem as if apathy has consumed public consciousness completely. Even as public confidence in government, business, and religious institutions has decreased in recent decades, the modest majority of Americans believe that income disparities will lessen (58 percent) and that health care will improve (51 percent). At the same time, majorities have become accustomed to accepting the inevitability of war and environmental catastrophe.[41] In overall terms, Pew Research reports that 56 percent say that in coming decades the U.S. economy will be stronger than it is today, although many worry about the prospects far future generations.[42]

Of course aggregate statistics say little about demographic variance in polling. And the contradictions and weak preferences on the above issues paint a picture of an uncertain public. Earlier in this book, I reviewed debates over the much-lamented notion of a "divided America," pointing out the ontologies of opposition and division dating to well before the nation's founding. Simply put, division can be a curse, a blessing—or both, or neither. Opportunities to effect change exist regardless of political orientation or agenda. The issue is one of acting. To Elizabeth A. Povinelli, spaces of resistance may be possible, but they are often difficult to see in such a blurred atmosphere. This doesn't mean that they won't emerge. As Povinelli puts this in relationship to neoliberalism, "potentiality and its perpetual variations never occur in a general way, but always … in specific *agacements*—arrangements of connecting concepts, material, and forces that make a common compositional unity."[43]

In other words, possibilities are out there if one seeks them out. The seemingly endless openness of networked society has sparked the utopian imagination in many quarters. My book *Worlding* was among many works in the early 2000s to speak about the new territories being staked out in social networking communities and the virtual spaces of game worlds. For better or for worse, the Internet has made it possible as perhaps never before for like-minded people to find each other—whether this is manifest in online dating or political organizing. Occupy Wall Street was able to stage actions based on its ability to instantly mobilize demonstrations. Some credit Twitter and Facebook for much of the activism surrounding the "Arab Spring." While the Internet revolution has increased the clatter of voices competing for attention, it has also allowed people to find common purpose—often in unlikely places. And just as those looking for hate or porn now have an easier time, so do people looking for soufflé recipes or pictures of puppies.

More to the point, what one might call the "author-function" has changed dramatically in an era in which relationships between writers and readers, producers and audiences, have been permanently altered. Debates over whether "texts" supersede "authorial" intent seem to be fading from view at a time when online postings have the substance of a wisp of smoke. Text-author-reader divides are but another set of lines that are now blurring. New kinds of writing and reading are constantly being invented and reinvented by people with little concern for such categories—even as they (admittedly) are still confined by the cultural constraints of language. But such matters increasingly have become contingent on time and location as much as anything one can name.

I was drawn to Alyssa Quart's book *Republic of Outsiders: The Power of Amateurs, Dreamers, and Rebels* because it promised to "rethink what it means to think differently."[44] And with chapters like "Beyond Hollywood," "Beyond Sanity," and "Beyond Normal," the book offered a wealth of first-person reporting on various groups and individuals often ignored or passed over by publications like the *New York Times* (which, ironically, gave the book a glowing review). As it turns out, a small cottage industry of these "outsider" books has been cropping up in recent years, perhaps due in part to the popularity of Malcolm Gladwell's best-selling *Outliers*. While Gladwell's book revealed the success "secrets" of idiosyncratic billionaires and star athletes, Quart's project focuses directly on "indie" culture—profiling groups ranging from upstart bloggers and shoe-string film producers to "Mad Pride" groups and transgender activists.[45] Indeed, *Outliers* and *Republic of Outsiders* offer radically different attitudes toward the notion of the "outside" itself. Gladwell's premise is all about the unique markings of high-achieving people, who by virtue of exceptional talents, obsessions, or life experiences are both cursed and blessed by their outlier personalities. Gladwell's premise is that what might look like misfortune can be the engine of success, especially if it is matched with hard work. *Outliers* also joins the chorus of voices celebrating "difference" as a marker of individuality.

In contrast, Quart's book argues that individualism is becoming a fuzzy concept—as consumers collaborate with makers of goods, personal and group identities merge, and audiences sometimes swap roles with producers of media. In one example, Quart reviews the enormous success of the online Etsy marketplace for people producing clothing and crafts. With a motto of "Buy, Sell, and Live

Handmade," Etsy's founders assert that "the connection between producer and consumer has been lost. We created Etsy to help them reconnect." And reconnect they have, with over seven million items sold each month.[46] In another compelling story, *Republic of Outsiders* discusses musician Amanda Palmer's collaborations with audience members who both perform with her and jointly fund concerts. Palmer sees this as a reversal of maker/audience roles, inasmuch as all parties collaborate in making the events occur. *Republic of Outsiders* also addresses the contradictions of outsider media producers who compete with large corporations so successfully that they become hybrid outsider/insiders. Quart argues that as renegades look for cultural spaces that the mainstream has neglected or underserved, they may sell out, going too far in their acceptance of certain aspects of the reigning modus operandi in order to get power and visibility. "When we rebel and resist, we must always remain mindful about the risks of co-optation—which today sometimes seems like an arcane preoccupation—while also valuing the new levels of access to the mainstream we now possess," Quart observes.[47]

As an ensemble, *Republic of Outsiders, Outliers*, and other new "outsider" books show just how far societal attitudes toward difference have matured. Five decades ago, Howard Becker's landmark *Outsiders* was defensive in its arguments about the social construction of bias and prejudice for those falling outside the parameters of "normalcy."[48] In the 1960s arguments for civil rights were just beginning to coalesce and the grip of the so-called consciousness industry over American culture had yet to be broadly acknowledged. Struggles over rights would follow, which would slowly improve conditions for women and minorities in the United States—although each advance would be met by opposition. History rarely travels in straight lines.

But if the new outsider books tell us something about the new "diversity as individualism," they also reveal how mired America still seems to be in the related values that neoliberalism seems to promote. The expansive licensing of free enterprise as a driving principle for nearly every social issue has been especially visible in the cultural realm—as media and communications have come to define the nation's economy at home and around the globe. America's obsessive fetishization and uncritical embrace of "freedom" is deeply tied to questions of speech and the press—so much so that many seemingly unrelated legal decisions have been decided on "speech" premises. The Citizens United case campaign over spending finance and the 2014 Hobby Lobby decision on contraceptive care are but two recent examples.[49]

In today's ongoing frenzy over expressive "freedom," little effective policy has emerged to address corporate growth and mergers in the communications sector—despite warnings dating back to the 1980s over a growing "media monopoly." Once a group of 50 powerful individuals and corporations, the media monopoly has tightened in the 2000s to a handful of companies controlling over 80 percent of broadcast media, publishing, movie production, and Internet services in the United States.[50] In many people's minds, the ubiquitous presence of corporations like AT&T, Comcast, Viacom, Time Warner, and Disney has become an accepted part of daily life.

The common mythology is that none of this really matters in the Internet age. Why should anyone worry about Hollywood when every 12-year-old can market homemade T-shirts or become a YouTube producer? The evidence of this "do-it-yourself" (DIY) spirit seems to be all around. Online merchandise forums like Etsy and eBay now compete with Amazon and Walmart. As movie theaters and broadcast TV continue to lose audiences, more and more people are watching what used to be called "alternative" media. It's important to remember that none of this is especially new. Economic downturns have always sparked such impulses. In historical terms, recycling and the production of homemade goods can be dated back to the Depression of the 1930s and later wartime eras.

Amateur photography is a perfect historical example of DIY culture. From the earliest days of George Eastman's first Kodak camera in the 1880s, people have taken image making into their own hands. Snapshot photography allowed people to avoid commercial portrait studios, while also reclaiming authorship of their personal likenesses. The ubiquity of snapshot cameras, and later of home movie equipment, allowed the general public access to the symbolic creativity of visual image making. But it also opened up all sorts of possibilities for artists, activists, and business as well. The key point is that a huge "space" has always existed between individuals and mega-producers. Not only did amateur media generate its own very large industries of equipment makers and magazines, but it also fostered camera clubs, film societies, and substantial aesthetic genres inside and outside the art world. While it is tempting to romanticize the Holy Grail of iPhone technology in changing people's lives and altering contemporary subjectivity, these relatively recent phenomena need to be seen as continuations of ongoing impulses for expression.

This is not to suggest that Hollywood has not played an enormous role in public aesthetics, nor to imply that corporate media is fading away. But even if one brackets the role of amateur "making" as a separate matter, there is an equally nuanced set of issues on the reception side of media. All storytelling involves the entry of a listener, reader, or viewer into the "virtual" world of the narrative. After all, language itself (including photographic representation) is little more than a system of symbolic signs and meanings. While it is commonplace to assume that readers take stories at face value, everyday interpretations of any narrative vary wildly according to who is reading, how they are reading, in what context, etc. Fan culture is one manifestation of the ways audiences appreciate and "play" with mass produced iconography.

What if someone turned a quintessential tale of neoliberalism back on itself? How about reversing the "corporations are people" concept on its own terms? Further delving into the history of incorporation shows that "people are corporations" is an equally valid proposition, but not commonly understood in such terms. Much as Dartmouth College was allowed to act as a "person" in protecting its property rights, incorporation was established to help individuals do likewise in business—allowing entrepreneurs, doctors, and other professionals to incorporate themselves as sole proprietors or in groups, thereby gaining certain benefits and protections. The same rights of "privacy" and property ownership were afforded to individuals and corporations alike.

But as artist Jennifer Morone notes, this apparent equity started to get out of balance in the information age, as the new commodity of "data" unexpectedly became a reality. Corporations began to collect consumer data and then sell it as their own property—as massive enterprises like Google, Amazon, and Facebook started to track, aggregate, and share information about people's search habits, consumer purchases, and online social behavior. These corporations were not simply invading people's privacy. In many instances companies began profiting from the sale of this information. Under current law, such exchanges of information are tolerated and even encouraged—as consumers/users and their behavior are quite literally treated as commodities.

The situation is quite different for corporations. All manner of intellectual property, trademark, and copyright laws protect private businesses from having their work products absconded or used by others. So, if corporations can guard their own information as private property, why can't individual citizens do likewise? What if every person became a private corporation? What could be more American? Hence was born Morone's JLM, Inc. for the purpose of assuming ownership of the personal data generated by her life. Beginning as a conceptual art exercise, JLM, Inc. morphed into an actual incorporation effort. In the process, Morone discovered the difficulties of even finding one's own "data," scattered as it is across a myriad of online repositories. Hence, Morone soon found herself developing a software program to accomplish the task.

Prior to this effort, almost no one had ever tried to push back against corporate data collection, aside from after-the-fact documentation of the kind offered by the credit scoring companies Experian, Transunion, and Equifax. Meanwhile, large corporations routinely turn huge profits on the buying and selling of this same information. When Google or Facebook harvest one's data, their "cost of materials" is practically nothing because the sources of that information (i.e., you and me) are largely unaware of the data's value or that it is being extracted. As computer guru Jaron Lanier has said, "The dominant principle of the new economy has been to conceal the value of information," adding, "We decided not to pay most people for performing the roles that are valuable in relation to the latest technologies. Ordinary people 'share,' while elite network presences generate unprecedented fortunes."[51] Morone's project has recently gone online at jenniferlynmorone.com, where she states: "Jennifer Lyn Morone, Inc. has advanced into the inevitable next stage of Capitalism by becoming an incorporated person. This model allows you to turn your health, genetics, personality, capabilities, experience, potential, virtues and vices into profit. In this system You are the founder, CEO, shareholder and product using your own resources."[52]

Whether or not the JLM concept catches on remains to be seen. But the project does seem to capture the essence of much of what has been discussed in this chapter. While many of the double binds of the new blurred neoliberal era can be traced to earlier histories, they have taken new turns in recent years. The current moment of financial capitalism and consumer citizenship may have been quickened by network society and virtual consciousness. But it would be a mistake to idealize the "virtual" as a purely technological phenomenon. While the shift to financial capitalism may be a relatively recent development, there is nothing especially novel about the present situation. The dynamic interplay between public and private interests has defined the structure of American society since the beginning. The periodic rise of labor movements, campaigns on behalf of the poor, rights movements for disenfranchised groups, anti-monopoly legislation, and banking reform always occurred at moments when the excesses of capital reached breaking point. And just as commonly, a cyclical amnesia seems to find its way into American consciousness, not unlike biblical losses of faith.

At such junctures a rupture is often required to bring the people back to their senses. Sometimes it comes in the form of a revolution, reform movement, or moderate legislative change. At other times it simply comes from within, as growing numbers of people incrementally become aware that something is changing. Even as huge corporations and big data encroach on collective sovereignty and personal privacy, more and more people in the United States are looking to each other as sources of information, entertainment, and mutual support in the Internet age. These are blurred and confusing times, to be sure. But the desire for something different is palpable. The task ahead lies not in vague hope or idealized dreams, necessary as these things are, but in locating the fibers that connect people with each other in ways they both know and have yet to realize.

Notes

1 See David Trend, *Worlding: Identity, Media, and Imagination in a Digital Age* (Boulder, CO: Paradigm, 2013) p. 100.
2 Anne Lowery, "The Wealth Gap in America is Growing, Too," *New York Times* (April 2, 2014) http://economix.blogs.nytimes.com/2014/04/02/the-wealth-gap-is-growing-too/ (accessed July 5, 2014).
3 "20 Facts about U.S. Inequality that Everyone Should Know," Stanford Center on Poverty and Inequality http://web.stanford.edu/group/scspi/cgi-bin/facts.php (accessed July 5, 2014).
4 Slavoj Žižek, *Absolute Recoil: Toward a New Foundation of Dialectical Materialism* (London and New York: Verso, 2014) p. 5.
5 Gilles Deleuze and Félix Guattari, *A Thousand Plateaus: Capitalism and Schizophrenia,* trans. Brian Massumi (London: Athlone, 1988).
6 Bruno Latour, *We Have Never Been Modern,* trans. Catherine Porter (Cambridge, MA: Harvard University Press, 1993); Jacques Lacan, *Écrits: A Selection*, trans. Alan Sheridan (New York: W.W. Norton & Co., 1977).
7 Quentin Meillassoux, *After Finitude: An Essay on the Necessity of Contingency*, trans. Ray Brassier (New York: Bloomsbury, 2010).

8 Alain Badiou, *Being and Event*, trans. Oliver Fentham (New York: Bloomsbury, 2013); *Absolute Recoil*.
9 David Harvey, *A Brief History of Neoliberalism* (Oxford: Oxford University Press, 2005) p. 2.
10 Terry Flew, "Michel Foucault's *The Birth of Biopolitics* and Contemporary Neoliberalism Debates," *Thesis Eleven* 108 (2012) p. 44.
11 Elizabeth Bernstein and Janet R. Jacobsen, "Gender, Justice, and Neoliberal Transformations," *S&F Online* 11, nos. 1–2 (Fall 2012–Spring 2013) http://sfonline.barnard.edu/gender-justice-and-neoliberal-transformations/introduction/(accessed July 4, 2014)
12 Jim Eckman, "Postmodern Morality among Today's Young Adults," *Issues in Perspective* (Oct. 8, 2011) http://graceuniversity.edu/iip/2011/10/11-10-08-2/ (accessed July 3, 2014).
13 "Words Denoting Number, Gender, and So Forth," Code of Laws of the United States (Title 1, Chapter 1, 1) http://uscode.house.gov/view.xhtml?path=/prelim@title1&edition=prelim (accessed July 4, 2014).
14 Michel Foucault, *The Government of Self and Others: Lectures at the College de France, 1982–1983* (Basingstoke: Palgrave Macmillan, 2011).
15 Jürgen Habermas. "Taking Aim at the Heart of the Present," in David Hoy, ed., *Foucault: A Critical Reader* (Oxford and New York: Basil Blackwell, 1986).
16 Fredric Jameson, "Progress versus Utopia; Can We Imagine the Future?" in Brian Wallis, ed., *Art After Modernism: Rethinking Representation* (New York: The New Museum, 1984) p. 239.
17 Antonio Gramsci, *Selections from the Prison Notebooks*, ed. and trans. Quintin Hoare and Geoffrey Nowell Smith (New York: International Publishers, 1972).
18 Henry A. Giroux, "Neoliberalism, Democracy and the University as a Public Sphere," Truthout (April 22, 2014) http://www.truth-out.org/opinion/item/23156-henry-a-giroux-neoliberalism-democracy-and-the-university-as-a-public-sphere (accessed July 4, 2014).
19 Victoria Harper, "Henry A. Giroux: Neoliberalism, Democracy and the University as Public Sphere," Truthout (April 24, 2014) http://www.truth-out.org/opinion/item/23156-henry-a-giroux-neoliberalism-democracy-and-the-university-as-a-public-sphere (accessed July 12, 2014).
20 Louis Althusser, "Ideology and Ideological State Apparatuses" (1970) in *Essays on Ideology*, trans. Ben Brewster (London and New York: Routledge, 1984).
21 David Trend, *Cultural Pedagogy: Art/Education/Politics* (New York: Bergin & Garvey, 1992).
22 U.S. Bureau of Labor Statistics, "Leisure Time on an Average Day," American Time Use Survey (2012) http://www.bls.gov/tus/charts/leisure.htm (accessed July 13, 2014).
23 "Desire," *Merriam-Webster.com*, www.merriam-webster.com/dictionary/desire (accessed July 14, 2014).
24 Jacques Rancière, *The Emancipated Spectator* (New York: Verso Reprint Editions, 2011).
25 Bernard Stiegler, "Care within the Limits of Capitalism, Economizing Means Taking Care," in Tom Cohen, ed., *Telemorphosis: Theory in the Era of Climate Change*, Vol. 1. (Ann Arbor, MI: MPublishing, 2012) p. 110.
26 Vilfredo Pareto, *Manual of Political Economy* (1906) trans. Ann S. Schwier (New York: Augustus M. Kelley, 1971).
27 Gregory Bateson, *Steps to an Ecology of the Mind: A Revolutionary Approach to Man's Understanding of Himself* (Chicago, IL: University of Chicago Press, 1969).
28 Gregory Bateson, "A Theory of Play and Fantasy," in Jerome S. Bruner, Alison Jolly, and Kathy Sylvia, eds, *Play: Its Role in Development and Evolution* (Hammondsport: Penguin, 1976) pp. 119–129.
29 George Gerbner, interviewed in Sut Jhally, et al., *The Mean World Syndrome* (video) (Northampton, MA: Educational Video Foundation, 2010).

30 "How Much Do You Know about Video Games?" Entertainment Software Rating Board (ESRB) http://www.esrb.org/about/video-game-industry-statistics.jsp (accessed July 8, 2014).
31 Gayatri Chakravorty Spivak, *An Aesthetic Education in the Era of Globalization* (Cambridge, MA: Harvard University Press, 2012) p. 1.
32 Terry Eagleton, *The Ideology of the Aesthetic* (London and New York: Blackwell, 1981); Pierre Bourdieu, *Distinction: A Social Critique of the Judgement of Taste*, trans. Richard Nice (Cambridge, MA: Harvard University Press, 1984).
33 U.S. Bureau of Labor Statistics, American Time Use Survey (2014) http://www.bls.gov/news.release/atus.toc.htm (accessed Nov. 20, 2014).
34 Paul DiMaggio and Toqir Mukhtar, "Arts Participation as Cultural Capital in the United States, 1982–2002: Signs of Decline?" *Poetics* 32 (2004) p. 177.
35 *How a Nation Engages with Art: Highlights from the 2012 Survey of Public Participation in the Arts* (Washington, DC: NEA, 2013).
36 Richard Florida, "The Rise of the Creative Class," *Washington Monthly* (May 2002) http://www.washingtonmonthly.com/features/2001/0205.florida.html (accessed Oct. 18, 2015).
37 Laura M. Holson, "We're All Artists Now," *New York Times* (Sept. 4, 2015) www.nytimes.com/2015/09/06/opinion/were-all-artists-now.html?_r=0 (accessed Oct. 18, 2015).
38 Isabelle Graw, "Questionnaire: The Contemporary" *October* 130 (Fall 2009) p. 120.
39 Sherry Turkle, *Alone Together: Why We Expect More from Technology and Less from Each Other*" (New York: Basic Books, 2011) p. 1.
40 Ibid.
41 "Confidence in Institutions," Gallup.org (June 5–8, 2014) http://www.gallup.com/poll/1597/confidence-institutions.aspx (accessed July 16, 2014)
42 "Public Sees a Future Full of Promise and Peril" (June 22, 2010) Pew Research Center for the People and the Press http://www.people-press.org/2010/06/22/public-sees-a-future-full-of-promise-and-peril/ (accessed July 16, 2014).
43 Elizabeth A. Povinelli, *Economies of Abandonment: Social Belonging and Endurance in Late Liberalism* (Durham, NC, and New York: Duke University Press, 2011) p. 16.
44 Alyssa Quart, *Republic of Outsiders: The Power of Amateurs, Dreamers, and Rebels* (New York: The New Press, 2013) p. ix.
45 Malcolm Gladwell, *Outliers: The Story of Success* (New York: Bay Back, 2011).
46 "Etsy Statistics: November 2013 Weather Report" (Dec. 13, 2013) https://blog.etsy.com/news/2013/etsy-statistics-november-2013-weather-report/ (accessed July 19, 2014)
47 *Republic of Outsiders*, p. 198.
48 Howard Becker, *Outsiders: Studies in the Sociology of Deviance* (Glencoe, NY: Free Press, 1964).
49 Adam Liptak, "Supreme Court Rejects Contraceptives Mandate for Some Corporations," *New York Times* (June 30, 2014) http://www.nytimes.com/2014/07/01/us/hobby-lobby-case-supreme-court-contraception.html?_r=0 (accessed Jan. 5, 2015).
50 Ben H. Bagdikian, *The Media Monopoly, 5th Edition* (New York: Beacon, 1997).
51 "The Incorporated Woman," *The Economist* (June 27, 2014) http://www.economist.com/blogs/schumpeter/2014/06/who-owns-your-personal-data (accessed July 19, 2015).
52 Jennifer Lyn Morone, "Life Means Business," http://jenniferlynmorone.com/ (accessed July 19, 2015).

6

MISTAKEN IDENTITIES

From Color Blindness to Gender Bending

"This school will no longer honor race or ethnicity," announced the high school principal in a speech that went viral on the Internet. "I could not care less if your origins are African, European, Latin American or Asian, or if your ancestors arrived here on the Mayflower or on slave ships."[1] The official continued: "The only identity this school recognizes is your individual identity—your character, your scholarship, your humanity. And the only national identity this school recognizes is American. This is an American public school." This now-famous address was written by LA radio talk show host Dennis Prager, who has never worked in education. But the fictionalized rebuff to political correctness spread across the conservative blogosphere like wildfire. That the speech was never made speaks to the nature of discourse in an electronic age. But the popularity of the message also says something about identity in the 2000s. Five decades ago President Lyndon B. Johnson signed the Civil Rights Act, outlawing discrimination based on race, religion, sex or national origin.[2] This came just a year after the passage of the Equal Pay Act of 1963 prohibiting differential pay scales based on sex. Now things are different—or so one hears from certain quarters. Across the political spectrum one hears that the U.S. has entered a new era, in which an African America can be president because prejudice has disappeared. Similar arguments suggest that the time has passed for feminism, gay rights, and concern for the disabled.

Imagine for a minute that the American dream of "equality" has become reality: that sexism, racial prejudice, homophobia, ableism, and anti-immigrant bias have disappeared. Then suppose that while the formally disenfranchised have won the day, they nevertheless keep asking for more—using the government to extract ever more resources from the rest of the citizenry. Such is the premise driving the backlash against affirmative action, assaults on public assistance programs, and continuing outcries over measures like the Affordable Care Act. What might support these widely held beliefs in the face of massive statistical evidence to the contrary? While conservatives are known for asserting that the marginalized have overreached in their claims, many liberals now also say that group-specific arguments are beginning to exhaust themselves. Disagreements have begun to emerge within progressive circles about the effectiveness of what has been termed "identity politics." After several decades of claims made on behalf of specific groups, this strategy is now being questioned. While "success" has been achieved on certain policy issues, the broader landscape of inequity has seen little improvement—and in some sectors matters seem to be getting worse.

Underlying current equality debates are conflicting views of what might be termed "American idealism"—defined as a set of consensus views about the nation's values, goals, and identity. But like most idealisms, the American version sometimes runs into problems, as generalities break down in specific application—and lofty principles fail to cohere uniformly in diverse populations. Democratic societies anticipate these disagreements, and build resolution mechanisms into the electoral process. Seen in this context, it's no surprise that many Americans disagree over what the ideal of "equality" means. Technically speaking, "equality" is defined as meaning "the same in number, amount, degree, rank, or quality."[3] When the U.S was founded in the 18th century, this idea of sameness made a lot of sense in its intention to level the playing field in voting and commerce. Little thought was given to how such factors as inclusion, exclusion, privilege, and bias might later come into play. Appeals to American founding doctrines or the language of original documents fail to take this into account, as manifest recently in debates over revolutionary-era constitutional "rights" to bear arms. This problem with the term equality has led to a more nuanced look at the goal of equality, which was a fundamental "fairness" for all people. Civil rights struggles throughout American history have been premised on addressing this issue of fairness in the face of structural issues that produce inequality. Voting rights might be equal by law, but access to polling places still varies from locale to locale. Anyone can open a business, but wealthy people start with a huge advantage. Public education is open to anyone, but poor kids often must attend lousy schools. In recent years, the term "equity" (meaning "fair and impartial") has replaced equality in many circles, premised on the idea that sameness does not always serve the goals of equality. Different populations may require different resources to achieve comparable outcomes.

None of this is news to the typical American household. Pretending that differences and inequities no longer exist in the U.S. may be possible in some alternative Tea Party universe, but seven in ten Americans say otherwise in recent polls.[4] As *U.S. News & World Report* recently put it: "There is a growing anger and alienation among Americans who are becoming convinced that the American dream is a mirage. It is no longer an article of faith that anyone who works hard and plays by the rules can get ahead."[5] Most people are upset about growing income disparities, which have been exacerbated during the economic declines of the last decade. Greedy bankers and corrupt CEOs have been pilloried in the news and such movies as *The Wolf of Wall Street* (2014), *Arbitrage* (2012), *Too Big to Fail* (2011), and *Margin Call* (2011), and television series from *Mad Men* (2007–2015) to *Billions* (2016–). Behind this generalized antipathy toward the wealthy lies the recognition that economic inequity is hitting some groups harder than others. Women earn 75 percent of what men make. Hispanic and African-American poverty has deepened. Racial disparities persist in education and employment opportunities in nearly every sector of the economy.[6] And people of color make up a disproportionately high percentage of America's prison population.

Many people regard the notion of "self" as a given, without giving the matter much conscious attention. They may reference jobs or relationship status, political beliefs or ambitions for the future, or otherwise reflect on place of birth, family origin, race, ethnicity, sexual orientation, social class, religious affiliation, or education. These are most of the ways that identity has been discussed in recent generations, although before 1900 reflections on personal identity were largely the domain of philosophers—as most people saw stations in life as matters of divine will or a natural order. The Age of Reason may have introduced certain notions of upward mobility, but beliefs in static social locations remained firmly entrenched until the 20th century. For much of human history, poverty was viewed as an inheritable condition—a consequence of birth or ancestral proclivity rather than an externally imposed circumstance. It has become customary in American studies scholarship to lay much of the blame for U.S. social inequity on the European Enlightenment. This follows from the role of European people and their thinking on the colonization of the Americas, the founding of the United States as a nation, and the dominance of European immigrants in U.S. society until well into the 20th century. In cultural terms, Enlightenment-era attitudes towards identity still exert a powerful influence, although they certainly can't tell the whole story of human history.

Welcome to "Post-Identity" America

What if the very categories that cause so much division in American society could be proven to be false? What if it was possible to show that the foundations of what people call "identity" in terms of race, gender, and sexual orientation are little more than fictions passed from generation to generation? You'd say that this was utopian silliness, a romantic fantasy that the world has become one great human family. And you'd be correct. Notions of a universal "humanity" have been critiqued ever since they reemerged following World War II. At the same time, it's fair to say that times have changed—and some prior forms of prejudice and discrimination have diminished or have been pushed underground. In an age in which "diversity" has become the norm, inequity and unfairness have become moving targets, shifting and changing in often-unexpected ways. In this new environment, underachievement or failure are no longer seen by most people as evidence of a prejudicial system, but instead as signs of personal shortcomings or inherent deficit. Sweeping aside the realities of ongoing discrimination, the utopian myth of a "family of man" is emerging again as it did in the wake of a prior period of turmoil.

As the globe came together in the establishment of the United Nations, many people romanticized ideals of a common "humanity." America in the 1950s reveled in idealized visions of the nuclear family, homogenized suburban culture, and a booming middle class. The art world remembers Edward Steichen's popular "Family of Man" exhibition at the New York Museum of Modern Art, mounted in 1955, which was roundly criticized in later years for oversimplifying the complexities of human diversity, especially as Cold War tensions were again driving nations apart.[7] Roland Barthes analyzed the "Family of Man" in his book *Mythologies*, zeroing in on the exhibition's representation of diversity. Likening the exhibition to a Tower of Babel parable, Barthes noted the "Family of Man" exhibition's mythological privileging of a human "nature" (common experiences of birth, death, and family life) over the particularities of "history" (specific experiences of joy, pain, play, and work). To Barthes the exhibition was one of many instances of cultural confusion resulting from mythological storytelling. "The myth of the human condition rests on a very old mystification, which always consists in placing nature at the bottom of history," he wrote.[8]

Issues of nature and history would inform the struggles over identity in the decades to come, as "natural" human differences were linked to actual historical injustices. Initially, feminists and civil rights activists would assert that they had been unjustly punished for their natural identities. This "essentialist" argument rested on traditional American claims of equality before the law, while also arguing the ethical imperative of diversity. It was simply wrong to punish people on the basis of race or sex. Identity-based empowerment movements would point out the subjective benefits of self-affirmation to their own constituents, while also asserting the overall benefits of multiple perspectives in a democratic society.

By the 1970s identity politics started to get messy, as it became apparent that what defined a group also separated it from others. Appeals to a single aspect of identity (like race, class, gender, or sexual orientation) might work well as a way to foreground a specific issue, but it failed to address ways that some issues work across multiple identities. African-American feminists noted that groups devoted to black power and women's rights often worked in mutual disregard. Initially this yielded coalitions and discussion of hybrid identities. Eventually the issue of categorical sorting itself came into question—with widening recognition that individuals possess many identities simultaneously. Scholars of language and media would point out how people's conceptions of themselves (as both individuals and groups) are determined by how they are spoken about, what they are called, and even the ways they are addressed. Soon the history of identity distinctions would be investigated and before long the "natural" origins of many categories had been debunked. Constructionist notions of the learned character of identity would be further extended by postmodern theory, which asserted the arbitrariness of meaning itself. If understanding of the "self" lies somewhere on a chain of endless signification, just how much of identity is imaginary and how much is real? While some were quick to argue that it is hard to debate basic facts of bodily materiality like skin color or genitalia, others responded that our attitudes toward these "realities" remain an open question. Soon a wave of theory began to further parse the idea of identity across the humanities and sciences.

By the late 1990s things were starting to reach a breaking point; as the journal *Post Identity* put it in its opening editorial: "Our culture has become so fragmented (ideologically and otherwise) so as not to allow for consensus about individual or community notions of identity. We began thinking about whether there ever was a time when 'cohesive' identity formations existed or whether all such claims were thoroughly constructed." To address this "identity crisis" within the field of identity, the journal tasked itself with opening conversations and broadening discussions of difference—in other words, expanding the discourse to an ever widening field of "positions." This strategy gave an early forecast of the way identity would subsequently evolve into an ever more dispersed constellation of subjectivities, or what some simply might call individual opinions. While this might have seemed a convenient way of dealing with contentious identitarians, the strategy had some flaws. Aside from its apparent referencing of a familiar realist/idealist divide, *Post Identity* was the product of a decade of turmoil within progressive circles over what might be called "strategy." In an often-quoted essay published in *Socialist Review*, the journal's editor, Leslie Kaufman, presciently had pointed to the balkanization of an American Left once unified by class antagonism, but then becoming "a fragmented mosaic of political groups."[9] Kaufman argued for yet-unnamed "radical pluralist politics" emerging from "the principle of solidarity, which exhorts progressives to organize against oppression, exploitation, domination, and exclusion—irrespective of whom they affect."[10]

The very fragmentation and balkanization lamented by members of the American Left itself bespoke a nostalgic yearning for totalizing political narratives of the kind envisioned by Karl Marx and others of his era. As an editor at *Socialist Review* at the time, I well remember the debates that emerged as identity came head to head with the time-honored struggles against economic exploitation. Anything not addressing class-based politics automatically became labeled a "cultural" issue or a matter of linguistic intellectual solipsism. Plenty of people took issue with this crude dichotomy. Judith Butler's book *Bodies That Matter: On the Discursive Limits of Sex*, published in 1993, extended her earlier work on the interplay of language and materiality as identity plays out in daily life, subject to various modes of repetition and disciplinary regimes.[11] Butler's point was that bodies and discourses can't be separated. Cornell West's *Race Matters* was published in the same year and made similar arguments, albeit in more populist terms, as he linked the subjugation of African-American people and their bodies to practices of power manifest in images, talk, education, and celebrity—as well as politics.[12] Indeed, West argued that a populist *ethics* (i.e., a discourse) was the best way to secure material change. This is hardly to suggest that the identity politics escaped internal critique. Utopian activists always have had disagreements.

With the dawning of the new millennium, the drumbeat continued to pronounce the subject of identity dead. In *American Quarterly*, Michael Millner put it this way in an essay entitled "Post Post-Identity":

> If the 1990s were characterized by a rich and sophisticated reconceptualization of identity—as performative, mobile, strategically essential, intersectional, incomplete, in-process, provisional, hybrid, partial, fragmentary, fluid, transitional, transnational, cosmopolitan, counterpublic, and, above all, cultural—the new millennium has been frequently marked by a sense of exhaustion around the whole project of identity.[13]

Part of the reason for the sense of exhaustion was the perception that certain battles had been won. A number of changes in American society supported these perceptions—although many of the changes had less to do with "winning" than they did with ongoing demographic changes, developments in communications technology, and the adaptability of neoliberal political economics. In many ways, formerly prominent group identities had become less visible, or at least less talked about. New objects of scorn and stigma (such as terrorists or the mentally ill) began to take the place of old ones. All of this contributed to a certain blurring of vision around the "project" of identity, if ever a single such thing ever existed in the first place.

The blurring of identities has only increased in the America of the new millennium. As populations shift and migrate within the nation's borders, fresh generations of newcomers mingle and assimilate, while the nation becomes increasingly ethnically diverse. Census figures show the once pernicious problem of residential racial segregation has improved significantly since 1980 in the American West and South, though less so in the nation's "rust belt" states of the Midwest and Northeast.[14] Geography itself has been transformed by online shopping, digital learning, workplace telecommuting. Social networks have radically altered the nature of friendship and community, enabling the consolidation of existing affiliations and the emergence of a multitude of virtual communities based on interest. It is widely observed that younger people feel less bound by the conventions that once defined identity. A more mobile and interconnected society has lessened the grip of history and tradition felt by prior generations. Women and men are now equally represented in America's workforce, as fathers increasingly assume domestic chores.[15] For more than a decade women have outnumbered men in college classrooms and degree completion.[16] Heterosexual marriage has dropped to its lowest point in a century, falling to less than half what it was in 1960—a reality not lost on those opposed to the widening legalization of same-sex unions.[17] According to Susan Brown, Co-Director of the National

Center for Family and Marriage Research, "Marriage is no longer compulsory. It's just one of an array of options. Increasingly couples choose to cohabit and still others prefer to remain single."[18] While Americans remain divided on many issues and sometimes still cling to prejudicial attitudes, recent research shows a country that is increasingly accepting of differences in religion, ethnicity, political opinion, and sexual orientation. One study even suggests that this openness was launched by aging baby boomers.[19]

In this new blurred environment, contests in the name of group identities have not so much been won as their terrain has been rearranged. Spurred by the economic downturns of the early 2000s, identity activists in recent years have begun to reengage political economy as manifest in the growing collusion between state and corporate interests. In an era in which the "official" policies of government and many businesses now champion diversity as a normative ideal, the punitive effects of identity-based inequity nevertheless persist. What's going on here? To some the answer lies in principles of alienation that Marx identified in *The German Ideology* when he wrote that "when the distribution of labor comes into being, each man has a particular, exclusive sphere of activity, which is forced upon him and from which he cannot escape."[20] Within his logic, the politics of identity looks for remedies within "exclusive spheres" without addressing larger issues of systemic exploitation. While this may sound a little bit like the worries about balkanization and fragmentation espoused by *Socialist Review* in the 1990s, things are a little bit different today.

Because many obvious forms of discrimination are perceived as "corrected," the impetus behind identity politics has been reduced. At the same time, "American" values of individualism, competition, opportunity, and free enterprise have never been stronger. As a nation, the U.S. is now a constellation of diverse individuals, each left to their own devices—or so the story goes. Failure in this system is less likely seen as a matter of identity these days as it is one of personal inadequacy, lack of drive, or character defect. And let's not forget how few of the former struggles over identity have been "corrected" by any means. Despite endless cycles of legislation in the interest of creating equity between men and women, the divided American political system seems to push history backward and forward. Meanwhile, a nation settled by immigrants seems relentlessly conflicted over the continuing arrival of newcomers to its shores. As globalization connects countries around the world as never before, groups within the U.S. are divided by national origin. And the persistent culture of fear in America relentlessly conjures new scapegoats: welfare cheats, substance abusers, crazy mass killers, Internet predators, out-of-control youth, lazy teachers, Muslim extremists, and so on.

The Race for Race

If the Western imagination can be credited with the idea of democracy, it also conceived ideas of biological unfitness for citizenship. As much as anything else, this paradigmatic notion of inherent inferiority drove European culture's integrated subordination of women, indigenous peoples, foreign nationals, the infirmed, the disabled, the poor or uneducated, and those considered mentally or morally compromised. But as discussed above, this program in the name of civilized progress was not without its contradictions and complexities, as the imperial mind found itself intrigued and drawn to its apparent opposite. Indeed, it is often said that in the purest form of dualism one is quite literally defined by what one is not. The subject *requires* the object, and vice versa, for its sense of meaning and self-definition. Of course it never occurred to anyone in the Enlightenment era that such roles might be interchangeable, partial, or fluid.

This longing for the other, which sometimes was laced with sexual desire, often expressed itself in colonial missionary consciousness. The Era of Exploration may have been driven by material acquisition, but divine purpose offered a further justification. Many expeditions were sponsored by Christian sects, notably the Vatican. Biblical narratives of religious conflict had driven the European Holy Wars and Crusades, giving early form to racist ideologies. But later quests for the new world or "promised land" acquired additional potency with metaphors of virgin territory, fertile ground, and populations often described in gendered terms. Native peoples were often seen in need of moral hygiene, spiritual guidance, regulation, and, most of all, sexual control. Remember that European religious law of the colonial period generally dictated celibacy as the ideal state for Christians, with sexual relations reserved for procreation. But this didn't remove sex from people's minds. Repression drives obsession, as Freud observed. While in 16th-century England it was considered improper to use the word "leg" in mixed company, one in five women in London made their living as prostitutes. Arriving in the new racial and ethnic landscapes of Africa and the Americas, Europeans carried with them idiosyncratic attitudes of patriarchal hierarchy, monogamy, heteronormativity, and fixed gender roles that often conflicted with social mores in the lands to which they ventured. In many instances indigenous societies were based on kinship and lineage, rather than traditions of competitive male dominance.

As imperial powers sought to impose principles of moral behavior on native populations, the colonizers' imaginations soon got the better of them. Accounts of virile indigenous men and sexually voracious women had made their way back to the Continent—as well as stories equating native nakedness with sexual invitation and promiscuity. All of this created confusion and contradiction in the colonial mind, as imperatives of religious purpose conflicted with fantasies of physical pleasure and "natural" freedoms. In these ways, early encounters with dark-skinned non-Europeans became erotically charged. That this historical intersection of ethnicity and sex is so little discussed today remains an artifact of selective memory, historical revisionism, and long-standing white shame. But it is also evidence of the shifting presence of race in sexual discourse.

To many people race seems to be one of the most obvious categories of human variation. In a culture heavily predicated on visuality, children learn to draw distinctions among people based on what they can see. Most commonly, variations in skin pigmentation become ways of categorizing self and other into groups, with associations of ethnicity, nationality, and behavior soon following. The problem is that the concept of biological races has failed to hold up under scientific scrutiny, and has been discarded by scholars in all academic fields for much of the last half century. As Michael Omi and Howard Winant wrote in their book *Racial Formation in the Unites States*, race has no innate psychological or trans-historical meaning, but instead resulted from what they term "racial projects" defining certain people and identities in particular ways.[21] Yet the myth of race persists as one of the most potent means through which societies define belonging and non-belonging. Like other myths about the human species—such as those pertaining to ability, aggression, competition, sex, and gender, among others—ideas about race have a long and varied history. Most early societies attributed differences in appearance to tribal or familial lineage, and to some extent geography. Hence, regional chauvinism has a long history in race thinking. The ancient civilizations of Babylonia, China, Egypt, and Greece held all those who didn't look like them in low regard.

But it took the Age of Discovery that began in the early 15th century to give "race" a name and much of the meaning it has today. Race really took hold as a concept with the development of the modern nation state—the establishment of countries defined by national populations and boundaries not limited by geographical demarcations. Subsequent divisions between the "people" of one country and another tended sometimes, but not always, to follow lines of local kinship, community, and ethnicity. But the separation of populations into nations allowed internal consolidation and external rivalries to grow were often bolstered by cultural factors like religion, tradition, and political ideology. Racial antipathy among European Christians during the Middle Ages toward Jews and Muslims provided an early form of modeling for later forms of overt racism resulting from nationalism.

As Europeans set out to build colonial empires in Africa, the Americas, and Asia, they also began to differentiate among the populations they encountered, often justifying the subjugation of these "others" in the process. The enslavement of African "heathens" flourished in the 1600s, rationalized further by Christian beliefs that dark skin was a mark of evil. In short order, Enlightenment science and optical reasoning reckoned that racial groups could be named and classified through processes of observation. This set off a debate between scientific proponents of polygenesis (races with separate origins) and creationist believers in monogenesis (a single original race), as a subset of broader incongruences between reason and faith that still persist today. Needless to say, the quest to map a racial taxonomy of the human species had begun. And from 1700 to 1900, scientists and non-scientists conjured up various schemes to sort people by skin color, body type, head shape, geographical origin, and other criteria. The sloppiness of these efforts is manifest even today in the categories used by the U.S. Census Bureau:

White, Black or African American, American Indian or Alaska Native, Asian Indian, Chinese, Filipino, Japanese, Korean, Vietnamese, Native Hawaiian, Guamanian or Chamorro, Samoan, Native Hawaiian or Other Pacific Islander.[22] As one can see, every category except "White" references some region of the world, some with more specificity than others. Rapidly growing demographic groups—including mixed race, hybrid or "hyphenated" Americans, immigrants and their offspring—increasingly point out the exclusionary character of antiquated census categories. This has led to calls for allowing people to identify with more than one race, a suggestion countered by worries that such a system would shrink the perceived size of racial minorities. No one seems able to solve this problem. But two things are clear. Government census statistics help to perpetuate misunderstandings about race. Yet these same statistics remain vital tools for documenting inequities and arguing for corrective measures.[23] The census dilemma is but one glaring example of problems caused by the myth of race. As a society America needs to develop a more nuanced understanding of difference as a dynamic phenomenon.

Culture matters in this discussion. To dismantle the myth of race, one needs to consider the way that people's thinking is organized by the very language they use. It's hard to conceive a topic without naming it—in a sense reinforcing pre-existing notions of its validity as an idea. Already in this discussion the word "race" has appeared many times, suggesting that its meaning has stability and is commonly recognized as a coherent concept. Sometimes people are tempted to substitute the term "ethnicity" for race. But the meaning of ethnicity is even more vague, referring, as it does, to ancestry, cultural heritage, physical appearance, nation of origin, religion, language or dialect, way of dressing, or even ideology. With race thinking one is beset with a priori thought processes—ideas that were put in one's head before conscious knowledge of them, often occurring in childhood. To get beyond them requires a determined effort of "unlearning."[24] This is not as simple as it sounds, since the operations of the mind are only partially available to rational thought. Throughout human history, philosophers, psychologists, clerics, and others have struggled with the problem of how to think oneself into a new state of consciousness. Common to most of these efforts is the belief that people can at least begin the process by talking about the problem—or reading about it.

At the heart of this is the process of dialogue, the act of engaging another someone besides oneself. This dialogical sensibility doesn't always come easily to those socialized in American values of independence and rugged individualism. Unlearning sometimes requires a willingness to look beyond the solipsism of the self. But *how* does one learn or unlearn something? Long ago linguistics pointed out that utterances function on denotative (literal) and connotative (symbolic) levels. In denotative terms, a "wealthy" person is simply someone with more than average resources. Connotatively, "wealthy" attaches to all sorts of positive and negative meanings, such as being deserving or undeserving, generous or greedy, and so on. Words like wealthy (and all words for that matter) rely on context for clarification, most immediately by the other words in a sentence. But in a more general sense, all speaking, imagery, behaviors are understood contextually—as denotative and connotative meanings are continually informing each other. Words describing human difference are particularly problematic in this way, inasmuch as denotative distinctions tend to drift so quickly into connotative valuation. This is what happens with terms about race. Even if one was to accept the legitimacy of race as a reality—that categories such as black, white, and Asian had some denotative biological origin—one still would have to sort out the connotative associations attached to such terms.

If Europeans invented the idea of race as a means of categorizing those they subordinated around the world, this history alone would be a reason for rejecting the idea. But principles of race, racism, and racial discrimination quickly became synonymous with the birth of the modern nation state, premises of nationalism, internal struggles within countries, and competition between them. Then there is the factor of time, as attitudes of one generation are transmitted to the next, and the next. Like language itself, racist thinking often moves forward silently as it shapes belief systems, interpersonal behaviors, institutional structures, economics, and political realities. Hence one arrives at the current moment in the U.S. On the one hand the nation finds itself deeply confounded by the meaning of race, yet on the other hand it is confronted by the material realities that the idea has made manifest. While the history of race makes it impossible to forget the concept, the imperative to move beyond race is equally inescapable. This contradiction is played out in daily life and in the culture that surrounds everyone.

The ascension of Barack Obama to the American presidency was evidence to many that the nation had truly entered a post-racial "color-blind" era. Within a few years of the election, the U.S. Supreme Court began openly questioning the legal validity of affirmative action, as groups across the country urged the dismantling of programs to compensate historically disadvantaged populations. In 2014 the U.S. Supreme Court overturned the use of race in college admissions in Michigan.[25] The court ruled that Michigan needn't give preference to minority applicants in the manner that it did to school alumni. But the justices stopped short of banning race-sensitive policies nationwide to increase student diversity. Meanwhile, continued immigration and other demographic factors now indicate that by mid-century so-called white people will lose their majority status as the nation becomes more multicultural.[26] Add to this the belief held by some that rising numbers of interracial children are destined to eliminate concepts of ethnicity altogether.

Against this backdrop, the very concept of "race" has come under heavy assault in recent decades, as biologists, geneticists, anthropologists, historians, and others have studied the ancestry and evolution of the human species. Here is what they've concluded with a broad degree of consensus. To an overwhelming extent, populations from all around the world share the same characteristics and variations therein. All sets of differences commonly attributed to different "races" are subsets attributable to early African peoples. While great genetic variation exists *within* each of the world's populations, the Human Genome Project has found minimal variation *between* populations.[27] Most of the generalized differences in the way people look have resulted from environmental factors, such as exposure to ultraviolet light at different latitudes. Other factors such as climate, nutrition, and culture have played a role in determining what are erroneously assumed to be inherent differences. This is not to suggest that differences don't exist. But it is to say that many of the characteristics people typically associate with race (i.e., skin color, cranial shape, body type and size) are largely independent variables that pop up in different mixtures throughout the human species—and hence can't be attributed to specific locales or societies in any scientific way.

Nor is this to say that race doesn't matter. While the empirical reality of race may be a fiction, the social construction of racism is very real, with positive and negative consequences, and all the shades in between. Knowledge of one's family history and origins are key elements of individual and group identity. Understanding the struggles and accomplishments of previous generations helps one to understand one's own upbringing and worldview. The common immigrant legacy of nearly all American citizens, as well as large population sectors around the globe, adds a particular potency to the recognition of migration in shaping human culture. All sorts of theories have tried to explain why so many cultures harbor suspicions about newcomers. Child development experts note the primordial anxieties experienced by youngsters when encountering someone unknown to them. Anthropologists point out the history of tribal conflicts over food and resources.

Capitalism and free market competition have become the underlying drivers of racism in contemporary America. In their book *After Race: Racism and after Multiculturalism,* Antonia Darder and Rodolfo D. Torres state that:

> The problem of the 21st century is the problem of "race"—an ideology that has served well to successfully obscure and disguise class interests behind the smokescreen of multiculturalism, diversity, difference, and more recently, whiteness.[28]

This is not to deny the "idea" of race or the historical reality of race-based discrimination—as much as it is to argue that race was simply another tool among many others (like sex, gender, sexual orientation, immigration status, age, education level) operating *inside* broader systems of social stratification.

It doesn't take much insight to recognize how racialized competition can translate into inequity. In a nation like the United States, where corporate CEOs often earn salaries 100 times greater than that of their typical employees, a lot of people end up at the short end of the stick. Large disparities persist between the wealth of "whites" within the United States and everyone else—although it's important to recognize the ambiguity and vagueness of the term white (generally functioning as a synonym for European ancestry). A recent study by the Pew Research Center of government data reveals the median wealth of white families is 20 times that of African Americans and 18 times that of Latino/Chicano households.[29] In 2009 the typical white household held $113,149 in accumulated resources; the typical black household had $5,677, and the typical Latino/Chicano $6,325. Statistics also showed that 35 percent of African-American and 31 percent of Latino/Chicano families had no surplus worth or were in debt, compared to 15 percent of white households. While in 2005 Asian households held resources of $168,103, four years later that amount had fallen by 54 percent to $78,066, partially due to the arrival of new Asian immigrant populations. Yet even without taking new immigration into account, Asian-American net wealth nevertheless dropped by 31 percent. A mere 11 percent of black students were proficient in math, as opposed to 50 percent of Asians, 42 percent of whites, 16 percent of Native Americans, and 15 percent of Latino students. And in reading, only 18 percent of Native-American students, 13 percent of black students and 4 percent of Latino students were proficient, compared to 40 percent of white students and 41 percent of Asian students.[30]

Here as elsewhere, statistical evidence seems to contradict the idea of a "post-racial" U.S. in which everyone has equal access to the American dream. If one can dispense with the notion of race as a biological reality and view it as a social construction, the matter of "natural" competition becomes the next question. Plenty of thinking has gone into this, with consensus across a broad intellectual spectrum increasingly asserting that the real key to human evolution has been people's ability to work together. Society is more than a set of isolated individuals working strictly in their own interests. Whether in families, tribes, interest groups, corporations, localities, or nations—collective endeavor multiplies human capacity to get things done. Moreover, individual and group interests need not always be mutually exclusive. In the United States individuals benefit from countless government programs—from national defense to student aid. But in a similar way, there is no doubt that communities gain a great deal from the achievements and innovations of individual citizens. The opposition of the one and the many is an illusion, another binary idea that contributes to myths about insiders and outsiders. In actuality, perhaps no idea is so deeply ingrained in the American ideal as the delicate balance between individuality and collectivity. Partisan polemics notwithstanding, a healthy tension between self and community is what keeps any political economic system going. Hence, rather than seeing the issue of individual competition as an all-or-nothing affair (as in familiar oppositions between capitalism and socialism), one might do better viewing self-interest and collective interest as interrelated. This is certainly what many biologists, anthropologists, and psychologists are now suggesting.

Contesting the Darwinist belief that self-centeredness derives from an animalistic character, Robert Augros and George Stanciu argue in *The New Biology: Discovering the Wisdom of Nature* that the natural world favors equilibrium and coexistence. For one thing, cooperation is simply more energy-efficient. And for that reason "nature uses extraordinarily ingenious techniques to avoid conflict and competition" nearly everywhere one looks.[31] Augros and Stanciu use science itself to point out that Darwin's theories of natural selection provide part, but not all, of the explanations for species evolution. And they cite dozens of examples in which what they term "systemic differentiation" occurs at a chromosomal level within a particular species, arising from latent potentialities within the organism itself. They also note cooperative behaviors among creatures ranging from honeybees to stickleback fish that seem to defy notions of inherent competition among nonhuman species. Turning to the thornier issue of social Darwinism, Augros and Stanciu make the quite self-evident observation that human beings possess a self-consciousness that other species don't have.

Pictures at an Exhibition

Images and vision have long played a vital role in the racial imagination, extending prior ideologies put in place by written texts and storytelling. Long before the invention of photography, European paintings were often decorated with background figures of dark-skinned servants, slaves, courtesans, entertainers—that is, when such figures were not featured as motives of colonial conquest or exotic fantasy. American painting of the plantation era was filled with depictions that naturalized and objectified the black body for white viewers. In the 1980s Edward Said broke new ground with his book *Orientalism*, which gave a name to the process through which the Western imperialist mind came to identify and represent those Others it encountered in North Africa, Asia, and especially, the Middle East. In a world historically occupied with North–South dichotomies, Said was instrumental in foregrounding East–West dialectic. Taking a long view of history, he described a 2,000-year lineage of Western domination—beginning with Grecian conflicts with what was then known as Persia. From that time forward, European writing about the Orient had characterized the East as irrational, feminine, and weak—as opposed to the rational, masculine, and strong West. These ancient Western paradigms would provide a justification of European colonialism around the world. Of particular relevance to our current moment, Said would focus on stereotypical representations of Muslim peoples in his later work, noting how easily long-standing ethnic tropes of the "Arab" could be mapped onto the figure of the "terrorist." As a scholar of language, Said spoke at length about the way meanings get associated with people and places, as all Eastern cultures come to be seen as identical to each other. In critiquing the overarching logic of Western expansionism around the world, Said was among the earlier theorists of postcolonialism—a school of thought directly addressing the bifurcation of the world through national and ethnic power asymmetries.

Stories and imagery of "primitive" peoples had long fascinated European readers, typified by travel literature by writers like Joseph Conrad and Rudyard

Kipling. With the invention of photography in the mid-1800s, imagery from far-away places quickly became a mainstay of publishing. George Bridges and Maxime du Camp popularized depictions of Asia and Africa, as U.S. photographers like Edward Curtis and John K. Hillers similarly photographed Native Americans. At the beginning of the 20th century the most prolific film-producing countries also ranked among the world's dominant imperial empires: Britain, France, Germany, and the United States. Part of the appeal of this imagery lay in its apparent authenticity in comparison to literary and cinematic fiction. It seemed the new "sciences" of photography and film had a unique ability to capture the realities of distant adventures and make them safe for home viewing. Each imperial filmmaking nation had its own genres of films depicting "darkest Africa," the "mysterious East," or the "stormy Caribbean."

Sex and race often converged in early movies. Aside from the generalized stereotypes conveyed in these moving pictures (with depictions always made from the colonizers' perspective), the films also often masked a racialized voyeurism of the dark body justified by populist anthropological pretenses. Ella Shohat and Robert Stam observed in their book *Unthinking Eurocentrism* that:

> Ethnographic science, then, provided a cover for the unleashing of pornographic impulses. The cinematic exposure of the dark body nourished spectatorial desire, while marking off imaginary boundaries between "self" and "other," thus mapping homologous spheres, both macroscopic (the globe) and microscopic (the sphere of carnal knowledge).[32]

Frontier expansion within the U.S. soon would emerge as a dominant paradigm in American filmmaking. Roughly one-fourth of all Hollywood features (both documentary and fiction) made between 1925 and 1965 were "Westerns."[33] These movies gave license to unprecedented levels of visualized violence against nonwhite people. Exaggerated depictions of native assaults would invariably trigger massive retaliation. But of course the cowboys often fought among themselves in movies, as American culture increasingly came to define itself through violent representation.

In one sense, the genre of American Western movies laid the groundwork for the popular genre of war movies that would extend the imagery of racialized violence even further in the name of national self-interest and defense. The Mexican-American War had already been a fixture of cowboy movies and continued to remain as such well into the 20th century. One of movie history's most famous examples of mass slaughter depicted a gunfight between American cowboys and Mexican soldiers in San Peckinpah's film *The Wild Bunch* (1967). Peckinpah gained notoriety for that film through his then-innovative use of multiple cameras, slow-motion photography, and bloody explosions from bodies torn apart by bullets. But without a doubt the popularity of *The Wild Bunch* also derived from its novel libidinous licensing of retributional violence visited on the Latino body. It goes without saying that plenty of movies also were made in the postwar period about the horrific history of America's wars with Japan, Germany, and to a lesser extent Italy, China, Russia, and Korea. The Vietnam era would generate yet another cycle of such movies. Without dwelling on this too much, it can be said that certain common denominators run through all such films made in the U.S. and Europe. These include the irrationality, inscrutability, or outright insanity of the enemy—with aggression against the U.S. uniformly categorized as a manifestation of evil. In this context, the figure of the terrorist in today's mediascape can be seen as an extension of wartime nationalist racism.

Evil has one further face in the racialized imagery of violence—the criminal. Police dramas remain one of the most popular genres on television, in such long-running series as *Bluebloods, CSI, Dexter, Law & Order, NCIS*, and *The Shield*. Until relatively recently the bad guys in the shows were invariably people of color. The one thing that hasn't changed very much in depictions of bad guys is the linkage of criminality and poverty. The stigmatization of poverty has a long history in the U.S. in depictions of what sociologist Michael B. Katz termed *The Undeserving Poor* in his book by the same title.[34] As discussed in Chapter 1, attitudes persist that a "taker" class continues to flourish in America, populated by those not meriting sympathy because they bring their poverty on themselves. Many Americans continue to see poverty as a personal failure, thus rationalizing the country's mean-spirited treatment of the poor. But if the recent recession has taught Americans anything, it is that poverty has many causes, can happen to anyone, and doesn't have an intrinsic sex, gender, race, or sexual orientation—despite the disproportionate vulnerability that some groups experience. It's now known that most welfare moms are white, as are most of the homeless, the mentally ill, and the addicted in American society.[35]

Considering this history, media representations of race and ethnicity are reaching a point of contradiction in the new millennium. Long-standing struggles for equal rights in the U.S. have pushed public consciousness and media representation in a positive direction, largely eradicating the most obvious forms of overt sexism and racism as such. This is not to say that these impulses have disappeared—only that they have been driven underground or otherwise transformed. As diversity becomes a mainstream value, differences of sex, gender, race, or ethnicity are no longer stigmatized in and of themselves, as they once were. But deviance from norms continues to be essentialized in the ways it always has been—with some interesting new twists. Black and Latino street gangs have replaced black and Latino criminals. Ethnic white crime syndicates from Eastern European countries have replaced the Italian Mafia. Women of all ethnicities are now joining the ranks of men in movie criminality. And now mental illness has become a popular theme in the construction of villains.

Bending Sex and Gender

Debates over sex and gender are always in the news, owing to their prominence as categories of identity. More than one historian has posited sexual difference as the dominant organizing principle in human thought, the ontological binary preceding philosophy, religion, or politics. This is what Luce Irigaray notoriously did in claiming sexual difference as *the* quintessential question of the age—inspiring later work by others dissecting the gendered dimensions of certain forms of knowledge and politics.[36] But this begs the question that ontologies are always written by someone, suggesting that sexual difference may have been a convenient framework on which to apply such metaphors as mind/body, active/passive, master/slave, and so on. Another way of looking at this might lie in acknowledging the difficulty of accounting for differences commonly explained in such simplistic terms—which is one reason why so much theoretical ink has been expended in the past two decades in mapping the substrata of sex and gender, exploring their imbrication with other forms of difference, or otherwise noting the futility of categorical bracketing altogether. In varying ways, modern science and philosophy sought to discard such clumsy dualisms, and eventually disregarded the matter of ontology itself—albeit by two different pathways. Objective scientific reason saw itself as neutral, disinterested, and unsullied by matters of mind, as scientists externalized hypotheses and proofs behind walls of observation and measurement. Meanwhile philosophical writing from Kant onward had questioned the idea of objectivity itself, owing to the impossibility of absolute "knowledge" beyond human perception and thought. These two approaches to ontology would become known as "realism" and "idealism," respectively. As might be expected, much subsequent thinking sought to bridge this divide, including recent attention to what have been called "new ontologies."

Old as it is, the realist/idealist divide pervades contemporary discussions of sex and gender, replete with time-honored appeals to scientific objectivity and philosophical subjectivity. Notably these have become manifest in a decoupling of sex and gender as matters of biology and human consciousness, respectively. In itself, this decoupling is a radical gesture in a society so accustomed to using the terms "sex" and "gender" interchangeably, or more precisely, favoring gender as a blanket term that avoids referencing sexuality. But biological sex and gender are different, with gender not automatically connected to physical anatomy. As an aspect of biology, *sex* includes such physical attributes as chromosomes, hormones, internal reproductive structures, and external genitalia. Individuals are typically identified as male or female at birth. *Gender* is considerably more complicated. Along with physical traits, gender inheres in the complex interrelationship between those traits and one's internal sense of self as female or male (or both or neither of these) as well as one's gender presentation and reception.

Within this nomenclature, sex and gender can be seen as overlapping but not coextensive categories, with plenty of space in the middle zones of both. Sex is generally considered the more immutable of the two, given the historical baggage of procreation in cultural belief systems. But in recent decades growing attention has been afforded to sex change and anatomical ambiguity. Since the 1950s gender has been recognized as an aspect of self-perception and experience, sometimes termed the "sex of the brain." While in most people's minds, a person's sex is fundamentally a matter of physical anatomy, a vast array of gender attributes get attached to it via culture and society. As soon as a child is born, a quick glance between the legs yields a gendered label that will follow the child henceforth.

Expectant parents gaze at the ultrasound screen to see whether their baby is a boy or girl. Embryos look pretty much the same until about nine weeks of development, with all babies possessing the same Wolffian and Mullerian ducts. After eight weeks chromosomes begin either to expand or reduce these ducts into what will become female and male reproductive hardware, typically visible at about 16 weeks of development. Just how this anatomy develops varies considerably, including manifestations of both male and female anatomy in "intersex" babies. While most cultures divide people into male and female categories, nature is not always so clear, even in terms of the body itself. Rather than a simple either/or matter, biological gender expresses itself across a continuum of possibilities. By itself this spectrum of anatomical variation would seem to refute the simplistic two-sex paradigm.

Western culture similarly tends to see gender as a binary concept, even as philosophers and scientists debate whether gender is a biological or environmental matter. In the public mind, threats to gender seem like threats the social order—which is one reason why so little variance from gender norms is tolerated in mainstream culture. Some parents (or most) begin treating their babies as male or female well before birth, decorating rooms with pink or blue and making gendered plans for the child's future. If you think about it, practically everything children experience is assigned a gender—names, toys, clothing, behaviors. By three years of age, children commonly begin expressing preferences and behaviors associated with their sex. In adulthood the world is defined further in gendered terms, whether manifest in work or relationships, movies and television, or gender-specific advertising. For many people female and male roles seem so "natural" that they are never questioned. In recent decades, the expression "gender diversity" has emerged in recognition of the fact that many people fall outside of commonly understood gender norms. After generations of battles over whether "nature" or "nurture" determine our genders, many conclude that the answer is both. It's more a matter of how *nature is nurtured* in differing ways.

Keep in mind this book's earlier discussion of normativity as a culturally constructed set of ideals. These ideals have very specific historical roots—largely related to worries over health and longevity. It's been less than 100 years since the great flu pandemic of 1918 wiped out 50 million people worldwide. Before then, centuries of plagues, wars, and other causes of human suffering had caused people to fear illnesses or injuries of any kind as incursions on the "great health." Anxieties about health were so great that the physically or mentally "deviant" were pathologized, not simply as objects of scorn or prejudice, but as a threat to the entire species. Darwin's theories of evolution had popularized beliefs that nature had processes of weeding out its errors. By the 1900s these principles had shaped public policies, as entire classes of people were ostracized in the interest of "cleansing" many societies.[37] Factor in ample measures of sexual repression and religious guilt and it's no mystery to imagine the related public antipathy toward nonreproductive sexual "inversion" (homosexuality) and gender variance in this atmosphere.

Before the 2000s the terms *transgender* and *transsexual* were obscure references in most people's minds, owing to their relative absence from public discourse and limited attention from academics. This apparent invisibility largely was held in place by popular misconceptions about gender as a seemingly "natural" correlate of biological sex, rather than a variable characteristic. Things have come a long way in recent years—owing in part to the visibility of high-profile transgender figures like Chaz Bono, Lavern Cox, Chelsea Manning, Lana Wachowski, and Caitlyn Jenner, as well as the new presence of transgender themes in popular TV series like *Orange is the New Black, Sense8*, and the award-winning *Transparent*. Notably most of the attention has been on male-to-female (MTF) transitions, although the exact breakdown of the nation's 0.5 percent transgender population has not been accurately calculated. In 2014 *Time Magazine* ran a cover story entitled "The Transgender Tipping Point," which noted that 9 percent of Americans say they have trans friends or family members.[38]

Facebook now lists 50 options in a gender checklist that once had only "female" and "male" options. With over 1.3 billion users, such a move by Facebook speaks volumes about broader social attitudes. Now one can identify online as androgynous, bigender, gender fluid, gender queer, pangender, transgender, trans female, trans male, transsexual, and so on.[39] One simply has to look at recent news headlines to see that gender variance has moved from the margins of mainstream consciousness to the center. And in 2012 the U.S. Equal Employment Opportunity Commission banned transgender job discrimination, a move backed up two years later by an Executive Order from President Obama.[40] Meanwhile, businesses and universities across the country (as well as many nations around the globe) have moved to include hormone replacement or gender-confirming surgeries in their health plans.

All of these changes reflect a growing weariness, irritation, or outright refusal with received categories of gender as traditionally defined. What began in the 1970s with feminist criticisms of women's objectification broadened in later decades with the recognition that stereotypical views of men had equally damaging effects. It seemed that every category of feminine gentleness, dependence, and emotionality had a masculine opposite of aggression, independence, and rationality. And these were hardly politically innocent categories. Even until recently, American marketing and entertainment seemed to suggest that anyone not conforming to stereotypical roles (or aspiring to do so) was out of step. A host of changes in public policy, reproductive rights, workplace demographics, and educational access led to broad-based changes in cultural perceptions of sex and gender roles—but not without resistance. The heterogeneity of the U.S.

population, regional isolationism, and the persistence of religious traditionalism are some of the factors creating ongoing pressures on equity advances, even today. Nevertheless, men and women now see flexibility in their options for gender expression as perhaps never before—whether this entails refusing the "beauty culture" of classic femininity or the "tough guise" of hyper-masculinity. "Androgynous" or "unisex" used to be the descriptors for the middle zones of the gender spectrum. But as more and more people have recognized their agency in gender expression, the notion of "bending" gender has become commonplace, especially as the fashion industry has followed suit. At the same time, the past decade has seen rising use of the term "cisgender" to mark normative gender expression in a way similar to categories like heterosexual and able-bodied.

Of course gender bending isn't exactly new. It's been a familiar theme in literature, explored by writers from William Shakespeare and Virginia Woolf to more recent novelists like Neil Gaiman and Ursula Le Guin. Pop performers from David Bowie to Lady Gaga have played with gender. Big-name clothing retailers like American Apparel, Yves Saint Laurent, and Barneys use transgender models, as demand for gender-neutral clothing continues to grow. And of course it is commonly known that millions of online gamers swap genders like changes of clothes. In his best-selling book on contemporary parenting, *Far from the Tree*, the author Andrew Solomon frankly discussed the rise of gender bending on college campuses. Many students now see little meaning in conventional gender expression, Solomon noted, including a growing number who "feel they can have no authentic self in their birth identity."[41] That Solomon made his comments in a book on raising children speaks to changing attitudes among Americans of all ages. As Solomon frames the matter:

> Western culture likes binaries: life is less threatening when we can separate good and evil into tidy heaps, when we split off the mind and the body, when men are masculine and women are feminine. Threats to gender are threats to the social order. If rules are not maintained, everything seems to be up for grabs.[42]

Evolving attitudes toward gender diversity are apparent at universities throughout the U.S., where many campuses have adopted gender-neutral policies toward athletics programs and public facilities. Similar accommodations also have been made in recent years in many secondary schools. In 2013 California governor Jerry Brown signed Assembly Bill No. 1266, making California the first state to make this basic accommodation a matter of law.[43] The legislation gave gender nonconforming students the freedom to join sports teams and to use locker rooms based on their gender identity. This sent conservatives and parent groups into a panic, with a group calling itself Privacy for All Students launching a virulent petition drive, largely organized through Californian churches, to overturn AB 1266.[44] While the Privacy for All Students effort failed, before long news stories began popping up all over the country about "men" using the new accommodations to sneak into women's restrooms. Among the many misunderstandings represented by the Privacy for All Students campaign was the persisting stereotype that gender variance is mainly about men changing their gender identities, and of course that this violation of nature masked deeper impulses of male sexuality.

This line of reasoning is well known in transgender circles, owing to an influential book written 20 years ago by radical feminist Janice G. Raymond entitled *The Transsexual Empire: The Making of the She-Male.*[45] A staunch proponent of biological essentialism, Raymond asserted that no amount of psychological awakening, hormone replacement, or surgical intervention could alter something as fundamental as male or female identity. Raymond's argument was that males who undergo gender confirmation procedures always remain deviant men and never become women. Worse still, these masquerading men use the appearance of the female body to infiltrate women's spaces, most egregiously lesbian feminist spaces, while continuing to exercise patterns of gendered dominance and sexual adventurism. Raymond's essay profoundly polarized feminism and transgender activism at the time—and its premises continue to do so. As Susan Stryker and Stephen Whittle write in the *Transgender Studies Reader*, "Janice Raymond's *The Transsexual Empire* did not invent anti-transsexual prejudice, but it did more to justify and perpetuate it than perhaps any other book ever written."[46]

While Raymond's essay fostered antipathy among some toward MTF identities, it also helped to launch a massive countermovement in the 1990s. Sandy Stone's "The 'Empire' Strikes Back: A Posttranssexual Manifesto" exemplified efforts to further theorize and articulate transgender subjectivity. Among other things, Stone pointed to the epistemological trap that Raymond entered by rigidly adhering to gender binaries. "To attempt to occupy a place as speaking subjects within a traditional gender frame is to become complicit in the discourse which one wishes to deconstruct," Stone wrote.[47] Besides critiquing essentialist views of sex and gender as natural categories of difference, Stone also questioned Raymond's premise that the ultimate goal of transgender identity is the swapping of positions in the male/female dichotomy—thereby "passing" as one's opposite and returning to "normal" society via masquerade. Ironically perhaps, Raymond and Stone agreed on the immutability of personal history in transgender identity, although while the former read transition as a crime against nature the latter saw it as a revolutionary act.

One of the biggest initial difficulties facing gender-variant youth, and many gender-variant young people in general, is disapproval and stigma within their immediate families. Aside from the risk of stress and abuse at home, this is one of the reasons for the disproportionate numbers of transgender young people living on the streets. According to UCLA's Williams Institute, 40 percent of homeless youth are LGBT, equivalent to 10 percent of the overall homeless population.[48] Transgender youth and adults are especially hard hit, with one in five reporting homelessness at some point in their lives. Unfortunately, transgender people facing homelessness also face discrimination from agencies that should be helping them, with nearly one in three reporting being turned away from a shelter due to their transgender status.[49] A recent federal government survey found that one in five transgender people experience a denial of service by a health-care provider as a result of their gender. In an especially sobering statistic, the Williams Institute finds that 45 percent of transgender adults attempt suicide between the ages of 18 and 44.[50] These numbers on homelessness, health care, and suicide point out the dark side gender nonconformity in America, as well as the often-unrecognized difficulties of transgender life.

If there is such a thing as a "transgender community" (and many would contest such a notion), it is hardly a monolithic entity. Indeed, radical heterogeneity lies at the very heart of the popular appellation of "genderqueer"—which is often used as an all-encompassing term for gender identities that resist strict binaries. From its original connotation as a term for eccentricity or strangeness, the term "queer" acquired a pejorative association with homosexuality in the 19th century, later to be appropriated and radicalized by gay pride movements of the late 1980s.[51] Soon afteward, activists, artists, and academics began using the term more broadly. Initially perceived as a reactive "pride" gesture, queer theory quickly moved to critique the very notion of gay/straight and male/female binaries—asserting that there are many varieties of sexuality and gender.

Heavily influencing the evolving discourse of genderqueer theory was the scholarship of Judith Butler.[52] Butler's formulation of gender as performance helped to clarify gender as a conditional aspect of the self, composed of both a priori aspects and situational contingencies informing one's relationship to bodily materiality. Butler spoke of gender more as an ongoing set of events than a fixed aspect of identity. Much queer theory of the early 2000s similarly framed queerness in terms of openness and refusal of definition, placing it on an endless signifying chain, pointing toward, but perhaps never reaching, a utopia or queer futurity.[53] While many found this premise inspirational, some critics said it was vague, and, worse still, that it intellectualized the very real discrimination and violence that was encountered by many in queer communities. Others countered that these criticisms were a misreading of a doctrine designed, in its openness, to always address both material and cultural matters. And Butler would add that such conceptual divisions were themselves part of the problem.

Let's not forget marriage: gay/straight, happy/unhappy, legal or unofficial, not to mention variations on partnering, family structure, separation, divorce, and child custody. Even as marriage equality debates often seemed to focus attention on matters of sexual orientation, underlying arguments of most conservatives attach to gender roles and reproduction. The complaint most commonly heard, especially from fundamentalist Christians, has been that same-sex marriage violates divine pairings of "one man, and one woman." In *Race, Monogamy, and Other Lies They Told You*, anthropologist Agustín Fuentes traces the roots of human "pair bonding" as it has been shaped by factors of sex, attachment, belief, and law. Concluding that "there is no real anthropological, biological, or psychological support for the notion that there is a pair perfect (or reasonably perfect) match for everyone, or for anyone," Fuentes attributes the long-standing institution of marriage to secular and religious conventions, worries about caring for children, and a fair amount of good old-fashioned patriarchy.[54] Noting how few couples stay married for an entire lifetime, Fuentes says that "we are not naturally monogamous, but we are frequently monogamous."[55]

Marriage equality is only one factor blurring the meaning of matrimony. As discussed in Chapter 2, despite the strong hold of "traditional values" in the nation (77 percent of Americans identity as Christian), the most common family unit today is a single person living alone.[56] In the United States 80 percent of the population get married at least once, although federal statistics show that half of all first marriages fail, and most second marriages fall apart as well.[57] In its 2013 rulings overturning the federal Defense of Marriage Act and California's Proposition 8, the U.S. Supreme Court said that those same-sex marriage bans were discriminatory. But the Court deferred from mandating marriage equality nationwide until 2015, thus triggering ongoing legal contests in state jurisdictions. Of course marriage is more than a social convention, inasmuch as it carries with it legal protections and benefits like rights of inheritance, hospital visitation, and child custody. Yet it may surprise some to know that in all the commotion over same-sex unions, transgender marriage has remained a genuine option for many. Heterosexual spouses who come out as transgender or transition to a new gender are not prohibited from remaining married in many non-marriage-equality states. And transgender individuals are often able to enter a heterosexual marriage after sex-reassignment procedures as well. Additionally, some states that do not recognize legal sex changes are among those recognizing same-sex marriages, affording couples other options.[58]

Varieties of Gazing

Media images of sex and gender are also blurring in a virtual sense, if not a literal one. The role of vision in human consciousness has been debated, reworked, and rethought in fields from art history and anthropology to media and gender studies. "Visuality" has been associated with people's fundamental sense of themselves as individuals, the desires they form for other people and possessions, not to mention the role of vision as a technique of mastery or control. It doesn't take much insight to recognize how vision and imagery influence the ways people think about sex and gender, the ways that visuality might reinforce norms and conventions, and how all of this might play into historical inequities. While visual media are sophisticated forms of language, vision itself is more than this—as what one sees links to conscious and unconscious thought.

Psychoanalyst Jacques Lacan described how infants perceive the attention of caregivers, typically their mothers, in mirroring a sense of the baby's selfhood.[59] When the infant later encounters an actual mirror, this self is experienced in image form—as the child's sense of identity becomes divided between "who I am" and "how others see me." To Lacan this doubling of the self has profound implications later in life, with reminders that one can be the "object" of another's gaze. Combine this with extant power differentials in a vision-based society (of gender, colonial rule, medical authority, etc.), and the stage is set for trouble of all kinds. Think about the ways animals use vision to find sustenance and keep themselves safe. People similarly learn to read the facial cues and body language of others in determining if someone is friendly or not. Historians note the cultural role of vision and images as human beings learned to recognize enemies or friends. Kings and even gods were rendered as pictures or statuary. The management of slaves was a visual process, as was surveillance of prison populations. Wealthy landowners often commissioned landscape paintings to document their estates. Portraiture allowed people to "own" likenesses of themselves or those they cared about.

Hence, from an early time pictures held meaning as copies of things of value. Being seen or pictured is to be captured by another's gaze and rendered as an object. From the outset, this raised intriguing questions about the roles of the person looking and the one looked at, the pleasure or discomfort inherent in these respective roles, not to mention what happens when the look itself becomes a thing—a picture. For a time it was assumed that the gaze possessed complete authority and that images had singular meanings. But Lacan also noted that the infant wants to be seen, knows it is being seen, and develops a sense of being in dialogue with the regarding caregiver. The resulting relationship can be asymmetrical, but not automatically so.

Decades ago film scholars began to analyze the prevalence of gender stereotyping in popular culture. In a famous BBC documentary, cultural critic John Berger stated that, "to be born a woman is to be born, within an allotted and confined space, into the keeping of men," to which he added the following often quoted passage:

> Men look at women. Women watch themselves being looked at. This determines not only most relationships between men and women but also the relation of women to themselves. The surveyor of woman in herself is male: the surveyed female. She turns herself into an object—and most particularly an object of vision: a sight.[60]

Berger illustrated his point not only with images from contemporary advertising and entertainment, but also with a full complement of paintings, sculpture, and other artworks from antiquity to the present. Without rehearsing this entire line of criticism, suffice to say that Berger popularized the notion of human "objectification" in representation: the practice of rendering selected people as passive objects rather than active subjects.

Feminist theorists had been discussing the phenomenon of the "male gaze" for some time. In 1973 Laura Mulvey noted how movies usually arrange female characters within the frame to be viewed in certain ways.[61] More often than men, women would be filmed facing the camera, with their appearance accented in various ways. Women would be watched by male actors as the story unfolded, just as camera operators (mostly male as well) would record the scenes. And of course stories themselves would often reinforce gendered relationships. All of this was striking at the time for two reasons. On a political level these criticisms were part of ongoing discussions about the prevalence of sex-based inequity throughout society. But in addressing media, critics like Berger and Mulvey drew attention to the unconscious ways that inequities traveled in the forms of entertainment and commerce.

Later theorists found aspects of "spectatorship" that seemed to contradict the early male gaze theories, especially since women and men were enjoying the same movies.[62] Was it simply that women had internalized their roles as objects? Certainly this might be part of the answer. But then scholars started to consider the "female gaze" more closely and the viewing process more broadly. Mary Ann Doane, among others, argued that women were looking at certain movies differently than men and deriving different meanings from them. Soon postmodern theories of "spectatorship" were arguing that gendered interpretations of media were not fixed, nor were any "readings" of texts consistent from viewer to viewer. Ideology might strongly push meaning in a certain direction. But it could also be pushed the other way, as viewers fanaticized during viewing or mentally argued against what they were watching. While pleasure in looking may link to one's sex or gender, enjoyment also might come from occupying the "wrong" viewing position. This meant that identification with a character or storyline need not always be tied to one's anatomy, gender, sexual orientation, age, race, ethnicity, social class, and so on.

As might be expected, this broadened view of spectatorship would eventually create controversies around the topic of pornography. From the 1980s onward, "sex-positive" feminists inside and outside of media studies asserted women's agency in sex and its representation. This conflicted with earlier views of pornography as the quintessential instrument of women's oppression—by asserting that voyeurism did not have a gender. Anyone might be drawn to porn, although not everyone would respond to the *same* porn. Queer theory of the 1990s would further problematize notions of static spectatorship, noting that lesbian and gay viewers had frequently read heterosexual narratives against the grain. It should go without saying that this also was a time when independent media producers and artists were actively contesting the hitherto white male heterosexual mainstream media system itself. Regionally and nationally scores of groups and organizations emerged like Women-Make-Movies and the Frameline Festival to support and exhibit new works. These groups fell alongside the huge outpouring of media activities among African Americans, Chicanos/Latinos, Asian Americans, and others making media in growing numbers. The popularity these films and video would show the enormity of audiences for different kinds of media—markets that later would be reached more fully in the 1990s by the fragmentation of broadcast television into cable and satellite viewing.

Taken as an ensemble, this new media activity from many quarters seemed to reflect back upon a single source—eventually raising the question of whether the "center" of the corporate boardroom did indeed have a singular organizing logic. When questions of women's objectification or racial stereotyping were put to business leaders or media executives, the answer would always be the same: "We have nothing to gain from alienating potential consumers." This issue of sales became all the more pressing as the purchasing power of women and minority groups became increasingly apparent in the 1970s and 1980s. Not only did women make buying decisions in the home, they were heading households in growing numbers, especially as more and more women entered the workforce. Meanwhile, the racial and ethnic demographics of the nation continued to change in the United States with growing immigration, internal population shifts, and the recognition of America as a multicultural society. Overt sexism and racism began to decline everywhere, as public policy advanced the rights of previously disenfranchised groups.

How could the corporate boardroom respond to this? Obviously something as huge as a national economy can't turn on a dime. Change would need to be incremental. The expedient way to begin would lie in making small changes to the system along with a limited number of symbolic gestures to show good faith. This became known as niche marketing or targeted media—two of the hallmarks of neoliberalism. Virginia Slims offered women their own brand of cigarette with the liberatingly suggestive slogan, "Have it your way, baby," but female smokers still had to look like fashion models in ads. The Cosby Show gave African-American families a positive presence on television, but replicated ideals of white bourgeois respectability in the process. In some ways these early efforts by Hollywood and corporate America illustrated Hegel's model of self and other. In that famous dualism, difference manifests in an anxiety in which oppositional pairs internalize aspects of each other as they seek synthesis. In asymmetrical relationships, the dominant party frequently brings parts of the other into itself. In her essay "Eating the Other," bell hooks put it exactly this way:

> To seek an encounter with the Other, does not require that one relinquish forever one's mainstream positionality. When race and ethnicity become commodified as resources for pleasure, the culture of specific groups, as well as the bodies of individuals, can be seen as constituting an alternative playground where members of dominating races, genders, and sexual practices affirm their power.[63]

Hooks didn't mince words in naming "white supremacist capitalist patriarchy" as the driver of this commodification of otherness. Key to this formulation was the recognition of multiple simultaneous mechanisms working *together,* rather as independent variables. In this intersectional analysis gender and race were as intertwined as class and capitalism, inasmuch as desires, fantasies, aspirations, fears, and taboos all play out across multiple vectors. As in the Hegelian dialectic, the concept of otherness is rooted in conscious knowledge and unconscious longing—the Western yearning for a unified subjectivity always just beyond reach.

In many ways, this struggle for unity has undergirded the American experiment and continues to do so. Color blindness and gender bending can be seen as two attempts to reconcile historical categories of difference with idealized visions of a society in which such distinctions have disappeared or changed. But as this chapter has detailed, ideals have a tendency to be sloppy and power-laden, for better or worse. Intersectional analyses of race, sex, and gender provided important tools for understanding the limits of conventional identity politics, even as its focus on subjectivity limited the dimensionality of its critiques. Recognition of the imbricated character of identity formations was an important step in the emergent address of boundary blurring now made more apparent in neoliberal times. But the rascal of the self still lurked in the background. In the chapters that follow, I will begin to untangle some other strands in these webs of meaning and mattering, noting in particular the tricky task of following a moving target. In this work, movement and change indeed may have become the only constants.

Notes

1 Dennis Prager, "A Principal's Speech," *Jewish Journal* (July 2, 2013) http://www.jewishjournal.com/dennis_prager/article/a_principals_speech_to_high_school_students (accessed July 20, 2014).
2 "Civil Rights Act of 1964," U.S. National Archives, http://media.nara.gov/rediscovery/02233_2011_001_a.jpg (accessed July 22, 2014).
3 "Equal," Merriam-Webster.com (2014) http://www.merriam-webster.com/dictionary/equal (accessed Jan. 14, 2015).
4 Drew Desilver, "Americans Agree Inequality Has Grown, but Don't Agree on Why," Pew Research Center (April 28, 2014) http://www.pewresearch.org/fact-tank/2014/04/28/americans-agree-inequality-has-grown-but-dont-agree-on-why/ (accessed Jan. 3, 2015).
5 Mortimer F. Zuckerman, "Solving America's Inequality Problem," *U.S. News & World Report* (Mar. 28, 2014) http://www.usnews.com/opinion/articles/2014/03/28/america-has-regressed-in-income-inequality-and-social-mobility (accessed July 22, 2014).
6 "Labor Force Statistics from the Current Population Survey," U.S. Bureau of Labor Statistics (2014) http://www.bls.gov/cps/earnings.htm (accessed Feb. 1, 2015).
7 Fred Turner, "The Family of Man and the Politics of Attention in Cold War America," *Public Culture* 24, no. 1 (Winter 2012) http://publicculture.org/articles/view/24/1/the-family-of-man-and-the-politics-of-attention-in-cold-war-america (accessed July 22, 2014).
8 Roland Barthes, "The Great Family of Man," *Mythologies*, trans. Annette Lavers (New York: Farrar, Strauss & Giroux, 1972) p. 101.

9 L.A. Kaufman, "The Anti-Politics of Identity," *Socialist Review* 20, no. 1 (Jan.–Mar. 1990) pp. 67–80.
10 Ibid.
11 Judith Butler, *Bodies That Matter: On the Discursive Limits of Sex* (New York: Routledge, 1993).
12 Cornell West, *Race Matters* (New York: Vintage, 1994).
13 Michael Millner, "Post Post-Identity," *American Quarterly*, 57, no. 2 (June 2005) https://muse.jhu.edu/journals/american_quarterly/v057/57.2millner.pdf (accessed July 24, 2014)
14 "Racial Segregation," U.S. Census Bureau http://www.census.gov/hhes/www/housing/housing_patterns/pdf/ch5.pdf (accessed July 24, 2014).
15 "Statistical Overview of Women in the Workplace," *Catalyst* (Mar. 3, 2014) www.catalyst.org/knowledge/statistical-overview-women-workplace (accessed July 24, 2014).
16 Mark Hugo Lope and Ana Gonzalez-Barrera, "Women's College Enrollment Gains Leave Men Behind," Pew Research Center (Mar. 16, 2014) www.pewresearch.org/fact-tank/2014/03/06/womens-college-enrollment-gains-leave-men-behind/ (accessed July 24, 2014).
17 "Marriage Rate Declines to Historic Low, Study Finds," *Huffington Post* (July 22, 2013) http://www.huffingtonpost.com/2013/07/22/marriage-rate_n_3625222.html (accessed July 24, 2014).
18 Megan Gannon, "U.S. Marriage Rate Drops to New Low," *LiveScience* (July 13, 2013) http://www.livescience.com/38308-us-marriage-rate-new-low.html (accessed July 24, 2014).
19 Philip Schwaden and Christopher R.H. Gareau, "An Age-Period-Cohort Analysis of Political Tolerance in the United States," *Sociological Quarterly* 55 (2014) http://onlinelibrary.wiley.com/store/10.1111/tsq.12058/asset/tsq12058.pdf?v=1&t=hy0lua6q&s=1bae6fafc704cbb833747899a1054fc3f21f09ff (accessed July 24, 2014).
20 Karl Marx, *The German Ideology* (1845) https://www.marxists.org/archive/marx/works/1845/german-ideology/ch01a.htm (accessed July 25, 2014).
21 Michael Omi and Howard Winant, *Racial Formation in the United States: From the 1960s to the 1990s* (New York: Routledge, 1994).
22 "2010 Census Questionnaire," United States Census (2010) http://www.census.gov/history/www/through_the_decades/questionnaires/2010_overview.html (accessed Jan. 3, 2015).
23 Kenneth Prewitt, "Fix the Census' Archaic Racial Categories," *New York Times* (Aug. 21, 2013) http://www.nytimes.com/2013/08/22/opinion/fix-the-census-archaic-racial-categories.html?pagewanted=all&_r=0 (accessed Jan. 31, 2014).
24 Sara Danius and Stefan Jonsson, "An Interview with Gayatri Chakravorty Spivak," *Boundary 2*, 20, no. 2 (1993).
25 Peter Schmidt, "Supreme Court Upholds Bans on Racial Preferences in College Admissions," *Chronicle of Higher Education* (April 22, 2014) http://chronicle.com/article/Supreme-Court-Upholds-Bans-on/146145/ (accessed July 21, 2014).
26 Eric Kayne, "Census: White Majority in U.S. Gone by 2043," NBC News (June 13, 2013) http://usnews.nbcnews.com/_news/2013/06/13/18934111-census-white-majority-in-us-gone-by-2043?lite (accessed Jan. 15, 2015).
27 Vence Bonham, "Race," in *Talking Glossary of Genetic Terms,* National Human Genome Research Institute (n.d.) http://www.genome.gov/Glossary/index.cfm?id=171 (accessed Feb. 5, 2015).
28 Antonia Darder and Rodolfo D. Torres, *After Race: Racism and after Multiculturalism* (New York: NYU Press, 2004) p. 1.
29 All statistics in this paragraph from: Rakesh Kochhar, Richard Fry, Paul Taylor, "Wealth Gaps Rise to Record Highs between Whites, Blacks, Hispanics: Twenty-to-One," Pew Research Center (July 26, 2011) www.pewsocialtrends.org/2011/07/26/

wealth-gaps-rise-to-record-highs-between-whites-blacks-hispanics/ (accessed April 15, 2012).

30 David A. Love, "Racial Inequality in Education Hurts America's Global Competitiveness," The Progressive (Sept. 8, 2011) http://progressive.org/education_racial_inequality.html.

31 Robert Augros and George Stanciu, *The New Biology: Discovering the Wisdom of Nature* (Boulder, CO: Shambhala, 1987).

32 Ella Shohat and Robert Stam, *Unthinking Eurocentrism: Multiculturalism and the Media* (New York and London: Routledge, 1994) p. 109.

33 *Unthinking Eurocentrism*, p. 115.

34 Michael B. Katz, *The Undeserving Poor: America's Enduring Confrontation with Poverty* (New York and London: Oxford University Press, 1989).

35 "Dynamics of Economic Well-Being: Poverty 2009–2012," United States Census (2013) www.census.gov/hhes/www/poverty/publications/dynamics09_12/index.html (accessed Jan. 12, 2015).

36 Luce Irigaray, *This Sex Which Is Not One*, trans. Catherine Porter (Ithaca, NY: Cornell University Press, 1985).

37 Michel Foucault, *The History of Sexuality*, Vol. 1, trans. Robert Hurley (New York: Vintage Reissue, 1990).

38 Eliza Grey, "The Transgender Tipping Point," *Time Magazine* (June 9, 2014) http://time.com/135480/transgender-tipping-point/ (accessed June 14, 2014).

39 Brandon Griggs, "Facebook Goes beyond 'Male' and 'Female' with New Gender Options," CNN.com (Feb. 13, 2104) http://www.cnn.com/2014/02/13/tech/social-media/facebook-gender-custom/ (accessed July 26, 2014).

40 Jennifer Bendery, "Obama to Sign Executive Order Protecting Transgender Federal Employees," *Huffington Post* (June 30, 2014) http://www.huffingtonpost.com/2014/06/30/obama-lgbt-executive-order_n_5545663.html (accessed Jan. 2, 2015).

41 Andrew Solomon, *Far from the Tree: Parents, Children, and the Search for Identity* (New York: Scribner's, 2012) p. 660.

42 *Far from the Tree*, p. 599.

43 "CA Governor Brown Signs Historic Transgender Students Bill into Law," Transgender Law Center (Aug. 12, 2013) http://transgenderlawcenter.org/archives/8756 (accessed Jan. 22, 2015).

44 "It's Not Over," Privacy for All Students (Feb. 25, 2014) http://privacyforallstudents.com/news/ (accessed Feb. 1, 2015).

45 Janice G. Raymond, *The Transsexual Empire: The Making of the She-Male* (New York: Teachers College Press, 1994).

46 Janice. C Raymond, "Sappho by Surgery: The Transsexually Constructed Lesbian Feminist," in Susan Stryker and Stephen Whittle, eds, *The Transgender Studios Reader*, Vol. 1 (New York: Routledge, 2006) p. 131.

47 Sandy Stone, "The 'Empire' Strikes Back: A Posttranssexual Manifesto" (1993) http://pendientedemigracion.ucm.es/info/rqtr/biblioteca/Transexualidad/trans%20manifesto.pdf (accessed Aug. 2, 2014) p. 11.

48 "America's Shame: 40% of Homeless Youth are LGBT Youth," The Williams Institute (July 13, 2012) http://williamsinstitute.law.ucla.edu/press/americas-shame-40-of-homeless-youth-are-lgbt-kids/ (accessed July 24, 2014).

49 "Housing and Homelessness," National Center on Transgender Equality (2013) http://transequality.org/Issues/homelessness.html (accessed July 24, 2014).

50 "Suicide Attempts among Transgender and Gender Non-conforming Adults," Williams Institute (Jan. 2014) http://williamsinstitute.law.ucla.edu/wp-content/uploads/AFSP-Williams-Suicide-Report-Final.pdf (accessed July 24, 2014).

51 "Queer," Oxford Dictionaries (2014) http://www.oxforddictionaries.com/definition/english/queer (accessed Nov. 25, 2014).

52 Judith Butler, *Gender Trouble: Feminism and the Subversion of Identity* (New York: Routledge Classics, 2006).
53 José Esteban Muñoz. *Cruising Utopia: The Then and There of Queer Futurity* (New York and London: New York University Press, 2009) p. 1.
54 Agustín Fuentes, *Race, Monogamy, and Other Lies They Told You* (Berkeley: University of California Press, 2012) p. 186.
55 *Race, Monogamy, and Other Lies They Told You*, p. 188.
56 Frank Newpost, "In U.S. 77% Identify as Christian," Gallup Politics (Dec. 24, 2012) http://www.gallup.com/poll/159548/identify-christian.aspx (accessed Aug. 1, 2014).
57 "Marriage and Divorce," Centers for Disease Control and Prevention (2011) http://www.cdc.gov/nchs/fastats/marriage-divorce.htm (accessed July 27, 2014).
58 "Transgender People and Marriage: The Importance of Legal Planning," Human Rights Campaign (n.d.) http://www.hrc.org/resources/entry/transgender-people-and-marriage-the-importance-of-legal-planning (accessed May 5, 2015).
59 Jacques Lacan, *Seminar XI: The Four Fundamental Concepts of Psychoanalysis*. (New York and London: W.W. Norton and Co., 1978).
60 John Berger, *Ways of Seeing*, BBC (1972). See Mira Popova, "Ways of Seeing: John Berger's 1972 Critique of Consumer Culture," Brainpickings.org (n.d.) http://www.brainpickings.org/index.php/2012/09/28/ways-of-seeing-john-berger/ (accessed July 25, 2014).
61 Laura Mulvey, "Visual Pleasure and Narrative Pleasure," *Screen*, 16, no. 2 (1975) pp. 6–18.
62 Mary Anne Doane, *Femmes Fatales: Feminism, Film Theory, Psychoanalysis* (London and New York: Routledge, 1991).
63 bell hooks, "Eating the Other: Desire and Resistance," in bell hooks, *Black Looks: Race and Representation* (1992) http://lit.genius.com/Bell-hooks-eating-the-other-desire-and-resistance-annotated (accessed July 28, 2014).

7

NO BODY IS PERFECT

Disability in a Posthuman Age

Millions of Americans struggle with body image. It's hardly a secret that today's media-saturated culture is obsessed with superficial visions of thinness, beauty, and youth. But beneath such preoccupations lie deeper values and assumptions. Underlying popular images of attractiveness or unattractiveness are a host of other beliefs about the kinds of bodies (and people) worthy of desire and acceptance in U.S. society—with Victoria's Secret's controversial "Perfect Body" campaign representing just one recent example.[1] Even as the so-called beauty industry has been critiqued for creating narrow standards of desirability, its idealized images make powerful statements about healthiness, social utility, and worthiness for *belonging* or *not belonging in America.* While "Perfect Body" purported to offer garments that could accommodate "any" body, what really upset many consumers and triggered a massive online backlash was the company's perplexingly tone-deaf use of the term "perfect"—and the age-old fantasy that perfection was an achievable goal.[2]

Dreams of physical perfection have a very long history, dating back to the statuary of ancient gods and mythical figures. Commonly considered in aesthetic terms, such representations of "perfect" bodies also linked to early thinking about health and longevity. Certain kinds of images stirred imaginary yearnings for immortality by visualizing it in symbolic forms—heightened in potency by the shortness of life centuries ago. Today's media present a similar set of fantasy images, pitching youth, thinness, and health to a population that is aging, overweight, and often unwell. This chapter will focus on heath as the underlying "body image" problem now facing America. Beneath the nation's widely known preoccupations with fitness and wellness lies the same nagging uncertainty that has troubled humanity throughout time: that the body may fail at some point, and that eventually all bodies succumb to this inevitability. Beauty always has been the public face of this anxiety.

Nobody wants to think about any of this. As a result, contemporary culture immerses itself in symbolic ideals of bodily perfection—often sexualizing and commodifying them along the way. Nearly half a century ago, Ernest Becker pointed out the long-standing "denial" of bodily frailty in what he termed "immortality" projects, manifest in elaborate human fantasies, myths, or religious beliefs about escaping death or finding eternal life in the hereafter.[3] Perhaps the real reason America's Affordable Care Act caused such controversy was that it brought care of the body to the forefront of public debate as never before. Underlying partisan squabbles over this or that technicality of Obamacare was the nation's confrontation with its own fears.

The conversation was long overdue. While life has few certainties, one thing everyone can expect is a progressive experience with illness—in oneself or with loved ones. While occasional reminders of this find their way into the news, public discourse largely ignores the enormity of medical need within the U.S. population, not to mention ongoing disparities in care, and the unfortunate stigma that still attaches to certain conditions and disabilities. Contrary to what most Americans think, the U.S. has one of the least healthy populations among high-income nations. Compared to 17 such countries, Americans face the second-highest risk for dying from noncommunicable diseases and the fourth highest for infectious diseases.[4] According to a 2013 study on American mortality entitled *U.S. Health in International Perspective: Shorter Lives, Poorer Health*, the National Academy of Sciences (NAS) reported that the U.S. falls below such countries as Austria, Australia, Canada, Finland, France, Germany, Italy, and Japan in these categories. Even more troubling, the U.S. had the highest losses of life due to suicide and drug abuse. Many of these disturbing realities result from America's size and the complexity of its population, which create widespread disparities in medical and mental health needs and care.

According to current research, life expectancy in the U.S. is now roughly 78 years of age—although race, sex, income, and other factors come into play.[5] With infectious disease on the decline, 50 percent of Americans eventually will die from cancer or heart disease, in about equal proportions. Right now 27 percent of American adults are defined as "sick"—meaning they are subject to a serious illness, medical condition, or disability.[6] But this figure of 81 million people only accounts for the *really* sick people in the country. An additional 133 million Americans (half of all adults) live with at least one chronic illness, according the U.S. Centers for Disease Control and Prevention (CDC).[7] Such chronic ailments include hypertension (31 percent of the population), obesity (34 percent), arthritis (22 percent) high cholesterol (15 percent), diabetes (11 percent), and drug/alcohol addiction (7.4 percent).[8] Add to this data from the National Institute of Mental Health (NIMH) reporting that 26 percent of Americans (78 million) suffer from a diagnosable psychiatric condition, with depression and anxiety disorders topping the list. And this doesn't include the 14 percent of children (10 million) with developmental disabilities and the 12 percent of seniors (5.2 million) with Alzheimer's.[9]

One way of coming to terms with these statistics lies in what is called comorbidity—or multiple intersecting ailments. Occurrences of comorbidity can appear in anyone, although often frequency tends to increase with age. Hypertension and heart disease often occur together, for example. Comorbidities are especially familiar to psychiatry, where the relational character of mental and physical illness is increasingly a topic of discussion. The Robert Wood Johnson Foundation reports that 30 percent of people with chronic health problems also have mental health disorders, and 68 percent who have a psychiatric diagnosis also have a medical problem.[10] Such comorbidities increase from an average of 15 percent for people under 30 to over 80 percent for people in their 60s. Comorbidity is a topic of great concern in epidemiological terms alone, inasmuch as physical and mental health correlate to a broad range of issues in human well-being, from socioeconomic status and employment to relationships and life expectancy.

More than half of those with chronic health problems also have other conditions: diabetics with mobility difficulties; cancer patients who are clinically depressed; arthritics hooked on pain pills; and so on.[11] The numbers of such people are escalating as the baby boomer generation ages. Experts anticipate that these intersecting problems will claim 75 percent of lives and will cost the American economy a fortune, especially in end-of-life care.[12] None of this gets much news coverage. Illness and disease make for unphotogenic and unappealing fare in a culture suffused with images of health and happiness. Media invisibility is part of why health-care legislation took nearly half a century to become law, despite the fact that medical care is one commodity that everyone uses or will use at some point.

Americans' unrealistic faith in their own good health allows them to forget about health care until they need it. This is one reason that studies of public opinion on the Affordable Care Act show disparities between general and specific views. While 53 percent of Americans continue to disapprove of an overall federal health-care mandate, these same respondents overwhelmingly support particular provisions (care for pre-existing conditions, coverage for adult children, etc.).[13] Support is higher among health care users, as well as the previously uninsured. In this latter finding, disagreements about Obamacare replicates aspects of the makers-and-takers oppositions discussed earlier in this book—as illness and its costs are cast in parasitic terms, or linked to broader antigovernment sentiments.

Of course there is nothing new in the attachment of stigma to illness. Throughout human history the sick or disabled have been cast out by fearful communities, especially when ideology serves as an accelerant. The politics of Obamacare illustrate one in an endless set of examples of ways the body becomes a screen on which deeper values and opinions are projected or performed. In today's America, almost no one seems willing to admit to anything less than perfect health. And when the body isn't healthy, it tends to be seen as a machine in need of repair. According to CDC statistics, 81 percent of American adults see a physician at least once per year, with six in ten reporting themselves in relatively "good" condition.[14] Drugs are increasingly prescribed and used. Researchers from the Mayo Clinic have found that 70 percent of Americans regularly receive at least one prescription medication, with more than half of the adult population using two such drugs. Of this number, 20 percent use five or more prescriptions. "Often when people talk about health conditions they're talking about chronic conditions such as heart disease or diabetes," stated the Mayo Clinic report. Yet the second most frequent prescription was for antidepressants, and the third most common drugs were opioids.[15] An estimated $250 billion per year is spent on prescriptions, just about half of the amount spent on over-the-counter medications. In both practical and statistical terms, nonprescription drugs are used by everyone—mostly for mundane things like cold symptoms, headaches, or upset tummies. Then again, use of over-the-counter medications sometimes signals more serious conditions, including abuse of the drugs themselves. Americans buy five billion nonprescription products each year, with about seven million people using them to get high.[16] In one way or another, drugs and drug policies affect everyone—although they are only one part of the discussion about America's health.

In *Illness as Metaphor*, Susan Sontag wrote: "Everyone who is born holds dual citizenship, in the kingdom of the well and in the kingdom of the sick. Although we prefer to use only the good passport, sooner or later each of us is obliged, at least for a spell, to identify ourselves as citizens of that other place."[17] But no one seems willing to think about this inevitability. Quite on the contrary, as Sontag points out, deep-seated worries about illness and mortality drive many into denial, or worse still, into forms of reaction formation that vilify both sickness and the sick. This thinking maps well onto extant American attitudes that people's difficulties are their own business and often due to their own failings. Sontag detailed the weird displacements often used to externalize illness as something that is alien, rather than a natural process. Witness the prevalence of military metaphors of sickness as "attacks" on the body or secret "invasions" by foreign diseases. As with national defense, Sontag explains that Americans are expected to guard against such things with the defenses of proper nutrition and hypervigilance about health. The crux of Sontag's book was in its identification of the blame people cast on themselves for illness—the cruelest of ironies: "Illness is interpreted as, basically, a psychological event, and people are encouraged to believe they get sick because they (unconsciously) want to, and that they can cure themselves by the mobilization of will."[18]

The body is a prime determinant of one's sense of self. But the experience of the body fragments along many vectors. In the general education art courses I teach, students often find themselves taken aback when I discuss the "self-portrait" people create in their morning routines of composing their appearances. These behaviors have become so routinized that many people think little about the decisions they make. Yet as discussed in Chapter 6, most people internalize expectations of being observed and evaluated throughout the day, some more consciously than others, depending on their social position, gender, age, professional role, and degree of ability or disability. This often repressed preoccupation with appearance runs deep. From Freud's assertion of the "corporeal" nature of the ego, Lacan would add the notion of an "ideal" image that individuals invariably fail to achieve. People spend their lives negotiating this gap with varying degrees of success and self-satisfaction, inhabiting identities over which they exercise partial degrees of autonomy. In his 1959 book, *The Presentation of the Self in Everyday Life*, sociologist Erving Goffman likened this "performance" of identity to a form of conscious role-play he called "impression management."[19] This idea was later refined by Judith Butler to entail unconscious predispositions and habits of mind.[20] In both accounts the body contributes to the sense of self, at least partially so, since mind and body exist in a state of continual interaction. Here as elsewhere, simple dualisms of identity construction become frustrated—whether one is talking about body/mind, male/female, inside/outside, or able/disabled.

No Body Is Perfect

While America deludes itself with fantasies of good health, the country also stigmatizes illness. When this happens, worries about certain medical conditions often get translated into prejudices. Perhaps no theorist in the postwar period has been more influential than Michel Foucault in writing about this. While many have charted the course of Enlightenment reason in political terms, Foucault recognized the body as the lightning rod of human consciousness, especially as the body became a site of visual analysis. In *The Birth of the Clinic*, Foucault contemplated the relationship between visibility and invisibility in the eyes of physicians and patients—as a model of modern subjectivity itself.[21] Foucault took on the sticky business of objective reason itself, pointing out that as generally understood, the concept presents an epistemological trap—inasmuch as there can ever be such a thing as an external "reality" that can be independently analyzed. Foucault noted that from Plato onward, Western philosophy has wrestled with the dilemma of the mind's inability to escape its hidden biases. Hence, contradictions between objectivity and subjectivity had been contested for centuries. Initially, this confusing opposition found popular resolution through religious belief or magical thinking. By the 1500s, at least in Western culture, the objective/subjective disagreement got more heated as science (and scientifically inspired philosophy) began dispelling superstitions through documented "truths" about the physical world and the body. The primacy of the human mind in defining and governing the natural world (including the body) would push subjectivity aside somewhat, although consensus on this was far from absolute.

Foucault applied these ideas in describing the rise of the physician as a figure of cultural authority and the growing social prominence of medicalized thinking. In elemental terms, the doctor replaced God as the arbiter of life and death, hence assuming a mystical role. "Are not doctors the priests of the body?" Foucault once asked.[22] At the same time, Foucault pointed to the primacy of vision in empowering the physician. "The eye becomes the depository and source of clarity," not only in comprehending disease, but also in making all sorts of other judgments about people, Foucault wrote.[23] Medical knowledge afforded a kind of "seeing" into the nature of a patient, a specialized capacity for insight lacking in the nonprofessional. Foucault is famous for reading worrisome implications in all of this. Hence he inferred that the physician's "medical gaze" tended to focus on visible symptoms at the expense of the patient's larger identity, with the body becoming simply the signifier of illness or its absence. This process of abstraction enabled the reduction of people to constellations of symptoms—hence facilitating labeling, stigmatization, and discrimination. In this new regime, patients were turned into "objects of instruction" or mere tools for medical teaching. Pain and suffering were thus rendered as spectacle and display, with anyone refusing to participate guilty of "ingratitude for partaking in social benefits without contributing back to the common good."[24]

The newly professionalized class of doctors intersected with the industrial rise of institutions to produce institutions for the "care" of the sick—hence "the birth of the clinic." Long-standing public anxieties about disease fed a policing of health and a segregation of the sick in the clinics. And physical health wasn't the only worry, as societies came to quarantine other classes of "undesirables" on the basis of mental illness (in the asylum) or moral bankruptcy (in the prison). To Foucault, the medical gaze derived from a larger system of control enabled by vision, observation, and surveillance: "A gaze that does not distinguish it from, but rather re-absorbs it into, all the other social ills to be eliminated; a gaze that isolates it, with a view to circumscribing its natural truth."[25] Ultimately, Foucault would conclude that the 18th century's privileging of "seeing" brought about a change in the character of knowledge itself. As it transformed social institutions and licensed new forms of power, there emerged "a language without words, possessing an entirely new syntax, to be formed: a language that did not owe its truth to speech but to the gaze alone."[26] It's important to point out that these were not merely abstract matters or historical conjecture to Foucault. Critiques of institutional discrimination were being voiced everywhere as Foucault was writing in the 1960s through the 1980s. Foucault also had discussed the classification of homosexuality as a "sickness" and its ongoing assessment by many as a pathology or perversion. Foucault himself contracted HIV at a time when public fears of HIV-AIDS as an inexplicable plague ran rampant, along with calls to isolate and legislate against those infected.

Foucault's views on medicine expanded on principles outlined by Friedrich Nietzsche, whose work influenced many of Foucault's contemporaries at the Parisian École Normale Supérieure. Nietzsche had critiqued many orthodoxies within Western culture—and often took issue with popular schools of thought of his time. In some accounts, Nietzsche's radicalism cleared the way for philosophers who followed him. Nietzsche had been among the first thinkers to name "the great health" as a dominant social ideal on a par with religion. Perhaps not surprisingly, Nietzsche also critiqued then-ascendant Darwinist thinking premised on survivalism and the primacy of capitalistic "competition" as a natural instinct—contending that conservation and stasis were what people were really seeking.

To these ends, Nietzsche said that medicalized reason really couldn't provide the psychic comfort and security that people sought. It would bring only existential emptiness. In famously stating that "God is dead," Nietzsche was not articulating a secularist polemic, but rather stating this very problem. He noted the ways that past cultures had used belief systems—like Christianity and Judaism—to specific ends, often changing these ideologies to suit their purposes. To Nietzsche, the demise of a deity did not provide the objective clarity of a lifted spiritual veil, but its opposite—a revelation of the contingent character of knowledge. He saw a progression of different sets of values throughout time and from culture to culture, concluding that the process of "esteeming" tended to be a constant in many societies. Nietzsche's insight lay in recognizing both the relativism of objective meaning and the ways that ideas of scientific "truth" had been subjectively exploited by the powerful. These ideas laid the groundwork for what would later be called "perspectivism," an important precursor to deconstruction.

Foucault and others took Nietzsche's principles of contingency into new dimensions. Among these was Foucault's dissertation sponsor, Georges Canguilhem, a philosopher who became a physician during World War II, and whose comprehensive analyses of normativity were discussed in Chapter 3. Canguilhem was intrigued by Nietzsche's suspicion of health as an ascendant, yet unexamined, cultural value. Engaging biology and medicine on their own terms, Canguilhem observed the vast diversity in the health status of individuals—and the many occurrences of various ailments over people's lifetimes. Canguilhem brought both critical precision and evidence-based inquiry to an analysis of genetics, epidemiology, and public health policy.[27] Bringing a then-uncommon interdisciplinarity to his analysis, Canguilhem would not only argue that perceptions of physical well-being were subjective, but that health and disease varied tremendously in empirical terms. Reversing conventional wisdom on these matters, Canguilhem pointed out that for most people, having some form of illness was just as likely as having none. Canguilhem asserted that being sick (that is, being diagnosed with a "pathology") was simply a part of being alive, and generally more common than being completely "well." Rather than viewing pathology as axiomatically part of a death trajectory, he would conclude that "In a sense one could say that continual perfect health is abnormal."[28]

The relativistic character of Canguilhem's thinking is significant, as he advocated against singular definitions of good health that would frame those outside as victims awaiting the salvation of a physician. For one thing, Canguilhem's own experience as a doctor had shown him that many maladies simply disappear on their own. And he also was troubled by the pervasiveness of sickness-related stigma, largely propagated by a medical profession that defined patients as ignorant sufferers incapable of understanding what ailed them. Countering the "invalidity of the sick man's judgment concerning the reality of his own illness," he argued for what he called a "pedagogy of healing" in which the physician and patient would become dialogical partners.[29] At the same time, he cautioned against romantic attachments to "the healing power of nature" that had come in and out of fashion ever since the times of Hippocrates. Repeatedly in his writing, Canguilhem addressed the problematic tendency in science and in human thought to seize upon solitary answers, foreclose discussion, and yield to apparent certainty. Concluding one essay, Canguilhem cited F. Scott Fitzgerald's famous line that "The test of a first-rate intelligence is the ability to hold two opposed ideas in the mind and still retain the ability to function."[30]

Constructions of Ableism

Needless to say, the issue of normality has taken a beating in recent decades—and with good reason. Whether the topic is the norms presented in mainstream media, those offered by politicians pandering for votes, or simple appeals to a universal "humanity"—the persistence of normativity appears everywhere. Earlier, I made the simple observation that, in fact, no one is normal. Or as discussed above, if there is anything one can say is common to the species, it is the infinite variability, mutation, and difference people see in each other and experience in their daily lives. In his landmark 1999 book, *The Trouble with Normal*, Michael Warner stated that "It does not seem possible to think of oneself as normal without thinking of some other kind of person as pathological."[31] In other words, normality itself is a kind of hallucination generated by statistics and an unexamined "common sense." It's used to sell products and reassure people they have a place in normal society. But also it promotes fear and an undeniable tendency toward intolerance.

Public awareness of disability has risen in the past decade, and with it a growing academic discipline to study public attitudes toward ability and disability. Changing demographics are part of the reason for this, driven by an aging U.S. population. It might surprise many to learn that people with disabilities now constitute one of the largest minorities in America, making up 15 percent of the country—or roughly 45 million individuals. Of these, one in eight is born with a disability, and about one-third of the disabled are over the age of 65. Half of all children put up for adoption have disabilities. There are 550 million people disabled worldwide.[32] Given these numbers, a rising disability rights movement now works for such goals as architectural accessibility, employment fairness, safety, and protection from abuse and neglect. Colleges and universities have seen the emergence of the field of "disability studies," generating new courses of study, conferences, journals, and widely selling anthologies like *The Disabilities Studies Reader*, now in its fourth edition.[33]

Majorities tend to define the world in their own terms, expecting outsiders to conform to their views. In the U.S. this impulse is especially strong, manifest in assimilationist traditions and a strong attachment to social norms. Many Americans like to think of themselves as ruggedly independent and ready for any challenge. In a nation defined by competition, failure to succeed often is attributed to individual defect rather than systemic error. Taken as an ensemble, these values have led to skewed thinking about variances in mental and physical abilities—as well as human differences of other kinds within the population. A society heavily premised on presumptions of full functionality "constructs disability" as a way to categorize deviations from the norm. Within this construction of disability, apparent deviations become labeled as deficits in need of correction, with responsibility falling to the disabled person to adapt or otherwise "fit in." The fallacy of this thinking is obvious, as disability activists have pointed out for decades. An "impairment" (like dyslexia or the paralysis of a leg) only becomes a problem if circumstances make it one. With the appropriate accommodation, a disabled person can found a company like Apple or become president of the United States.

The social construction of disability is now widely accepted—meaning, in other words, that "disability" largely is defined by the group creating the label. All kinds of characteristics can make one less able in someone else's eyes. Difficulties with walking, seeing, or hearing are what most people call to mind when they think of disabilities, as well as impairments of intellect. But in a broader sense, impairments of almost any kind can be constructed as disabilities. One can think of poverty, illiteracy, old age, extreme youth, or obesity as disabling conditions, for example. Or consider the disabling potential of shyness, anxiety, religious zeal, greed, obsession with power—and the list of potentially disabling conditions gets longer. Certainly for much of American history, being a woman or a person of color rendered one less than fully able in many ways. Being a lesbian or a gay man was considered a disability, quite literally, in the 19th century, and in psychiatric circles much later than that.

The social construction model also draws attention to the unrecognized workings of majorities in establishing mainstream values or what many people regard as "common sense." This nearly always takes place in the implicit referencing of an opposite. Disability activist Rob McRuer has discussed the way this operates across various forms of difference, noting, for example, that the unacknowledged meaning of "able-bodied is to be 'free from physical disability,' just as to be heterosexual is to be 'the opposite of homosexual.'"[34] More perniciously, such categorization often functions to render its own workings invisible. As McRuer puts it, "Compulsory able-bodiedness functions by covering over, with the appearance of choice, a system in which there actually is no choice."[35] McRuer theorizes this as an aspect of a neoliberal obsession, endlessly deferred, for an idealized unified subjectivity. In the U.S. one sees this obsession in nostalgic calls for a return to a mythical "traditional America." In this light, ideals such as able-bodiedness, heterosexuality, and even capitalism itself—all reflect yearnings to achieve a "healthy" body, a "natural" sexuality, or an "efficient" system in a world where differences and contingencies will always preclude that possibility.

Another way of connecting stigmatized identities lies in the common logic that locates people *Elsewhere in America*. Whether through medical reason premised on erasing illness in favor of an idealized "good health," or more politicized efforts to segregate, deport, or otherwise discourage non-hegemonic groups—the over-arching scheme is an opposition to difference. Discriminatory attitudes about race, gender, and sexuality all find common origin in 18th- and 19th-century "scientific" studies of human beings. A key conceptual strategy connecting all of these was the philosophy of "eugenics," broadly writ. While the concept is no longer acceptable in polite circles, the rationale for eugenics lives on in attitudes bent on eliminating less-than-perfect people and their problematic behaviors.

Owing to the legacies of 19th-century panics over public health and the rise of policies to protect fearful populations, prejudicial attitudes toward the disabled and otherwise different reached well into recent history, often propped up by government policies and laws. Even in today's purportedly enlightened era, it's worth noting that laws aimed at racial purity in the U.S. weren't eradicated until 2001, when Alabama finally overturned its antimiscegenation statute. The persistence of such laws, despite rulings by the Supreme Court decades earlier, reveals deep-seated antipathy over the "breeding" of inferior types of people. Writings by eugenicist Charles Davenport continued to be read into the 1900s, as he wrote about the risks of immigrants presumed to render the U.S population darker in skin tone, smaller in size, and more prone "to crimes of larceny, assault, murder, rape, and sexual morality."[36] Reports in the press frequently drew upon the terminology of germ theory in speaking of "contagions," "infections," and "plague spots" in impoverished communities. To Herbert Spencer, such sickness was a necessary part of social evolution:

> Having, by unwise institutions, brought into existence large numbers who are unadapted to the requirements of social life, and are consequently sources of misery to themselves and others, we cannot repress and gradually diminish this body of relatively worthless people without inflicting much pain. Evil has been done and the penalty must be paid. Cure can only come through affliction.[37]

Linkages between disability and mental illness found expression in popular beliefs in a "depraved class," the characteristics of which were both genetic and contagious. Poverty, crime, and other social "defects" were all seen as potentially solvable by eugenic means. And this wasn't a fringe movement. Subscribers to eugenics included such widely respected figures as Neville Chamberlain, Winston Churchill, H.G. Wells, John Maynard Keynes, and Theodore Roosevelt, among others. While the United States could never muster the political will to enact sweeping federal eugenics legislation, the same cannot be said for Europe. During the 1930s bills were introduced in the British Parliament to regulate the disabled, and by the end of that decade Nazi genocide had begun in Germany. While remembered largely for the Holocaust, Germany's eugenics programs (with research funded in part by America's John. D. Rockefeller Foundation) was responsible for the forced sterilization or execution of an additional 675,000 people deemed "unworthy of life" through the rulings Germany's Heredity Health Courts. The unworthy included the disabled, homosexuals, the mentally ill, political dissidents, and habitual criminals, among others.

Lest one assume that such thinking is simply a relic of history, the state of California practiced forced sterilizations of the "enfeebled" and "depraved" through state prisons and psychiatric institutions through 1963. Eugenics debates reignited in the 1980s and 1990s in reaction to civil rights and equal opportunity claims from disenfranchised groups. The 1994 publication *The Bell Curve: Intelligence and Class Structure in American Life* by Richard J. Herrnstein and Charles Murray set off controversies in its purportedly "scientific" findings that intelligence was largely an inherited trait, that people's successes in life were tied to their native intelligence, that American society was growing increasing stratified by intelligence-related inbreeding, and that this inbreeding could be tracked racially.[38] Remnants of this thinking persist to this day in right-wing assertions that programs like "No Child Left Behind" do little to correct genetic "deficiencies" in minority populations.[39]

Eugenics-oriented thinking persists in other significant ways, especially in terms of disability. The central premise of the Human Genome Project was the possibility and advisability of perfecting the living organism by eliminating birth defects and other anomalies before they happen. It is difficult to argue with such thinking from the perspective of parents wanting only the best for the new lives they are creating, not to mention public policy concerns over the expense of accommodating those disabled from birth. Prenatal screening allows expectant parents to know, for example, if an embryo is likely to be born with Down syndrome, Tay-Sachs disease, or spina bifida. The American College of Obstetrics and Gynecology now recommends that all pregnant women, especially those over the age of 35, receive "fetal chromosome testing," and if indicated, additional prenatal diagnostic analysis.[40] Groups like the National Down Syndrome Council argue that such testing protocols carry the implicit assumption of terminating pregnancies, thus reducing the unborn child to a condition rather than an identity as a person. Beyond this, many people living with congenital abnormalities contend that they lead independent and productive lives, possessing unique knowledge and the capacity for empathy that "normal" people lack. These disparate views and agendas on genetic testing are complicated further by factors like socioeconomic status, access to screening, and personal belief systems that make the option of elective abortion highly variable.[41]

Other controversies begin at birth—with new surgeries allowing immediate remediation of heart conditions, breathing difficulties, or intestinal problems.

Hearing-impaired newborns now routinely receive treatment with cochlear implants, sometimes known as "bionic ears." Research shows that the earlier a cochlear implant is administered the more likely it is that a child will grow up with a near "normal" sense of hearing. But what about the "patient's" choice in the matter? At first glance this might seem like a silly question. Why would anyone want less than full hearing? In the 1950s approximately 80 percent of deaf children went to special residential schools and learned to use American Sign Language (ASL). Now that number stands at 14 percent.[42] Despite this, ASL remains the third most widely used language in the United States among deaf and hearing people.[43] Segments of the deaf community argue that the rapidly diminishing number of deaf people using ASL signals the loss of a unique language and vibrant deaf culture. For example, deaf activists Tom Humphries and Carol Padden assert that ASL is part of a specific culture for deaf people, which allows them to see themselves as "not so much adapting to the present, but inheriting the past. It allows them to think of themselves not as unfinished hearing people but as cultural and linguistic beings in a collective world with one another."[44] Very few non-deaf people know that ASL contains many words, expressions, and shades of meaning for which there is no spoken equivalent. In the interplay between hand gestures and facial expressions, some have compared ASL to a combination of speech and dance.

The flip side of this argument is the stigma and outright discrimination that deaf people face. In the U.S., over 34 million people have significant hearing loss, of whom six million are profoundly deaf.[45] In 2013 a dozen deaf Starbucks customers sued the chain for discrimination at two New York City locations, where they were refused service, mocked by employees, and ejected from the sites. Over a period of months, Starbucks employees had refused to fill hand-written orders handed to them by deaf customers and called police to break up a "Deaf Coffee Chat" meeting at which customers were discussing deaf culture.[46] Employment discrimination against the deaf is common, despite federal laws against it. In 2013 Toys "R" Us was charged in a high-profile case by the Equal Employment Opportunity Commission (EEOC) after failing to provide interpreters and otherwise discriminating against a deaf job applicant. But Toys "R" Us is hardly alone.

Employment discrimination remains a serious problem for disabled people of all kinds. Last year nearly one-quarter of EEOC hiring bias and workplace discrimination claims came from disabled workers. The enormity of this number (23,397 cases) is noteworthy, when one considers that the EEOC also manages workplace unfairness based on race, sex, disability, national origin, religion, and age. And contrary to what most people would assume, employment discrimination against the disabled is on the rise—increasing by 25 percent from 1997 to 2014.[47] Employment discrimination partly explains why people with disabilities are disproportionately poor. The U.S. Census Bureau reported in 2010 that nearly 28 percent of people with disabilities aged between 18 and 64 lived in poverty, compared to a 12.5 percent rate in the general population. Comparably lower earnings are found at almost every income level. The median income for men with disabilities stood at $41,500, compared to $48,000 for those without. Women with disabilities had incomes of just under $32,000, while the national average was $37,000.[48]

Bias against the disabled extends to other areas of life. In another rising statistic, disability-related fair housing complaints now account for 44 percent of cases.[49] While great attention has been given to accommodating the disabled in public schools, anyone trying to obtain assistance elsewhere knows how challenging this can be. Given the enormous regional inequities in the way America funds social programs, services for the disabled are unevenly distributed. In areas where school resources are scarce, those wanting accommodations often must resort to lawsuits. The situation is worst in the prison system, especially as it affects people with mental health challenges. According to the Bureau of Justice Statistics, 56 percent of state prisoners and 45 percent of federal prisoners have a diagnosable psychiatric illness.[50] Rates of serious mental illness such as schizophrenia, bipolar disorder, and major depression among the incarcerated are two to four times higher than among members of the general public. The current professional consensus is that as many as 20 percent of prisoners have psychiatric disorders that manifest in functional disabilities, with an additional 15 to 20 percent requiring some form of psychiatric intervention during their time behind bars.

"Though individual differences can be isolating, the fact of difference is nearly universal," Andrew Solomon wrote in *Far from the Tree: Parents, Families and the Search for Identity*.[51] Appearing in 2012, *Far from the Tree* was a landmark volume in the exploration of disabled identities—compiled by Solomon during a decade of interviews with family members of children considered "different" (far from the tree) in some way. Reading the book, one is struck by the exceptional character of certain conditions and the quite varied responses of families to them. Introducing the book, Solomon wrote of what he termed "horizontal identities," defined as conditions shared with a peer group but not with one's family of origin. The factual significance of the 962-page *Far from the Tree* lay in its detailed accounts of families adjusting to autism, deafness, dwarfism, Down syndrome, schizophrenia, among other conditions. Solomon documented the relentless passion with which families struggle (often imperfectly) with what many initially do not understand. While Solomon does not varnish over the difficulties, ambivalent feelings, and occasional regrets of his subjects, he finds a remarkable resiliency in the families of the disabled. Sometimes this resilience emerges from support communities, but just as often families simply figure it out on their own.

Faced with the intractable fact of "abnormality," the families Solomon studied come to terms with their new reality. "Ability is a tyranny of the majority," Solomon observes: "If most people could flap their arms and fly, the inability to do so would be a disability. If most people were geniuses, those of moderate intelligence would be disastrously disadvantaged. There is no ontological truth enshrined in what we think of as good health; it is merely convention."[52] In summarizing his findings, Solomon finds that disability is not predictive of happiness or unhappiness in either children or parents. Nine out of ten parents of disabled children feel they get along as well as other families. Over 80 percent say that their disabled child had made the family closer. Perhaps more significantly, a full 100 percent report "increased compassion for others" attributed to their direct experience with disability.[53] Solomon concludes on a philosophical note in suggesting that for able-bodied people disability is unmapped territory:

> Nirvana occurs when you not only look forward to rapture but also gaze back into the times of anguish and find in them the seeds of your joy. You may not have felt that happiness at the time, but in retrospect it is incontrovertible. For some parents of children with horizontal identities, acceptance reaches its apogee when parents conclude that while they supposed that they were pinioned by a great and catastrophic loss of hope, they were in fact falling in love with someone they didn't yet know enough to want.[54]

The Dismodern Condition

The Disability Pride movement sometimes is dated to its first parade in Chicago in 2004. Today such events take place around the world each July. Partly a celebration of an identity, Disability Pride also works to maintain public visibility for the differently abled, as well as to push for suitable legislation in the face of persistent opposition. As with environmental protection laws, a key sticking point with the 1990s Americans with Disabilities Act (ADA) has been the economics of living up to its provisions. While public agencies have little choice in the matter, the situation is quite different in the private sector. Many people don't know that lawsuits by well-known corporations like United Airlines and Toyota Motors have succeeded in weakening the ADA in the workplace. At issue have been definitions of "disabled," broadly defined by the ADA as "a physical or mental impairment that substantially limits a major life activity."[55] In 1999 the U.S. Supreme Court invalidated portions of the ADA based on corporate assertions that an employee was not disabled if the impairment could be corrected by mitigating measures. This negatively affected the availability of accommodations for growing segments of the population—those with diabetes, for example. Owing to the efforts of disability activists and with support from the Obama administration, an enhanced version of the ADA—the Americans with Disabilities Act Amendments Act (ADAAA)—came into law in 2009. The revised legislation specifically defines impairments *regardless* of ameliorative measures. The ADAAA also broadened the law's definitional categories of disability to include difficulties with such "major life activities" as "caring for oneself, performing manual tasks, seeing, hearing, eating, sleeping, walking, standing, lifting, bending, speaking, breathing, learning, reading, concentrating, thinking, communicating, and working."[56]

The ADAAA story says much about the social construction of disability and points to an ongoing dilemma in the ways that disabled people are able to identify as such. Keep in mind that many disabilities are not immediately visible, and hence can require active efforts for accommodation. For people with both visible and invisible disabilities, this can mean making a choice and accepting the consequence of such disclosure. In some instances, articulation of a disabled identity can be the pathway to accommodation, legal rights, and more options in life. But in other cases, the same choice can foreclose opportunities and protections. One need only consider the histories of the women's movement, racial equality, and LGBT rights to see that legislation does not always change deeply entrenched attitudes. Referencing such histories, Solomon writes that

> Defective is an adjective that has long been deemed too freighted for liberal discourse, but the medical terms that have supplanted it—*illness, syndrome, condition*—can be almost equally pejorative in their discrete way. We often use *illness* to disparage a way of being and *identity* to validate that same way of being. This is a false dichotomy.[57]

Hence, one sees various efforts to locate common ground among forms of difference—which has proven difficult. Continuities and discontinuities among traits of identity have been elaborated and contested in recent years, pointing to the risks over drawing equivalences. At the same time, recognition has risen of the multiplicity of human identity—for example, of age, gender, race, income, sexual orientation, occupation, geography, education level, and so on.

Many of the thinkers discussed in this chapter—Foucault, Canguilhem, Warner, and Solomon, among many others—have wrestled with society's tendency to marginalize, segregate, stigmatize, romanticize, or celebrate human variation. Common among many constructions of stigmatized identities is the parallel construction of their invisible opposites. Part of what makes social norms so confounding is not only that they exclude almost everyone, but that their naming of aberrant "others" shifts attention elsewhere. In 1988 feminist Peggy McIntosh named this problem in her essay "Unpacking the Knapsack of White Privilege," famously stating that "White privilege is like an invisible weightless knapsack of special provisions, maps, passports, codebooks, visas, clothes, tools and blank checks."[58] McIntosh's point was not so much to highlight the existence of privilege per se, as it was to differentiate between benefits gained by struggle and benefits accrued without effort.

Evolving understandings of the constructed character of disability (and ability) lay behind three overlapping phases of disability movement politics, as recounted by veteran activist Lennard Davis. The first phase occurred in the 1970s and 1980s, manifest in resistance to then-largely unchallenged bodily standards. During this period activism often took the form of direct opposition to discriminatory practices, inequities, and negative stereotypes. These resistant impulses fostered groups promoting policy changes and positive images (Disability Pride, Deaf Power, etc.). Many activists of the time would say that the disabled wanted to be recognized on their own terms—not to be corrected, altered, or repaired in ways dictated by the able-bodied. By the 1990s a second phase of activism began to build upon the first, but with a new self-consciousness about differences within the disability movement. Rather than a monolithic identity, the experience of disability could vary according to age, gender, ethnicity, and social class—and these often affected each other. This intersectional awareness caused a certain destabilization of the very idea of disability as a discrete identity category.[59] In a somewhat controversial move, in 2002 Davis proposed a third phase of disability activism that embraced this very contingency. Davis called this phase "dismodernism"—a concept defined by an overarching continuity between ability and disability. With the recognition that to different degrees most people will fall prey to health challenges at some point in their lives, to Davis disability has become the "new normal." As he wrote:

> This new way of thinking, which I'm calling dismodernism, rests on the operative notion that postmodernism is still based on a humanistic model. Politics have been directed toward making all identities under a model of the rights of the dominant, often white, male, "normal," subject. In a dismodernist mode, the ideal is not a hypostatization of the normal (that is, dominant) subject, but aims to create a new category based on the partial, incomplete subject whose realization is not autonomy and independence but dependency an interdependence. This is a very different notion from subjectivity organized around wounded identity; rather all humans are seen as wounded. Wounds are not the result of oppression, but rather the other way around.[60]

Davis was not alone is such assertions, with theorists like Jasbir Puar stating that "illness and disability can be posited as the most common identity because we will all belong someday," Robert McRuer concurring that "It is clear to me that we are haunted by the disability to come," and David Mitchell suggesting that a view of disability "not as exception, but the basis upon which a decent and just social order is founded."[61] Niko von Glasow's film *Nobody's Perfect* (2011) succinctly named the reality that anyone can be regarded as disabled by someone else—that the designation of disabled is always situational and contingent on the cultural interpretation of "impairment." Moreover, disability is already a functional norm in many poor and working class communities.

Davis's dismodernism initially resonated in pointing out the breadth of a hitherto largely disregarded social category, arriving as "disabilities studies" was ascending as an area of interest in academic research and publishing. A degree of controversy over dismodernism would ensue in the years following Davis's initial presentation of the concept. In part, this had to do with Davis's philosophical critiques of what he had termed "oppression" and "pride" phases of prior disability activism. The resulting debates reflected broadly on discussions about identity, ontology, and politics. While acknowledging the value of oppression and pride models in struggles against discrimination and prejudice, dismodernism said that these strategies also self-limit when they foreclose broader visions of commonality. Both models are premised on a fragmented view of society for purposes of collective interest or political purpose. At issue is the fact that individuals carry numerous identities in the highly complicated cauldron of selfhood—not infrequently resulting in contradictions and confusions due to the exclusive terms in which identity politics so often is framed. The result has been that "identity" as commonly deployed has become highly unstable, and fraught with antagonism, while also losing a certain practical utility. In recognition of the commonality of bodily complaints (from inside and outside) and limitations of oppression/pride models of identity, Davis's dismodernism would turn the eugenic model of stigma on its head. In other words, Davis suggests a societal acknowledgment of bodily deficits, diseases, and differences—call them disabilities, if you will—and a movement toward a limited form of post-identity. This doesn't mean that difference or identities disappear, but rather, that they simply become a common currency. As he puts it, rather than repressing the ubiquity of disability, or rather than trying to hide these qualities from view, "we should amplify that quality to distinguish it from other identity groups that have … reached the limits of their projects."[62]

Critics of dismodernism quickly pointed out how closely it resembled a universalizing humanism, especially as it seemed to overlook issues of race, gender, and sexual orientation. Or worse still, it might generalize a specific set of human attributes into an overarching social condition. Davis would later respond that dismodernism had never suggested such absolutism (as to suggest that "We are all disabled," for example), but instead had argued for inclusion of disability in discussions of identity and subjectivity.[63] Davis would argue that, in fact, "Those who pushed identity had very strong Enlightenment notions of the universal and the individual. The universal subject of postmodernism may be perceived and narrative-resistant but that subject was still whole, independent, unified, self-making, and capable."[64] In such terms the entire argument about "difference" changes. After all, the issue of difference always implies the underlying question of "different from what?" An immediate self/other dichotomy underlies the concept. This dichotomy is reinforced by oppositional paradigms, as many difference theorists have pointed out.

If the ontology of opposition is rooted in the "self"—call it "individuality," "ego," or "self-image"—then this atomized view of personhood is behind much of the competition, conflict, and fear that permeates social consciousness, drives consumer culture, and animates political division. Davis doesn't mince words here. The concept of subjectivity autonomy manifest in the "reason" of individual citizens undergirds the histories of democracy and constitutional government. So there's no easy casting away of such ideals in legislative terms or "official" methodologies. To Davis, the:

> dismodern era ushers in the concept that difference is what all of us have in common. That identity is not fixed but malleable. That technology is not separate but part of the body. That dependence, not individual independence, is the rule. There is no single clockmaker who made the uniform clock of the human body.[65]

One issue remains, however. And it is here that Davis credits thinking in what has been termed "post-positivist realism" of the kind discussed by such scholars as Linda Alcoff, Paula Moya, and Michael Hames-Garcia.[66] This work has sought to stake out a compromise between premises of materialism and constructionism. This is especially apropos considering the phenomenology of disability, which often exceeds the constraints of language in experiential terms. While material impairment can be socially constructed as "disability," the lived experience of disability (immobility, cognitive difficulty, physical pain) is non-discursive. This seems to be the major difference within the "difference" that is disability.

Whether one has a legally defined disability, a chronic health problem, a psychiatric diagnosis, an injury, or a transient condition, it is clear that the ideal of perfect health is as elusive as that of absolute beauty. Why then do so many people live in a state of denial about their own frailties and why is prejudice against the sick and disabled so prevalent? Worries about one's mortality certainly provide part of the answer—at least on a superficial level. And there is plenty of historical evidence and contemporary anecdote to support the notion that people want to stay away from disability, contagion, or reminders of their effects. But what about the idea that everyone is in this together, that they might help and support each other? There seems to be a disconnection between the notions of illness as normality and illness as pathology. A veteran physician recently observed to me that everyone lives in a state of being "temporarily abled," although few see themselves as such. Rather than seeing this in universal terms, it seems fair nevertheless to accent the issue of interdependence. This returns the discussion to belonging, non-belonging, and the stakes implicit in the matter. At some point in most people's lives, circumstance or the aging process will render them unwell and vulnerable. Deep in their hearts they all know this, but often pretend that it isn't so. If personal experiences of disability and illness have an upside, it lies in the recognition that wellness is a mercurial commodity—here one day and perhaps gone the next—like life itself.

The Posthuman Body

The story of Olympic athlete Aimee Mullins is now well known, although her name is less familiar than the technological advances that brought her to prominence. Mullins was born without fibula bones and had both legs amputated below the knee when she was one year old. With conventional prosthetic legs she learned to walk, ride a bike, and swim like other kids. But things changed radically when Mullins received a set of experimental carbon fiber Cheetah legs in 1996. She became the first amputee to compete in NCAA sports, setting world records as a sprinter. Technical innovation had turned a disabled woman into a superwoman—so much so that nondisabled athletes protested Mullins's unfair advantage. Similar controversies arose more recently involving the prosthetically enabled runner Oscar Pretorius, dubbed the "Blade Runner" in the 2012 Olympics. For her part, Mullins rose to the occasion and became a national voice for the disability community, asserting the ubiquity of assistive technology in the daily lives of the abled and disabled. "A cell phone is a prosthetic device," Mullins once told an interviewer.[67] More than a decade since she made history as an athlete, Mullins is now an international advocate for disabled people around the world. She sits on the President's Council to Empower Women and Girls through Sports. But through it all, she remains an activist.

Mullins actively reminds her audiences that the wide variety of prosthetics available to her remain unavailable in underdeveloped nations, where economic disadvantages and stigma drive many families to hide or abandon disabled children. Named by *People Magazine* as "One of the 50 Most Beautiful People in the World," Mullins speaks out against conventional beauty norms.[68] Asked how she responds when people now say to her "You know, I have to tell you, you just don't look disabled," Mullins responded, "I know that they're confused, and they're telling me this because they know I'm missing both legs from the shin down, but they're presented with this package of a highly capable young woman. This has happened all over the world. I tell them it's interesting because I don't feel disabled." Mullins subscribes to the notion that people are not born disabled. "It's society that disables an individual by not investing in enough creativity to allow for someone to show us the quality that makes them rare and valuable and capable."[69] Mullins asserts that terms like "abled" and "disabled" are no longer adequate to describe physical differences. "Our language just hasn't caught up with the opportunities technology is providing for people," Mullins has stated. "I feel like today there's a different sense, so much more widespread, of people feeling like they don't want to be negated, they don't want to be marginalized, they want to make their own definitions of their identity. They want to identify themselves."[70] While Mullins's story is exceptional, her message about subjectivity resonates for many people living with an embodied difference.

At issue here is the perennial question of defining what it means to be fully human—an exercise historically prone to separating people into desirable and undesirable categories. *How We Became Posthuman* by N. Katherine Hayles appeared a few years after Aimee Mullins's initial notoriety in the late 1990s as a technologically enhanced person with a disability. Keep in mind that this period also marked the rise of the Internet as a social phenomenon, replete with new concepts of virtual identity and electronic communities. As hard as this is to imagine, at the dawn of the new millennium Google was still in its test phase and Facebook did not yet exist. At this moment in history, Hayles argued that new technologies had disrupted the ideal of a self that is separated from the world around it. Rather than autonomous "humanist" subjects, Hayles proposed that all people now function as cybernetic creatures to the extent that their existences are mediated by some form of external intervention.

While technology always has transformed human capacity, Hayles argued that computers, the Internet, and bioscience have accelerated this subjective transformation. Like Mullins, Hayles advocated new definitions of this "posthuman" way of being, untethered to obsolete notions of "natural" (or normal) life: "The posthuman view thinks of the body as the original prosthesis we all learn to manipulate, so that extending or replacing the body with other prostheses becomes a continuation of a process that began before we were born."[71] Underlying this proposal is the more radical principle that the body itself is but the "material instantiation" of a posthuman informational pattern and that what people call "consciousness" is a similarly mutable by-product of the informational matrix. The philosophical and political consequences of this are manifold. For one thing, the contingent character of bodies and consciousness implies an interrelatedness and interdependence among people. People are not only "helped" by technology, but also by other humans, creatures, and the environment.

The posthuman as postulated by Hayles is stridently opposed to notions of owning one's freedom—or one's body for that matter. The principle of exceeding the limitations of what it is to be "human" per se, has been central to the arguments of many, who, for one reason or another, have found themselves outside such definitions, especially as such terrain has shifted and changed from place to place and over time. Slavery, genocide, and the eugenics movements were all premised on changing definitions of what constituted a full human being. While these views may seem hopelessly ignorant and anachronistic today, questions of "humanness" continue to provoke debate in such areas as fetal viability, abortion, brain death, Alzheimer's disease, and severe intellectual disability. Well known in these debates is the ethicist Peter Singer, who has argued that in "practical" terms human life itself does not equate with what he terms "personhood." Citing the U.S. Supreme Court's 1973 *Row v. Wade* decision, for example, Singer contends that in historical terms under U.S. and English common law "the unborn have never been recognized … as persons in the whole sense."[72] What's gotten Singer into trouble is his assertion that "rationality, autonomy, and self-consciousness" are what really defines personhood—and that these attributes should be weighed in difficult life-and-death situations.[73] Anyone who has watched a loved one suffer through the end stages of life knows the difficult mixed emotions of such personhood questions, as Singer himself experienced with his mother. But what of the profoundly intellectually disabled child? Or the yet-unborn fetus diagnosed with a severe lifelong impairment? This is where the interests of the "person," caregivers, and society at large begin to get murky.

In recent years so-called wrongful life suits have been filed against physicians by parents seeking compensation for the care of severely disabled children. French courts sided with the complainants in several of these cases, until disability activists successfully argued that such litigation should not be permitted. In the U.S., anyone can sue anyone else for just about anything, although no successful wrongful life suit has been brought since the 1990s. This hasn't stopped opportunistic attorney groups such as Becker Law in Cleveland, Ohio, which points out that 25 U.S. states still will entertain these cases. Winning over $85 million in such suits, Becker explains that "These lawsuits are usually filed following the birth of a child with holoprosencephaly, cystic fibrosis, Down syndrome, or spina bifida," adding that it is the physician's responsibility to advise parents about whether or not to complete pregnancies where such outcomes are likely.[74] A recent case was successfully brought in New York State, which argued on behalf of the mother, claiming that she had been denied the information to make an informed decision about her pregnancy. One common approach among attorneys these days is to repackage the wrongful life cases as obstetric malpractices suits, based on technical errors in prenatal care or deliveries. Beverly Hills attorney Bruce Fagel advertises that he has collected over $1 billion in such "birth injury" or wrongful death suits.[75] While no one would discount the importance of safeguarding families against negligent providers, critics argue that wrongful birth litigation implicitly promotes the idea that people with significant disabilities shouldn't exist at all, and that it promotes a eugenics-based approach to abortion.

All of this is indicative of what has been termed the "designer baby" phenomenon. In an age of sophisticated genetic counseling, prenatal screening, sonograms, and amniocentesis, it is more possible than ever before for parents to actively choose the kind of baby they want to produce. At the other end of the continuum from birth injury complainants are parents who value certain disabilities as a unique expression of humanity. Anecdotal evidence abounds of deaf couples or those with dwarfism who would like to raise children who resemble them at some level. Indeed, the central premise of Solomon's *Far from the Tree* was the question of how families adapt to children who are different from themselves, whether the children arrive via birth, adoption, or other means. A survey of 200 American clinics offering preimplantation genetic diagnosis (PGP), a procedure that has been available for 20 years, recently reported a 3 percent rate of parents selecting in favor of an embryo with a disability.[76] Children have always been an emotional lightning rod in American society, often exploited in the public imagination to trigger adult anxieties, aspirations, and projections about anticipated futures. The iconic Jerry Lewis Muscular Dystrophy (MD) Telethon, which ran on television each Labor Day weekend for over 40 years, saw its last broadcast with Lewis as host in 2009, amid rising sentiment within the MD community that Lewis was "exploiting his 'kids,' portraying them as pitiable victims who just need a big charity to take care of or cure them."[77] Lewis's work may well have brought unprecedented attention to a condition otherwise off the radar of most Americans. But the question of whether Lewis did more damage than good reveals the fault lines between subjectivity and objectivity in disability, especially as it pertains to the many varied ways that disability is constructed in the minds of the abled population. In many ways, the controversies over the MD telethon have less to do with the blurry line between empathy and pity than they do with representation and power.

This chapter's discussions of ability, disability, and posthuman futures all impinge on a very old idea, but one of extreme potency: *interdependence*. Rather than perpetually viewing life as a contest, rather than valuing individual achievement and accumulation as the ultimate goal, perhaps people's collective habitation of the world should drive the agenda. The simple reality that citizens are both social creatures and individual beings needs to be kept in balance at a time when so many pressures seem to be pushing people apart. Easy as this is to say, the psychic shift to interdependence is very difficult to achieve in practice. Everywhere one is measured, quantified, and pitted against others—in school, the workplace, the housing market, the search for companionship, and so on. Davis took a risk in positing dismodernism as a unifying super-identity, and was criticized narrowly and widely for the apparent privileging of disability in his model. Some noted the inattention to other forms of difference in dismodernism, for example, as well as the implicit humanism in a vision that would include "everyone" in universal terms. With these cautions in mind, others have stepped forward, however, reiterating the premise of connection in a time of social dislocation. Jim Ferris wrote that "Disability culture, which values interdependence over the illusion of independence, privileges not a uniform perspective but the validity and value of a wide range of ways of moving through the world—and the varied perspectives those different experiences engender."[78]

As the above discussion has detailed, despite decades of critique of disability as a cultural construction, long-standing biases persist in a nation in which nondisabled people hold disproportionate authority. This is hardly a neutral issue when definitions of health, happiness, and human worth remain narrowly proscribed. But day-to-day materiality should never be forgotten. One can theorize about the social construction of disability, as well as resistance to it, all one wants. But at the end of the day there is actual experience and genuine impairment. Whether experienced as physical discomfort, difficulty in functioning, material inequity, or the consequence of stigma, this fundamental phenomenon often serves to distinguish disability from other identities. This is not to privilege one body over another in terms of access to what is "real." But it does suggest important differences in knowledge about the meaning of abled and disabled bodies, and all of the many variations that lie outside this imaginary dichotomy.[79] Almost any characteristic can be regarded as an identity or a disability. But by virtue of history and habit, many find difficulty with this dual perspective. With the conviction to do so, it is possible to discover that while individual differences can be solitary, the fact of difference is something that everyone shares.

Notes

1 Nina Bahadur, "Victoria's Secret 'Perfect Body' Campaign Changes Slogan after Backlash," *Huffington Post* (Nov. 6, 2014) http://www.huffingtonpost.com/2014/11/06/victorias-secret-perfect-body-campaign_n_6115728.html (accessed Jan. 18, 2015).
2 See "The Dove New York for Real Beauty," Dove: Social Mission (2104) http://www.dove.us/Social-Mission/campaign-for-real-beauty.aspx (accessed July 1, 2014); David Grinner, "5 Reasons Why Some Critics Are Hating Dove's Real Beauty Sketches Video," *AdWeek* (April 19, 2013) http://www.adweek.com/adfreak/5-reasons-why-some-critics-are-hating-doves-real-beauty-sketches-video-148772 (accessed July 1, 2014).
3 Ernest Becker, *The Denial of Death* (New York: Simon & Schuster, 1974).
4 National Academy of Sciences, *U.S. Health in International Perspective: Shorter Lives, Poorer Health*, (2013) pp. 26–27, http://obssr.od.nih.gov/pdf/IOM%20Report.pdf (accessed Jan. 13, 2015).
5 According to U.S. Census figures, a "white" woman will outlive a "black" man by a decade. See "Life Expectance by Sex, Age, and Race" *2012 Statistical Abstract*, U.S. Census (n.d.) http://www.census.gov/compendia/statab/cats/births_deaths_marriages_divorces/life_expectancy.html (accessed July 29, 2013).
6 "Sick in America," NPR/Robert Wood Johnson Foundation/Harvard School of Public Health (May 2012) p. 2, http://www.npr.org/documents/2012/may/poll/summary.pdf (accessed July 29, 2013).
7 "Chronic Diseases," U.S. Centers for Disease Control and Prevention (2010) http://www.cdc.gov/chronicdisease/resources/publications/aag/chronic.htm (accessed Feb. 6, 2015).
8 "U.S. Health Statistics: Health in America, by the Numbers," *Huffington Post*, http://www.huffingtonpost.com/2011/02/22/us-health-statistics-_n_826171.html#s243767&title=Heart_Disease (accessed May 22, 2015); "Drug Facts; Treatment Statistics," NIH (2011) http://www.drugabuse.gov/publications/drugfacts/treatment-statistics (accessed Apr. 2, 2015).
9 "Developmental Disabilities Increasing in the U.S.," U.S. Centers for Disease Control and Prevention (accessed July 30, 2013) http://www.cdc.gov/features/dsdev_disabilities/; "Alzheimer's Facts and Figures," Alzheimer's Organization (n.d.) http://www.alz.org/alzheimers_disease_facts_and_figures.asp" (accessed July 29, 2013).
10 "The Synthesis Project," Policy Brief #21, Robert Wood Johnson Foundation (Feb. 2011) http://www.rwjf.org/content/dam/farm/reports/issue_briefs/2011/rwjf69438.
11 James H. Thrall, "Prevalence and Costs of Chronic Disease in a Health Care System Structured for Treatment of Acute Illness," *Radiology* (2005) http://radiology.rsna.org/content/235/1/9.full (accessed July 1, 2014).
12 Ibid.
13 "Looking beyond Opinion Polling on the Affordable Care Act," Health Policy Center of the Urban Institute (Feb. 26, 2014) http://hrms.urban.org/briefs/aca-opinions.html (accessed Jan. 10, 2015).
14 "Summary Health Statistics for US Adults, National Health Interview Survey, 2011," U.S. Centers for Disease Control and Prevention (Dec. 2012) http://www.cdc.gov/nchs/data/series/sr_10/sr10_256.pdf (accessed July 30, 2013).
15 "Nearly 7 in 10 Americans Take Prescription Drugs," Mayo Clinic (June 19, 2013) http://www.mayoclinic.org/news2013-rst/7543.html (accessed July 29, 2013).
16 "Fact Sheet: The Use of Over-the-Counter Medicines," http://www.bemedwise.org/press_room/sep_2003_fact_otc.pdf (accessed July 30, 2013).
17 Susan Sontag, *Illness as Metaphor* (New York: Vintage, 1977) p. 3.
18 *Illness as Metaphor*, p. 35.
19 Erving Goffman, *The Presentation of the Self in Everyday Life* (New York: Doubleday, 1959).

20 Judith Butler, *Bodies That Matter: On the Discursive Limits of "Sex"* (London and New York: Routledge, 1993).
21 Michel Foucault, *The Birth of the Clinic*, trans. A.M. Sheridan Smith (New York: Vintage, 1963).
22 *The Birth of the Clinic*, p. 22.
23 *The Birth of the Clinic*, p. xiii.
24 *The Birth of the Clinic*, p. 84.
25 *The Birth of the Clinic*, p. 43.
26 *The Birth of the Clinic*, p. 69.
27 Georges Canguilhem, *Normal and the Pathological* (1966), trans. Carolyn R. Fawcett (New York: Zone Books: 1989).
28 *Normal and the Pathological*, p. 137.
29 *Normal and the Pathological*, p. 91.
30 Georges Canguilhem, *Writings of Medicine,* trans. Todd Meyers and Stefano Geroulanos (New York: Fordham, 2012) p. 66.
31 Michael Warner, *The Trouble with Normal: Sex, Politics, and the Ethics of Queer Life* (Cambridge, MA: Harvard University Press, 2000).
32 Statistics in this section from Andrew Solomon, *Far from the Tree: Parents, Children, and the Search for Identity* (New York: Scribner, 2012) p. 23.
33 Lennard J. Davis, "The End of Identity Politics: On Disability as an Unstable Category," *The Disabilities Studies Reader*, 4th ed. (New York: Routledge, 2013).
34 Robert McRuer, *Crip Theory: Cultural Signs of Queerness and Disability* (New York: New York University Press, 2006) p. 8.
35 *Crip Theory*, p. 9.
36 Charles Davenport, as cited in *The Disabilities Studies Reader*, p. 7.
37 Herbert Spencer, *The Principles of Ethics*, Vol. 1 (New York: Appleton, 1904) p. 93.
38 Richard J. Herrnstein and Charles Murray, *The Bell Curve: Intelligence and Class Structure in American Life* (New York: Free Press, 1994).
39 Dennis Carlson, "Tales of Future Past: The Living Legacy of Eugenics in American Education," *Journal of the American Association for the Advancement of Curriculum Studies*, 5 (Feb. 2009) http://www2.uwstout.edu/content/jaaacs/Vol5/Eugenics_Carlson.htm (accessed Jan. 9, 2015).
40 "Routine Testing in Pregnancy," American College of Obstetricians and Gynecologists (2007) http://www.acog.org/~/media/For%20Patients/faq133.pdf (accessed Feb. 3, 2015).
41 Carol Bishop Mills and Elina Erzikova, "Prenatal Testing, Disability, and Termination: An Examination of Newspaper Framing," *Disabilities Studies Quarterly*, 32, no 3.
42 *Far from the Tree*, p. 55.
43 "American Sign Language," National Institute on Deafness and Other Communication Disorders (NIDCD) www.nidcd.nih.gov/health/hearing/pages/asl.aspx (accessed July 1, 2014).
44 *Far from the Tree*, p. 56.
45 "Quick Statistics," National Institute on Deafness and Other Communication Disorders (NIDCD) http://www.nidcd.nih.gov/health/statistics/pages/quick.aspx (accessed Jan. 20, 2015).
46 Geetika Rudra, "Customers Sue Starbucks for Discrimination," *ABC News* (July 17, 2013) http://abcnews.go.com/Business/deaf-customers-sue-starbucks-discrimination/story?id=19679652.
47 "Charge Statistics FY 1997 through FY 2012," *EEOC*, http://www.eeoc.gov/eeoc/statistics/enforcement/charges.cfm (accessed Mar. 24, 2015).
48 Shaun Heasley, "More than 1 in 4 with Disabilities Living in Poverty," *DisabilityScoop* (Sept. 14, 2011) http://www.disabilityscoop.com/2011/09/14/more-1-in-4-poverty/13952/ (accessed Jan 23, 2012).

49 "Disability Rights in Housing," U.S. Department of Housing and Urban Development (2014) http://portal.hud.gov/hudportal/HUD?src=/program_offices/fair_housing_equal_opp/disabilities/inhousing (accessed Jan. 18, 2015).
50 "Mental Illness, Human Rights, and US Prisons," *Human Rights Watch* (Sept. 22, 2009) http://www.hrw.org/news/2009/09/22/mental-illness-human-rights-and-us-prisons.
51 Andrew Solomon, "Son," from *Far from the Tree*, Internet reference, http://www.farfromthetree.com/son (accessed Aug. 4, 2013).
52 *Far from the Tree*, p. 29.
53 *Far from the Tree*, p. 24.
54 *Far from the Tree*, p. 47.
55 See ADA.gov (Dec. 1, 2014) http://www.ada.gov/ (accessed Dec. 1, 2014).
56 "The Americans with Disabilities Act Amendments Act of 2008," EEOC (2008) http://www.eeoc.gov/laws/statutes/adaaa_info.cfm (accessed Jan. 12, 2015).
57 *Far from the Tree*, p. 5.
58 Peggy McIntosh, "Unpacking the Knapsack of White Privilege," http://www.nymbp.org/reference/WhitePrivilege.pdf (accessed Aug. 4, 2013).
59 "The End of Identity Politics," p. 263.
60 "The End of Identity Politics," p. 275.
61 Jasbir K. Puar, "The Cost of Getting Better: Ability and Disability," in *The Disability Studies Reader*, p. 182; McRuer, *Crip Theory*, p. 207; David Mitchell, as cited in "The Cost of Getting Better," p. 179.
62 "The End of Identity Politics," p. 273.
63 Lennard J. Davis, *The End of Normal: Identity in a Biocultural Era* (Ann Arbor: University of Michigan Press, 2013) p. 20.
64 Ibid.
65 Ibid.
66 Robert Young, "Postpositivist Realism and the Return of the Same: The Rational Subject and Post(post)modern Liberalism," *Clogic* (2002) http://clogic.eserver.org/2002/young.html (accessed Oct. 21, 2015).
67 Richard Galant, "You Just Don't Look Disabled," *CNN News* (March 9, 2010) http://www.cnn.com/2010/OPINION/03/09/mullins.beyond.disability/ (accessed Jan. 23, 2015).
68 "Biography," *AimeeMullins.com*, http://www.aimeemullins.com/about.php (accessed Aug. 11, 2103).
69 In "You Just Don't Look Disabled."
70 Ibid.
71 N. Katherine Hayles, *How We Became Posthuman: Virtual Bodies in Cybernetics, Literature, and Informatics* (Chicago, IL: University of Chicago Press, 1999) p. 3.
72 *Roe v. Wade,* Legal Information Institute: Cornell University Law School (1973) http://www.law.cornell.edu/supremecourt/text/410/113 (accessed Jan. 3, 2015).
73 Peter Singer, *Practical Ethics* (New York: Cambridge University Press, 1993) p. 192.
74 Michael F. Becker, "Pursuing a Birth Injury Medical Malpractice Case" (June 14, 2014) http://www.birthinjuryjustice.org/legal-options/ (accessed July 1, 2014).
75 "Medical Malpractice Is All We Do," Dr. Bruce G. Fagel & Associates (n.d.) http://www.fagellaw.com/About_Us/Dr_Bruce_Fagel/ (accessed Feb. 4, 2015).
76 *Far from the Tree*, p. 681.
77 Eddie Deezen, "A Brief History of the Jerry Lewis Telethon" (2011) http://mentalfloss.com/article/12397/brief-history-jerry-lewis-telethon (accessed July 1, 2014).
78 Jim Ferris, "Keeping the Knives Sharp," *Beauty Is a Verb* (El Paso: Cinco Puntos Press, 2011) p. 91.
79 See Tom Siebers, *Disability Theory* (Ann Arbor: University of Michigan Press, 2008) p. 81.

8

ON THE SPECTRUM

America's Mental Health Disorder

As I began to write these words I could hear the television in the next room, with coverage of Robin Williams's death playing on all the news channels. At that moment a bit of controversy had been stirring over the way that the coroner released the grisly details of the comedian's suicide. But most of the coverage focused on what a funny guy Williams had been—and the tragedy of his passing. A few stories briefly mentioned that Williams had been depressed in recent months, and that for years he had had problems with alcohol and drugs. But little explicit discussion about Williams's underlying depression made it into the press that day, although allusions to his state of mind infused the details of the coverage—implying an inevitability to his ultimate demise.[1]

The way America first discussed the Robin Williams tragedy spoke volumes about the way popular culture foreshortens discussions of mental health, reducing pervasive life-threatening illnesses to metaphor and clichés—or choosing not to talk about such difficult questions at all.

In those initial hours after Williams's death, little discussion of his psychiatric diagnosis would occur—not the way a celebrity's long battle with cancer or history of heart attacks would be detailed. One heard no thoughtful discussion of Williams's treatment protocols or the course of his mental illness, as it progressively worsened over the course of his lifetime.[2]

Within the general population, white men of Williams's age are the most likely group to take their own lives. Major depression, mood disorders, and substance abuse problems lead the list of causes named by the National Center for Suicide Prevention.[3] "Suicide now kills twice as many people as homicides, yet receives only a fraction of the attention," said Dr. Thomas Insel, Director of the NIMH, adding that the "suicide rate has been stubbornly high for decades, with more than 39,000 annual deaths—a number that has been growing even as deaths from other causes have fallen."[4]

On the day of Robin Williams's death, 22 American veterans also committed suicide, although none of those deaths made it into the headlines. Most Americans remain unaware that more soldiers have died by their own hands than in combat during the past decade, and that this terrible phenomenon is accelerating.[5] While those in military service make up 1 percent of the American population, they now account for 20 percent of suicides. Mental health experts say that one of the greatest challenges in the veteran suicide epidemic is that those suffering don't seek treatment. Conditioned on a military culture stressing fitness for duty, the stigma of mental illness also plays a big role—compounded even further by American values of self-reliance and the widespread belief that asking for "help" is a form of weakness.

As the sensation of Williams's death began to subside, voices from the mental health community began to be heard, with many expressing hope that Williams's death might foster a renewed conversation about mental illness in the U.S. All told, over 26 percent of Americans (78 million) suffer from a diagnosable psychiatric condition, with depression and anxiety disorders the most common diagnoses.[6] From the UCLA Semel Institute, Dr. Andrew Leuchter quantified the issue further in saying that:

> 15 million people in this country at any given time suffer from depression, but only about a quarter of these people seek and receive adequate diagnosis and treatment. One of the biggest reasons for this is that people do not want to be labeled as having a mental disorder.[7]

American Psychiatric Association (APA) president Dr. Paul Summergrad observed, "It's very important that we stop seeing these illnesses as faults and blames, and see them as what they are, medical conditions, genetic conditions, brain disorders which require appropriate diagnosis, treatment, care and support."[8]

But let's face it, psychiatric conditions are among the most stigmatized identities of our time, with public worries over mental illness heightened in recent years following several highly publicized mass shootings by young men purportedly living with undertreated problems. In a nation with the most powerful military in the world, Americans continue to worry about a creeping madness in the people around them. As a society, the U.S. finds itself profoundly divided on the issue of mental illness, amid a myriad of conflicting attitudes and laws. Despite the enormous variance in the population and broad prevalence of transient or chronic mental health problems, psychiatric diagnoses remain shrouded in mystery, misunderstanding, and fear. Many states have laws in place that restrict the rights of people with mental illness in such fundamental exercises of citizenship as voting, public service, jury duty, or holding elected office. At the federal level, concerns about the privacy of people's mental health histories drove the passage of the 1996 Health Insurance Portability and Accountability Act (HIPAA), which was partly implemented to protect employee medical records from the eyes of employers.[9] HIPAA regulations remain a vital firewall against unwarranted job discrimination based on matters like chronic illness, pregnancy, or a mental health diagnosis.

Without a doubt, histories of mental health treatment constitute many people's most closely guarded secrets—and with good reasons. Even as celebrities and public figures have publicized their mental health conditions, an atmosphere of social stigma persists, often with very real consequences. While federal legislation prohibits discrimination on the basis of physical and mental disability, such laws only apply to companies receiving public money. The *New York Times* recently detailed a study revealing that as many as 50 percent of workers reporting mental health conditions to their employers found themselves passed over for promotions, treated differently, or bullied in the workplace.[10] Disclosures about psychiatric diagnoses can end a career, foreclose advancement, or even preclude employment in the first place—even though such discrimination is legally prohibited. This has meant that people working in certain professions decline to speak or write about the matter—especially in fields like education and health care. One academic working in medicine recently wrote of the risks of "writing a book that so explicitly describes my own attacks of mania" for fear of losing licensing and hospital privileges.[11] These worries run through every profession.

And things get worse when drug or alcohol dependence accompanies a mental health condition, which it does an astonishing 43 percent of the time. According to the U.S. Substance Abuse and Mental Health Services Administration (SAMSA), nine million Americans have co-occurring mental health and substance abuse problems.[12] Certainly none of these people want to talk about their problems in any way. "Few academics have dared to engage this topic," writes Dennis Schepp, "to protect their reputations, if not their income."[13] But all of this silence doesn't begin to address the subjective experience of the individual with the mental health condition. Lost in the discourse of privacy, nondisclosure, and professional standing is the phenomenology of the person with the disease. Being differently "abled" may sound reassuringly politically correct, but it doesn't change the reality that the label makes life harder for some than for others. America's relentless emphasis on happiness and achievement tells everyone that being anything less that "okay" is unacceptable and unmentionable.

This is the double burden of disability, the naked fact that in addition to a person's individual struggle with illness, society often adds the cruelty of negative assessment or even moral judgment. Consider for a moment what it is like to endure the darkness and frequently fatal neurochemical condition of depression, while also knowing that one must hide this from nearly everyone in one's life. A handful of writers have spoken about these matters, the most prominent of whom are Kay Redfield Jamison and Andrew Solomon. Jamison's *An Unquiet Mind* and Solomon's *Noonday Demon* systematically detail what life is like with bipolar disorder and chronic depression, respectively.[14] Jamison likened the struggle of hiding her condition to living in a perpetual "war against myself."[15] Of course there has been no shortage of famous writers and artists with similar diagnoses, many of whom died from their illnesses: Ernest Hemingway, Georgia O'Keefe, Pablo Picasso, Sylvia Plath, Jackson Pollack, Anne Sexton, Paul Simon, to name but a few.

In recent years, the issue of diagnosis has moved from an area of academic interest to a broad-based public concern, as issues of privacy have come into conflict with worries over public safety. Further complicating matters, Obamacare's universalization of health insurance has opened a floodgate of concerns over disclosures of medical histories to insurance providers. But privacy and disclosure aren't the only worries. At issue as well are the very questions of normality and pathology discussed above. If conceptions of illness and abnormality are contingent on groups assigning such labels, the relative meaning of mental "health" becomes even more unstable. Who decides whether a person is "sick" or "well"? By what standards? From the professional point of view, such questions are complicated further by the transient character of some psychiatric conditions. Grief over the loss of a loved one will often trigger a depressive episode in an otherwise "healthy" individual, an episode that will probably subside with therapy or simply the passage of time. Yet chronic depression can be a progressive illness that only worsens with age, and if untreated can completely incapacitate someone.

Media representations of mental illness don't help matters, as they extend Western culture's long-standing fascination with "madness" as a signifier of everything from artistic genius to monstrous criminality. In his book, *Seeing Madness: Insanity, Media, and Visual Culture*, W.J.T. Mitchell discussed the historical othering of the mentally ill in literature and film, from *Hamlet* and *The Brothers Karamazov* to *Psycho* (1960) and *Shutter Island* (2010). Mitchell hones in on the age-old question of visibility, observing that "madness and insanity do not have any intrinsic, essential nature, but are products of knowledge/power formulations—elaborate strata of discursive statements and visible institutions and spaces, accessible to an archeology of the seeable and sayable."[16] Regrettably, this means that most movies still pathologize mental illness in the interest of spectacle, as in horror and crime genres of the *Silence of the Lambs* (1991) variety. But Mitchell also notes a growing trend toward institutional critique, famously launched with *One Flew Over the Cuckoo's Nest* (1975). Mitchell notes an emerging movement to "reverse the psychiatric gaze" in foregrounding the subjective experience of the mental patient. In Mitchell's exegesis, key dichotomies stand out in popular formulations of madness/sanity and doctor/patient as stable and impermeable oppositions. Neither of these binaries squares well with increasingly nuanced diagnostic principles in the fields of psychiatry or treatment protocols that bring patients and therapists together as collaborators.

In 2013 the APA released the fifth edition of its *Diagnostic and Statistical Manual of Psychiatric Disorders (DSM-5)*, which replaced the *DSM-IV* that had been in use since 2004. The new *DSM* created a storm of controversy in reorganizing the ways that it defined conditions meriting or requiring treatment, changes that upset groups newly included, excluded, or simply recategorized. At issue is the murkiness of psychiatry itself, which derives diagnoses from both medical and behavioral evidence. In the discipline's nomenclature, diagnosis hinges on both "*symptoms,* a person's subjective report of an abnormality, and *signs*, objective findings of abnormality."[17] These two approaches have been converging in recent years with the rising influence of neurobiology, imaging technology, and the growing recognition that many disorders can be empirically documented by looking at the brain. At the same time, psychiatrists continue to be trained to base their treatments on symptoms in the patient's actions or verbalizations. And this latter methodology remains important. Critics of the *DSM-5* argue that it didn't go far enough in recognizing the biochemical bases of mental illness, and that it mostly reshuffled its categories. But this reshuffling had one major theme. Across a wide swath of diagnoses, the *DSM-5* eliminated usage of the terms *disease* and *illness* in favor of the more general term *disorder.* This was done to forestall the rising tide of empiricism and to recognize the interplay of biological, social, cultural, and psychological factors involved in mental health. And the list of disorders is a long one, literally categorizing hundreds of conditions and sub-conditions. Even an abbreviated listing of *DSM-5* disorders is bewildering, including, as it does, such disorders as anxiety, depression, stress, mania, panic, delusion, obsession, anorexia, hypochondria, narcolepsy, agoraphobia, and psychosis, among scores of others.

Keep in mind that many of these disorders intersect with or cause each other. Given these nuances, another change in more recent versions of the *DSM* was to place conditions on "spectra" rather than simple black-and-white descriptions. This reflects the views of many patients and doctors that conditions can be weak or strong, transient or ongoing. The consensus on the spectrum concept is reflected in a recent book entitled *Better than Normal: What Makes You Different Can Make You Exceptional*, which argues that *all people* have *all elements* of the *DSM* categories present in their minds, but the amounts of these qualities simply differ.[18] The stated goal of the *DSM-5* was to "harmonize" extant approaches. As one APA guidebook to the *DSM-5* put it, "By their nature, psychiatric signs and symptoms often exist in the borderlands between what is normal and what is pathological."[19] Another not-so-widely discussed goal of the compromise was to make the *DSM* relevant to its field. A couple of psychiatrist friends confessed to me that they hadn't actually *read* the *DSM* for years and that many colleagues use the manual only to look up diagnostic definitions for insurance claims. The practical orientation of the *DSM-5* led to charges that the book had been watered down by the hundreds of authors, commentators, and committees that had influenced its creation, with some critics arguing that it was "unscientific" or even "unsafe."[20] Others added that brain science, while promising, simply hasn't reached the threshold of practicality or accuracy necessary to supplant in-person examination.

Stigma and Discrimination

"The more I become immersed in the study of stigma attached to mental illness, the more it astonishes me that any such phenomenon should exist at all," writes Robert Lundin, a member of the Chicago Consortium for Stigma Research. "I believe that serious and persistent mental illnesses, like the one I live with, are clearly and inexorably no-fault phenomena that fully warrant being treated with the same gentleness and respect as multiple sclerosis, testicular cancer or sickle-cell anemia."[21] Here Lundin names a central problem in the social construction of mental illness: the misunderstanding of conditions affecting the mind as somehow different from other biological illness. The misrecognition renders mental illness prone to the judgmental attributions discussed by Susan Sontag in her 1973 book *Illness as Metaphor*. To Sontag, contemporary society reverses ancient views of sickness as a reflection of the inner self. In this new view, the inner self is seen as actively causing sickness—through smoking, overeating, addictive behavior, and bad habits: "The romantic idea that disease expresses the character is invariably extended to exert that the character causes the disease—because it is not expressed itself. Passion moves inward, striking within the deepest cellular recesses."[22] But as before, the sick person is to blame for the illness.

Such sentiments are especially vindictive when a mentally ill person commits a crime. Understandably perhaps, clinical terms like "mental illness" quickly acquire malevolent meanings in the public mind—even though the mentally ill statistically are no more prone to criminality than anyone else. Sometimes this semiotic slippage causes public panic over commonplace disorders. Consider the case of Adam Lanza, the young man who in 2013 shot 26 children and adults at the Sandy Hook Elementary School in Newtown, Connecticut. While mental health analysts speculate that an acute psychotic episode prompted his violence, Lanza never had been diagnosed with a serious mental illness. As reporters scrambled for a story, much was made of Lanza's childhood symptoms of Asperger's syndrome, a form of high-functioning autism. The repeated mention of this disorder in news coverage triggered wrong-headed fears nationally of the murderous potential in other autistic kids. According to the CDC, approximately 1 in 50 people (1.5 million) fall somewhere on the autistic spectrum, 80 percent of whom are boys.[23] In recent years, improved diagnostic measures have resulted in an apparent rise in autism cases—up 78 percent from a decade ago—and made autism a source of acute anxiety for many new parents.[24]

No link between autism and violent behavior has ever been shown. National crime data place autistics at precisely the same rates (1.6 percent) as the general population, with many experts stating that autistic people are, in fact, *less likely to commit violence* than the average person.[25] Ironically, in this context, because of their social difficulties autistic children are far *more likely to be the victims* of bullying and assault than others. One study found that autistic children are 49 percent more likely to wander from safe settings due to "social referencing" impairments.[26] Also, because autistic kids are taught compliance from an early age, they are more often victimized by domestic violence and sexual abuse than the general population. The Sandy Hook autism story shows how a psychiatric condition—in this case a nonthreatening developmental disorder—is vilified in the sensationalizing dynamics of moral panic.[27] Simple as this process sounds, it raises a host of secondary questions, not the least of which concerns the actual risks posed by the mentally ill to the rest of us and by what criteria a nonprofessional makes such an assessment in our current culture of fear.

Here is what statistics show: fewer than 5 percent of people with serious mental health problems commit violence against others.[28] Almost none who do so have developmental disabilities like autism. Violent offenders usually fall within narrower diagnostic categories like schizophrenia, which at best only partially accounts for their antisocial behavior. This is not to deny the legitimate threats posed by delusional psychotics. One's instincts about the person muttering on the subway are not always unfounded. But often such impressions are based more on perceived unpredictability of behavior rather than on a rational assessment of risk. Statistically speaking, the likelihood of a violent episode is surprisingly low—even as public fear of individuals with mental illness has increased in recent decades.[29] Also, the interplay of alcohol and drug use with psychiatric conditions is a major factor in violence and crime. The NIMH estimate that 4.6 percent of the population falls under the classification of having a "serious" mental illness—of whom half also have a substance abuse disorder. [30]

In today's America there are more mentally ill people in prisons than in hospitals. In fact, the nation's largest psychiatric ward is the Los Angeles County Jail.[31] By current Bureau of Justice Statistics (BJS), more than 50 percent of all jail inmates in the U.S. have a psychiatric disorder, with major depression and psychotic conditions topping the list. Over the past two decades, government budget cutbacks have led to more formerly institutionalized people with mental illness being on the streets, resulting in a 154 percent increase of mentally ill people in the criminal justice system.[32] According to Patrick W. Corrigan, a well-known advocate for the mentally ill, "Criminalizing mental illness is a way in which the criminal justice system reacts to people with mental illness, contributing to the increasing prevalence of serious mental illness in jail." As a result, those with psychiatric diagnoses are "more likely than others to be arrested by police" and can be expected "to spend more time incarcerated than persons without mental illness."[33] Women with mental illness are 50 percent more likely than men to land up in jail, with many female inmates reporting histories of abuse as children.[34] Looking at the mentally ill who commit violent acts, a MacArthur Foundation study pointed to the pivotal role of social context. Typical targets of such violence were family members—87 percent—with most assaults occurring in the home and characterized by "mutual threat, hostility, or financial dependence." Fewer than 10 percent of attacks were against strangers.[35]

Mentally ill people do more violent harm to themselves than they do to others, according to the NIMH. Suicides occur at more than twice the rate of murders nationally, with the mentally ill accounting for the vast majority of self-inflicted deaths.[36] Self-harm isn't the only way that the mentally ill or developmentally disabled are at risk. Although murders committed by the mentally ill are widely reported and studied, less attention has been afforded to murders of them. One study by American and Swedish researchers found that as many as 20 percent of homicides are committed *against* people with psychiatric diagnoses. The risk of being murdered was highest among the mentally ill who also abused drugs, although it's also increased among those with personality disorders, depression, anxiety, and schizophrenia. Analysts think that these high rates of murder result in part from common fears that the mentally ill are "unpredictable" or "dangerous." This creates "feelings of uneasiness, fear and a desire for social distance and may increase the risk of victimization."[37] Here again, social context matters—but in a broader sense. Mentally ill people are more likely than the general population to live in risky neighborhoods or to be homeless, which in itself can make them more likely to be victimized. Many of America's two million "long-term mentally ill" live in inadequate housing and without social support.[38] To make matters worse, some psychiatric disorders cause people to be less cognizant of their surroundings and therefore less cautious about personal safety.

Socioeconomic status matters a lot in mental illness. For people with a psychiatric diagnosis, work can be a key factor in promoting health and social inclusion, as well as financial independence. Most people with mental illness want to work and are among the largest cohort served by the federal Vocational Rehabilitation system. But employment discrimination can make this difficult. When steady jobs can be found, they have proven to be one of the best therapies for reducing the symptoms of mental illness. Nevertheless, the unemployment rate for adults with a major psychiatric diagnosis is three to five time higher than the general population. The National Alliance on Mental Illness estimates that 60 to 80 percent of the mentally ill are unemployed, with rates running as high as 90 percent for those with severe impairments.[39] Half of the latter group lives at the national poverty level of $11,490 for a single person. The costs of such unemployment are huge, with an estimated $25 billion paid annually in the U.S. in disability payments to the mentally ill.

While the stigma of mental illness directly influences the way in which an individual is treated by others, the effect of the label on a person's self-image creates one of the biggest challenges for the mental health field. As a group, the mentally ill are highly prone to hiding their conditions, avoiding treatment, and deferring support options. A 2007 study conducted by the journal *Psychiatric Services* found that two-thirds of patients believed that their problems "would get better on their own" and that 71 percent were convinced they could cure themselves without help.[40] These tendencies are most pronounced with those in the grip of substance abuse. Often the problem starts at home, as the mentally ill struggle to hide their conditions from family members, or to minimize them. Studies have shown that 30 percent of those with a psychiatric condition try to conceal it from family members.[41] In addition to the individual's belief that he or she can somehow "manage" an illness perceived as a personal failing, there is an additional tragic rationale for this, as the "associated" stigma of having a "disturbed" child or parent can affect the way an entire family is treated. Approximately 25 percent of families with a mentally ill member report instances of avoidance from others. This means that some families will collude in maintaining the illness as a "private" matter, often exacerbating the individual's reluctance to seek professional care. This can be a deadly move, especially considering that many common conditions like depression and bipolar disease become progressively worse over time.

In one national study, less than 40 percent of those with serious mental health conditions received stable treatment during the prior year.[42] According to the Bureau of Labor Statistics, 89.3 million Americans live in federally designated Professional Mental Health Shortage areas—nearly twice the number in areas with similar shortages for general health care.[43] During the past 20 years the way in which mental illness is treated has changed significantly as well, with inpatient care dropping from 42 to 19 percent of expenditure and prescription drugs jumping from 7 percent to 27 percent.[44] Worries persist among the mentally ill over the consequence of being labeled, channeled into counseling, or obliged to take prescription medications. But resistance to mental health treatment is but a part of the problem, since it seems that people with psychiatric diagnoses are less likely to receive health care of all kinds. Until the passage of the Affordable Care Act, a psychiatric diagnosis was the kind of "pre-existing condition" that could preclude an individual's eligibility for health insurance. With new regulations, many in the mental health field say that communication difficulties, resistance to treatment, and subtle biases among health-care providers lessen the likelihood of people with psychiatric illness receiving routine health screenings and care.

Some populations resist care more than others. The health risks and reduction in life opportunities related to mental illness are intersectional problems, more heavily affecting the economically disadvantaged and those affected by other forms of social stigma and discrimination. Mental illness among military personnel and veterans is especially problematic in this way. In general terms, public attitudes toward returning members of the military are mixed. While Vietnam-era resentment of returning military personnel is now a relic of history, misperceptions and misunderstandings of the veteran experience persist. For every scene of flag-waving heroic celebration there is a matching image in many people's minds of violent unpredictability, possibly induced by war trauma. And military culture discourages mental health care. Unlike in civilian life, the privacy firewall between employer and employee medical knowledge is largely missing in the military chain of command, where supervisors often have responsibility for assessing troop readiness. The omniscient character of the military chain of command has recently come to public attention in the area of sexual abuse, where supervisors sometimes are both perpetuators and adjudicators of such offenses. The film *The Invisible War* brought this issue to light in noting that since 2006 over 95,000 such instances had been documented, with less than 14 percent reported and 5 percent brought to prosecution.[45] Add to this military social pressures involving toughness, which often persist after service ends, and the stage is set for widespread denial of mental health conditions, the most common of which is Post-Traumatic

Stress Disorder (PTSD). It is now documented that few service personnel return from active duty without being affected by the stress of war, with as many as 20 percent showing PTSD symptoms.[46]

On Invisibility and Passing

Those with mental illness often find themselves caught between impulses of disclosure and nondisclosure. In recent decades an expansive literature has emerged on the dynamics of "passing," largely attached to multiethnic and queer identities, and to some extent, to disability. Recent titles include Warren Hoffman's *The Passing Game*, Mattilda's *Nobody Passes*, Jeffrey A. Brune and Daniel J. Wilson's *Disability and Passing*. [47] Writing about passing in psychiatric terms has been less robust, although a list of works is beginning to emerge in disability studies and "crip theory," drawing attention to continuities and discontinuities among invisible identities.[48] Despite antidiscrimination laws and evolving social attitudes, the ability to hide psychiatric diagnosis (or other chronic illness) can make the difference between success and failure in work, school, and many other contexts. In his classic work *Stigma*, Erving Goffman distinguished between what he termed "discredited" and "discreditable" identities.[49] In this formulation, a discredited person's distinguishing characteristics are marked in visual or behavioral terms—and thereby known to others. In contrast, the discreditable individual is unmarked—and can "pass as normal" without notice. While Goffman's writing in the 1960s took place well before invisible identities would be politicized and, ultimately, subject to legal rights and protections, he presciently foregrounded the distinction between visual meaning and what he termed "known-about-ness." It's also worth noting that like Canguilhem, Goffman zeroed in on the damaging hegemony of normativity in a world of ubiquitous deviation. "It is not to the different that one should look for understanding our differentness, but to the ordinary," Goffman wrote, adding that, "The question of social norms is certainly central, but the concern might be less for uncommon deviations from the ordinary than for ordinary deviations from the common."[50]

"Passing" takes many forms and has many purposes. In theoretical terms, passing can be seen as a blurring or refusal of categorical difference, often as defined in terms of race, ethnicity, sex, social class, or age. Typically, passing entails being seen as a member of a social group other than one assigned. But in practice, passing also can imply the creation of hybrid or in-between spaces that play with or against conventional categories. Passing can be partial or complete, active or passive, casual or strategic, transient or long-standing. And in all of this, passing weighs heavily on belonging or non-belonging. For people with a psychiatric diagnosis, questions of passing and disclosure often intersect with a host of conflicting variables—as rights, benefits, and accommodations are weighed against stigma, exclusion, and discrimination. Most seriously in medical terms, impulses to pass often correlate with reluctance among those with a mental illness to seek treatment.

Even if one accepts the dismodern premise that most people become bodily compromised in some form or at some time, questions of degree and disclosure remain. Not only do psychiatric conditions exist along a spectrum of impairments, but they are much more likely to be temporally contingent. It is common for the mentally ill to "cycle" between levels of wellness and symptomology, just as it also is not unusual for a severely ill person to pass as functional. "Within the contingent and malleable category of disability, psychiatric disability raises perhaps the most perplexing questions about identity," writes legal scholar Susan Stefan. "Although almost every disability has some effect on social functioning, psychiatric disability is, from the point of view of the external observer, completely characterized by difficulties, deficits, or aberrations and social functioning."[51] Yet if the person manages to cope and function "normally," this frequently triggers suspicions among employers, coworkers, or others. As Stefan writes, "If someone reporting a severe psychiatric difficulty continues to function, the person is likely to be disbelieved or criticized for self-pity, exaggeration, or overdramatization."[52] There is nothing new in the privileging of the observable over the unobservable, especially given the recognition bias afforded to ocular reasoning in Western epistemology.

Invisibility is hardly a simple matter—especially in the contingent relationship between observer (subject) and observed (object). People render aspects of themselves invisible for lots of reasons, including many that are completely involuntary. From the observer's side, invisibility can be a source of uncertainty in a world predicated on seeing—and from this uncertainty all sorts of suspicions and worries can emerge. Long-standing fears about the invisibly diseased took new form in the 19th and 20th centuries in worries over mental illness, social deviance, foreign subversion, and espionage. From the perspective of the observed, the term "invisibility" has long been used in reference to groups unrecognized by middle-class America, as in Ralph Ellison's book *The Invisible Man* (1953) about racism in America, and in Michael Harrington's famous advocacy for "the invisible poor."[53] Complicating matters further, the term invisibility has been used in recent decades to describe inabilities of groups to "see" themselves—in such "unmarked" categories as whiteness, heterosexuality, and able-bodiedness. All of this has begun to introduce a productive uncertainty in a solid reliance on the observable, especially as faith in the visual image has been shaken in a postmodern age. In this shifting terrain, the premises of "invisibility" and "passing" have become unstable—their visual metaphors inadequate for the representation of thinking, identity, and politics.

Some writers have cautiously drawn parallels between disclosures of invisible disabilities and other forms of coming out. Often such similarities can be linked to traditions pathologizing disparate forms of "embodied difference." In most instances, the implication of a clear "in/out" dichotomy is itself a limiting concept, inasmuch as coming out is often neither a singular nor a complete process, but instead something that can occur over time and in different degrees. Gender theorist Ellen Samuels is among a growing field of scholars charting the relationship of disability and other identities—not as discrete categories, but as intricately imbricated constellations. Binary views of coming out are like other dualisms, such as those that minoritize/universalize identities or cast people into normal/deviant categories.[54] Contrasting the benefits and risks of analogizing "coming out" in disabled and queer identities, Samuels notes that the unmodified phrase "coming out" can refer to a process of self-actualization as well as articulation, but "coming out to" implies a subject/object relationship that is frequently asymmetrical.[55] One comes out to family, friends, coworkers, the media, etc. in different ways. In almost every instance of coming out, there is often some measure of cost/benefit analysis. Suffice to say that the processes and effects of coming out can vary greatly among the chronically ill, those with mental illness, people with learning disabilities, and so on.

All of this creates a social economy surrounding conditions that can be seen and externally verified. As Samuels writes, the societal "focus on the visual continues to render nonvisible disabilities *invisible* while reinforcing the exact cultural reliance on visibility that oppresses all of us."[56] This again raises the issue of passing, and the variable stakes in the clash between visible and invisible. Daily life for people who are capable of passing can entail a continual negotiation between doing so deliberately or by default, with value judgments attached to either option. In some contexts, passing (as able-bodied or "sane" for example) has been read as a denial of self or community and a manifestation of internalized oppression. In other instances, passing is seen as a contextual and practical occurrence—or a matter of personal autonomy or privacy. And in some situations, passing is a matter of safety or survival. Historically, in the U.S. revelations of biracial passing could be an excuse for violence. Today's transgender population faces similar risks.

Passing as non-disabled also can reflect a desire to assimilate or otherwise belong, as seen in historical patterns of immigrant Americanization. On the other hand, passing can become its own quite variable form of identity—conformist in some instances, transgressive in others, but always confounding the idea of categorical difference in some way. Metamorphosis and changeability can limit, liberate, or both.[57] Nella Larson's 1920s-era novel *Passing* illustrates this variability in its story of two mixed-race women of nearly equal skin tone, one of whom passes for black in New York's Harlem community and the other who lives in Manhattan white high society.[58] Issues of solidarity and personal ethics emerge in the story, which ends tragically when the "white" woman's deception is discovered. In its plot and character development, *Passing* is a fictionalized case study of how invisible identities are nevertheless visible as they are performed. The book evokes the often-unrecognized "voice" that speaks through silence—as exclusion and absence generate political effects and qualities of subjective articulation. Even more potently, Larsen's *Passing* narrativizes processes through which those deemed invisible can be surveilled and controlled. Hence, in the work there is an ever-present awareness in both women that they are being *watched* and are always at risk of discovery.

For the invisibly disabled person, passing can mean a trade-off between social stigma and accommodation, with one diminishing at the expense of the other. Temporality often figures in passing as non-disabled in ways that are different from racial, gender, or queer passing. Some disabling conditions can be mediated with therapies or medications, while others may occur episodically, as in the case of many chronic illnesses. It's also important to keep in mind extant social pressures to pass in such areas as institutionalized rehabilitation and educational mainstreaming. And at some point, almost everyone must pass standardized employment assessments, school exams, or other instruments of normative measurement. For the unmarked disabled person, this can create a conflicting array of choices. Passing can occur for purposes of self-interest, convenience, or simply to minimize discomfort for others. Additional differences between disabled and other passing identities involve issues of degree, credibility, and, ultimately, of legibility. While queer theory has helped to soften the line between such distinctions as gay/straight and male/female, the existence of middle zones or hybrid identities remains a foreign concept to most people. Those with chronic illnesses, neurological conditions, or psychiatric disabilities often meet with resistance in requests for assistance in school, time off from work, or other accommodations. As Susan Wendell writes, "Suspicion surrounds people with chronic illnesses—suspicion about how ill/disabled we really are, how and why we became ill, whether we are doing everything possible to get well, and how mismanaging our lives, minds, or souls may be contributing to our continuing illness."[59]

This creates a silencing paradox for people with invisible conditions. On the one hand, there is resistance toward the medical construction of impairment as disability, which often indiscriminately labels people with certain conditions as damaged or dysfunctional. This conflicts with the need to claim impairment in the absence of visible evidence to support it. These dual pressures against disclosure emerge from the able-bodied or otherwise unafflicted, living in transient states of "good health." Without doubt this is one of the most wrenching aspects of unmarked disability. Not only is it time to abandon prejudices toward sick and disabled people, but it becomes imperative to change social attitudes toward the experience of illness itself. Not only has the moment arrived to recognize that debility is in fact the new "normal," but it is necessary to explore the vast dimensionality of disabled experience. As Wendell writes, "I do not think that those of us who appreciate having become ill are making a mistake or deceiving ourselves. Illness is not by definition evil. People fear or try to avoid illness because of the suffering it causes."[60] And yes, suffering is real, challenges can be enormous, and mortality eventually visits everyone. But illness and disability are also not *only* suffering. Those who have become aware of bodily and mental difference often want things to be otherwise, but they also are cognizant of the continuum between states of wellness. Many would not trade their conditions with those of normatively "healthy" people. And most would never want to exist in a state of ignorance about the afflictions of others. Disability often brings unique lessons of empathy, shared understanding, and community.

The Shame Game

Many conditions carry degrees of stigma that generate isolation, nondisclosure, and the avoidance of treatment. But mental health disorders have a unique relationship to stigma's shaming effects. In a more direct sense than physical disability or many other illnesses, psychiatric conditions can be worsened by stigma-related exclusion or negative attitudes from others. While attitude may be a factor in recovering from any illness, in conditions like anxiety and depression, attitude itself can be a major symptom. This can cause a damaging cycle, in which internal and external consequences of an illness feed each other. Social science has extensively has examined stigma as material fact and social construction. But less attention has been afforded to the lived experience of those stigmatized. The phenomenology of stigma gets hidden, which is perhaps one of the reasons the term "stigma" remains so underused in popular discourse, remaining largely an artifact of medical or sociological research.

But just the opposite has happened with "shame," which often gets woven into the experience of stigma. Shame is not a diagnosis or illness, but rather a mental state that everyone occasionally experiences in such common feelings as embarrassment, inadequacy, and underachievement. And thanks to the self-help industry, a booming literature has emerged on shame in recent years. One can speculate that shame became more widespread in the hard economic times of the 2000s, even as shame was loudly condemned by feminists and various pride movements. Rising public awareness of misplaced shame occurred in tandem with the rise of "affect theory" in academic circles. In recent years, shame has made widely seen appearances in such movies as *Walk of Shame* (2014), *Shame the Devil* (2013), *Shame* (2011), and *I'm Not Ashamed* (2011)—not to mention the wildly popular Showtime series *Shameless* (2011–), and dozens of popular music titles. Best-selling novels by Nora Roberts and Salman Rushdie address shame, along with hundreds of blogs, apps, websites, and digital resources on the topic.[61] Shame fits within this chapter on mental illness precisely because of this ubiquity, not to mention its relationship to life *Elsewhere in America.*

Perhaps the most prominent figure in the shame world is Brené Brown, whose is best known for her viral TED talk *Listening to Shame* (2012). Brown's rise to prominence is instructive in this chapter's discussion of mental health, stigma, and invisibility. Briefly stated, Brown described shame and vulnerability as consequences of a culture of competitive individuality and fear. Comparing American society to a family emerging from violence (9/11 and subsequent wars) and deprivation (2007–2008 recession), Brown adapted the concept of "resiliency" from victim-therapy and trauma-treatment protocols. Deftly distancing herself from the discourses of motivational "how-to" prescriptions or positive psychology, Brown wrote that "If 'how-to' worked, we would not be the most obese, in-debt, medicated, and addicted adults in human history. If 'how to' worked, we wouldn't be struggling as much as we are feeling lonely and discontent. If 'how to' worked, we would not be struggling all the time feeling we are not enough."[62]

Brown's success as a public figure lies in the way she makes shame "ordinary"—something everyone knows about on some level. Yet in acknowledging the common experience of shame, Brown gives it an interesting twist. As the above quotation suggests, she works shame into a critique of a set of "American" values that place members of a consumer society in a continual cycle of comparison with one another. Like many other commentators on shame, Brown is quick to draw a distinction between shame and guilt. Guilt may derive from a bad thing one has done, but shame is about the bad person one really is. For example, as Brown says, imagine having too much to drink one night and showing up to work hungover, missing a meeting. Someone experiencing guilt will think to themselves, "That was a really stupid thing to do. I wasn't thinking." In contrast, someone experiencing shame will say, "I'm an idiot. I'm such a loser." In other words, guilt focuses on behavior while shame focuses on self.[63] Children learn to play shame scripts within themselves when they are raised in judgmental or perfectionistic households where they can never win. To Brown this same dynamic plays out in a society in which unachievable ideals of wealth, beauty, strength, popularity, achievement and other measures of "success" are relentlessly drilled into people. Let's face it, the inescapable message of most advertising pitches is that something is missing in one's life. There is some desired object, relationship, or state of mind just beyond reach—and a product will bring it closer. Unfortunately the product proves to be a transitional object in this unrelenting desire. And the failure to obtain the goal becomes a quiet source of shame.

But here is the really bad news about shame. It can be more than a causal "feeling" that everybody gets. Statistically speaking, shame is highly correlated with addiction, depression, eating disorders, violence, bullying, and aggression. Guilt, on the other hand, is inversely correlated with such conditions. Shame is the condition of mind that tells people they are unimportant, unlovable, defective, fake, undeserving, or simply bad. Shame results in a plethora of compensating behaviors that run the gamut from people pleasing and attempting to "fit in"—to perfectionism and hyper-competitivism. Shameful people often try to be something they feel they are not. A guilty person is able to let things go, delimit the damage to self, and is more likely to learn from the guilt-producing experience. Shame is something people carry with them, usually scrupulously attempting to hide it from others. Some people even speak of being ashamed of feeling shame itself.

Shame means different things to different people—and has been interpreted variously across academic disciplines. One can speak of individualized accounts of shame as a consequence of impropriety, guilt, stigma, or bias. The word *shame* derives from the Germanic *Scham,* which refers to the act of covering one's face. In this sense, shame has everything to do with the topic of mental health discussed in this chapter. It resonates with notions of visibility and invisibility, external and internal, body and mind, self and other—even as dualities themselves confuse and hide their operations. Then there is the kind of shame that people experience in groups. Wars often produce a residue of shame, as do other forms of collective violence such as racism, genocide, police brutality, and selected incarcerations like those occurring at the Guantánamo Bay Naval Base. The relational and relative character of collective shame was manifest after World War II in reports of its experience by both German nationals and Jewish Holocaust survivors. Soldiers returning from wars often feel ashamed about what duty has compelled them to do, as civilian populations at home feel shame for having forced them to do it. Shame accrues to the perpetrators of crimes but also to its victims. The residue of a national "white shame" is still felt by many in the U.S.—a country built on the eradication of one race and the enslavement of another.

Of course the etiology of shame in the Western mind can be traced to the biblical origins of the sexes in Genesis, so contested in recent political debates over marriage. Notably in this account shame is gendered by the misdeeds of woman's "original sin," which caused the primordial couple to be ashamed of their bodies. Plato spoke of shame frequently in his *Dialogues* and topics of shame and guilt figure prominently in religious texts from around the globe. The ancient Chinese philosopher Mencius wrote, for example, that "Men cannot live without shame. A sense of shame is the beginning of integrity."[64] The body figures prominently in recent discussions of shame, as either the source or manifestation of stigma—with visible difference and observed behavior playing reciprocal roles. Here becomes manifest the penchant for making visible even that which is not apparent to the senses: the need to make shame public, to disclose it. Charles Darwin famously wrote about shame in his 1872 *The Expression of Emotions in Man and Animals*.[65] Darwin saw that shame makes some people want to hide.

One can't really avoid psychoanalysis as a backdrop for further thinking to evolve surrounding shame. Freud would locate shame in the intersection of libidinous drives, cognition, and the superego.[66] In this model, Freud saw shame in a dialogue with narcissism, as both its opposite and one of its motivators. Later analysts would extend this double notion of shame as both confirmation of an idealized subjectivity and a symptom of internalized crisis. Michel Foucault famously historicized a type of societal shame in his discussions of sexuality.[67] Accordingly, bourgeois society since the 18th century had been in the throes of what Foucault termed a "repressive hypothesis" in which pleasure becomes subordinate to utility. In this scheme, heterosexual marriage functioned as a control mechanism to perpetuate joyless procreation while simultaneously prohibiting other sexual practices. It goes without saying that Foucault would have been the last person to universalize this theory, which he presented, after all, as a conditional supposition. Yet the contemporary undercurrents of the repressive mindset are hard to deny, especially in a media culture that alternately celebrates and condemns erotic impulses depending on who is speaking to whom. The repressive hypothesis served and continues to function as a series of questions about Western discourses on sexuality as a means of getting at larger questions about knowledge and power. In this sense, even raising such questions can be seen as an intervention, albeit usually an academic one.

The Affective Turn

Attention to shame as an object of study has risen in recent years with the growing popularity of affect as a category of analysis in critical theory, the humanities, or the more broadly interdisciplinary field of cultural studies. This is hardly to suggest that *emotions* and *feelings* had been ignored in these fields. But often such matters had gotten less attention than plot, author, reader, history, language, and in some circles, the psychoanalytic implications thereof. In a familiar dynamic within academic culture, emotion was regarded as old-fashioned, obvious, and not deserving of serious attention. As a term, "affect" remained buried in the lexicon of social science until a small number of theorists began examining it in the 1990s and 2000s. In the opening pages of the *Affect Theory Reader*, from Duke University Press, the book's editors describe affect in a poetic language of invisibility, speaking of its "in-between-ness," "beside-ness," or "the name we give to those forces—visceral forces beneath, alongside, or generally *other than* conscious knowing, vital forces insisting beyond emotion—that can serve to drive us toward moment, toward thought and extension, that can likewise suspend us (as if in neutral) across a barely registering accretion of force-relations."[68] In her book, *Depression: A Public Feeling,* Ann Cvetkovitch has described the "affective turn," not so much as a "new" movement, but as an important consolidation of ongoing questions and concerns. To Cvetkovitch, affect theory offers a novel way of examining topics ranging from cultural memory, sentimentality, everyday life, and public fear to "the ongoing legacy of identity politics as another inspiration for the turn to the personal" and "continuing efforts to rethink psychoanalytic paradigms."[69]

This interest in affect brought new attention to the thinking of the psychologist Silvan Tompkins—a somewhat marginal figure, who mapped out a typology of affects in the 1960s. Tomkins identified nine pairs of affects ranging from those he counted as *positive* ("interest-excitement," "enjoyment-joy," etc.) to *negative* ("fear-terror," "shame-humiliation," etc.). Part of what gives Tompkins's writing on shame its contemporary appeal lies in its clinical neutrality and willingness to depart from prior psychoanalytic views. To Tompkins shame is not necessarily a function of guilt, superego, or narcissistic crisis—but rather, the result of deprivation. Observing the behavior of infants, Tompkins concluded that the complex set of feelings adults associate with shame derive from early experiences of absence, unmet needs, and disappointed expectations. A person doesn't even need to know the exact source of shame in order to feel it. Tompkins conceptualized shame on a deeper structural level, implicitly abstracting it from notions like guilt.

Tompkins put shame on an experiential spectrum rather than a presence/absence binary. Tompkins's originality, if one can call it that, derived from his delimited account of shame, as when he stated, for example, that "Any affect may have any object."[70] Among other attributes, this emphasis gives Tompkins's work a strangely depoliticized tenor, not unlike Goffman's work, even as it addressed topics that elsewhere might be tied to oppression and discrimination. In her book, *Blush: Faces of Shame*, Elspeth Probyn summarized Tompkins's thesis in stating that "Shame can appear only once interest and enjoyment have been felt and when they have been ripped from you. At that moment the sheer disappointment of loss translates into shame that attacks your sense of self: the entrails of who you thought you are suddenly displayed for all to judge."[71]

Here the connection to stigma becomes evident as well, as yet another impulse for hiding invisible identities. Whether internally maintained or externally perceived by others, stigma can block or rip away the interest or enjoyment one might feel, leaving a residue of shame. Interestingly Tompkins thought that shame might result from the experience of contempt projected by others, but only if something more positive had been anticipated: "If the other expresses contempt for me, I may respond with counter-contempt, with self-contempt, with anger, with fear, with distress, with surprise, with interest, with enjoyment or amusement, with indifference, or with shame. In order for the contempt of the other to evoke shame rather than one of the above alternatives, the other must be an actual or potential source of positive affect, which is reduced by the contempt of the other."[72] In other words, shame is unlikely to circulate around an impartial source. This isn't always a bad thing. It's worth reiterating that shame invariably bears a relationship with "interest in the world." In other words, one would hardly be ashamed if something or someone didn't matter. And here Probyn makes an essential point: that aside from the discomfort of a negative self-assessment:

> equally, shame compels an involuntary and immediate reassessment of ourselves: Why am I ashamed? Why did I say or do that? Can I rectify the actions that have either brought shame upon myself or caused someone else's shame? Shame in this way is positive in its self-evaluative role; it can even be self-transforming.[73]

This open-ended and productive aspect of shame is useful in thinking through what to do with shameful thoughts. One can learn from shame by examining its sources. What sense of impending loss brought this feeling of shame? By what mechanisms are shameful events subjectively internalized as constitutive elements of one's identity? Pride movements often function to reverse the polarities of externally imposed shame. But in reversing the polarities of shame, its structure remains in place nevertheless. Eve Kosofsky Sedgwick wrote at length about the pernicious problem of such binary oppositions as shame/pride. The introduction of Sedgwick's *Shame and Its Sisters: A Silvan Tompkins Reader*, assembled with Adam Frank, explored the use of Tompkins's work in reconceptualizing subjective dualisms. "Tompkins is valuable as one of the repertoire of ways that such a psychology has of displacing the Freudian emphasis on Oedipality and repression," Sedgwick stated.[74] Sedgwick found in Tompkins a refreshing approach in modeling "the self" without recourse to a Foucauldian repressive hypothesis of inescapable power asymmetry, adding, "How supremely alien Tompkins' own work remains to any project of narrating the emergence of a core self."[75] The epistemological trap Sedgwick saw in Foucauldian theory lies in its displacement and inherent replication of a dualism, even as it denies this operation. A distinct moralism has made Foucault appealing to a generation of academics, especially what Sedgwick saw as his implied promise "that there might be ways of stepping outside the repressive hypothesis, to forms of thought that would not be structured by the question of prohibition in the first place."[76] Sedgwick was one of the first scholars to suggest leaving open the question of identity—a dynamic contingency exemplified in Tompkins's formation of shame that can attach to "any object" in which one finds "interest."

Political Feelings

This raises several issues about the shame/pride opposition in collective terms. In the first place, societies throughout history have used shame as a means of social control, whether in the service of national identity, utilitarian ethics, or the reification of other norms like "success" or the "work ethic." And no one needs reminding of the deployment of shame in religious practices. Many faiths cast life itself as a contest between shame and redemption. As this point makes clear, especially as collective affect plays out in daily life, experiences of shame, their articulation in the public sphere, and their strategic deployment for political gain vary wildly in expression among individuals and groups.

Despite these variations, shame is evident everywhere in media discourse. In an Internet age of near-instantaneous communication, one is bombarded daily with accounts of celebrity misbehavior and politicians casting aspersions on each other's beliefs. While corporations and governments will occasionally admit their shameful histories and make public apologies, administrative practices more frequently tend to minimize or deny wrongdoing. In other instances, what many perceive as shameful behavior toward the environment or foreign enemies, for example, is rationalized in the interest of jobs, corporate profits, national security, or patriotic self-righteousness. Meanwhile, a self-help industry continues to expand in the form of radio advice programs, television talk shows, and the thousands of websites and books appearing each year to minimize personal shame.

Probyn and Sedgwick, among others, pointed out the dangers of denying or rigidly dichotomizing shame. This is not to pretend that shame doesn't exist or to minimize its consequences. The thesis of this book hinges in large part on exposing the very real forms material damage and psychic violence exacted on people through the obscured, hidden, and otherwise "unmentionable" spaces of difference, stigma, and their related affects. The recent academic interest in shame derives from recognition of its usefulness in explaining certain under-examined aspects of both personal subjectivity and collective life. These discussions have done much to help to elucidate, not only shame's painful manifestations, but also its origins, motivations, and lessons. Again, as Tompkins recognized, shame reveals what provokes "interest," and it takes a psychic toll when those interests are put at risk. One can learn from shame, mediate its sources, and change the pathways of shame in one's world/s.

Crude oppositions can get in the way of this project in two ways. On the one hand, they obfuscate the extraordinary nuances, flavors, and shades of shame. More pernicious than the shame cast on a convicted criminal is the subtle embarrassment that might preclude a depressed person from seeking help, or stop a traumatized service member from disclosing to a peer or therapist. The shame of stigma is slowly becoming acknowledged as a pervasive, and sometimes deadly, fact of life. And as I have outlined in this chapter, the reach and complexity of stigma in the current era is enormous. The second difficulty with shame dichotomies, related to the first, is their occlusion of what Sedgwick called "the middle range of agency." Sedgwick quite appropriately links this all-or-nothing approach to shame with consumer capitalism:

> One's relation to what is risked is becoming reactive and bifurcated, that of a consumer: one's choices narrowed to accepting or refusing (buying, not buying) this or that manifestation of it, dramatizing only the extremes of compulsion and voluntarity. It is only the middle ranges of agencies that offer space for effectual creativity and change.[77]

All of this points to the role of affect in political life. What does it *feel* like to exist in an economic system premised on relentless competition and comparison? What does it *feel* like to be caught in a cycle of work and consumption in which one never produces enough or has enough. What does it *feel* like to be a political subject in an increasingly authoritarian land where people hate their leaders but never vote? Is it any wonder that extremist groups at both ends of the political spectrum find common cause in their resentment of the invisible reach of corporations and government? The inescapable answer to these questions is that something is wrong, broadly *felt* as such, but lacking a coherent explanation. These questions of public affect have long been the topic of cultural studies, which remains a marginal field within intellectual discourse and largely unknown outside the academy. But generally speaking, the broad-based discomfort, sense of inadequacy, and estrangement from power felt by so many still largely remains unnamed—its workings invisible or hidden.

Discussions of affect represent yet another important move to articulate what Raymond Williams described 50 years ago as a "structure of feeling," which he saw manifest in the lived experience of a population rather than its overt institutional or political organization. Remember that much of Williams's cultural studies enterprise of the 1960s was motivated by a strong critique of social stratification. In the context of aristocratic traditions of what counted as "culture," Williams sought to reclaim the trivial, the "ordinary", and the everyday—and their implicit phenomenology. He describes this structure of feeling:

> as firm and definite as 'structure' suggests, yet it operates in the most delicate and least tangible part of our activity. In one sense, this structure of feeling is the culture of a period: it is the particular living result of all the elements in general organization.[78]

Lots of discussion has taken place in recent years about this generalized sense of a hidden problem—from recent scholarship on affect, to sociological accounts of "moral panics" and the "culture of fear," to analyses of popular uprisings in nations around the world, to the increasing polarization of politics in the United States, and to unresolved campaigns for social justice everywhere. In the context of invisibility, Williams's legacy holds a special relevance as an early gesture at bringing forward issues frequently relegated to silence. This program would later be elaborated in the discourses of civil rights and multiculturalism, feminism and gender equity, poststructuralism and performativity, decolonization and critical race studies, and queer theory. As this thinking has become more nuanced and complex, the elusiveness of anything like a singular "answer" has become increasingly evident—despite theories of intersectionality, transdisciplinarity, convergence culture, and the like. But if this work has yielded anything, it is that the difficulty of a task may in some ways signal its importance. The elusiveness of adaptive inequities reminds us to be wary of what is hidden, covert, or even unconscious.

Notes

1 See Andrew Weinstein and Stuart Oldman, "Robin Williams Found Dead in Possible Suicide," *Variety* (Aug. 12, 2014) http://variety.com/2014/film/news/robin-williams-found-dead-in-possible-suicide-1201280386/ (accessed Aug. 12, 2014).
2 See Amber Hildbrand, "Robin Williams Death: Are Comedians More Prone to Depression?" *CBC News* (Aug. 12, 2014) http://www.cbc.ca/news/health/robin-williams-death-are-comedians-more-prone-to-depression-1.2734500 (accessed Aug. 13, 2014).
3 "Facts and Figures," American Foundation for Suicide Prevention (2012) https://www.afsp.org/understanding-suicide/facts-and-figures (accessed Aug. 13, 2014).
4 Liz Szabo, "Advocates Hope Robin Williams' Death Will Spur Discussion," *USA Today* (Aug. 12, 2014) http://www.usatoday.com/story/news/nation/2014/08/12/robin-williams-spurs-suicide-discussion/13965293/ (accessed Jan. 4, 2015).
5 Michael Vincent, "More US soldiers Dying from Suicide than Combat," *ABC News* (Nov. 12, 2013) http://www.abc.net.au/news/2013-11-12/more-us-soldiers-dying-from-suicide-than-combat/5085070 (accessed Aug. 13, 2014).
6 "Developmental Disabilities Increasing in the U.S.," U.S. Centers for Disease Control and Prevention (n.d.) http://www.cdc.gov/features/dsdev_disabilities/ (accessed July 30, 2013); "Alzheimer's Facts and Figures," Alzheimer's Organization (n.d.) http://www.alz.org/alzheimers_disease_facts_and_figures.asp (accessed July 29, 2013).
7 Dr. Andrew Leuchter, "Letter to Friends of the Semel Institute for Neuroscience and Human Behavior," unpublished e-mail (Aug. 13, 2014).

8 "APA Reaches Out in Wake of Robin Williams' Death," *Psychiatric News* (Aug. 14, 2014) http://alert.psychnews.org/2014/08/apa-reaches-out-in-wake-of-robin.html (accessed Aug. 15, 2014).
9 "Health Information Privacy," U.S. Department of Health & Human Services (n.d.) http://www.hhs.gov/ocr/privacy/ (accessed Jan. 7, 2015).
10 Alina Tugend, "Deciding Whether to Disclose Mental Health Disorders to the Boss," *New York Times* (Nov. 14, 2014) http://www.nytimes.com/2014/11/15/your-money/disclosing-mental-disorders-at-work.html?_r=0 (accessed Jan. 9, 2015).
11 Kay Redfield Jamison, *An Unquiet Mind: Memoirs of Moods and Madness* (New York: Vintage, 1997) p. 7.
12 "Rates of Co-occurring Mental and Substance Use Disorders," Substance Abuse and Mental Health Services Administration (n.d.) http://www.samhsa.gov/co-occurring/topics/data/disorders.aspx (accessed Oct. 15, 2014).
13 Dennis Schepp, *Drugs: Rhetoric of Fantasy, Addiction to Truth* (Dresden and New York: Atropos, 2011) p. 11.
14 See *An Unquiet Mind* and Andrew Solomon, *Noonday Demon: An Atlas of Depression* (New York: Touchstone, 2002).
15 *An Unquiet Mind*, p. 3.
16 W.J.T. Mitchell, *Seeing Madness: Insanity, Madness, and Visual Culture* (Kassel, Germany: Hatje Cantz, 2012) pp. 6–7.
17 Abraham M. Nussbaum, *Pocket Guide to the DSM-5 Diagnostic Manual* (Arlington, VA: American Psychiatric Association, 2013) p. 3.
18 Dale Archer, *Better than Normal: What Makes You Different Can Make You Exceptional* (New York: Crown Archetype, 2012).
19 Ibid.
20 Allen Frances, "Is Criticism of DSM-5 'Anti-Psychiatry'?" *Huffington Post* (May 24, 2013) www.huffingtonpost.com/allen-frances/is-criticism-of-dsm-5-ant_b_3326980.html (accessed Dec. 12, 2104).
21 Robert Lundin, "Foreword," in Patrick W. Corrigan, ed., *On the Stigma of Mental Illness: Practical Strategies for Research and Social Change* (Washington, DC: American Psychological Association, 2005) p. xi.
22 Susan Sontag, *Illness as Metaphor* (New York; Vintage, 1977) p. 45.
23 See "Autistic Spectrum Disorders," U.S. Centers for Disease Control and Prevention (n.d.) http://www.cdc.gov/ncbddd/autism/data.html (accessed Feb. 3, 2015).
24 Miriam Falco, "CDC: U.S. Kids with Autism Up 78% in Past Decade," *CNN News* (March 29, 2012) http://www.cnn.com/2012/03/29/health/autism (accessed Jan. 12, 2015).
25 "Are Autistics Natural Born Criminals?" *The Autism Crisis* (Oct. 10, 2010) http://autismcrisis.blogspot.com/2010/10/are-autistic-people-natural-born.html (accessed Jan. 1, 2015).
26 April Choulat, "Why Do Autistic Children Wander?" *Autism Remediation for Our Children* (Aug. 11, 2013) http://autismremediationforourchildren.blogspot.com/ (accessed Aug. 22, 2014).
27 Sociologists have mapped such progressions: from *signs* ("the person muttering in the subway must be crazy"), to *stereotypes* ("crazy people can be dangerous"), to *discrimination* ("I won't hire a crazy person").
28 "Violence and Mental Illness," *World Psychiatry*, 2, no. 2 (June 2003) pp. 121–124. http://www.ncbi.nlm.nih.gov/pmc/articles/PMC1525086/ (accessed Jan. 12, 2015).
29 Patrick W. Corrigan, in Patrick W. Corrigan, ed., *On the Stigma of Mental Illness* (Washington, DC: American Psychological Association, 2005) p. 20.
30 "Prevalence of Serious Mental Health Illnesses among U.S. Adults by Age, Sex, and Age" (2010) http://www.nimh.nih.gov/statistics/SMI_AASR.shtml (accessed Oct. 15, 2014).

31 Dina Demetrius, "Exclusive: Inside the US's Largest Psychiatric Ward, the LA County Jail," *Al Jazeera America* (July 28, 2014) http://america.aljazeera.com/watch/shows/america-tonight/articles/2014/7/25/l-a-county-jail-psychiatricward.html (accessed May 1, 2015).
32 *On the Stigma of Mental Illness*, p. 20.
33 Ibid.
34 "Study Finds that Half of All Prison and Jail Inmates Have Mental Health Problems," Bureau of Justice Statistics (2010) http://www.bjs.gov/content/pub/press/mhppjipr.cfm (accessed Oct. 10, 2014).
35 "Violence and Mental Health: An Overview," National Institutes of Health (2003) http://www.ncbi.nlm.nih.gov/pmc/articles/PMC1525086/ (accessed Jan. 9, 2015).
36 Tom Insel, "Understanding Severe Mental Illness" (n.d.) www.nimh.nih.gov/about/director/2011/understanding-severe-mental-illness.shtml (accessed Dec. 15, 2014).
37 Jeremy Laurence, "Mentally Ill People Nearly Five Times More Likely to Be Victims of Murder than General Population," *The Independent*, (Mar. 6, 2013) http://www.independent.co.uk/life-style/health-and-families/health-news/mentally-ill-people-nearly-five-times-more-likely-to-be-victims-of-murder-than-general-population-8521493.html (accessed Feb. 4, 2015).
38 *On the Stigma of Mental Illness*, p. 18.
39 "The High Costs of Mental Health: Unemployment," National Alliance on Mental Illness (Jan. 2010) http://www.nami.org/Template.cfm?Section=About_the_Issue&Template=/ContentManagement/ContentDisplay.cfm&ContentID=114540 (accessed Dec. 20, 2014).
40 Sarah Kliff, "Seven Facts about America's Mental-Health Care System," *Washington Post* (Dec. 17, 2012) http://www.washingtonpost.com/blogs/wonkblog/wp/2012/12/17/seven-facts-about-americas-mental-health-care-system/ (accessed. Jan. 4, 2015).
41 *On the Stigma of Mental Illness*, p. 23.
42 The number in treatment for schizophrenia, one of the most problematic conditions, was somewhat higher at 60 percent. See *On The Stigma of Mental Illness*, p. 28.
43 "Seven Facts about America's Mental-Health Care System."
44 Ibid.
45 *The Invisible War*, http://www.notinvisible.org/about (accessed Jan. 5, 2015).
46 Sarah Peters, "Veterans Groups Encourage Returning Service Members to Seek Mental Health Care Early" *Express-Times* (July 30, 2013) www.lehighvalleylive.com/breaking-news/index.ssf/2013/07/veterans_groups_encourage_retu.html (accessed Aug. 20, 2014).
47 Warren Hoffman, *The Passing Game: Queering Jewish American Culture* (Syracuse, NY: Syracuse University Press, 2009); Mattilda (a.k.a. Matt Bernstein Sycamore), *Nobody Passes: Rejecting the Rules of Gender and Conformity* (Berkeley, CA: Seal, 2013); Jeffrey A. Brune and Daniel J. Wilson, *Disability and Passing: Blurring the Lines of Identity* (Philadelphia, PA: Temple University Press, 2013).
48 Robert McRuer, *Cultural Signs of Queerness and Disability* (New York: New York University Press, 2006).
49 Erving Goffman, *Stigma: Notes on the Management of a Spoiled Identity* (1963) (New York: Touchstone Reissue, 1986) p. 4.
50 *Stigma*, p. 127.
51 Susan Stefan, "Discredited and Discreditable: The Search for Political Identity by People with Psychiatric Disabilities," *Williams and Mary Law Review*, 44, no. 3/9 (2003) p. 1345.
52 Ibid.
53 Peter Dreier, "Poverty in America 50 Years after Michael Harrington's *The Other America*," *Huffington Post* (Mar. 25, 2012) http://www.huffingtonpost.com/peter-dreier/post_3167_b_1378516.html (accessed Jan. 15, 2015).

54 Eve Kosofsky Sedwick, *Epistemology of the Closet* (Berkeley: University of California Press, 1990) p. 22.
55 Ellen Samuels, “My Body, My Closet: Invisible Disability and the Limits of Coming Out,” in Lennard Davis, ed., *The Disabilities Studies Reader*, 4th ed. (New York and London: Routledge, 2013) pp. 316–322.
56 “My Body, My Closet,” p. 327.
57 See Judith Butler, “Passing, Queering,” in *Bodies That Matter: On the Discursive Limits of “Sex”* (New York and London: Routledge, 1993) pp. 167–186.
58 Ella Larsen, *Passing* (1928) (New York: Martino, 2011).
59 Susan Wendell, “Treating Chronic Illnesses as Disabilities,” in *The Disabilities Studies Reader*, p. 169.
60 “Treating Chronic Illnesses as Disabilities,” p. 171.
61 Salman Rushdie, *Shame: A Novel* (New York: Random House, 1984); Nora Roberts, *Born in Shame* (New York: Berkeley Trade, 2013).
62 Brené Brown, *The Power of Vulnerability: Teachings of Authenticity, Connection, and Courage* (Audiobook) (Sounds True, 2012).
63 “Dr. Brené Brown on Shame, Guilt, and Addiction,” *Huffington Post* (Apr. 18, 2013) http://www.huffingtonpost.com/2013/04/18/brene-brown-shame-guilt-addiction-oprah_n_2966351.html (accessed July 7, 2013).
64 See Ying Wong and Jeanne Tsai, “Cultural Models of Shame and Guilt” (2007) http://psych.stanford.edu/~tsailab/PDF/yw07sce.pdf (accessed Jan. 2, 2015) p. 209.
65 See Charles Darwin, *The Expression of Emotions in Man and Animals* (London: John Murray, 1872) p. 320. http://darwin-online.org.uk/content/frameset?pageseq=1&itemID=F1142&viewtype=text (accessed July 3, 2013).
66 See Joseph Sandler, Ethel Spector Person, and Peter Fonagy, eds, *Freud’s “On Narcissism: An Introduction”* (1914) (New Haven, CT: Yale University Press, 1991).
67 Michel Foucault, *The History of Sexuality, An Introduction*, Vol. 1 (New York: Vintage Reissue, 1990).
68 Gregory J. Seigworth and Melissa Gregg, “An Inventory of Shimmers,” in Seigworth and Gregg, *The Affect Studies Reader* (Durham, NC: Duke University Press, 2010) p. 1. See Ann Cvetkovitch, *Depression: A Public Feeling* (Durham, NC: Duke University Press, 2012) p. 4.
69 *Depression: A Public Feeling*, p. 3.
70 Silvan Tomkins, *Affect Imagery Consciousness*, Vol. 1: *The Positive Affects*; Vol. II: *The Negative Affects* (New York: Springer, 2008) p. 347.
71 Elspeth Probyn, *Blush: Faces of Shame* (Minneapolis: University of Minnesota Press, 2005) p. xii.
72 *Affect Imagery Consciousness*, p. 421.
73 *Blush*, p. xii.
74 “Introduction” to *Shame and Its Sisters*, as republished in Eve Kosofsky Sedgwick, *Touching Feeling: Affect, Pedagogy, Performativity* (Durham, NC: Duke University Press, 2003) p. 98.
75 Ibid.
76 *Touching Feeling*, pp. 12–13.
77 Ibid.
78 Raymond Williams, *The Long Revolution* (London: Broadview, 2001) p. 164.

PART III

Belonging Elsewhere

The Subject of Utopia

If *Elsewhere in America* has described the country's struggle with inclusion, Part III: "Belonging Elsewhere: The Subject of Utopia" is about the gaps between the nation's aspirations and actualities. This book has examined ways America's infamous "independence" came embedded with epistemological baggage: philosophical yearnings for wholeness and universality, habits of tribalism and protectionism, narrative structures of linearity and completion, psychological memories of trauma and desire, scientific legacies of rationality and empiricism, economic habits of competition and accumulation, and political histories of domination and resistance. Taken as an ensemble, this baggage defines many in the U.S. as "belonging elsewhere."

Unresolved conflicts have a nagging way of returning, often rearing their heads in different shapes and forms. Late in his career, Derrida wrote a short book about a pattern he had noticed throughout his work, a returning question he found himself unable to answer completely. He titled his book *Aporias*, using the term from ancient Greek meaning "impassable."[1] In *Aporias*, Derrida detailed the confounding recurrence of paradoxes, antimonies, and double binds in his life—concluding that some matters are impossible ever to figure out. The challenge is how to live with contradictions. Pertinent to this discussion, Derrida spoke of the "foreigner" as simultaneously a welcomed guest and an alien stranger: in other words, a boundary figure whose existence between identities is never completely resolved in one direction or another.

As a nation of perennial newcomers, the U.S. has a special relationship with boundary identities, especially as it encounters new dimensions of difference within its ranks. Each American is a stranger in the eyes of someone. And in a global context, "Americans" are some of the strangest creatures on earth. The irreducible boundary between guest and stranger is examined in the following chapters as a recurring paradigm of difference and alterity. This section of *Elsewhere in America* looks at various strategies for reconciling (or living with) the singularities and generalities of belonging—as they play out in the national, linguistic, and cultural terms. The individual chapters will examine the nation's cultural anxiety manifest in manic accumulation and consumption, repetitive patterns of vilification, a compulsive hunger for relief and medication, and a tendency to externalize internal conflicts.

The 2000s brought the autochthonic idea of "homeland" into the popular vocabulary. The "new" threat of terrorism allowed Americans to forget the fascist origins of the term, as the idea of a national "home" also appealed to deeper anxieties festering in the national psyche. Many citizens worrying over public safety and defense found succor in the powerful metaphor of a "border fence," promoted with protectionist zeal as a repellent against such "foreign" elements as crime, drugs, disease, and even unemployment. And in broader terms, "Homeland Security" similarly would become a perfect antidote to the culture of fear that had gripped the nation for decades. Of course the U.S. has always been an anxious nation—owing to its fractious and violent history and prehistory, as well as the doubts and uncertainties it carries to the present day.

Traumatized groups are prone to disquiet. Despite a 20-year decline in crime rates and the relative rarity of terrorist incidents, public anxieties continue to escalate—often driven by political opportunism and media sensationalism. Frightening news stories abound about mass killers, crazy people, drugs smugglers, welfare cheats, and urban gangs—as well as those pandering to fears about unhealthy foods, sickness, and the ravages of aging.[2] Meanwhile, genuinely widespread problems like poverty, alcoholism, domestic violence, and environmental pollution get little attention. Worries about violent harm intersect with insecurities of a collapsing economy. It's now known that risky banking behavior and bad corporate investments by big banks had a lot to do with what went wrong. But these revelations brought little solace to a country suffering as a result of tighter budgets, joblessness, or outright poverty. America needed people to blame.

The nation's edginess also reflects a generalized worry about the future: the expectation of threats yet to come, but nevertheless experienced in the present.[3] Imagined in the current moment, these anticipated dangers are often driven by memories—or manipulated images of past events. And as might be expected, the consequences of this are hardly neutral. While the culture of fear may be an aspect of affect, it is much more than a subjective experience. Distress almost always attaches to an object—to an actual someone or something to be scared about. In this way, a fearful "structure of feeling" nearly always translates into suspicion, scapegoating, prejudice, and antagonism—and sometimes leads to violence where none previously existed.[4]

Health concerns are common in times of stress, both for individuals and societies. Earlier in this book I discussed the roots of dogmatic normativity, as medical practices and statistical science converged in the interest of optimizing public health. Concerns over health and longevity are no less present in today's America, manifest in the nation's obsessions with fitness, diet, and appearance. While debates continue over the effectiveness of the U.S. medical system, one fact is indisputable. Americans consume more drugs and medicines than any other people on earth. This is due to the availability of prescriptions and the heavy marketing of over-the-counter remedies—both driven by a powerful pharmaceutical industry. Add to this the huge volume of recreational substances consumed by millions (often addictively), and it's clear that technologies of medication play a definitional role in modern culture, challenging definitions of nature and technology, real and artificial, and inside and outside.

Democracy is always a work in progress, even when people think they agree on what the idea means. This is to say that in theoretical terms democracy is characterized more as an ongoing condition than a singular moment. This inherent instability partly explains why some reach for founding documents, historical precedents, moral high ground, money, or even guns in an effort to tame the wildness that democracy implies. And of course nations like the U.S. long ago figured out that to make a philosophical ideal like democracy functional, dozens of constitutional instruments, party structures, and representative schema would be necessary. In all of this, tensions between individual and community, so deeply entrenched in American consciousness, seem to animate many of the nation's divisive struggles. For many people, something seems to get in the way of being able to hold both of these ideas in their minds simultaneously.

How does one build a society premised on the conflicts and aporias of belonging? Is it possible to negotiate the ongoing state of being one and many, inside and outside, or singularity and plurality?[5] One answer might lie in recognizing that difference itself is America's common currency, although many seem wired to think otherwise. Another route seems to reside in acknowledging a common interdependence and vulnerability. Both of these hinge on a recognition that the specific and general, the individual and collective, have a tendency to push people apart, rather than toward a future in which multiple forms of belonging animate collectivity. Affinity is one way of thinking in terms of the kinds of alliances, large and small, that people form with each other all the time. Without surrendering the particularities of anyone's experience, it seems possible to imagine ways of thinking together along multiple vectors of self-interest and collectivity, anxiety and hope, in approaching a future of radical openness based on connection rather than disconnection.[6] Perhaps a future not yet imagined.[7]

Notes

1 Jacques Derrida, *Aporias*, trans. Thomas Dutoit (Stanford, CA: Stanford University Press, 1993).

2 Barry Glassner, *The Culture of Fear: Why Americans Are Afraid of the Wrong Things* (New York: Basic Books, 1999).

3 Brian Massumi, "Everywhere You Want to Be: An Introduction to Fear," in Brian Massumi, ed., *The Politics of Everyday Fear* (Minneapolis: University of Minnesota Press, 1993).
4 Raymond Williams, *The Country and the City* (London: Chatto and Windus & Spokesman, 1973).
5 Jean-Luc Nancy, *Being Singular Plural* (Stanford, CA; Stanford University Press, 2000).
6 José Esteban Muñoz, *Cruising Utopia: The Then and Now of Queer Futurity* (New York: NYU Press, 2009) p. 11.
7 Ernst Bloch, *Literary Essays*, trans. Andrew Joron et al. (Stanford, CA: Stanford University Press, 1998) p. 341.

9

GAMING THE SYSTEM

Competition and Its Discontents

Americans celebrate contest as perhaps no other people, lauding the competitive marketplace as the true source of the nation's greatness in the world. Competition is seen as a crucial reward system, an engine of production, and, in its capitalistic manifestations, a driver of quality, innovation, and efficiency. Many see competition as embedded in human nature and an inescapable aspect of the "game of life," with one writer calling competition the U.S. "state religion."[1] Further incentivizing competition is a culture animated by American dreams of achievement and prosperity, purportedly achievable by anyone. Yet outside the dream, a certain paradox emerges in difficult economic times. When so many people seem to be losing the game, why do they still want to play? Or more profoundly stated: Can the game of life be imagined without competition?

Louis Althusser is known for describing ideology as a fictional rendering of society, which draws people into imaginary relationships to one another.[2] More than a narrowly political concept, Althusser used the term ideology to describe the broader ways that experience is rendered into mental images, much as Plato had suggested in his theory of forms. In extending this classical philosophical premise, Althusser noted the subjective character of "ideals" in shaping people's social outlooks, especially their attitudes to such "apparatuses" as the state and the marketplace. Althusser saw such ideologies and apparatuses as mutually constitutive, capable of reinforcing each other even in the face of contradiction or resistance. This explains, at least in part, why many Americans see a fundamental justice in their market economy, even as standards of living continue to fall. Time after time many working Americans vote against their economic interests, convinced that they have only themselves to blame for their downward mobility.

So strong is the ideology of the marketplace that individuals rarely think of questioning the apparatus that pits them against each other. Althusser's contemporaries made no bones about calling this a collective delusion—a form of ideological madness.[3] But Althusser saw the matter of ideology more deeply, as a function of the way people make meaning in their lives. Something about capitalism seemed to speak to their innermost desires and needs. Drawing on psychoanalysis, Althusser explained competition as a way of answering anxieties over imagined losses or absences. Even without the actual occurrence of a loss, many people sense that one might occur. Often this anticipation comes from early memories of absence, or perhaps an unnamed desire for something never acquired. But in either case, competition and material acquisition become not so much contests for specific gains or goods as signals of latent yearnings or cravings—for which no particular event or object can ever provide satisfaction. And because almost everyone experiences these yearnings, they do not always rise to the level of madness. Considering this broader view, is America's delirious love affair with competition (and capitalism) really a sign of insanity? Or does the nation simply need more insight about its wants and desires?

No Contest

Let's return to childhood for a moment. Think of all the ways that competitive ideals are promoted in school, sports, behavioral reward systems, and the market economy—and then consider the assumptions that lie beneath them. Alfie Kohn, one of the leading figures in U.S. progressive education, has argued that doubt and insecurity are the real drivers of American competition. Along with other values, adults project fears of scarcity and loss onto the young. Kohn writes in his book *No Contest: The Case against Competition (Why We Lose Our Race to Win)* that Americans are caught in a vicious circle in which individual anxieties and structural conditions reinforce each other. Children are conditioned in preparation for a world of presumed scarcity, based on the following contradictory ontology: "If I must defeat you in order to get what I want, then what I want must be scarce," Kohn states, explaining that when "competition sets itself as the goal, which is to win, scarcity is therefore created out of nothing."[4]

Of course this imaginary relationship to scarcity is reinforced in periods of economic decline, as manifest in the recent recession. In this way, transient scarcity appears more like an ongoing condition, giving credence to beliefs that competition and aggression among human beings is somehow "natural," in the way it sometimes appears to be in certain animal species. Scientists in the 17th century—notably Thomas Henry Huxley, Charles Darwin, and Herbert Spencer—advanced principles of "the survival of the fittest" in an age in which human agency and rationality were gaining ground as alternatives to magical views of social hierarchy. These new ideas fit well with emerging principles of capitalism and democracy. It was a neat package. And humankind was off to the races—metaphorically and literally. It wasn't until the industrial era that doubts about competition became widespread. But by then the free market had firmly established its grip on Western society—so much so that many saw capitalist competition as the defining ideology of the modern era. Hence, subsequent explanations of competition would place it at the intersection of material need, psychic desire, and the enormous social apparatus holding it in place.

Not that competition is evenly distributed in cultural terms. Nearly every demographic group in U.S. society comes with its own competitive assumptions, often varying according to age, ethnicity, and national origin. America's fondness for competition often carries unfortunate racial dimensions, owing to lingering social Darwinist beliefs in natural selection among human species. This thinking got a boost in the 1960s and the 1970s with the publication of books like *On Aggression* by Konrad Lorenz and *The Selfish Gene* by Richard Dawkins, both purportedly offering new scientific proof of innate human tendencies toward aggression, violence, and self-preservation. Lorenz popularized the "beast and man" comparison, with a healthy dose of determinism about gendered conflict among men. His reasoning would later take a bit of a beating itself when his sympathy with Nazi eugenics was made public. Dawkins similarly would be criticized for his book title which seemingly implied that molecular substances carried sentient consciousness.[5] Dawkins himself refuted this widespread misinterpretation, noting his more modest Darwinist arguments. But this didn't stop millions from believing that genes alone could be blamed for a vast array of behaviors—from aggression to gambling.

Everyone has a story of competition gone wrong. I can still remember the sadness I felt at my child's graduation from middle school. Parents, teachers, students, and family members had gathered in the assembly room for what many of us assumed was a celebration of collective accomplishment and individual effort. After platitudes were exchanged about the value of knowledge and personal integrity, an unexpected moment arrived—unexpected by me anyway—the "awards" ceremony. I had been naïve not to know this was coming. But before long kids were called to the stage for recognition as the school's best soccer player or scientist. To my surprise, my own child was honored with the year's writing award. I imagine that like other parents, the award brought me a momentary happiness. But then something caught my eye. One of my child's friends sat with her face in her hands, her body shuddering with tears. Then I noticed many others similarly crying in disappointment—and the horrific effect of this ritual hit me. In the psychic economy of this class of sixth graders, the few had been separated from the many in such a public way as to stigmatize the majority of students as non-meritorious. I knew that the moment of pride I felt would soon pass. But I wondered how long the sad memory of that day would linger in the memories of those crying students—the ritual of graduation so profoundly marked by differentiation rather than shared accomplishment.

Americans historically have made gendered assumptions about competition and cooperation, assigning aggressive/acquisitive tasks to boys and passive/nurturing ones to girls. While these archaic gender divides have fallen out of favor in the

21st century, it seems that competition has become the default setting for men and women alike. Sheryl Sandberg's highly influential recent book *Lean In: Women, Work, and the Will to Lead* is but one recent text telling women that they can play the game of life to win just like men.[6] While Sandberg advises women to see the "corporate ladder" more like a "jungle gym," the goal of getting to the top remains the ultimate reward. Here again, it bears mentioning that there is plenty of new scholarship and research indicating that human beings have never been "natural" competitors and that people's minds are not "wired" to require them to combat each other. Anthropologists have discovered plenty of societies that have gotten by without competition. And contemporary neuroscience is finding that empathy and compassion for others are among humanity's most fundamental instincts, even today.

"Competition is destructive to children's self-esteem, it interferes with learning, sabotages relationships, and isn't necessary," Kohn writes.[7] Most parents either believe in competition completely or believe it can be healthy if kept in perspective, Kohn explains—but next to none think it's a bad thing. After all, competition builds character, incentivizes effort, rewards achievement, instills teamwork, and perhaps most importantly, it introduces children to the real world of competition they will encounter as adults, or so people say. Kohn argues that in fact not one of these "life lessons" requires competition—and that the real lesson instilled by competition is one of personal inadequacy. In this light, it's no mystery that so many people comfort themselves with the easy satisfaction of instant entertainment or an online purchase. If this is the kind of character that losing builds, perhaps America would be better off with less of it. Winning doesn't build character either. Like the awards at the graduation ceremony I mentioned, such triumphs are short-lived moments of self-satisfaction derived from external evaluation, implying that one's character rises in proportion to the number of those beaten. The transitory character of such winning means that any gain is fragile and contingent on the outcome of the next contest, setting off a repeating cycle, until one ultimately fails to win. The external character of the evaluation can also make young people feel they are not in control of what happens to them, as researcher Carole Ames has noted. Ironically the very system of competition thought by many to instill a sense of subjective autonomy actually does the reverse. Agency can become weakened even among successful students, but it takes a greater toll on those who fail. This tends to produce lower achievement in both groups, along with a plethora of esteem-related problems.[8]

Much of America's love of competition is based on the assumption that people do their best when they are in a horse race—and that without the contest they would be complacent and lazy. In study after study conducted in schools over much of the past century, this simply has proven to be false. School competition, grade pressures, and high-stakes testing make young people anxious and often distract them from genuine learning. It discourages kids from sharing their knowledge and working together. Competition can even transform the school curriculum itself, as complex ideas are reduced to formulaic answers via "teaching to the test" mentality (that itself results from school accountability pressures forcing teachers to compete against each other to achieve standardized metrics). At a deeper level, competition can be a recipe for hostility. This has social implications, as youngsters come to regard other people as obstacles to their success. Trust and empathy begin to atrophy in a system in which one person's loss is another person's gain. Antagonism and aggression rise, with one study showing that competitive children are less generous and less willing to accept those who are different from them. This is not to say the kids can't be taught *about* competition and achievement. It is only to suggest the notions of growth, improvement, teamwork, and mastery don't need to be linked to scenarios of winning and losing.

Sports play a huge role in America's culture of competition—whether one is discussing kiddie soccer leagues or the mega-industry of televised sports. Add to this the booming expansion of the computer game industry, and there can be little doubt about the role of competitive "play" in American culture. Statisticians report that 72 percent of children in the U.S. play organized sports outside of school, 64 percent of adults watch NFL football, and 67 percent of households play video games.[9] So ubiquitous are sports that they are often considered too ordinary for critical analysis—their manifestations of competitive role play or simple "fun" so transparent as to require no explanation whatsoever. In this way, sports have become naturalized and depoliticized like many other aspects of everyday experience, much in the way that domestic life was once considered outside the realm of serious study. But what if one took sports seriously as sources of pleasure, engagement, and relational modeling? In recent years, a new generation of scholars has been doing just this, seeing sports as a lens through which issues of politics, nationality identity, gender, race, and social equality play themselves out. So powerful are sports in American society that they inhere deeply in the processes of neoliberalism, globalization, and cosmopolitanism that lie at the center of belonging in the United States. In this sense, sports function as what Robert Putnam in *Bowling Alone* called a "bridging capital" in integrating different groups across cultural boundaries.[10] Sports divide, exclude, and otherwise delegitimize huge cohorts of people, even as they seem to bring them together. The apparent innocence of sports is their greatest danger.

But times change—and in recent years the troubling aspects of sports have been in the news as never before. While success in sports has always correlated to youthful fitness, until recently little attention has been given to the toll that high-pressure competition puts on players' bodies. The widespread use of steroids and other illegal performance enhancements became impossible to ignore when seven-time winner of the Tour de France bicycle race Lance Armstrong was finally proven to have cheated in this way. While head trauma and brain damage long had been associated with boxing, stories now abound in the media about the Alzheimer's-like symptoms and lowered life expectancy of professional football players. America's pattern of denial about the long-term health risks of certain sports has been driven, at least in part, by the huge amount of money at stake. The millions paid to top athletes account for but a fraction of the $422 billion in revenues deriving from broadcasting, advertising, ticket sales, concessions, souvenirs, gambling, and the gigantic market of sports-related products, clothing, drinks, and other items.[11] Labor disputes now are common at every level of the industry. In the past year owners of three different leagues have locked out members of four different unions (NFL players, National Basketball Association players, NFL referees, and National Hockey League players). A federal court in 2014 ordered universities to create trust accounts for money made from the likenesses and names of individual players—profits the schools had formerly absorbed under "amateur" sports rules.[12] Meanwhile, after years of tolerating sexual misconduct by athletes and aggressive fans, numerous cases have come to light of harassment and abuse by coaches, notably Penn State coach Jerry Sandusky.

The time of denial is over for America's favorite escapist pastime. While no one doubts that sports and games can yield many benefits, the evidence is clear that this "escape" can also expose what is most troubling in the American psyche—from unbridled greed and exploitation to the brute exercise of power and violence. Enter Dave Zirin, sports columnist for *The Nation* magazine and author of the book *Game Over: How Politics Has Turned the Sports World Upside Down*. Zirin begins his book by quoting legendary sportscaster Howard Cosell, who famously said that the "number one rule of the jockocracy" is that sports and politics just don't mix. As Zirin stated in a recent interview:

> It's as though being political in itself is somehow antithetical to being an athlete or a sports fan—that somehow caring about what goes on in the world, or questioning and wondering and thinking critically about the role of sports in the wider culture, is somehow abnormal, uncool, and unmanly. And it's just this attitude that throughout the history of American sports has marginalized entire groups of people.[13]

Much of what Zirin reveals won't surprise many people: deeply ingrained patterns of sexism that excluded women for many years; ongoing racial inequities in which people of color struggled to join leagues only to now find themselves on teams owed by white millionaires; persistent homophobia on and off the field.

But beyond these specifics, Zirin makes two important general points: that the commercial imperative to "sell" sports viewership has driven its depoliticization by a corporate infrastructure with much to gain from its innocent enjoyment; and that violent competition on a mass scale reinforces an aggressive nationalism that maps perfectly onto a militaristic culture. Without giving the matter very much thought at all, viewers of the nation's most popular spectator sport—NFL football—are immersed in metaphors of ground and air attacks, blitz strategies, bullet and bomb passes, or coaches described as generals or field commanders. The U.S. national anthem often opens games, frequently followed by thanks to American service members. Super Bowl opening ceremonies regularly feature a flyover by Air Force combat jets. This is problematic for a number of reasons, not the least of which is its trivialization of war and actual military service. As Tracee Hamilton wrote in a recent *Washington Post* editorial, "War is hell. Football is a game. It's insulting to portray football as war, just as it's insulting to portray war as a game."[14] In response to such criticisms, NFL Films has removed direct war references from its products. But it isn't clear whether this is going to do much good. Ideology isn't shifted so easily in a nation enveloped in unsettling images everywhere it looks, especially when ideas as ubiquitous as worry and competition are so deeply woven into cultural attitudes, national mythology, peer behavior, shared beliefs, and the consumer economy.[15] Add to this the active *denial* of politics from a sports culture that so deeply supports particular narratives of power and nationalism.[16]

In this sense, sports culture can be seen as one piece of a larger system of integrated messaging about competition—its agenda so normalized as to become invisible. Roland Barthes wrote about the symbolic economy of sporting competition, noting the prevalence of moral investments by fans in their teams and heroes, the exhilaration in viewing the "spectacle" of conflict played out, and, most of all, that satisfaction of witnessing a form of "justice" culminating in the conclusion of the contest. Cognizant of the many popular justifications of sports (as moral lesson, or celebration of the body, for example), Barthes saw sports instead as a form of collective ritual—drawing communities or nations together for a shared experience. But the collective experience Barthes saw was not exactly what one might expect. "What wins the race is a certain concept of man and the world," Barthes wrote, "The concept is that man is proven by his actions, and man's actions are aimed, not at the domination of other men, but at the domination of things."[17] In enabling this control of the objective world, sports provide a powerful means of coming to terms with feelings of powerlessness. Most poignantly, Barthes noted the common objective in games like soccer, hockey, basketball, and football: the empty space of the "goal." The ultimate source of value registered in a game's score is the erasure of the void. In this way, sports function like many belief systems (religion, nationalism, capitalism) in providing metonymic displacements for deeper desires. This is why no single sports outcome (or any sports outcome, for that matter), ever satisfies the enthusiast's hunger for the game. The process of spectatorship in its endless indeterminacy is the actual attraction.

Doing God's Business

Though no one likes to admit it, Christianity is a fiercely competitive faith—and as such plays a largely unexamined role in the continuing advancement of American capitalism and other competitive ideologies. Along with other Abrahamic faiths, Christianity embodies deeply engrained doctrines of persecution, retribution, and personal transcendence, as well as a singular tendency for sectarian rivalry—manifest especially in its expansion in the U.S. This competitive ethos conflicts with principles of compassion and generosity espoused in biblical texts. And of course Christianity has adapted itself to all sorts of social and political contexts. It managed to accommodate the Roman Empire, feudalism, and early nationalism before conforming to democratic capitalism and laissez-faire neoliberalism. In its early iterations, Western Christianity thrived in societies premised on kinship structures, and later in those organized around principles of social obligation. Familial metaphors of fathers, mothers, "brotherhood," and "sisterhood" emerged in times when partnering, childrearing, descent, and lineage defined social and economic life. In tribal Christian societies, people shared or cooperated within extended families to compete against others for resources. But it's important to remember that such rivalries were often mediated or eliminated by intermarriage or other forms of accommodation. Nevertheless one finds in the Christian Bible, especially its Judaic Old Testament sections, an overarching self/other referencing, manifest in recurrent discussions of intergroup conflict, persecution, and exile.

With the rise of the secular state came the separation of religion from government. This was part of a larger dichotomization of private and public experience in Western epistemology. As capitalism took hold throughout Europe and the Americas, Christian theologians soon began to criticize the excesses taking place in the secular realm. In the 19th century American Gospel theologian Walter Rauschenbusch would write: "Capitalism has overdeveloped the selfish instincts in us all and left the capacity of devotion to larger ends shrunken and atrophied."[18] Pope Leo XIII would similarly criticize the rising tide of accumulation in quoting Thomas Aquinas: "Man should not consider his material possessions as his own, but as common to all, so as to share them without hesitation when others are in need."[19]

In this heated atmosphere Max Weber would write his opus *The Protestant Ethic and the Spirit of Capitalism*, published in installments in the first decades of the 20th century.[20] One of the architects of modern sociology, Weber was quick to point out that greed and material gain were not unique to capitalism, in temporal or spatial terms. Plenty of wars had been fought over land, money, and resources. Weber adapted Marx's theory of ideology in pointing to ways that labor and goods were "rationalized" as people came to want more than they needed, even as they were obliged to work for whatever wages they could get. And of course Protestant teachings would tell them not to complain, sinners that they were. Weber was notably cautious about generalizing about Christianity, noting that Calvinist and Puritan traditions promoted capitalism more directly than Catholicism, for example. But as Anthony Giddens would observe in discussing Weber's work, Judeo-Christian attitudes toward guilt and salvation played an important role in the molding of the Western mind. In his own *Capitalism and Modern Social Theory*, Giddens would praise Weber for providing early insights linking capitalism "to the study of social institutions brought into being by the industrial transformation" which culminated in the 20th century.[21]

Fast-forward to the new millennium. One of the little discussed realities of neoliberal ascension has been the collusion of the Christian church in the process. While Hobby Lobby may have gotten some headlines for inserting its fundamentalism into the company's employee benefits policies, lots of other high-profile corporations promote faith-based agendas in even more obvious ways. In-N-Out Burger prints Bible verses on its cups and wrappers, Forever 21 does the same thing with its shopping bags, Chick-fil-A locks its doors on Sundays, Tyson Foods employs chaplains to preach in its factories, Mary Kay cosmetics trains employees that God is its business partner. Christian business schools are so widespread that they even have their own ranking system, similar to that of universities and technical schools. Christian business magazines are everywhere, as are a myriad of books with titles like *Doing God's Business, Kingdom Calling, Christian Business Secrets, Work as Worship, Business for the Glory of God, Business Mission*, and *The Gospel at Work*. As Jeff Van Duzer writes in *Why Business Matters to God*, "Business exists in society in order to provide a platform where people can express aspects of their God-given identity through meaningful and creative work and to provide goods and services to a community to enable it to flourish."[22] While it is tempting to think that Christian business people would be governed by the impulses of fairness, generosity, and charity often associated with their faith, it turns out that many of them either leave their faith at the door or use it to justify their avaricious behavior. For example, Hobby Lobby billionaire David Green has said, "If you have anything or I have anything, it's because it is given to us by our Creator."[23]

Earlier I described competition as a symptom of anticipated threat or loss, linked to deeply held desires for security and wholeness. Emerging in the minds of individuals, these common yearnings call forth social structures to answer them—often in an imperfect way. There are clear reasons why democratic capitalism became the prevailing doctrine of the United States, given the nation's turbulent past and its messianic ambitions. But there are equally clear explanations for why the system periodically has spun out of control in ways that some have called simply crazy. Competition defines the self in a peculiar relationship to what lies around it, not merely as external, but often as malevolently so. In a sense, competition depends on the separations it creates—and melts away when the boundaries become permeable.

It is commonly assumed that competition implies the absence of cooperation and vice versa. But it also goes without saying that no contest is possible without a commonly held point of comparison—that in any sport, for example, no competition could take place without a mutually agreed upon set of rules. Even "competing with oneself" requires a relational benchmark or an imagined pairing as a basis of comparison. In a similar way cooperation is generally defined as an activity for mutual benefit, but it always implies a gain that must be wrested from somewhere—through a competition with nature, other people, or antagonistic interests of some form. These contradictions play into the primordial tension between individual and collective interests concretized in American-style democracy, but also in play in nearly every society throughout the world. The U.S. valorizes individual interest in the widely held belief that its capitalist system gives everyone a fair chance at success. Yet citizens also cooperate as groups to build families, corporations, or unions because collective enterprises empower individuals to do more than they can by themselves. But these days no one needs reminding that this theoretically "fair" system is broken—and this is not the first time that such sentiments have arisen.

Frank Capra's Depression-era film *American Madness* (1932) tells the story of banker Tom Dixon, whose generosity toward struggling clients makes him seem insane to his corporate peers. As Dixon's efforts for the "little guy" become known, his board of directors becomes increasing anxious that Dixon "is not interested in profits" and sees his depositors as "friends" rather than customers.[24] Eventually Dixon is blamed when money goes missing from the bank—and the irrationality (and dishonesty) of Dixon's peers is revealed. The message of the film would become a familiar one—that the U.S. had descended into a form of capitalistic delusion, driven by obsessive materialism and structural unfairness. In doing so, *American Madness* builds on long-standing legacies of liberal/conservative economic conflict, as well as tendencies of both sides to label each other as crazy, immoral, or otherwise out of touch with reason or truth. Similar assertions of socioeconomic insanity have arisen in the 2000s. On the heels of the recent recession, Henry A. Giroux captured the staying power of this debate in an essay entitled "America's Descent into Madness."[25] Giroux used a language of pathology in describing a U.S. that "celebrates a narcissistic hyper-individualism that radiates a near sociopathic lack of interest in—or compassion and responsibility for—others."[26] He is hardly alone in these sentiments.

In his book, *American Mania: When More Is Not Enough*, psychiatrist Peter Whybrow discussed American competition as an instinctual habit transformed though culture into a machine now out of control, noting what he terms the nation's "dysfunctional" obsession with solitary achievement and personal gain. "We must strive to understand the roots of the growing conflict that exists in American culture between our instinctual striving for more and the reward system of the affluent society that we have built for ourselves," Whybrow writes.[27] Employing mental health terminology and metaphors, Whybrow discusses a public mind bursting with energy, agitation, impulsivity, and irritability. Leaving the legacy of Adam Smith's famous prescriptions for free markets intact, Whybrow points out that what might have seemed "reasonable" in the 1700s may not apply in the 2000s. Rather than framing competition and cooperation in oppositional terms, Whybrow summarizes the utopian vision of democratic capitalism thus:

> A market culture is essentially an ordering of human instinct and competition by those traditional cooperative, sharing practices that our forebears found to be fruitful and successful. Through the give-and-take of social interaction, and through the internalization of the conventions and customs it promotes, instinctual self-interest is liberated and molded to the common good.[28]

Like many utopian visions, America's grand experiment in democratic capitalism would falter in practical application. A few decades after the founding of the republic, Alexis de Tocqueville wrote in *Democracy in America* of a system degenerating into a "game of chance" with citizens facing a "daily battle" for their material necessities.[29] Of course, no student of American history needs to be reminded about what happened next, as industrialization and urbanization fueled growing class division and exploitation by the modern corporation. Factor in the role of the media in shaping public consciousness and the stage was set for the "mania" of an information age of one-click shopping, instant viewing, cyber-dating, online trading, telecommuting, and ubiquitous workaholism. The result is a generalized social malaise, and what Whybrow now sees as a lurking danger:

> For many Americans the sense of exhilaration and the reward-laden opportunities afforded by the manic society are compelling, indeed even habit forming. But for those mentally unprepared or unwilling to impose personal constraint, there are dangers in such a demand-driven, helter-skelter existence. As any individual who has suffered mania knows, despite the seductive quality of the initial phases of the condition, life at the manic edge is impossible to sustain in any coherent fashion.[30]

Less extreme explanations of consumer "mania" have been part of psychoanalytic discourse for decades. Many of these ideas derive from Freud's modeling of various human drives and desires. Prominent in contemporary critical discourse is the concept of libido, as discussed briefly in Chapter 5. Child development experts had long observed that infants are born into conditions of need and dependence, hungering for sustenance and craving the comfort of another being. Noting that babies first develop a sense of self through a relationship with an early caregiver, Freud identified an initial recognition of a "you" and a "me" in that initial dyad.[31] Gratification from this early contact forms the basis of libidinal wanting, which evolves into various stages of sexual desire, according to Freud. Almost from the beginning the libido is regulated by the unconscious ego, later supported by a governing superego. But central to all of these processes is the underlying dynamic of lack: the hunger for something needed but temporarily withheld—be that food, warmth, recognition, erotic satisfaction, or material possessions. Freud famously described the ways that this hunger operates at an unconscious level, manifest in latent yearnings, symbolic desires, and fantasies. These days contemporary advances in neurobiology and brain imaging have confirmed Freud's theories in locating the libido in the brain region of what is known as the limbic system and the superego in the prefrontal cortex governing system. These two systems correspond to our "emotional" and "rational" selves, roughly speaking, although scientists also tell us that our different brain regions constantly interact. While I'm oversimplifying this description somewhat, the point is that Freud formulated a model, now confirmed by contemporary neuroscience, in which self-interested libidinous drives are constrained by a supervening superego. In what follows I'll describe how more recent theory has asserted that this system has gotten out of whack.

Capitalism and Schizophrenia

Postmodernists started sounding the alarm in the 1990s, as theorists in many fields began to worry that something was shifting in the character of American subjectivity. Contemporary culture was losing its moorings, many said, and was drifting into a vacuous state of confusion. Mass media and consumerism got a lot of the blame, although many said the crisis of meaning ran deeper. The delicate balance between individual and community also had been disturbed, unhinging people's understandings of themselves and their relationships to others. Fredric Jameson was among the first to label this shift a kind of schizophrenia overtaking the American psyche.[32] Extending fundamental Marxist premises of alienation and false consciousness, Jameson looked to psychoanalytic theory to further explicate the transformation of the self in a postmodern age of blurred meanings, image bombardment, and manic consumerism. To put it simply, Jameson argued that postmodern culture interferes with people's ability to know themselves and develop a coherent ego structure. This leaves them vulnerable to the seductions of the marketplace and the fantasy worlds of images—all of which reduce the mind to a "schizophrenic" state.

This schizophrenic confusion results from a person's inability to "accede fully into the realm of speech and language," Jameson wrote.[33] And due to this confusion, the schizophrenic can't differentiate between itself and the world—and hence has an unstable or nonexistent identity. Postmodern neoliberal capitalism instills schizophrenic consciousness by operating in so many simultaneous realms that it is impossible to track. This is especially problematic in an image-based society, since pictures present people with more information than they immediately can process. With the mind overloaded by stimuli one grasps for fleeting meanings, yet remains unable to critically analyze what flashes before one's eyes. All the while, fragments of advertisements, romantic fantasies, and violent news reports accumulate in an incoherent jumble—paralyzing any ability to make coherent assessments or combat their effects on the libidinous unconscious.

Digging a little deeper into this analysis of identity confusion, Barthes spoke about the ways that viewers project themselves into the media images of advertising and entertainment.[34] At least in part, audiences "narcissistically identify" with the people seen in advertisements, movies, or online—momentarily imagining themselves in the role of the fashion model, narrative protagonist, or game avatar. Communication scholars in the area of reception theory have studied this process of identification in film viewing, for example, as viewers enter stories, seeing themselves in dramatic portrayals, anticipating narrative progression, predicting outcomes, and even imagining alternative scenarios. As anyone who has been moved by a good book or movie knows, the effects of this identification can be meaningful and long lasting. When one experiences such events dozens or hundreds of times in the course of a day, the effect also can be jarring and disorienting. One is drawn to this process of identification as a means of knowing and confirming who one is, but its rapid disruption shakes the ability to hold a sense of identity and place—again, producing a quasi-schizophrenia.

Not everyone sees this as a completely bad thing. Contrarians have pointed out that schizophrenic disconnection from meaning and identity can have both negative and positive effects, or a combination of both. Pessimists say that schizophrenic dislocation leaves people vulnerable to powerful forces like capitalism or dominant ideologies. This is not unlike certain Marxist analyses of culture, which see audiences and consumers as unknowing pawns or passive victims of oppressive systems. But a more positive view counters that when the mind is in flux these forces never take over completely. Possibilities always exist to grasp, negotiate, or resist any forces trying to take advantage—allowing mediation, resistance, or the invention of new systems. In *A Thousand Plateaus: Capitalism and Schizophrenia,* Gilles Deleuze and Félix Guattari theorized both individual subjectivity and the larger society as infinitely differentiated, yet connected, in the manner of an organic rhizome.[35] Because of their complex architecture, social apparatuses like capitalism have the potential to disaggregate as their "codes" shift over time. Using the analogy of a map, Deleuze and Guattari spoke of the "deterritorialization" and "reterritorialization" of consciousness and social formations. A club is an example of such territorializing, although the concept has been used more recently to describe the ways that telecommunications and multinational capitalism reorganize groups and entire populations.

Globalization has reterritorialized commerce and culture across national boundaries and reshaped the world into one giant marketplace. The resulting "new" economy plays by the same "old" rules of supply and demand (for goods and labor alike), except that it operates in extralegal spaces between or beyond the regulatory capabilities of individual countries. Hence American companies constrained by U.S. labor laws can sell goods made for pennies by factory workers in Bangladesh or China, as cogently documented in Robert Greenwald's film *Wal-Mart: The High Cost of a Low Price* (2005) and hundreds of other journalistic accounts.[36] Economic reterritorialization has produced another "third world" right here in the United States—quite a few third worlds to be exact—as what used to be called "labor" has been transformed by technology and the marketplace. Even though "unemployment" has been decreasing in recent years, little mention is made that seven times more part-time jobs have been created than full-time ones.[37] Seen in these terms, the psychic dislocations of consumer culture are further aggravated by people's fragmented work lives, not to mention the fact that so many are simply underemployed. Add to this that so many new jobs have been created in the disembodied realm of online networks, creating what is been called the "homework" economy. Businesses save on workplace costs and employees don't need to punch a time clock—or so proponents of homework assert. But put another way, individual homes have now become factories that workers can never leave at the end of the day. Not only does this install the supervisor in the worker's very dwelling and mind, such new arrangements also make it nearly impossible for employees to organize in collective bargaining.

But Deleuze and Guattari worried more about deterritorialization as a process of psychic dislocation made ubiquitous in contemporary capitalist culture. This dislocation interfered with psychoanalytic principles of drives and desires described by Freud and Lacan—in effect, refuting their premises as well. In naming schizophrenia as a broadly experienced condition of postmodern existence, Deleuze and Guattari argued that people were more than the sum of neuroses and complexes gotten from mommy and daddy. Following this reasoning, they criticized the therapeutic "treatment" of patients aimed at helping them to recognize and come to terms with reductionist diagnostic categories. Rather than seeing people mired in internal psychological battles over what is "real" or "imaginary," for example, Deleuze and Guattari said that the postmodern schizophrenic has the ability to invent new worlds—much as artists, revolutionaries, and innovators have always done. This "worlding" capability of the schizophrenic has made Deleuze and Guattari's ideas popular to a millennial generation often dismayed by the seemingly inescapable conditions of contemporary neoliberalism. In this admittedly intellectualized form, schizophrenia is seen as both the illness and the cure.

How does any of this play out in practical terms? Is this radical schizophrenic postmodernism having an effect anywhere, or is this simply an intellectual finger exercise? The answer is that this radical subjectivity is accessible to anyone who can recognize it for what it is. Earlier in this book, I discussed the blurring of distinctions between makers and consumers, manifest in the transformations of the marketplace resulting from online sales of homemade goods, the DIY movement in general, and the growing popularity of recycled commodities. So-called slacker living has moved the social margins to the mainstream, especially as many Americans learned to get by with less and less in the recession of the early 2000s. Not that putting off buying the latest iPhone is an especially new concept. Hand-me-down jeans were well known to working people long before they started selling for $200 a pair in high-fashion boutiques. In this sense, it's worth remembering that popular resistance to market commodification has a very long history dating back to the earliest days of industrial mass production. In his intriguing 2010 article "Towards a Radical Anti-Capitalist Schizophrenia?" Jonah

Paretti reviewed various forms of non-commodified exchange and alternative models of community endemic in American cultural traditions of independence and self-reliance, when noting how in the current moment "media-savvy youth consume the accelerated visual culture of late capitalism yet do not develop ego-formations that result in consumer shopping."[38] Paretti observed that an articulated political program was often lacking in today's slacker culture, however. In contrast, he pointed to the work of queer activists and postmodern artists as examples of more pointed critiques of neoliberalism.

Let's not forget Occupy Wall Street (OWS), the movement launched in 2011 in New York City's financial district, but which quickly spread to other cities around the world. With the iconic slogan "We are the 99%," Occupy spoke to the class-based legacy of the American New Left—but with an important twist for neoliberal times. While contesting corporate agendas and their enabling hierarchies, OWS also "refused" the system's schizophrenic ideology in meeting postmodern neoliberalism with a suitably deconstructionist critique. The very use of the term "occupy" evoked a sense of provisional control, rather than permanent sovereignty. Of course OWS's complex platform frustrated critics and journalists alike—leading to a certain incoherence in press coverage. Commentators had trouble describing a movement with no center. For example, Occupy's populist egalitarianism extended to the very organization and program, with the movement eschewing a vanguard leadership structure or singular list of demands. As J. Jack Halberstam observed, "They don't want to present a manifesto, they actually are themselves the manifesto of discontent. The 99 percenters simply show up, take up space, make noise, witness. This is a form of political response that doesn't announce itself as politics."[39]

In this way, OWS demonstrations exemplified the performativity of the "carnivalesque" outlined by Russian philosopher Mikhail Bakhtin in the 1960s. To Bakhtin the carnival was a celebratory disruption of daily routines and social conventions in which the presence of participants, manifest through their bodies, was foregrounded. OWS's "Declaration of the Occupation of New York City" began by stating:

> As one people, united, we acknowledge the reality: that the future of the human race requires the cooperation of its members; that our system must protect our rights, and upon corruption of that system, it is up to the individuals to protect their own rights, and those of their neighbors; that a democratic government derives its just power from the people, but corporations do not seek consent to extract wealth from the people and the Earth; and that no true democracy is attainable when the process is determined by economic power. We come to you at a time when corporations, which place profit over people, self-interest over justice, and oppression over equality, run our governments. We have peaceably assembled here, as is our right, to let these facts be known.[40]

Elegant in theoretical terms, Occupy proved in practice to be a flash in the pan. OWS's initial months were ones of frenzied success, as scores of "occupations" occurred in Amsterdam, Atlanta, Boston, Chicago, Los Angeles, Madrid, Montréal, Paris, Philadelphia, Rio de Janeiro, Sydney, Toronto, and many other places. For a while it seemed as though the 99 percent really was rising up and would take the day. But within the U.S., the Occupy movement failed to find a foothold in the mainstream two-party political system. Because it had no leaders, no OWS representative ran for office. Because its concerns were so diverse, no OWS legislation was ever proposed. Meanwhile, the upstart conservative Tea Party movement could point to OWS as evidence of the anarchistic depravity spreading through American youth culture. Within little more than a year, the Tea Party would become a formidable force as OWS drifted into oblivion. Researchers would later link Occupy's demise to a vulnerability common to many progressive coalition movements. "Liberals tend to underestimate their similarity to other liberals," the researchers stated, "while conservatives overestimate their similarities."[41] Appearing in the journal *Psychological Science*, the study said that OWS's reluctance to reach closure on its goals and ambition not only made it's program difficult for outsiders to support, but it also eroded OWS's own internal solidarity.

Adorno might have described OWS's downfall as a problem of "negative dialectics," meaning that the movement chose not to organize around the very coherences that drove the Tea Party.[42] Occupy was not, in fact, a warmed-up version of New Left solidarity movements arguing for workers' rights or economic justice alone. OWS saw neoliberal capitalism as the structuring agent of consciousness itself, reinforcing the very illusions of autonomous subjectivity that held it in place. Rather than promoting independence, freedom, and a "correct" pathway to liberation, Occupy simply called for a refusal of business as usual—as a way of opening space for a future yet to be written. If Occupy had a shortcoming, it might have been in overestimating the prevailing zeitgeist of disaffection it sought to mobilize. But viewed more philosophically, it would be incorrect to read a failure into OWS's demise—because that history has yet to reach its end.

The Power of Giving

Let's assume humanity is more than a rat race of individuals, as Margaret Thatcher once claimed in famously stating that "there is no such thing as society."[43] Even the most extreme conservatives and libertarians concede that some level of government is necessary to build roads and provide national defense, for example. And a longer view of history shows that the human need for cooperation runs deeper than this—if for no other reason than one of basic survival. But these days the idea of cooperation remains a deeply contested issue, especially when it comes to money. To many Americans, ideals of equal opportunity and limitless acquisition don't always square with the realities of structural inequity and downward mobility. In the mythic construction of the American left and right, "big government" is often juxtaposed with "small government," with little space in between. As the recession of the 2000s pushed growing numbers into categories of need, so did tensions over how to help them—with America's balance of individual and collective values put to the test in conflicts over "public" assistance versus "private" charity.

Many Americans believe that philanthropy is guided by the sense of reciprocity, whereby those who prosper feel obligated to give back. But behind such altruistic ideals lies a more fundamental set of exchange relationships, which in one way or another inform the principle of economy itself. In his classic 1923 work, *The Gift: Forms and Functions of Exchange*, the anthropologist Marcel Mauss studied economies existing before or outside of capitalism in tribal societies in Asia, Australia, and the Americas. Mauss described a symbolic economy of giving in which a psychic exchange undergirds a material one. Perhaps the most striking finding that Mauss made involved the impermanence of possession. To put it simply, not all cultures get hung up on the idea of owning things forever. A lot of this had to do with the fact that primitive societies needed to share food, tools, and shelter simply to survive. But this sharing also invariably brought with it certain rituals and belief systems. Malaysian and Trobriander peoples saw themselves with three obligations: to give, to receive, and to reciprocate. This meant that one was expected not only to give to others, but also to graciously accept things one was given, and that cycles of giving and receiving were ongoing and mutually reinforcing. In nearly all cultures examined, Mauss found that such giving often was sacralized in relation to a god or the dead—much in the way that "alms" practices would evolve in Buddhist and Christian theology. Mauss limited his work to those he studied, and refrained from extrapolating his findings to contemporary Western cultures. But he identified what to many seems a fundamental insight: that when people get something, they often feel like giving back, and vice versa.

Mauss also observed patterns of competition in what one would now call philanthropy, as social capital would accrue to those making the gifts as in the form of admiration or respect. Even in non-capitalistic societies, public recognition of giving functioned as a personal and tribal value that only intensified as the size of the gift increased. And with the prestige of recognition, other forms of social capital would attach to the giver: gratitude, respect, and admiration. In stratified capitalistic societies these exchanges take on added meaning, amplifying asymmetrical relationships of authority and control. Recipients of gifts are still expected to "give back." But when they lack the material means to reciprocate, they are often expected to return the favor with prescribed behaviors. Hence, in Western societies philanthropy has often produced literal or symbolic economies based on market principles.

Consider the case of Andrew Carnegie. Memorialized by the foundations, museums, and schools bearing his name, Carnegie was also a ruthless titan of American industry. Before his legendary generosity kicked in, Carnegie was famous for exploiting his workers and crushing unions—often by violent means.

These tactics reached a breaking point in 1892, when his agents shot seven strikers dead at his Homestead Steel Mill. Shortly afterwards, Carnegie launched a public relations campaign to rebrand himself a Christian humanitarian, notably by circulating an essay entitled "The Gospel of Wealth" to leading newspapers. While labor leaders at the time branded him the consummate hypocrite, Carnegie clearly knew the power of positive messaging.[44] Carnegie's "Gospel" flattered ascendant industrialists of his time by saying that they themselves were the best stewards of their riches. Excoriating government welfare and the scourge of European-style socialism, Carnegie preached the value of an ownership society: "Upon the sacredness of property civilization itself depends—the right of the laborer to his hundred dollars in the savings bank, and equally the legal right of the millionaire to his millions," he wrote.[45] A harsh man to the end, Carnegie saw philanthropy as a tool of social engineering—a means of inducing productive behavior with a financial reward system. Should a recipient fail to respond, support was to be withdrawn quickly. Carnegie scorned anyone who would sustain the poor indefinitely, agreeing with Herbert Spencer that poverty came from flawed character and that wealth was a sign of virtue. Sustained charity "is unwisely spent; so spent, indeed as to produce the very evils which it proposes to mitigate or cure," Carnegie wrote.[46] Today such calculated behaviorism persists in much private sector giving and even public "welfare-to-work" programs.

But not all giving is so directly manipulative. Many philanthropic contributors will say they give to causes they "care" about—often for personal reasons. Churches pitch to their congregations, schools fundraise from alumni, and hospitals solicit former patients. And in broader terms, charity is seen by some people as a form of contributing to the public good. But as everyone knows, such participation often veils a latent self-interest of some kind. While some patrons will make anonymous donations or content themselves with passive support, others will demand personal favors, board memberships, or other roles in the governance of the places they sponsor. In an age in which nonprofit organizations increasingly are encouraged to behave in an "entrepreneurial" spirit, donations are now termed "investments" rather than gifts—in a veiled concession to the market system from which the money was generated.

At the end of the day, most people give money to things they believe in. And most often this giving comes in the form of small donations from people without huge incomes. According to the National Philanthropic Trust, 95 percent of American households have given to charities of some kind.[47] Of the $335 billion contributed in 2013, less than 5 percent came from corporations and 14 percent from foundations. Individual gifts accounted for 72 percent of giving. One out of every three dollars went to religious institutions, with the next largest category being education. It's also worth noting that money wasn't all that people gave—with one in four American adults donating volunteer time. When asked about why they contributed, most people spoke of "giving back" to the community. But in fact people's reasons are often more complex.

Private philanthropy doesn't like distance, which is one reason that people give so much to their own churches and schools. In other words, there is a strong tendency to give money to causes that return a tangible benefit to the donor or to those the contributor knows or recognizes as deserving. Such "enlightened self-interest" occurs when one literally sees a personal benefit in helping someone else. This can range from the direct benefit of giving to a school that a family member attends—to the ideological advancement of giving to a favored cause or a political organization. While nonprofit organizations are supposedly "nonpolitical" according to IRS regulations, the selective enforcement or nonenforcement of such provisions has been the subject of great scrutiny in recent years.

Also, an emotional payback from giving often lurks behind many fundraising appeals. Increasingly, savvy charities and foundations enlist psychologists as consultants for their campaigns. "Altruism isn't exactly simple," explains consultant Krystall Dunaway in discussing the many forms of payback that come from philanthropy. According to Dunaway, common ideals of "pure" altruism often underestimate the extent to which "performing the selfless act (i.e., giving to a charity) also benefits the self (mainly through positive feelings about doing a good thing)."[48]

She adds that the "good feeling" often associated with giving also can be described as a narcissistic reward or a complement to the philanthropist's social status, achievement, power, and authority. In this regard, it is no surprise the people giving to institutions want to be recognized with their identities listed in reports, on wall plaques, or even in the names of buildings or programs.

What about other motivations for giving? While many people report a positive psychological benefit to "helping others," what does this mean exactly? Certainly, giving can bolster the philanthropist's sense of agency described by Mauss—through ego gratification, competitive recognition, and implied (or literal) obligation to the benefactor. While the notion of giving back can be seen as a form of gift reciprocity, it's often little more than good old-fashioned guilt. The recent rise in anonymous philanthropy is a curious phenomenon in this regard. In purely practical terms, some rich people donate in secrecy to hide their wealth. According to a recent *Wall Street Journal* article, they either don't want to be assaulted by other charities or don't want to seem different from neighbors struggling in a flagging economy. Charities walk a fine line these days—between protecting the identities of some donors while simultaneously broadcasting the names of others whose generosity might inspire peer gifts.[49] Guilt always has been the favorite tool of the charity fundraiser—from the wide-eyed kids in Save the Children ads to PETAs shocking images of mutilated animals. "Innocence" is a major ploy in such campaigns—which implicitly suggest hierarchies of need and moral purpose in giving. Also, the photogenic aspects of some problems make them much more marketable than others.

Precious little money in the United States is donated to causes like diabetes, obesity, mental illness, and substance abuse—even though these are among the leading killers of Americans today. Meanwhile, outfits like the Kids Wish

Network are pulling in tens of millions of dollars with their hyperbolic ad campaigns on behalf of dying children and their families. This year it became public knowledge that the Kids Wish Network spends less than three cents to the dollar on its stated goals, with the rest of its contributors' money fueling its massive fundraising and administrative edifice. Newspapers in Florida concerned about charities that scam seniors with such pitches drew up a list of the "50 Worst Charities," defined as those that budget less than 4 percent of their income on their "causes." Appearing among the top ten were the Kids Wish Network, the Children's Wish Foundation, the Children's Cancer Fund, the Firefighters Charitable Foundation, and the National Veteran Service Fund.[50] It is estimated that 1,800 of the nation's 76 million children will die from cancer in the coming year—about 1 in 36,000.[51] But 1 in 10 of them will die before middle age from obesity-related problems.[52] American society shouldn't be in the business of weighing the relative value of illnesses or lives—of children or adults—against each other. Unfortunately, highly publicized private charities do exactly this.

As you might expect, guilt has gotten a lot of attention in the literature of giving psychology—whether one is looking at rich kids who inherit their fortunes or people making windfall profits in business. While American culture may be driven by a mind-set that "more is not enough," an undertow of Protestant work ethic and communal responsibility lurk beneath the surface. Also keep in mind that most religions—especially the Christian ones that dominate America—preach the evils of greed and sloth, nagging at the collective superego even as people work and spend at a manic pace. Many of America's early settlers were consumed by such beliefs. They tempered their colonizing impulses with rationales that they were sharing God's word with indigenous people. Ironically the natives often greeted arriving ships with actual gifts of food and handicraft. The point is that both cultures exhibited the kind of reciprocal attitudes toward exchange described by Mauss, even though understood in different terms.[53]

Game Over

It is sometimes said that the denial of politics is politics in its most dangerous form. Such denial often resides in ideological structures seen as harmless, natural, or simply part of a normative "common sense." Americans tend to depoliticize competition this way, or fold it into presumed consensus values like democracy and free enterprise. But dig a little deeper into the ideology of competition, and one finds deeply entrenched oppositional (and often prejudicial) values writ large, valorizing historically privileged groups over others. American narratives of competition pull people in with promises of winning if one plays by the rules and does one's best in a system one writer calls "casino capitalism."[54] The dramatic lure of the contest is maintained through the endless repetition of struggles large and small. Many are reluctant to admit that, like the game of mortality itself, the house always wins in the end. In this state of denial, Americans feel compelled to battle each other even as the realities of the contest become glaringly apparent. But in recent years faith in the system appears to be wavering.

Opinion surveys reveal that millennial youth are far more likely than previous generations to worry about their future. Many of these young people have come of age listening to family members fretting about jobs and money. Significant numbers of those aged 18–35 report anxiety about finding employment (66 percent), paying the bills (60 percent), being able to support a family (59 percent), and affording a college education (56 percent).[55] According to the Pew Research Center, "Millennials are burdened with higher levels of student loan debt, poverty, and unemployment than previous generations had at that same age. Millennials are also currently experiencing lower levels of wealth and personal income than the generations that preceded them."[56] While symptoms of the problem may abound, solutions for fixing America's competitive society remain elusive. Most people feel that the issue is just too big—that competition is so ingrained in American culture that options are unthinkable. At the same time lingering worries abound that yet another economic "crash" is just around the corner, and that eventually the corporate house of cards will collapse, as Marx once predicted.

Amid growing uncertainty about the legitimacy of the American dream, popular culture seems riven with stories of paranoia, suspicion, and even direct critiques of competitive culture. The popularity of dystopian computer game narratives says something about a growing undercurrent in U.S. society, especially among younger audiences. Book series like Suzanne Collins's *The Hunger Games* (2008–2010), Veronica Roth's *Divergent* (2011–2013) and single titles like Lois Lowry's *The Giver* (1993)—all recently adapted for film—have become cult classics in their depictions of protagonists pitted against a malevolent corporate state. Near the end of Collins's *Catching Fire*, heroine Katniss Everdeen shoots an arrow into the sky, shattering the invisible bubble containing contestants in an artificial arena. The metaphor resonated for obvious reasons. While on some level, *Hunger Games*–type books and movies can be seen as classic coming-of-age narratives, they can be read just as reasonably as the quintessential stories of our times. Futuristic dystopias commonly critique their present moment, as when George Orwell's *1984* (1944) illuminated the manic-nationalism of its day, manifest in pervasive Big Brother surveillance, censorship, and propaganda. Today's popular television series like *The Blacklist, House of Cards, Nikita, Scandal,* and *Revolution* all hinge on resistance against invisible regimes of oppressive power linked to corporate-state collusion. In other words, these popular entertainment products seem to name neoliberalism as the enemy.

Meanwhile, within academia a determined subculture is emerging to analyze the effects of a rigged system. "We are all used to having our dreams crushed, our hopes smashed, our illusions shattered," wrote Judith Halberstam in *The Queer Art of Failure*, "but what comes after hope?"[57] Halberstam argues against all-or-nothing views of success and failure, while also asserting the positive value of disappointment in opening the door to alternative thought. "Under certain circumstances failing, losing, forgetting, unmaking, undoing, unbecoming, not knowing may in fact offer more creative, more cooperative, more surprising ways of being in the world."[58] Ann Cvetkovich made a similar point in her book *Depression: A Public Feeling*. At a historical moment when the contradictions seem to be widening between America's optimistic ideals and its pessimistic realities, Cvetkovich used a language of possibility in describing "a utopia that doesn't make simple distinctions between good and bad feelings or assume that good politics can only emerge from good feelings; feeling bad might, in fact, be the ground for transformation."[59]

Without a doubt, educators make a good point in accenting the intergenerational character of competition—and the potential for intervention in the cycle. This has been a major incentive behind the progressive school movement for much of the last half century, although the idea of noncompetitive schooling also has been criticized by many sides (as inconsistent with American values, as a conceit of economic privilege, as unresponsive to new immigrants, etc.). On the other hand, it seems reasonable to propose that families and schools might model cooperative behaviors and teach *about* competition as a potential risk factor, much as schools today warn students about bullying and drug use. Along similar lines, if one understands that competition and related issues of comparative self-worth inhere within myriad identity structures, competition can be addressed in exactly those adjacent territories. For example, advertising images promoting gender stereotypes do so via implicit points of comparison. Deconstructing the stereotype dismantles the competition. In other words, it seems thinkable to break down many kinds of competition by understanding the foundational premises on which they reside. In what follows I will discuss the relationship of this drive, symptomized by consumer behavior, to other factors related to belonging or not belonging *Elsewhere in America*.

Notes

1 Pau Wachtel, *The Poverty of Affluence: A Psychological Portrait of American Life* (New York: Free Press, 1983) p. 284.
2 Louis Althusser, "Ideology and Ideological State Apparatuses (Notes Toward an Investigation)," *Lenin and Philosophy and Other Essays*, trans. Ben Brewster (New York: Monthly Review Press, 1971).
3 Friedrich Engels, "Letter to Franz Mehring," *Marx and Engels Correspondence* (1893) http://www.marxists.org/archive/marx/works/1893/letters/93_07_14.htm (accessed Jan. 17, 2015).
4 Alfie Kohn, *No Contest: The Case against Competition (Why We Lose Our Race to Win)* (Boston, MA and New York: Houghton Mifflin, 1986) p. 4.
5 Konrad Lorenz, *On Aggression* (New York: Harvest Books, 1974); Richard Dawkins, *The Selfish Gene*, 30th Anniversary Edition (New York: Oxford University Press, 2006).
6 Sheryl Sandberg, *Lean In: Women, Work, and the Will to Lead* (New York: Knopf, 2013).
7 Alfie Kohn, "The Case Against Competition," *Working Mother* (Sept. 1987) http://www.alfiekohn.org/parenting/tcac.htm (accessed Aug. 10, 2014).
8 Carole Ames, "Children's Achievement Attributions and Self-Reinforcement: Effects of Self-Concept and Competitive Reward Structure," *Journal of Educational Psychology* 70 (1978).

9 "The Hidden Demographics of Youth Sports," *ESPN* (July 13, 2013) http://espn.go.com/espn/story/_/id/9469252/hidden-demographics-youth-sports-espn-magazine; Bill Gorman, "No Surprise: 64% of Americans Watch NFL Football; 73% of Men, 55% of Women," *TV by the Numbers* (Oct. 14, 2011) http://tvbythenumbers.zap2it.com/2011/10/14/no-surprise-64-americans-watch-nfl-football-73-of-men-55-of-women/107308/; "How Much Do You Know About Video Games?" Entertainment Software Rating Board (2014) www.esrb.org/about/video-game-industry-statistics.jsp (all accessed Aug. 10, 2014).

10 Robert Putnam, *Bowling Alone: The Collapse and Revival of American Community* (New York: Simon & Schuster, 2001).

11 "The American Sports Industry Is Worth $422 Billion and Employs 1% of the Population!" *OMG Facts.com* (2012) http://www.omgfacts.com/Sports/The-American-Sports-industry-is-worth-42/53738 (accessed Aug. 11, 2014).

12 Ben Strauss and Marc Tracy, "NCAA Must Allow Colleges to Pay Athletes, Judge Rules," *New York Times* (Aug. 8, 2014) http://www.nytimes.com/2014/08/09/sports/federal-judge-rules-against-ncaa-in-obannon-case.html?_r=0 (accessed Aug. 10, 2014).

13 Dave Zirin, speaking in Jeremy Erp, director, *Not Just a Game: Power, Politics and American Sports* (Northampton, MA: Educational Video Foundation, 2011).

14 Tracee Hamilton, "Time to Blow Taps on Football-as-War Metaphors," *Washington Post* (Sept. 12, 2012) http://www.washingtonpost.com/sports/redskins/time-to-blow-taps-on-football-as-war-metaphors/2012/09/08/6eb00924-f936-11e1-a073-78d05495927c_story.html (accessed Aug. 10, 2014).

15 Dave Zirin, "The Exploitation of Pat Tillman," *Bohemian* (June 27–July 3, 2007) www.bohemian.com/northbay/the-exploitation-of-pat-tillman/Content?oid=2171356 (accessed Aug. 10, 2014).

16 Dave Zirin, "'Like He Died Twice': Mary Tillman's Lonely Quest," *The Nation* (May 28, 2008) http://www.thenation.com/article/he-died-twice-mary-tillmans-lonely-quest (accessed Aug. 10, 2014).

17 Roland Barthes, "Of Sports and Men," trans. Scott MacKenzie, *Cine-Documents* 6, no. 2 (1962) p. 80.

18 Walter Rauschenbusch, "Daily Reading," in *Christianizing the Social Order* (New York: Macmillan, 1912). http://www.episcopalcafe.com/thesoul/daily_reading/commonwealth.html (accessed Aug. 8, 2014).

19 Pope Leo XIII, "Encyclical of Pope Leo XIII on Capital and Labor" (1891) http://www.vatican.va/holy_father/leo_xiii/encyclicals/documents/hf_l-xiii_enc_15051891_rerum-novarum_en.html (accessed Aug. 9, 2014).

20 Max Weber, *The Protestant Ethic and the Spirit of Capitalism* (1904–1905) trans. Talcott Parsons and Anthony Giddens (London and Boston, MA: Unwind Hyman, 1930).

21 Anthony Giddens, *Capitalism and Modern Social Theory* (Cambridge: Cambridge University Press, 1971) p. 132.

22 Jeff Van Duzer, *Why Business Matters to God* (New York: IVP Academic, 2010). As cited in Hugh Whelchel, "Four Ways Christians Live and Work in the Marketplace," Institute for Faith, Work, and Economics (May 13, 2013) http://blog.tifwe.org/four-ways-christians-live-and-work-in-the-marketplace/ (accessed Aug. 9, 2014).

23 David Green as cited in "Christian Billionaire Entrepreneurs," Mykingdombusinss.com (Feb. 24, 2014) http://www.mykingdombusiness.com/christian-billionaire-entrepreneurs/ (accessed Aug. 9, 2014).

24 Mikita Brottman and David Sterritt, "American Madness," *TCM.com* (n.d.) www.tcm.com/this-month/article/150144%7C0/American-Madness.html (accessed Jan. 3, 2015).

25 Henry A. Giroux, "America's Descent into Madness," in *The Violence of Organized Forgetting: Thinking beyond America's Disimagination Machine* (San Francisco, CA: City Lights Books, 2014) pp. 9–24.

26 *The Violence of Organized Forgetting*, p. 9.

27 Peter C. Whybrow, *American Mania: When More Is Not Enough* (London and New York: Norton, 2005) p. 5.
28 Ibid.
29 *American Mania*, p. 9.
30 *American Mania*, p. 11.
31 Sigmund Freud, *A General Introduction to Psychoanalysis* (New York: CreateSpace, 2013).
32 Fredric Jameson, "Postmodern Culture and Consumer Society," in *The Anti-Aesthetic: Essays on Postmodern Culture,* Hal Foster, ed., (Port Townsend, WA: Bay Press, 1983).
33 "Postmodern Culture and Consumer Society," p. 118.
34 Roland Barthes, *Image, Music, Text*, trans. Stephen Heath (New York: Hill and Wang, 1978).
35 Gilles Deleuze and Félix Guattari, *A Thousand Plateaus: Capitalism and Schizophrenia*, trans. Brian Massumi (Minneapolis: University of Minnesota Press, 1987).
36 Robert Greenwald's film *Wal-Mart: The High Cost of a Low Price* (New York: Brave New Films, 2005).
37 Stephen Dinan, "Obama Economy: Part-time Jobs Swamp Full-time Jobs," *Washington Times* (Aug. 5, 2013) http://www.washingtontimes.com/blog/inside-politics/2013/aug/5/obama-economy-part-time-jobs-swamp-full-time-jobs/ (accessed Aug. 15, 2014).
38 Jonah Paretti, "Towards a Radical Anti-capitalist Schizophrenia?" *Critical Legal Thinking* (Dec. 21, 2010) http://criticallegalthinking.com/2010/12/21/towards-a-radical-anti-capitalist-schizophrenia/ (accessed Aug. 7, 2014).
39 J. Jack Halberstam, *Gaga Feminism: Sex, Gender, and the End of Normal* (Boston, MA: Beacon, 2012) p. 134.
40 "Declaration of the Occupation of New York City," Occupy Wall Street, NYC General Assembly (Sept. 29, 2011) http://www.nycga.net/resources/documents/declaration/ (accessed Aug. 7, 2014).
41 Travis Gettys, "Study Suggests Occupy Wall Street Movement Undone by Liberals' Need to Feel Unique," *Raw Story* (Dec. 2, 2013) www.rawstory.com/rs/2013/12/02/study-suggests-occupy-wall-street-movement-undone-by-liberals-need-to-feel-unique/ (accessed Aug. 8, 2014).
42 Theodor W. Adorno, *Negative Dialectics*, trans. E.B. Ashton (London and New York: Routledge, 1966).
43 Margaret Thatcher, "Interview for *Woman's Own*" (Sept. 23, 1987) http://www.margaretthatcher.org/document/106689 (accessed Aug. 8, 2014).
44 "Carnegie's Conversion," *Brotherhood of Locomotive Firemen and Enginemen's Magazine*, 16 (1892) pp. 1067–1068.
45 Andrew Carnegie, "The Gospel of Wealth" (1886) http://carnegie.org/fileadmin/Media/Publications/PDF/THE_GOSPEL_OF_WEALTH_01.pdf (accessed Aug. 8, 2014).
46 Ibid.
47 Charity statistics in this section from "Charitable Giving Statistics," National Philanthropic Trust (2014) http://www.nptrust.org/philanthropic-resources/charitable-giving-statistics/ (accessed Aug. 8, 2014).
48 Darice Britt, "Philanthropic Psychology Sheds Light on Charitable Giving," *South Source* (n.d.) http://source.southuniversity.edu/philanthropic-psychology-sheds-light-on-charitable-giving-128334.aspx (accessed Jan. 2, 2015).
49 Robert Frank, "Rich Feel Guilty about Giving to Charity," *Wall Street Journal* (May 9, 2009) http://blogs.wsj.com/wealth/2009/05/18/rich-feel-guilty-about-giving-to-charity/ (accessed Aug. 8, 2014).
50 Kris Hundley and Kendall Taggart, "America's Worst Charities," *Tampa Bay Times* (June 6, 2013) http://www.tampabay.com/topics/specials/worst-charities1.page (accessed Aug. 8, 2014).

51 "Cancer in Children and Adolescents," National Cancer Institute (2010) http://www.cancer.gov/cancertopics/factsheet/Sites-Types/childhood (accessed Aug. 8, 2014).
52 "Child Obesity Facts," U.S. Centers for Disease Control and Prevention (2014) http://www.cdc.gov/healthyyouth/obesity/facts.htm (accessed Aug. 8, 2014).
53 See Jay Lindsay, "Religion and Giving: More Religious States Give to Charity," *Huffington Post* (Aug. 8, 2012) http://www.huffingtonpost.com/2012/08/20/study-less-religious-stat_n_1810425.html (accessed Aug. 9, 2014).
54 Susan Strange, *Casino Capitalism* (Manchester: Manchester University Press, 1987).
55 Jim Hobart, "Millennials Express Mixed Views on the Economic Future," *Public Opinion Strategies* (June 18, 2014) http://pos.org/2014/06/millennials-express-mixed-views-on-their-economic-future/ (accessed Aug. 11, 2014).
56 Ibid.
57 Judith Halberstam, *The Queer Art of Failure* (Durham, NC: Duke University Press, 2011) p. 1.
58 *The Queer Art of Failure*, p. 2.
59 Ann Cvetkovich, *Depression: A Public Feeling* (Durham, NC: Duke University Press, 2012) pp. 2–3.

10

TO AFFINITY AND BEYOND

The Cyborg and the Cosmopolitan

If identity politics is dead, it seems that its enemies didn't get the memo. Pick up any newspaper and you'll find a continuing frenzy of assaults on immigrants, women, youth, and the poor. If anything, it seems that the list of social scapegoats is expanding, with growing fears about school shooters, the mentally ill, and the entire Muslim world. Meanwhile, American society remains deadlocked in two-party conflicts that alienate citizens from their neighbors, as they drift into the consumerist solipsism of individual interest. The sense of isolation parallels the paradoxical place of the U.S. in the world—a nation entwined with other countries in a global economy, yet playing by its own rules in the name of "American exceptionalism."

This chapter looks at strategies of reconnection in an age of social atomization and distrust. Beginning with a philosophical consideration of the primordial figure of the "stranger," the discussion then turns to emerging models for finding "affinities" with other people or groups. Sometimes this can be as simple as finding a shared interest or goal, which tends to work when people get along with each other. But things get more complicated in oppositional contexts, which so often are seen in either/or conflicts. Historically, solutions sometimes have come through compromise or finding a third way. In what follows, I will expand the notion of third approaches in discussing some ways that concepts of identity and self have been reworked in recent decades in the discourses of critical pedagogy, cyborg ontology, alternative politics, queer theory, disability culture, and cosmopolitanism.

Americans seem like strangers to each other. In a country divided into red and blue states, "real" Americans and those who don't fit in—it seems that everyone is someone else's opponent, oppressor, or villain. These feelings of estrangement are reinforced by competition and self-interest, which erode values of community and collective concern. As the gulf between rich and poor widens, citizens are told that failure to reach the American dream is a product of personal inadequacy, lack of will, or even moral deficit. Unable to name what is wrong, more and more people feel that the system somehow is broken. But where is the problem? In growing numbers many blame the one institution that might fix things—their government.[1] That the Tea Party could gain traction by equating duly elected representatives with a totalitarian regime is symptomatic of the schizophrenic state of the American psyche. Feeling powerless and confused in the face of an authority they cannot name, citizens lash out against each other and every institution they can find.

Neoliberalism is the 21st-century term for the marriage America's quintessential ideals of democracy and capitalism, now spinning out of control in a fast-paced world of multinational commerce, media mergers, high-frequency trading, and billionaire campaign funding. As power aggregates in the hands of corporate CEOs and their legislative cronies, citizens find themselves more and more on their own—seeking comfort in one-click shopping rather than the ballot box. People need to find ways to break out of these patterns of disunity and morbid selfishness. Where can the nation find ways of belonging at a time when so many forces push people apart? This is hardly a simple question. In these times of alienation, loneliness, and doubt, Americans need a new paradigm for connecting with one another.

But this isn't easy in a culture conflicted between impulses of making and taking, of taking care of oneself and reaching out to others. Jacques Derrida took up these kinds of relational contradictions in discussing the paradoxical construction of *l'étranger* (the stranger) as a welcome/unwelcome or trusted/suspected figure. People tell themselves that they care about their fellow citizens and that everyone is in this together. But when push comes to shove, as it so often does, these ethics go out the window. So choices get made and certain paradoxes result, as Derrida suggests when he writes that "I am responsible to anyone (that is to say, to any other) only by failing in my responsibility to all the others, to the ethical or political generality. And I can never justify this sacrifice; I must always hold my peace about it." This creates an obvious moral quandary, about which Derrida concludes that "What binds me to this one or that one, remains finally unjustifiable."[2]

Throughout this book I've discussed the growing sense among many Americans that they are not a part of a greater collectivity. Think about newcomers to our "nation of immigrants" being told by "real" Americans that they don't belong, that they might "self-deport."[3] While women now outnumber men in the workplace, few advance to leadership positions—the message being that they don't belong in roles of authority. Certainly, poor people on welfare don't belong. If incarceration statistics tell us anything, they suggest that people of color don't belong on the streets, but should be in jail. Hostilities lingering in some communities tell LGBTQ people they don't belong. Discomfort with the disabled says they don't belong. But these are simply the most obvious cases. Kids who aren't normal don't belong. Overweight people don't belong. Anyone who is sick doesn't belong. The elderly don't belong. The wealthy only belong in their gated communities. You get the idea. Add up all of these numbers and you've got a lot of people who don't belong—the majority of Americans. Are there new ways of finding one another in an era of non-belonging? One place to start is with the very idea of dividing the world into groupings of friends or strangers, allies or competitors, family members or outsiders, and so on. Often these are arbitrary distinctions, based largely on unfamiliarity. Another place is with a culture of individualism that encourages views of others as separate entities or objects, especially those one doesn't know or understand.

As mentioned earlier, in recent years the most common "family" unit in America has become a single person living alone.[4] In historical terms, the rise in living alone stems from the cultural change that Émile Durkheim called "the cult of the individual," which grew in the transition from traditional agrarian communities to modern industrial cities, where individuality became, according to Durkheim, "a sort of religion."[5] Writing in the 1800s, Durkheim could not have predicted the way economies and technologies would later shape contemporary life, nor the changes in social attitudes that would send women into the workforce and weaken the grip of marriage.

The rise of "singletons" has its defenders and critics. In his book, *Going Solo: The Extraordinary Rise and Surprising Appeal of Living Alone*, Eric Klinenberg argues that the once transitional stage of solitary existence has now become a permanent fixture of American life—and that this is a good thing. "Not long ago, it might have made sense to treat living on our own as a transitional stage between more durable arrangements, whether coming up with a partner or moving into an institutional home. This is no longer appropriate."[6] Focusing largely on upwardly mobile urban professionals, Klinenberg says that young people now can afford to go it alone. He writes:

> The rise of living alone has been a transformative social experience. It changes the way we understand ourselves and our most intimate relationships. It shapes the way we build our cities and develop our economies. It alters the way we become adults, as well as how we age and the way we die. It touches every social group and nearly every family, no matter who we are or whether we live with others today.[7]

In an interview following the release of his book, Klinenberg noted that "we need to make a distinction between living alone and being alone, or being isolated, or feeling lonely. These are all different things."[8] Apparently singletons spend more time going out than those who live with others. And of course they find sociality on the Internet. Others writing about the singleton phenomenon have been less enthusiastic. In *Bowling Alone,* Robert Putnam described "going solo" as a symptom of a decline in "social capital" accelerated by growing self-interest.[9] Putnam linked this decline to a broader hardening of Americans toward mutual responsibility, generosity toward others, and community involvement. And in a familiar refrain, Putnam put much of the blame for this on too much time with the television and computer.

In *Alone Together: Why We Expect More from Technology and Less from Each Other*, Sherry Turkle directly took on the issue of technology and social networks. "Technology is seductive when what it offers meets our human vulnerabilities. And as it turns out, we are very vulnerable indeed. We are lonely but fearful of intimacy," Turkle observed.[10] Ultimately concluding that new social networks have both positive and negative effects on collective sensibilities, Turkle also makes the following point: "Our networked life allows us to hide from each other, even as we are tethered to each other. We'd rather text than talk."[11] Turkle adds that technology has allowed many Americans to do their jobs at home, while losing the benefits of friends at work. Social networks may let people "connect" online, but as a consequence many don't leave their homes as much. Face-to-face interaction is lower than it has ever been, as fewer and fewer people meet in public places, go to churches or synagogues, join clubs, and so on.

There is little disagreement among these authors that America is becoming a more solitary society. But few of these commentators address the extent to which Durkheim's "religion" of the individual has become a national obsession. In our neoliberal era, the extreme ideologies of Milton Friedman, Ayn Rand, and Margaret Thatcher have become the new normal—as belonging and non-belonging have become radicalized as perhaps never before. At a time when old ways of joining together have become blocked or outmoded, American society has a profound need to develop new strategies for collectivity, sharing, and working together on problems. As detailed throughout this book, Americans seem to have no problem identifying, naming, and acting against opponents throughout the world or in their very neighborhoods. Children are raised with competitive values urging them to win at any cost in a society in which everyone is out for their own gain. The social character of consumption tells people that they are worth less if a neighbor has more. Then tragically, those who actually do have less now are conditioned to believe that their conditions result from their own failings rather than a system designed to make them fail. In such an environment, a search for scapegoats becomes common. The search is always elusive. Some may find villains in the corporate boardroom or at the border crossing, but the real enemy may be much closer at hand. Can it be that the actual problem lies within each of us? Might it be possible that our very separation from each other is what pushes us further apart, makes us suspicious, and causes us all to feel that we don't belong to something larger?

Where can America look for answers? Most people recognize that the American dream of unbounded freedom and equality remains just that: a utopian dream. Part of the problem is that the dream rests on profoundly contradictory impulses—with the balance between its competitive and cooperative values, the dynamic tension between individual and community, seriously undermined in recent decades. In previous chapters of this book, I've discussed many of the philosophical and practical reasons that America has become a culture divided against itself: Western epistemologies, capitalist impulses, power asymmetries, regimes of othering, scapegoating, and stigma. I've also pointed out the naïvety of assuming that the United States was ever a unified totality—and that, in fact, such grand ideals often have functioned more in the service of nationalist fantasy than of any essential wholeness. Marx may have inherited Hegel's ontological models, but perhaps more than anyone he helped to reify oppression/resistance approaches to political economy, which Freud would map onto a psychic landscape. These thinkers explained that authority exists as much in the mind as it does in the body, and that nobody is innocent in these operations. Oppression can come via external means in both obvious and not-so-obvious ways, some so subtle and complex that they reached into the capillaries of daily life. Postmodernists later would observe that the pressures of power were not always absolute—that they could be reversed or even flow back and forth.

In his classic work, *Pedagogy of the Oppressed*, Paulo Freire outlined just such a fluid approach to authority in what he termed "critical pedagogy."[12] As developed by Freire, critical pedagogy was used by colonized citizens to analyze their own roles in oppressive situations and to devise programs for social change. To Freire, this analytical process grew directly from an ordinary process of dialogue among disempowered people, rather than from the top-down prescriptions of an intellectual vanguard. The premise of "dialogue" proved an ideal antidote for citizens who had always been told what to do by those in control. Rather than subordinate "objects" in a one-directional system of command from above, participants in a dialogue become "subjects" who could jointly share ideas. As a term synonymous with "education," pedagogy implied that people could learn from one another. In practical application, Freire linked this philosophy to the idea of "praxis," which links theory to action. As Freire put it:

> A revolution is achieved with neither verbalism nor activism, but rather with praxis, that is, with reflection and action directed at the structures to be transformed. The revolutionary effort to transform these structures radically cannot designate its leaders as its *thinkers* and the oppressed as mere *doers*.[13]

During the 1970s and 1980s critical pedagogy's vocabulary of "empowerment," "dialogue," and "voice" would enter the lexicon of Western social reform movements. The premises of critical pedagogy owe much to the writings of Antonio Gramsci. Just as Freire sought new applications for Marxist theories through methods of learning, Gramsci saw social change as a process in which ordinary people might formulate revolutionary plans. Gramsci emphasized what he termed "creative" knowledge in which "learning takes place especially through a spontaneous and continuous effort of the pupil, with the teacher only exercising a function of a friendly guide."[14] Gramsci foresaw radical consciousness emerging from the oppressed themselves. To Gramsci, every relationship of "hegemony" emerges from some kind of educational encounter, broadly conceived. In this context Gramsci was not only referring to the kinds of teaching that occur in the classroom. He was discussing the profoundly political dynamic through which citizens are socialized to recognize and validate state power. This process takes place everywhere: the home, the office, the church, and particularly the school. If one considers these institutions as sites of potential ideological influence, then Gramsci's view of education becomes significant. Obviously one is practically always in a process of learning.

Critical pedagogy remains important as a way of rethinking the self/other dichotomies that place groups, individuals, and societies in opposition to one another. Naming an opponent can be important, but it doesn't always resolve the issues underlying an antagonism. Critical pedagogy begins with the idea of talking with one another, rather than going it alone. The simple premise is that each of us has only our own perspective on the world, and we rely on others to help us learn and grow. Most of the great social movements of our time have been made possible by people coming together in just the kind of dialogue that Freire talked about. While the world may seem a very big place to change, most of the changes that have been made have often begun with simple conversations among small groups, where shared ideas begin to resonate more broadly.

A Cyborg Manifesto

Dialogue among friends or with opponents can be helpful, but it only goes so far in a complex society that isolates individuals within myriad self/other oppositions. New models seem to be needed for finding common purpose and moving beyond old forms of antagonism. The beginning of a new activist paradigm began decades ago, with the recognition of the intersecting character of social inequities and identities—that factors like race, class, and gender often linked to each other and made resolution of one problem contingent on others. By the 1990s it became clear that the old forms of opposition (Marxism, feminism, the civil rights and LGBTQ movements) to the old forms of oppression (capitalism, patriarchy, racism, homophobia) were losing traction. The search began for new "strategies" to combat what seemed like an assault from all sides, which could change shape the minute it came into sight. I was among those arguing for a "radical democratic" approach of the kind espoused by Ernesto Laclau and Chantal Mouffe in their classic book *Hegemony and Socialist Strategy*.[15] In what would be termed a "post-Marxist" approach, Laclau and Mouffe urged a view of politics outside the conventional view of socialist base/superstructure models. This strategy provisionally embraced matters of identity, but perhaps more importantly, also focused on the "politics" of everyday life and the domestic sphere. In other words, revolutionary struggle could begin at the breakfast table just as much as it might on the street. As Mouffe would later observe, "What is liberal democracy? Just another name for capitalist democracy? Can one imagine a non-capitalist liberal democracy? This is the most pressing question for the left today, and it cannot be answered without a new understanding of the nature of the political."[16] As I wrote in my book

Radical Democracy, Radical Democrats argue that traditional democracy has failed to deliver on its promises of equality and civic participation. They accuse liberal democracy in particular of being too willing to sacrifice the interests of diverse groups in the name of a broad consensus. Most importantly, Radical Democrats claim that Democratic principles underlie critiques of capitalism and the creation of an egalitarian society will entail extending those democratic principles into ever-expanding areas of daily life: work, education, leisure, and the home.[17]

At the time, no one could have predicted the ways that democratic capitalism would be transformed by the forces of globalization, neoliberalism, and their acceleration via digital networks. Nobody had heard of one-click shopping and stock market flash trading, although some prescient observers were keeping an eye on science and technology. With this in mind I recently reread Donna Haraway's canonical essay, "A Manifesto for Cyborgs," originally published in *Socialist Review* in 1985.[18] Very much a product of its time, Haraway's essay sought to reconcile already-emerging tensions over identity politics within the class-based program of the American New Left. Haraway rooted her premises in a postmodern critique of Western self/other epistemology, yet also refused to ignore the very real problems she saw around her in Reagan-era America. Her critique of the New Left was simple, yet devastating in its implications. Haraway said that oppositional movements against this or that "oppression" engage in the same binary game that caused the oppression in the first place. In this sense, fighting the enemy on its own turf was already a concession to the rules of engagement. Haraway also said that proponents of identity politics were making just this mistake, important as their voices were in revealing new sites of struggle. Battles might be won by feminists or people of color, but the overarching logic of the system would continue with business as usual.

Haraway used the metaphor of the "cyborg" to argue for a radical space outside Western worldviews. Noting the blurring of such distinctions as nature/technology, male/female, and physical/nonphysical, Haraway proposed a radical form of subjectivity: "We are all chimeras, theorized and fabricated hybrids of machine and organism; in short we are cyborgs. The cyborg is our ontology; it gives us our politics."[19] What gave the cyborg its radicality was not merely its in-between-ness, but also its refusal to engage the desire (often unconscious) of the Western mind for a unified subjectivity. The cyborg did not want to be whole, singular, autonomous, or in control of anything. It was half machine after all, tempered only partially by that stuff that some call human. Haraway would observe that "To be One is to be autonomous, to be powerful, to be God. But to be One is an illusion, and so to be involved in a dialectic of apocalypse or the other. Yet to be other is to be multiple, without clear boundary, frayed, insubstantial. One is too few, but two are too many."[20]

Haraway's focus on cybernetics was hardly incidental, given the centrality of technology (as tool making and scientifically rationalized effort) in "human" epistemology. It is commonly observed that technology and symbolic cognition are what separate people from other species. Whether or not this is true, it's fair to say that attitudes toward technology say a lot about what Western society values. Science and technology are often seen as more "real" areas of study than philosophy, humanities, and the arts. In this way, science and technology have been rationalized for centuries as neutral, factual, and disinterested pursuits, wanting little more than to help to cure diseases or build better bridges. Of course many now argue that this is nonsense, recognizing that these innocent tools can drive the engines of war and death as well as those of peace and a better life. In making her cyborg proposal, Haraway recognized that science can work in both directions, although when she wrote her essay digital technology and network communications had yet to demonstrate just how far this could go. One now can see the astonishing instability of a world rendered to any form imaginable. The susceptibility of the digital image to manipulation is simultaneously its curse and its blessing, enabling both infinite rhetorical excess and irreducibility at the same time.

"Affinity" is the term Haraway chose in discussing how cyborg politics might play out—and in recent years affinity has been pinging in activist discourses as perhaps never before. As conventionally defined, *affinity* means "related not by blood but by choice, the appeal of one chemical nuclear group for another."[21] But as Haraway used the term, affinity "marks out a self-consciously constructed space that cannot affirm the capacity to act on the basis of natural identification, but only on the basis of conscious coalition, of affinity, of political kinship."[22] This entails the active creation of mechanisms inducing affinity, while staying away from appropriation, incorporation, and categorical identifications. More specifically, Haraway wrote that:

> The theoretical and practical struggle against unity-through-domination or unity-through-incorporation ironically not only undermines the justifications for patriarchy, colonialism, humanism, positivism, essentialism, scientism, and other unlamented -isms, but *all* claims for an organic or natural standpoint. I think that radical and socialist/Marxist-feminisms have also undermined their/our own epistemological strategies and that this is a crucially valuable step in imagining possible unities. It remains to be seen whether all "epistemologies" as Western political people have known them fail us in the task to build effective affinities.[23]

Keep in mind that this "manifesto" was both sketching a philosophical model *and* laying out a political program. But if one follows its logic, keep in mind one caveat. Affinity represents a powerful concept in rethinking politics beyond the realm of domination/incorporation. The concept also links nicely to recent work exploring the role of affect, feeling, care, and other subjective states in forging alliances, inspiring action, and bringing people together. Perhaps more than any other idea, affinity articulates this constellation of elements needed for progressive change. It is both practical and utopian, historically informed yet forward-looking, and inclusive without being exclusive. The beauty of cyborg affinity lies in its reflexivity.

Yet the magnetism of affinity can be reversed, its very affective attractions turned on end. One sees this all around today in the growing fields of disaffinity that separate neighbor from neighbor, group from group, and individual from society. Just as affinity can be a powerful tool for building connection without category, disaffinity can break those same connections in ways not so easy to name. Disaffinity emerges from the powerful mythos of normativity, for example. This is how a statistically minoritarian Euro-American heterosexuality became seen as the standard against which others were measured, judged, and often punished. It's important to understand this process, not so much as a strategy of any particular group, but as a symptom of primitive belief systems specific to Western culture. Anthropology and world history have shown that not every society chose to follow crude self/other models of understanding the universe. Western views of world domination are not the only game in town.

In historical terms, affinity was and continues to be linked to insights emerging from African-American feminists and other women of color in the United States. As discussed in Chapter 6, "intersectional" theory, as set forth by Kimberlé Crenshaw in the late 1980s, pointed out the multiple, simultaneous, and often-partial character of particularized "identities" within individuals and groups. Responding to what was perceived as a Euro-American brand of bourgeois feminism, women of color asserted that people are more than one aspect at any given time, even as certain oppressions may sometimes foreground themselves. Phenomena like sexism, racism, ableism, homophobia, or transphobia do not operate independently, but frequently interrelate and reinforce each other in both obvious and not so obvious ways. Hence, intersectionality problematized older views of "identity politics," especially as they were argued via existing taxonomies. What gave intersectionality its real teeth was the recognition, for example, that men, who were also white, and who were also straight, might have several "invisible knapsacks" helping them. It's important to remember the historical moment in which intersectionality arose, as identity politics was largely in a reactive mode. It seemed that every time a coalition was formed to combat a problem like sexism or racism, gaps would become apparent. Intersectionality provided an important paradigm for identifying affinities between and among disparate groups. At the same time, intersectionality still placed the locus of revolutionary consciousness within the resistant subject. Whenever this is done, the subject runs the risk of over-determination and the continual need for revisitation. Hence, even as intersectionality has become the dominant paradigm in American feminism, it also has been criticized for having nationalistic blind spots, for example.

Third Person Plural

This meant that trouble was brewing in paradise. While intersectionality fitted well within emerging understandings of mixed or hybrid identities, it seemed to be promoting the further fragmentation of the New Left that many socialists had cautioned against. Without overarching paradigms like economic class, what would be the super-identity that bound people in common struggle? Could it simply be their shared estrangement from power? Such a premise might work until power (or the illusion of power) was achieved. Then what? As America lumbered through the 1990s, an apparent answer came with the election of Bill Clinton to the White House. The crowd-pleasing Clinton held office through much of the decade owing to a strategy of third way compromise. Prime Minister Tony Blair successfully used the same approach in Great Britain. Clinton termed his third way of "pragmatic centrism" as the only viable national strategy following the collapse of the liberal consensus during the Reagan years. As might be expected, the third way effectively neutralized certain segments of the right and the left, while further enflaming others. But perhaps more than anything else, third way politics represented neoliberalism by another name. In his book, *Surrender: How the Clinton Administration Completed the Reagan Revolution*, Michael Meeropol describes Clinton's contradictory election promise "to stimulate the economy and reduce the deficit at the same time" as inherently doomed.[24] Something would have to give. Clinton would propose spending measures, only to be forced into compromise by the legislature, as grand plans for social programs gave way to tightened controls over spending, often linking welfare assistance, for example, to "individual responsibility." In true neoliberal fashion, this provided the illusion of accommodation even as life got tougher for millions of Americans. In many ways, Clinton's third way represented exactly the kind of problem identified in "A Manifesto for Cyborgs" when the essay spoke of Western culture's hunger for wholeness, manifest in practices of sublation, absorption, incorporation, and other means of subverting difference in the interest of unity. It's probably no surprise that as Clinton and Blair were engineering middle-ground compromise through a politics of concession, not everyone was finding solace.

The problem of "thirdness" has a long history in philosophy, sociology, geopolitics, and the study of interpersonal dynamics. Thirding also has been used as a premise in education, family studies, nonprofit organizations, everyday culture, and environmental activism. This multiplication of thirds into a category one might call thirdness—and the conflict between specific to general—was identified by the ancient Greeks in what was termed "The Third Man Problem." For Plato, what binds items in any pair together is the ideal form of their togetherness. But as soon as this ideal form is identified, it takes on a life of its own—becoming a third entity. Because the third entity resembles the other two, the form of three can generate a fourth, and so on. While The Third Man Problem has been of interest to classical philosophers as a logical conundrum, the construction also breaks down in more contemporary reasoning. The notion of an ideal form seems a sloppy way of talking about entities as complex as people, for example. And it also provides insight into the ways that classical European philosophy compressed difference into neat categories. The concept of the ideal form would later become the philosophy of idealism, which dealt with ethereal concepts and values beyond the realm of the actual or "real." Plato's dialogues with Socrates were riddled with the kinds of dualisms (good/evil, true/false, man/god, master/slave) that established binary reasoning at the center of European thinking. In this consciousness, the third man was a problem from the start. At its most primary mathematical level, binary codes are made from zeros and ones, which also correspond to the off/on switches in circuit boards. Contemporary neuroscience has shown that the brain and body operate with such electrical circuitry, leading some to conclude that "nature" is defined by this essential structure of plus and minus, presence and absence. But even at the atomic or cellular level this matter is more complicated. In fact, it is the dissimilarly in atoms and the variability of charges that allows electrical currents to flow. But the tendency to look at such things as atoms and circuit boards as templates for human consciousness points to a valuable lesson, which Plato himself pointed out: the yearning to make sense of a bewildering world with the tools of analogy one has at hand.

Derrida saw a certain magic in third positions—in the ways they wreaked havoc on binary logic. To Derrida, thirdness ruptured the logic of opposed pairs by introducing a radically exterior element. As he writes in *Dissemination*:

> The dual opposition (remedy/poison, good/evil, intelligible/sensible, high/low, mind/matter, life/death, inside/outside, speech/writing, etc.) organizes a conflictual, hierarchically structured field which can be neither reduced to unity, nor derived from a primary simplicity, nor dialectically sublated or internalized into a third term. The "three" will no longer give us the ideality of the speculative solution but rather the effect of a strategic re-mark, a mark which, by phase and by simulacrum, refers the name of one of the two terms to the absolute outside of the opposition, to that absolute otherness which was marked—once again—in the exposé of *differance*.[25]

Classical sociologists looked at the "third" person as an interloper in social dyads—drawing different conclusions about the ways outsiders are embraced, rejected, or otherwise negotiated by groups.[26] In the 1950s George Simmel focused on the value of external perspectives in suggesting that third party newcomers often bring fresh eyes to long-standing local problems. Without the burden of historical memory, outsiders often have the ability to view an unfamiliar situation with a certain degree of criticality, perhaps even objectivity. Artists coming to the U.S. frequently have been credited with such skills. Swiss photographer Robert Frank's book *The Americans* (1958) became an art world classic for its disinterested observations of American patriotism, materialism, and exclusionary tendencies.[27] While Frank was canonized for his work later in life, the initial response to *The Americans* was not completely friendly. In the Cold War era of rabid nationalism in the U.S., Frank was branded an anti-American outsider. This antagonism toward Frank fits with the view of third parties discussed by Alfred Schütz, who examined the marginalization of "strangers" when they are seen as threats or destabilizing influences to an existing group. Later, sociologists began to look more closely at the workings of this acceptance or rejection of third persons, with some observing the role of familiarity in the process. It seemed that if the stranger had some connection—perhaps one of kinship or prior friendship—the stranger's knowledge would be valued over his or her difference from the local group. As I will discuss later, this ability to find correspondences seems a key component in breaking down one person's sense that another might pose a threat. These correspondences need not be comprehensive perceptions of equivalence, but instead they can be found in the minutia of shared knowledge, experience, history, or other relationships. Ulf Hannerz described this as a "cosmopolitan" movement in certain societies, sometimes instigated through the aggregation of diverse populations in urban settings. Hannerz described cosmopolitanism as "the willingness to become involved with the Other" resulting from impulses to develop shared competencies.[28]

Earlier sections of this book dealt at length with the Western mind's struggles with the self/other dialectic. Viewing the world in binary terms, difference creates a tension that demands appeasement, as the Hegelian dialectic would frame it. To get around this Hegel proposed a process in which aspects of the other are incorporated into the self, as each side of the dyad adapts in the interest of achieving stasis. Of course the problem is that dimorphic entities rarely manifest themselves in perfect symmetry, and Hegelian sublation gives way to whatever power dynamics inform the exchange. Hence, colonized people were obliged to adopt the languages, cultures, and economic mandates of their masters; youngsters the mandates of their elders; the poor the values of the privileged; and women the interests of men. In many cases the powerful side of the dyad would cast its opposite in all sorts of negative or incomprehensible terms: inferior, irrational, weak, feminine, deviant, dishonest, inscrutable, or evil—all as a consequence of an underlying anxiety. Freud, Marx and others would use this dual construction in trying to decipher the working of the mind and politics. Modern science would only make matters worse in efforts to confirm the dualistic mind-set it unconsciously had been built upon.

Given this legacy, it is no surprise that thirdness upset matters even further in its challenge to the marriage of the self/other couple. Following this metaphor, it's no surprise that the birth of a child is commonly a disruptive event in most couples' lives—causing a splitting of their attention, resources, affection, and famously, their sex lives. Invariably the third entity makes a permanent change in the lives of the two, often described with mixed emotions by parents. In geopolitical nomenclature, "First" and "Second" world emerged as terms following World War II, referring to the Western and Eastern alliance, respectively. The "Third" world was the neglected child produced via imperialism, replete with custody disputes as powerful nations clamored for control of this or that nation. But if globalization has shown anything, it is that such divisions as First, Second, Third or even Fourth Worlds are sloppy and inaccurate ways of looking at global societies of radical interconnection and mutual interdependence. In crude economic terms, poor countries can't buy the goods that rich ones make. This has led more than one theorist to observe, as Zygmunt Bauman has done, that "the question is no longer how to get rid of the strangers and the strange once and for all, or declare human variety but a momentary inconvenience, but how to live with alterity—daily and permanently."[29]

Though hardly the only source of such critique, postcolonial theory deconstructed the assumptions of Western idealism and its self-righteous premises of ownership, authority, and benevolence. In this discourse, radical versions of thirdness came forward even as concessionary third options were being advanced in mainstream politics. In a global political economy in which all nations had in some way been touched by the legacies of colonialism and imperialism, figures of the "Third World" and Third World people were exposed as yet further evidence of generalizing paradigms that contain non-Western difference into manageable terms.

Some would choose to reclaim third territories for the cause of alterity—even as thirdness itself was problematized and revised. Third spaces were proposed as new positions, hybrids, spectra or continua, temporal/spatial configurations, or outright refutations of positionality itself. Homi K. Bhabha proposed a third space specifically as an alternative to Western thinking in eschewing the logics of domination and absorption manifest in colonialism. Significantly for Bhabha, this also meant looking critically at the very ways language and history worked to flatten difference in singular narratives of serial time. Bhabha's third space challenged "historical identity of culture as a homogenizing, unifying force, authenticated by the originary past, kept alive in the national tradition."[30] Drawing on postmodern theory, Bhabha was careful not to suggest anything resembling a pure "outside" position in a third space, but rather a set of negotiated inside/outside locations manifest in doubling, appropriation, metonymy, and "mimicry." Meanwhile, writers like Chela Sandoval cautioned against the idealization of the "Third World" as a potentially nostalgic move, noting the limits of analogy.[31] The postmodern geographer Edward Soja took up the notion of heterotopia more specifically as a space of radical fusion—of mind and body, structure and agency, abstract and concrete, knowable and unimaginable, conscious and unconscious. Soja wrote of a "Thirdspace" producing "what might best be called a cumulative trialectics that is radically open to additional otherness, to a continuing expansion of spatial knowledge."[32] Drawing together many of these principles, Trinh T. Minh-ha put the matter this way:

> Third is not merely derivative of First and Second. It is a space of its own. Such a space allows for the emergence of new subjectivities that resist letting themselves be settled in the movement across First and Second. Third is thus formed by the process of hybridization which, rather than simply adding a here to a there, gives rise to an elsewhere-within-here/there that appears both too recognizable and impossible to contain.[33]

Such receptivity to otherness finds recognition in recent writing on cosmopolitanism. By standard definition, a "cosmopolitan" person is someone unbound by local or provincial ideas, attachments, or prejudices of a particular "polis." Often associated with urban sensibilities, cosmopolitans take a broader worldview. While the idea of the cosmopolitan can be dated to Diogenes, who said, "I am a citizen of the world," the idea gained further currency in the context of Enlightenment ideals of a universal humanity. This gave the cosmopolitan a transcendental flavor in being something bigger than what any nation or tribe might value or fight over. Immanuel Kant proposed cosmopolitanism as a quasi-religious ethnic that might prevent wars in the broader interest of the world. Kant thought that cosmopolitanism might "finally bring the human race ever closer to a cosmopolitan constitution."[34]

Later, philosophy would point out the problems of universal ideals, but would hold onto the notion of the cosmopolitan as a potentially important ethical principle. Emmanuel Levinas would speak of cosmopolitanism as an explicit engagement with otherness in a nonviolent encounter.[35] To Levinas, there was nothing natural about violence or aggression, inasmuch as they are destabilizing events in an otherwise neutral space of freedom. People are born "good" by default rather than choice, but this also means that they inherit a "responsibility" not to harm others. Persecuting a victim or becoming one are optional outcomes of self/other interaction. Derrida would take Levinas's ethical cosmopolitanism a step further in discussing the other as a foreigner or stranger. Particularly well known as a radical relativist, Derrida nevertheless said that philosophers ought to stake ethical positions. Derrida famously did this in his writings on hospitality and gifts, among other things. He pointed out that people's ethics get confused from the start when they're taught to believe in a single God—especially when this promotes a singular allegiance superseding all others. Such beliefs set up hierarchies of caring and compassion that replicate themselves when people start to think about others. Both Levinas and Derrida stressed the detraining function of "proximity" (manifest in group membership, kinship, shared interest, or geographical nearness) as people tend to care more about those close to them. And when it comes to hospitality, distinctions get made between temporary visitors and those who decide to move in permanently. All of this shows that cosmopolitanism is inherently fraught with tensions—especially as it generates singular and plural impulses.

These days the word "cosmopolitan" is generally associated with the magazine bearing its name, or even more so the publication's reputation for explicit imagery and content, presumably intended for a female audience. *Cosmopolitan* also is a good example of how cosmopolitanism can go wrong. Today few people know that *Cosmopolitan* was launched in 1886 as a "first-class family magazine," catering to the education and household needs of American bourgeois society. With short stories by leading authors of the time, *Cosmopolitan* also carried articles on cooking, childcare, and fashion. The magazine's clear intention was to identify the

American family as a quintessential cosmopolitan entity—a model of global humanism. To cut a long story short, *Cosmopolitan* and other magazines began to lose readers in the television age. So in 1965 the magazine hired Helen Gurley Brown to give *Cosmopolitan* a facelift. This is when the publication was reinvented as a magazine for the liberated single career woman. Adopting a language of empowerment, Brown would write that women should have men to complement their lives, but not to take them over. Sex without shame would become a familiar theme in the magazine. Over time it was observed that despite its inclusive name, *Cosmopolitan*'s content more often addressed a privileged cohort of Euro-American heterosexual women, while uncritically replicating a stereotypical "beauty culture." In the eyes of many critics, *Cosmopolitan* became a symbol of the way purportedly universal ideals—of the "human family" or "every woman"—can become transfigured into narrowly exclusionary conceits.

Queering Heterosexuality

The new millennium has seen shifts in long-standing public attitudes toward sexuality and gender, brought about in large part by decades of LGBT civil rights activism. While the campaign for marriage equality often was seen as the public face of this movement, underlying principles of queer theory challenged both the hegemony of heterosexuality and the dualistic mind-set supporting it. Much of the emotionalism over marriage derived from its implications for the "family," and what some argued were natural, eternal, or heavenly ordained premises of heterosexual coupling. And this particular form of sexuality inheres deeply in paternal and maternal traditions in many cultures. From Freud onward it has been observed that sex and sexual repression have driven societies in both obvious and not so obvious ways, linking as sex does both conscious desires and subliminal fantasies. Everyone is familiar with how sex and romance drive narratives, as audiences anticipate symbolic or literal unions at the end of stories. And of course sex "sells" everything from clothing and skin care products, to vacations and sports cars, to diet and fitness programs, to cosmetic surgery and erectile dysfunction medications. Western culture is obsessed with sex, but shy to talk about it directly, owing to many factors—not the least of which are religious traditions that fetishize sex as a gift from God that can only be practiced in proscribed ways.

In many accounts, discourses on homosexuality and heterosexuality emerged in the context of Victorian-era religious beliefs about what is and isn't a couple or family unit.[36] But this isn't completely accurate. The fact is that gay/straight distinctions didn't exist before the 19th century. People might marry or remain single, but what they did in bed was rarely discussed outside of bawdy storytelling—largely because the idea of sexual identity had not been spelled out. As Hanna Blank discuses in *Straight: The Surprisingly Short Story of Heterosexuality*, it took the convergence of several social changes to concretize straightness as a social norm that had a name and a prohibited opposite.[37] The famous moralism of the era was really only partly about sex. It also had more to do with worries that society was coming unglued. The agrarian family was dissipating into urban enclaves, religious faith was wavering, and countries like Britain and France were increasingly stressed over maintaining control over their colonial empires. Bourgeois culture needed propping up, many thought. More specifically, men were needed who were physically ready and morally grounded. As populations migrated to cities, opportunities for sexual experimentation had opened up. Men went to taverns, had affairs, met prostitutes, and sometimes had sex with other men. So public policies emerged that adapted preexisting religious doctrines about sex and sodomy into the new "religion" of the secular state. With the rise of scientific categorization, sexual practices were divided into two categories used today—with one labeled a normal, healthy, and sanctified expression of love; and the other a form of deviance, a mental illness, and moral failings. Even today, arguments are made by fundamentalist Christian groups that with enough prayer and counseling, homosexuals can undergo a "conversion" process to heterosexuality much in the same way that people can be "born again" through religious epiphanies.

Given these prejudicial histories and their persistence in American culture, it is not surprising that a broad-based understanding of homosexuality has been a long time in coming. To some extent homosexual relationships had been referenced in art and literary works in many cultures. But in practical terms, sexual orientation remained largely a personal matter until the urbanization of the industrial era. Dozens of gay coffeehouses would emerge in London in the 1800s, for example, as well as in other cities. Yet owing in part to the long-standing Judeo-Christian views on sodomy, early gay culture was often clandestine. Keep in mind that the terms "heterosexual" and "homosexual" themselves did not come into usage until scientists of the late 19th century began their attempts to map out social and psychological types. All of this resulted in a generalized ignorance about sexual orientation of any kind well into the 20th century. Confusions about the relationship between gender and sex drew sexologist Havelock Ellis in 1927 to describe homosexual attraction as an "inversion" of natural impulses. Borrowing the term from French and Italian scientists of the prior century, Ellis wrote of inversion as a "contrary sexual feeling" made possible as one same-sex partner "inverts" in assuming an opposite-sex role. While focusing primarily on what he saw as frequent feminization among male homosexuals, Ellis also spent a portion of his book *Sexual Inversion* talking about masculine expressions in "The School Friendships of Girls."

At the same time, even opposite-sex sex wasn't talked about very much. Well into the first years of the 20th century, sexuality itself still remained very much the stuff of medical textbooks. This is to say that heterosexuality had not been named as a norm—since, until the 1920s, sex of any kind was considered private and potentially sinful. Even underwear was termed an "unmentionable." In fact, a 1901 medical dictionary used the term "heterosexuality" to describe what it termed an "abnormal or perverted appetite toward the opposite sex."[38] Twenty years later, *Merriam Webster's New International Dictionary* would define heterosexuality as "a morbid sexual passion for one of the opposite sex." According to historian Jonathan Ned Katz, the modernization of the U.S. during this period, along with the growth of media and advertising, began to transform the American family from a producing unit to a consuming one. Images of mom, dad, and the kids began to animate a growing array of domestic goods. But there was trouble in paradise as well, evidenced by falling birthrates, the growing prevalence of divorce, and a nascent "war of the sexes." This atmosphere validated certain aspects of heterosexuality, while also introducing a certain level of anxiety. The strain of economic collapse in the 1930s didn't help the national mood, and the war that came in the following decade made matters worse. By the time the fighting ended, America was ready to get back to normal—whatever that was. But as everybody knows, conformist suburban procreation soon became synonymous with the new American dream.

Demographic studies of sexuality (including sexual orientation) began in earnest in the post–World War II era, with studies by biologist Alfred C. Kinsey remaining some of the best known. In the 1940s and 1950s Kinsey and his staff conducted 18,000 interviews on sexual behavior, which would later be published in separate volumes on male and female sexuality.[39] Surprising many at the time, Kinsey discovered widespread variations between presumed sexual norms and the sexual behaviors of those interviewed. Among numerous findings, Kinsey would conclude that categories of heterosexual/homosexual were not always as clear-cut as many had believed. To Kinsey, sexual orientation existed on a continuum rather than the commonly thought either/or model. Kinsey also introduced the elements of time and degree in his analysis, noting that sexual orientation can modulate with age. Perhaps most significantly, this research for the first time quantified homosexuals as 10 percent of the population—although the Kinsey surveys also found that 37 percent of men reported homosexual experiences at some point in their lives. Obviously issues of self-perception and frankness in reporting have a great bearing on these statistics, especially in a culture laced with homophobia and gender anxiety. One recent survey by the CDC put the number of people who "say" they are gay/lesbian at less than 2 percent. Another study showed that up to two-thirds of Americans stray from heterosexual norms at some point.[40]

The key point to keep in mind is that "normal" sex always has been a myth. After all, there are a limited number of things people can do with their bodies, and most heterosexual and homosexual couples make use of all of them. Same-sex erotic encounters occur regularly or occasionally with much more frequency than most people know. And even what counts as "having sex" (as casual flirtation, sexual fantasy, pornographic indulgence, or physical act) varies wildly from person to person. The fact is that sex and sexuality are and always have been much more expansive, complex, and nuanced than the ways they are stereotyped in popular culture. And if one adds to this the remarkable variations in biological sex and gender expression that exist in the human species, the familiar bifurcations of sex, gender, and sexual orientation really should be tossed out the window.

Enter "queer theory," a field of study that has come a long way since first given a name by Teresa de Lauretis in 1991.[41] In the decade that followed, writers such as Judith Butler, David Halperin, José Esteban Muñoz, Eve Kosofsky Sedgwick, and Michael Warner, among others, began mapping "queer theory" as a direct response to widely held views of normalcy and deviance, especially those pertaining to sexuality and gender.[42] Initially an expression of the resistant impulses of LGBTQ liberation and rights movements, "queer" has come to represent a comprehensive critique of larger systems of categorization and their frequent assignment of negative values. Queer is one of those words that have taken on many different meanings—from a term referencing eccentricity, to its later use as a pejorative epithet, to its appropriation as positive affirmation. It's no secret that language changes over time. In historical terms, at first the term queer served the cause of minority affirmation in a world of heterosexual hegemony. But very soon, queer theory went beyond this "minoritizing" approach in later critiquing "heteronormativity" itself. In other words, rather than engaging heterosexuality strictly in oppositional terms, queer theory approached sexual orientation and gender performance as components of a larger doxa of the "normal."

The term "doxa" was coined by the early Greeks to describe common beliefs or popular opinions that come to hold sway over populations. Often originating from inherited mythologies or pronouncements, doxa takes on a life of its own as it becomes naturalized as "common sense." Doxa becomes what "everybody" knows, even though most people forget their sources. As such, doxa is often invisible even as it exerts a continuing influence over attitudes and behavior. Beliefs in the laziness of poor people, the emotionality of women, and the violent proclivities of Muslim people are examples of doxa. The tricky thing about doxa is that it doesn't always link to one's rational mind. And doxa can be an important political tool inasmuch as it forms a constant undercurrent below the surface of what is being discussed. Queer theory named the common sense of the normal for what it was—narrow and historically specific sets of ideologies that had been expanded, naturalized, and applied to everyone.

But queer theory does more than this in critiquing the very notion of inside/outside identities. This is exactly how Diana Fuss put the problematic in the introduction to her 1991 anthology *Inside/Out: Lesbian Theories/Gay Theories*: "The figure inside/outside cannot be easily or ever finally dispensed with; it can only be worked on and worked over—itself turned inside out to expose its critical operations and interior machinery."[43] Queer theory emerged in the context of broader discussions about identity, especially in emerging views that concepts of the self were partly or completely "constructed" by culture. In other words, variables like skin color or sexual anatomy might play an important part in determining who one was, but other factors worked on identity as well. One's natal body, genetic inheritance, and upbringing might point in one direction, but individuals ultimately "perform" their identities in daily life in ways affected by their surroundings, social circumstances, attitudes, beliefs, and desires. Or put another way, anatomy may be something one "has," but identity is something one "does." Of course normativity exerts a powerful influence on how any individual "does" their gender, race, or sexual orientation—and large numbers of people simply follow the prevailing templates of social norms. But what about those who want or need to follow a different path? Queer theory opened the doorway by arguing that much of doxa was in fact a social fabrication—that mainstream rules and conventions came from somewhere and that somewhere could be tracked down and analyzed. In his book, *The Problem with Normal*, Michael Warner made this point explicit by using the term *normal* in place of the term *heterosexual.* [44]

The critique of heteronormality was more than a simple attack on the status quo, although that strategy remained central. Perhaps just as importantly, this new vocabulary was a critique of normativity itself—pointing to the "trouble" that any overarching "common sense" that "everybody knows" can cause. Time and time again throughout much of the past century, ideas of "universal" definitions of humanity have been proven faulty. The time had come to stop thinking in insider/outsider terms, as Christien Garcia put the matter:

> While I often hear "queer utopia" being described along the lines of a critical space in which we might (finally) be brought to the table, I imagine it somehow as the opposite. … I venture instead to suggest that what a queer utopia might look like is a place where no one has to stand in *as* the opposition that is a necessity of social critique. For that matter, it is a place where, as in any utopia, the ethical necessity of opposition itself is dissipated.[45]

Many queer histories credit Lee Edelman with this fundamental insight. Edelman applied Lacanian theory in proposing queerness as *absence* in the domain of heteronormativity, rather than opposition to it. Significantly, Edelman and other queer theorists named this absent place ("nothingness") as a site of radical possibility, owing to its implicit lack of definition. Rather than insisting on any singular definition, Edelman generalized this absence as experience shared by many people in their negotiation of the Lacanian Symbolic. Queerness would claim the space between Real and Imaginary, a space that exists in the play of signification, which sometimes does and at other times doesn't accept the closure of particular meanings. As Edelman wrote, "our queerness has nothing to offer a symbolic that lives by denying that nothingness except an insistence on haunting excess that this nothingness entails."[46] This meant rejecting such limiting identifications as "heterosexual" or "homosexual" in a more open, multiple, fragmentary, and temporal view of sexual orientation.

As a historian, Edelman also was critical of linear concepts of time, especially as manifest in idealized notions of the family and procreation (i.e., "children are the future") in the implication of human "progress," ambitions, and achievement.

The title of Edelman's book, *No Future*, explicitly articulated a continuously moving present as the means of analyzing both past and future—rather than the projection of an idealized time yet to come. As Edelman put it, "This paradoxical formulation suggests a refusal—of every substantiation of identity, which is always oppositionally defined."[47] Queerness represents a refusal of closure, a denial of the epistemic violence of definition as "gay" or "straight" or anything else. The subversive implications of this are obvious. In many ways, queer theory brought a strategy to identity politics which went beyond antagonisms of resistance per se. Incorporating poststructuralist ideas about language and meaning, queer theory questioned the very grounds of the argument itself.

Judith Halberstam's book *The Queer Art of Failure* was largely about the value of queer theory in saying "no" to overdetermined meanings of all kinds. Specifically, Halberstam pointed to American values of success and positivity in times of profound inequity and misery.[48] In this view queerness is not so much a negative value, as Halberstam's book title implies, as it is a refusal of certain forms of idealism like the American dream and the nuclear family. One of the most inspirational voices in queer theory was the late José Esteban Muñoz. In his book, *Cruising Utopia: The Then and There of Queer Futurity*, Muñoz spoke of queerness as its own idealism of a time not yet achieved, perhaps never to be completely found, but one that demanded to be sought. The boldness of Muñoz's book lay in its embrace of utopia and hope. He wrote, "Queerness is essentially about a rejection of a here and now and an insistence on potentiality or concrete possibility for another world." [49]

Queer theory provided an important template for thinking about affinity; first, by calling into question the rules of the game that would insist on certain doxa of sexual orientation and gender; and second, by presenting "queer" as an all-purpose term for anyone not following those rules. In doing so, queer theory also pointed out that the rules themselves were messy, inconsistently applied, and often themselves unclear. But in practical terms, queer offered a name for a radical "something else." This "something else" proved enormously attractive, especially for a younger generation hungry for new affinities. In the early 1990s the organization Queer Nation would state in its founding document: "Being queer is not about the right to privacy: it is about the freedom to be public."[50] During the past two decades queer collectives, arts groups, and student organizations have been built in communities, schools, and universities around the nation. On the University of California campus where I work, Irvine Queers organize events, weekly information meetings, and maintain a robust online presence. Notably, one element of Irvine Queers involves "allies."

PFLAG is the nation's largest ally group dedicated to LGBTQ issues—driven by the principles of "proximity" discussed above. Formerly known as Parents and Friends of Lesbians and Gays, PFLAG switched to using the acronym as its name in the interest of broader inclusion. PFLAG began in 1972, when New York elementary school teacher Jeanne Manford reacted to the beating and hospitalization of her son Morty as he participated in a gay rights protest. Manford wrote a letter published in the *New York Post* and accompanied her son months later in New York's Gay Pride March carrying a banner that read, "Parents of Gays Unite to Support Our Children." Since then PFLAG has grown into an organization of 350 chapters and 200,000 members, spanning multiple generations of families in major urban centers, small cities, and rural areas in every state in America.[51] While significant in its own right, PFLAG also says something important about affinity. In the past 20 years, numerous heterosexually identified entertainers and other public figures have come forward in support of LGBTQ causes. Liberal politicians (such as Steny Hoyer, Dick Gephardt, and Deval Patrick) have been more likely to voice such views than conservatives (including Dick Cheney, Alan Keynes, and Rob Portman).

What is an ally in these situations? Implicit in the name PFLAG is the recognition of an affinity resulting from familial proximity. Bonds of kinship—notably the parent-child relationship—typically precede and override subsequent identities, although this is not always so. Friendship may work similarly, although friendship alliances also can form from mutual interest of some kind—as in the strategic alliances of nations. In the case of international treaties and trade compacts, two or more parties work toward a commonly identified goal such as trade or military defense. Commonality of interest is critical, even when the partners may be unequal in other terms. This raises the tricky issue of power asymmetries in family, friends, and ally relationships. Straight people who enter the field of LGBTQ alliance do so from a majoritarian position. This asymmetrical relationship opens up the potential misrecognition and romanticization of the Other of the sort reviewed in the previous chapter's discussion of charitable benevolence.

Allies and benevolent parties often speak of "identifying" with those they help. This idea also requires some parsing. In most instances, those who identify mean that they recognize characteristics that they share with someone else. The common default position in many people's minds is the notion of a shared humanity, although all sorts of other conscious or unconscious factors can color identification ("We are all God's children;" "We are all Americans;" etc.). In these instances one sees the intersection of difference and similarity, of the specific and general, in play. Perhaps more than anywhere else, this is where Haraway's theorization of affinity meets its test as the dissolution of boundaries becomes apparent and necessary.

Crip Analogies

Disability activism has been on the rise in recent decades, as discussed in Chapter 7, notably manifest in its critique of normative ableism. In the 2000s the term "crip" came into use as an appropriation of the derogatory term for incapacitation. One might say that "crip" is to disabled what "queer" is to homosexual, as both terms reference an assertive reclaiming of formerly stigmatized identity. The similarities of crip and queer movements go beyond nomenclature, although the question of just how far these resemblances go has been the subject of considerable debate among activists and scholars, evoking historical disputes over the uses and limitations of analogy and coalitions among stigmatized groups. To what extent can affinities operate or not operate in such contexts?

In his book, *Crip Theory: Cultural Signs of Queerness and Disability*, Robert McRuer noted that queer and disabled identities share a common relationship to the contemporary "normal," as well as similar histories of exclusion and stigma with the roots in 19th-century scientism.[52] As McRuer explained, neither of these outsider identities originated initially from a conscious choice. Perhaps most importantly, crip theory carved out a space for LGBTQ people who *also* were disabled—and whose voices had rarely been heard. In making this intersectional point, McRuer noted that heterosexual and able-bodied privilege shared more than a common historical lineage, and that in certain ways they were in fact deeply intertwined. Frequently the "compulsory" doxa of heterosexuality and ableism come together in conflating or controlling homosexual and disabled bodies. Most obviously, mainstream culture and media generally depict a universally straight and fully functioning subject. Heroes and heroines usually are *both* heterosexual and able-bodied—as queer and disabled characters are frequently cast as victims, villains, unemployed, impoverished or otherwise "cripped."

Beyond this, McRuer implicates neoliberalism as an accelerant. In focusing on the "signs" of queer invisibility, McRuer foregrounds both the visualization and commodification of identity, along with its material manifestations. He notes that neoliberalism has a special way of marking queer and disabled as invisible, devalued, and disposable in contrast to a "flexible" heterosexual and able-bodied subject. Noting the relationship of neoliberalism to actual or imagined crisis, McRuer sees this flexibility as prerequisite admission to the normative realm. The effect is pernicious, given neoliberalism's adaptive capabilities and its tendencies to pressure similar adaptations of selected populations. Today LGBTQ and disabled people are no longer uniformly cast as outsiders as they once were. But those who gain admission to normative society sometimes do so at a cost.

Here the intersectional character of normativity requires some unpacking, as its dictates play out variously for different groups. With the passage of marriage equality laws in many states, same-sex couples can form the same kind of unions as their straight counterparts. But marriage carries with it a range of associations about normative family roles, relationship stability, and of "making it legal"—not to mention the consumerist orientation of everything from wedding planners to home buying. This can narrow the definitions of relationship and family in favor of tightly drawn images of respectability. Complicating matters further, normative pressures within queer culture sometimes minimize other forms of difference—suggesting, for example, that one would never want to be both gay *and* disabled. Normative assumptions inform both policy and discourse aimed at allowances for the disabled. This positions embodied difference as always in need of assistance, repair, correction, or some form of change aimed at restoration to a presumed standard. Among other things, this view fails to acknowledge the enormous variations in states of ability and disability, the continuities between them, and the often-transitory character of either one. Put another way, little attention is given to the relationship of "impairment" (bodily limitations) to "disability" (the way society treats the impairment). As noted earlier in this book, thinking about the body is heavily loaded, and often driven by quite specific interests, power dynamics, and their attendant ideologies.

"Neither queerness nor disability are monolithic," McRuer writes as a caution, noting that neoliberalism operates differently in each domain. "Converging or diverging, it's no longer possible to say *one* thing about either. But the fact that it's no longer possible to say one thing is perhaps not at all defeatist, but rather a crucially important queer-crip insight: We are continually generating a multitude of ways of being queer and crip, and of coming together."[53] These comments by McRuer are hardly casual observations, considering prior and continuing tensions within LGBTQ and disability discourses over issues of mutual intersection or exclusion, equivalence or non-equivalence. Recall that solipsism was one of the ongoing critiques of identity politics—that a focus on one object implied a disregard of others. While this argument sometimes has been an epistemological smoke screen, it nevertheless has brought to light that much early queer discourse implicitly assumed a non-disabled body, just as much disability writing steered clear of discussions of gender or sexual orientation. To some extent these lacunae have been addressed in more recent discourse, with savvy university presses and conference organizers addressing queer disability for much of the past decade. But the question of parallel, overlapping, or mutually occurring identities is worth considering, given the long history of analogizing impulses among those working for social change.

Analogy looms large in the idea of affinity, as it has in coalition politics more generally. As defined in *Merriam-Webster's Dictionary*, an analogy is a "comparison of two things based on their being alike in some way."[54] Historically the figure of the "common enemy" has functioned analogously, drawing disparate groups together. During the 1960s and 1970s the women's liberation movement famously evoked a "race-sex" analogy in asserting that early feminist struggles were like the struggles of African Americans for civil rights. These analogous assertions came mostly from white feminists, who subsequently came under fire from women of color. It seemed that in their zeal to find common cause through the figure of the domineering white man, white women's liberation groups tended to collapse racial identities into convenient stereotypes to create "fantasies of coalition," as one critic put it. [55] For example, the complicated civil rights struggles of African Americans—replete with their own internal gender politics—would be papered over with nostalgic slogans that also rendered black people as a homogenous totality without contradiction, particularity, or history.

Analogy has a tendency to fantasize equivalence, especially in political struggles against a common opponent. This kind of imagined equivalence has the effect of flattening difference, or at least minimizing it, in the interest of a broader cause. Problematic as this can be, it's important to point out that analogy itself is not the problem. Psychologists speak of analogy as one form of "heuristics" ("rules of thumb") that people all use every day. Everyone uses heuristics to extrapolate from one situation to the next, or to formulate general rules of meaning. Obviously this doesn't always work perfectly. Analogy heuristics are subject to distortion when the primary variable is overly vivid, appears too often, or is tainted by bias.[56] Research on cognition notes frequent problems emerging from the "representativeness heuristic" (assumptions that one object in a group is like all others), as well as "confirmation bias" (interpreting evidence to match pre-existing beliefs), and a variety of other rules of thumb of the kind in play in the race/sex analogy, among others.

This is how good intentions can go wrong, especially as analogies have and will continue to be used to organize all manner of causes. It's not that analogy must be abandoned, per se. But it means that caution needs to be observed as analogies are mapped. As Ellen Samuels has pointed out in discussing queer/crip formulations, analogy remains inescapably part of the communicative realm, despite its endemic flaws.[57] Appearances of resemblance or structural isomorphism can lead anyone to assume that different entities can be more or less transformed by analogy into an equivalence. Yet one point of distinction should never be surrendered: *an analogy is not an identity*. This was one of the key points of intersectionality: that identity can't be reduced to a single characteristic analogized as another. Rather than through correspondences among separate analogous aspects, intersectional subjects share a multiplicity of characteristics. Whether as common heuristics or linguistic devices, analogies follow people everywhere nevertheless. Their commonness makes them convenient tools, especially when the emotionalism of political purpose would have one overlook their sloppiness—as in confrontations with a common foe.

The common enemy affinity also has the epistemological problem of framing relationships in oppositional terms. What happens when the enemy is defeated and the source of solidarity is gone? Does this foster an inward examination within the coalition, perhaps a new way of finding common purpose? Or does it simply mean a new enemy has to be found? More than one observer of American foreign policy has said that the United States *needs* wars to maintain nationalistic coherence. Notwithstanding such concerns, the common enemy strategy remains a familiar figure in political organizing, especially in mainstream American politics. The Rainbow Coalition, the Tea Party Movement, and Occupy Wall Street stand as recent examples of this, although National Republican and Democratic parties also use specified objects of opposition as mean of consolidation. In part this is a manifestation of a sound-bite culture, although the compression of meaning also inheres in the very way that language often reduces complexity to symbolic legibility—often at the expense of someone. Suffice to say that ever since the 1970s, savvy activists have been very careful about going too far in claiming correspondence or analogy in their varied struggles.

Realms of Mattering

Recent conversations over queer and crip identities are part of a broader body politics driving many current debates in American culture. In one way or another, such contested issues as health care, reproductive rights, racial profiling, marriage equality, and immigration reform all revolve around the regulation of certain bodies in particular ways. The term "body politics" first emerged in the 1970s as feminists were contesting objectification of the female body, violence against women, and restrictions on reproductive freedom. The racial dimensions of body politics confronted prejudice and discrimination based on skin color, physiognomy, and related stereotypes. Since those days, the body has remained a site of contest—especially in a culture predicated on visual markers of difference. More recently the mind is recognized as a part of the body as well, making the body even more central as a political object.

"Bodies that matter" was the phrase employed by Judith Butler to capture the coalescence of the biological and the constructed, the material and the performative. "In this sense, what constitutes the fixity of the body, its contours, its movements, will be fully material, but materiality will be rethought as the effect of power, as power's most productive effect," Butler wrote.[58] Put another way, Butler's "mattering" was stated not merely as a product of discourse, as was so frequently evoked by others in the 1990s, but as an element of her now famous formulation of a broader range of subjective elements as they play out. More recently, Butler has written of the body in more overtly political terms, as bodies assemble in crowds, organizations, and publics—directly using the physicality of presence to claim space and "appear" in contesting effacement, disenfranchisement, and abandonment.[59]

Put this all together and the contest over the body becomes huge: the laboring body, the gendered body, the racialized body, the disabled body, and the queer body. Add to this another one worthy of consideration: the disposable body. In his now widely read work *Homo Sacer*, Giorgio Agamben brought forward the ancient Roman concept of the person "set apart" from society.[60] The category of homo sacer included oath breakers, outlaws, or others who violated prevailing norms of their time. Inclusion in the category of homo sacer depended on a key distinction. Was a person "barely" alive and simply carrying on day to day? Or did the individual live politically and contribute to the reproduction of society? In its hunger to establish binary categories, as Agamben states: "The fundamental categorical pair of Western politics is not that of friend/enemy but that of bare life/political existence, zoë/bios, exclusion/inclusion."[61] To Agamben, this principle informs the negative imperatives of contemporary political economy. As neoliberalism represents biopower in serving the "interests of the people," it does so by rewarding productive bodies and shunning the homo sacer. Beyond this, Agamben details how throughout the 20th century huge cohorts of people became cast as either non-contributory or burdensome to contemporary Western societies: the unemployed, the welfare recipient, the refugee, the childless, the sick and disabled, the mentally ill.

The concept of homo sacer has been articulated further by a growing number of intellectuals in the 2000s, translated into such notions as outlaw society (bell hooks), fugitive culture (Henry A. Giroux), expulsions (Saskia Sassen), dispossession (Judith Butler and Athena Athanasiou), disposable people (Kevin Bales), and wasted lives (Zygmunt Bauman).[62] In one sense, these debates have been ongoing for half a century, as outlined in this book's discussion of Howard S. Becker's *Outsiders*, Erving Goffman's *Stigma,* and other works.[63] Keep in mind that these earlier writings emerged in the context of postwar capitalist consolidation and the rise of normalcy as a governing ethos in American society. As a prolific commentator on these debates today, Zygmunt Bauman recently has appropriated the term "collateral damage" from the military lexicon to describe neoliberalism's "consequences that are unplanned but nevertheless damaging and often very costly in human and personal terms." Bauman explains that collateral damage can be applied broadly in the following manner, using the example of poverty:

> The inflammable mixture of growing social inequality and the rising volume of human suffering marginalized as "collateral" is becoming one of the most cataclysmic problems of our time. For the political class, poverty is commonly seen as a problem of law and order—a matter of how to deal with individuals, such as unemployed youths, who fall foul of the law. But treating poverty as a criminal problem obscures the social roots of inequality, which lie in the combination of a consumerist life philosophy propagated and instilled by a consumer-oriented economy, on the one hand, and the rapid shrinking of life chances available to the poor, on the other. In our contemporary, liquid-modern world, the poor are the collateral damage of a profit-driven, consumer-oriented society—"aliens inside" who are deprived of the rights enjoyed by other members of the social order.[64]

The implicit question these analyses raise is whether any singular strategy can be used as an organizing affinity against a countervailing neoliberalism. In one way or another, all of the authors referenced above have advocated forms of consciousness raising as a precursor to social change—whether this takes the form of political activism or a simple refusal to play neoliberalism's game. Certainly, the many iterations of alternative markets, DIY production, antinormativity, disability activism, slacker culture all represent important strains of this resistance. Is there anything one can say that these impulses have in common? Perhaps it is an alternate value system.

These questions continue to percolate in critical discourse, as themes of power, relationships and networks try to get at the complexities of contemporary consciousness and continuing inequity. This chapter has been a long account of the search for affinity—of the struggle to find familiarity in the unfamiliar. In certain registers, what one doesn't know can generate curiosity and anxiety, often simultaneously. Approaching what seems strange can be an act of faith and even sometimes courage. In different ways post-identity, radical democracy, cyborg feminism, intersectionality, postcolonialism, queer activism, crip theory, and dismodernism each gesture toward this leap of faith. One of the lessons to be gleaned from these different approaches is simply their importance as tools, each having a utility for a certain aspect of the job at hand. In talking about Donna Haraway's "Manifesto for Cyborgs," Jasbir Puar noted that Haraway had ended her essay by saying, "I'd rather be a cyborg than a goddess."[65] Puar reads this closing statement as a juxtapositioning of two sets of ideas. In the goddess one can envision the model of a transcendental subject, the heroine of radical feminist struggle finally prevailing. But at the end of the day, the goddess is a subject defined through signification as a coherent entity, ethereal as she might sometimes appear. It is these qualities of "being" and linguistic determination that set the goddess apart from the cyborg. Remember that the cyborg Haraway described resisted subjectivity in refusing reduction to a gender or even to language. The cyborg was simply a form of embodiment existing in the realm of mattering and performativity.

As discussed elsewhere in this book, recent history has shown how frequently useful strategies nevertheless often return to marginalized subjectivity as the center of truth. One may refine and correct how one sees this subject, but it keeps dragging the conversation back into the realm of the known, the specified, and ultimately to some form of opposition to an object. And again it's important to remember that often one *needs* to be oppositional in a world so heavily defined in such terms. At the same time, such thinking only serves to replicate the strange/familiar dichotomy that has been the topic of this chapter. Puar adroitly contrasts the subjectivity of the goddess to the nonrepresentational realm of "matter itself." In this usage matter is not a synonym for materiality, but rather a reference to meaning inside and outside of representation. In other words, matter does not manifest by signification alone. This is mattering in the sense that Deleuze and Guattari used in their principle of *agencement*, commonly translated as assemblage." The term agencement "means design, layout, organization, arrangement, and relations—the focus being not on content but on relations, relations of patterns, and connections," Puar explains.[66] The key point in Puar's analysis is not to create yet another opposition between contesting theories, but to instigate a conversation. She notes that there has yet to be a serious consideration of whether theories of matter and mattering can inform understandings of intersectionality, for example: "Intersectionality attempts to comprehend political institutions and their attendant forms of social normativity and disciplinary administration, while assemblages, in an effort to re-introduce politics into the political, asks what is prior to and beyond what gets established." [67]

Strange becomes familiar through engagement. In a world in which language seems to be the only form of engagement, it is difficult to avoid being compromised in this task, however. Affinity seems to be one way of looking at this challenge in a manner that both uses the tools available but also reaches into realms of mattering and feeling that lie outside the self, or even the "us." This reaching out is always partial and uncertain, but it is also something that most people also know about on some level. The task of making the strange familiar inheres in the will and desire to stretch one's hands into the spaces that lie between us. The key point in this chapter's discussion of the "stranger" is the recognition of everyday experience and human interaction in what actually influences people's thinking. Government programs and high-minded studies might affect people from above, but what takes place in mundane day-to-day interactions is just as important. With this in mind, it seems that several strategies warrant consideration in advancing a better *Elsewhere in America*. The first is discursive in the sense of opening a middle space to create the kind of conversations that have been lacking. The second is material in the sense that difference occurs in degrees as well as extremes, but also appears, diminishes, or becomes mediated by various means throughout the lives of so many. Finally, the seeking out of both an affective and political third space makes room for the agency of the majority of a population either partially implicated or perhaps unaware of its stakes in these matters.

Notes

1 Rebecca Rifkin, "Americans Say Government, Economy Most Important Problems," Gallup Research (Nov. 12, 2014) http://www.gallup.com/poll/179381/americans-say-government-economy-important-problems.aspx (accessed Jan. 5, 2015).
2 Jacques Derrida, *The Gift of Death*, trans. David Willis (Chicago, IL: University of Chicago Press, 1991) p. 70.
3 "Romney on Immigration: 'I'm for Self-Deportation,'" *CBS News* (Jan. 24, 2012) www.cbsnews.com/news/romney-on-immigration-im-for-self-deportation/ (accessed Jan. 19, 2015).
4 Tim Henderson, "More Americans Living Alone, Census Says," *Washington Post* (Sept. 28, 2014) www.washingtonpost.com/politics/more-americans-living-alone-census-says/2014/09/28/67e1d02e-473a-11e4-b72e-d60a9229cc10_story.html (accessed Jan. 20, 2015).
5 Émile Durkheim, *The Elementary Forms of Religious Life*, trans. Joseph Ward Swain (London: Allen & Unwin, 1915).
6 Eric Klinenberg, *Going Solo: The Extraordinary Rise and Surprising Appeal of Living Alone* (New York: Putnam, 2011) p. 4.
7 *Going Solo*, p. 6. Klinenberg has been criticized for insensitivity to the economic recession, increase in poverty, and the data on college graduates returning home to live with their families.
8 Joseph Stromberg, "Eric Klinenberg on *Going Solo*," *Smithsonian* (Feb. 2012) http://www.smithsonianmag.com/science-nature/eric-klinenberg-on-going-solo-19299815/ (accessed Aug. 21, 2014).

9 Robert Putnam, *Bowling Alone: The Collapse and Revival of American Community* (New York: Simon & Schuster, 2001).
10 See also Sherry Turkle, *Alone Together: Why We Expect More from Technology and Less from Each Other* (New York: Basic Books, 2011) p. 1.
11 Ibid.
12 Paulo Freire, *Pedagogy of the Oppressed*, 30th Anniversary Edition (New York: Continuum, 2000).
13 Ibid.
14 Antonio Gramsci, *Selections from the Prison Notebooks*, ed. Quintin Hoare (New York: International Publishers, 1972) p. 33.
15 Ernesto Laclau and Chantal Mouffe, *Hegemony and Socialist Strategy: Toward a Radical Democratic Politics* (London: Verso, 1985).
16 Chantal Mouffe, "Radical Democracy or Liberal Democracy," in David Trend, ed., *Radical Democracy: Identity, Citizenship and the State* (New York and London: Routledge, 1996) p. 19.
17 *Radical Democracy*, p. 3.
18 Donna Haraway, "A Manifesto for Cyborgs: Science, Technology, and Socialist Feminism in the 1980s," *Socialist Review*, 80 (1985) pp. 66–108.
19 "A Manifesto for Cyborgs," p. 67.
20 "A Manifesto for Cyborgs," p. 90.
21 "Affinity," *Oxford Dictionaries* (n.d.) http://www.oxforddictionaries.com/us/definition/american_english/affinity (accessed Jan. 20, 2015).
22 "A Manifesto for Cyborgs," p. 66.
23 "A Manifesto for Cyborgs," p. 73.
24 Michael Meeropol, *Surrender: How the Clinton Administration Completed the Reagan Revolution* (Ann Arbor: University of Michigan Press, 2000).
25 Jacques Derrida, *Dissemination*, trans. Barbara Johnson (London: Althone, 1981) p. 25.
26 Marinus Ossewaarde, "Cosmopolitanism and the Society of Strangers,"*Current Sociology* 55, no. 3 (May 2007).
27 Robert Frank, *Les Americains* (Paris: Robert Delpire, 1958).
28 Ulf Hannerz, "Cosmopolitans and Locals in World Culture," in *Theory, Culture, and Society* 7 (Aug. 2009) p. 239.
29 Zygmunt Bauman, *Postmodernity and Its Discontents* (London: Polity, 1997) p. 30.
30 Homi K. Bhabha, *The Location of Culture* (London: Routledge, 1994) p. 202.
31 Chela Sandoval, *Methodology of the Oppressed* (Minneapolis: University of Minnesota Press, 2000).
32 Edward Soja, *Thirdspace: Journeys to Los Angeles and Other Real-and-Imagined Places* (Oxford: Basil Blackwell, 1996) p. 6. Trinh T. Minh-ha similarly would clarify that thirdness is more than a synonym for addition, famously writing that there is a "Third World in every First World, a Third World in every Third World, and vice versa." See Trinh, *Woman, Native, Other: Writing Postcoloniality and Feminism* (Bloomington: Indiana University Press, 1989) p. 98.
33 Trinh T. Minh-ha, *Elsewhere, Within Here: Immigration, Refugeeism and the Boundary Event* (New York and London: Routledge, 2011) p. 37.
34 Immanuel Kant, "Toward Perpetual Peace in Practical Philosophy," in M.J. Gregor, ed. and trans., *The Cambridge Edition of the Works of Immanuel Kant* (Cambridge: Cambridge University Press, 1999) p. 329.
35 Emmanuel Levinas, *Humanism of the Other*, trans. Nidra Poller (Chicago, IL: University of Illinois Press, 2005).
36 Jonathan Ned Katz, *The Invention of Heterosexuality* (Chicago, IL: University of Chicago Press, 2007).
37 Hanna Blank, *Straight: The Surprisingly Short History of Heterosexuality* (Boston, MA: Beacon, 2012).

38 "Heterosexuality," *Dorland's Medical Dictionary* (Philadelphia, PA: Dorland, 1901).
39 Alfred C. Kinsey, *Sexual Behavior in the Human Male* (1948; repr., Bloomington Indiana University Press, 1998); Alfred Kinsey, *Sexual Behavior in the Human Female* (1953; repr. Bloomington: Indiana University Press, 1998).
40 Jan Hoffman, "How Many Americans Are Lesbian, Gay, or Bisexual?" *New York Times* (July 21, 2014) http://well.blogs.nytimes.com/2014/07/21/how-many-americans-are-lesbian-gay-or-bisexual/?_php=true&_type=blogs&_r=0 (accessed July 28, 2014).
41 Richard Scherer, "Introduction: Queering Paradigms," in Richard Scherer, ed., *Queering Paradigms* (Bern: Peter Lang 2010) p. 1.
42 The origin of the term "queer theory" is commonly attributed Teresa de Lauretis, who used the expression when organizing a 1990 conference and subsequent special issue entitled "Queer Theory Lesbian and Gay Sexualities" of *Differences: A Journal of Feminist Cultural Studies*, 3, no. 2 (1991).
43 Diana Fuss, *Inside/Out: Lesbian Theories, Gay Theories* (London and New York: Routledge, 1991) p. 1.
44 Michael Warner, *The Trouble with Normal: Sex, Politics, and the Ethics of Queer Life* (Cambridge, MA: Harvard University Press, 2000).
45 Christien Garcia, "General Queer; or, Lee Edelman and the Oppositional Meaning of Queer," in *Queering Paradigms*, p. 13.
46 Lee Edelman, *No Future: Queer Theory and the Death Drive* (Durham, NC: Duke University Press, 2004) p. 31.
47 *No Future: Queer Theory and the Death of Drive*, p. 4.
48 Judith Halberstam, *The Queer Art of Failure* (Durham, NC: Duke University Press, 2011).
49 José Esteban Muñoz. *Cruising Utopia: The Then and There of Queer Futurity* (New York and London: New York University Press, 2009) p. 1.
50 "Read This," Queer Nation (1990) http://www.actupny.org/documents/QueersReadThis.pdf (accessed Aug. 23, 2014).
51 "About PFLAG," PFLAG (2014) http://community.pflag.org/page.aspx?pid=191 (accessed Aug. 23, 2014).
52 Robert McRuer, *Crip Theory: Cultural Signs of Queerness and Disability* (New York: New York University Press, 2006) p. 9.
53 Robert McRuer, "Cripping Queer Politics, or the Dangers of Neoliberalism," *S&F Online* 10, no. 1–2 (Fall 2011/Spring 2012) http://sfonline.barnard.edu/a-new-queer-agenda/cripping-queer-politics-or-the-dangers-of-neoliberalism/ (accessed Aug. 27, 2014).
54 "Analogy," *Merriam-Webster Online* (2014) http://www.merriam-webster.com/dictionary/analogy (accessed Aug. 25, 2014).
55 Lisa Marie Hoagland, "*Invisible Man* and Invisible Women: The Race/Sex Analogy of the 1970s," *Women's History Review* 5 (1996) p. 46.
56 Daniel Kahneman, Paul Slovic, Amos Tversky, eds, *Judgment under Uncertainty: Heuristics and Biases* (New York: Cambridge University Press, 1982).
57 Ellen Samuels, "My Body, My Closet," in Lennard J. Davis, ed., *The Disabilities Studies Reader*, 4th ed. (New York: Routledge, 2013) p. 318.
58 Judith Butler, *Bodies That Matter: On the Discursive Limits of Sex* (New York: Rout ledge, 1993) p. 2.
59 Judith Butler, "Bodies in Alliance and the Politics of the Street," *Transversal Texts* (Oct. 2011) http://www.eipcp.net/transversal/1011/butler/en (accessed Oct. 6, 2015).
60 Giorgio Agamben, *Homo Sacer: Sovereign Power and Bare Life* (Stanford, CA: Stanford University Press, 1998).
61 *Homo Sacer*, p. 12.
62 bell hooks, *Outlaw Culture: Resisting Representations* (New York and London: Routledge, 2006); Henry A. Giroux, *Fugitive Cultures: Race, Violence, Youth* (New York and

London: Routledge, 2012); Saskia Sassen, *Expulsions: Brutality and Complexity in the Global Economy* (New York: Belknap, 2014); Judith Butler and Athena Athanasiou, *Dispossession: The Performative in the Political* (New York: Polity, 2013), Kevin Bales, *Disposable People: New Slavery in a Global Economy* (Berkeley: University of California Press, 2012); Zygmunt Bauman, *Wasted Lives: Modernity and Its Outcasts* (New York: Polity, 2003).

63 Howard S. Becker, *Outsiders: Studies in the Sociology of Deviance*, (New York: The Free Press, 1963); Erving Goffman, *Stigma: Notes on the Management of Spoiled Identity* (New York: Simon & Schuster, 1963).

64 Shelley Walia, "The Crisis of Modernity" (Review of Zygmunt Bauman, *Collateral Damage: Social Inequalities in a Global Age*, Cambridge, MA: Polity, 2013). *India Tribune* (Feb. 23, 2013) http://www.tribuneindia.com/2014/20140223/spectrum/book1.htm (accessed Aug. 28, 2014).

65 "A Manifesto for Cyborgs," p. 94.

66 Jasbir K. Puar, "'I Would Rather Be a Cyborg than a Goddess': Intersectionality, Assemblage, and Affective Politics," European Institute for Progressive Cultural Policies—eipcp.net (Jan. 2011) http://eipcp.net/transversal/0811/puar/en (accessed Aug. 29, 2014).

67 Ibid.

11

MEDICATING THE PROBLEM

America's New Pharmakon

America has a drug problem, but it's not the one you imagine. The issue isn't so much with drugs themselves, as it is the ways people think about them. U.S. society is consumed by medications or enhancements of one sort or another, whether taken for health or recreation, obtained legally or illegally. And in a broader sense, it's fair to say that the United States has an addictive personality—a nation of shopaholics and workaholics—famously "hooked" on its favorite foods, TV shows, and computer games. But like many addicts, the U.S. lives in denial about its guilty pleasures—just as it also neglects its own health. On one hand, America's compulsive shoppers and voracious entrepreneurs are championed as economic drivers, job creators, or embodiments of the American dream. At the same time, substance abusers (or alcoholics) are scorned as the very epitome of self-indulgence, moral weakness, and threat.

This chapter will discuss America's conflicted attitudes toward drugs and addictive behavior—as these views divide citizens against each other and confuse many in the process. As the nation continues along the road of economic recovery, is it possible for the U.S. to find some deeper "recovery" in these areas? In many ways, U.S. culture valorizes extreme desire as an expression of a zest for life. Americans obsess over wellness and fitness, as they drive their minds and bodies in the relentless pursuit of success, pleasure, and consumer goods. Of course I am speaking of people with the money to buy gym memberships or organic foods—and not the percentage of the population for whom "health" may fall behind rent or food as a spending priority. Keep in mind that the number of poor and disadvantaged people has grown steadily in the past decade, with $47 million Americans now living below the federal poverty line.[1] And although substance abuse in the U.S. is equally distributed across all socioeconomic groups, low-income people are far more likely to end up in prison over drug charges.[2]

The roots of America's addictive proclivities lie buried in contradictions deep in the American psyche—over what constitutes health and happiness—and how to achieve these elusive ideals. Might it be possible that the very values that give America its vaunted strength and vitality also create the nation's greatest vulnerabilities? In a manic society where "more is never enough," is it possible to find a way out? One of the first "steps" in many rehab programs is the acknowledgment of a problem—followed by the recognition that a connection to others is a prerequisite for getting better. While some recovery programs have their philosophical faults, this fundamental message of mutual care suggests a subjective shift in the breaking of an addictive cycle—as individuals find solace in recognizing their interdependence.

Part of the problem is how Americans talk about drugs—or don't talk about them. No matter one's age, the expression "war on drugs" has a certain meaning. Particular kinds of substances, their use, and misuse get all of the attention in public discourse, while the nation tends not to discuss ways drugs-as-medicines implicate everyone. After all, broadly speaking a "drug" is simply a chemical with a biological effect on the body (or mind). Lots of drugs are naturally occurring agents that simply raise or lower body chemistry, like insulin does for diabetics. But it isn't simply that the country doesn't talk about drugs. The conversation also comes loaded with crazy beliefs, values, superstitions, medical jargon, and a fair amount of good old-fashioned ignorance. Public debates about drugs tend to focus on the subset of medications that affect the brain—the infamous "mind-altering substances"—as opposed to those helping the body with things like blood pressure and infections. Most people tend to view medicines for bodily matters with impunity. It's the drunks, pill poppers, and junkies that get all the scorn in "Just Say No" campaigns.

For obvious reasons, cultural attitudes toward medicines and drugs weigh heavily on questions of belonging and not belonging in America. One way or another, just about everyone is "addicted" to some favorite food, consumer behavior, or exercise routine—partly because American culture encourages excess in work and play, whether anyone admits this or not. Some of these addictive behaviors keep people happy and healthy. Yet at both a behavioral and medical level, guilt about being "dependent" on anything makes people feel conflicted. At what point does too much become a problem in a culture that valorizes overindulgence? When does obsession become a sign of weakness or cause for scorn in a society so predicated on values of individual autonomy? In many ways, subservience to *any* need seems antithetical to American ideals of freedom and liberty.

When it comes to substance abuse, demographic data paint a mixed picture—suggesting no clear overall reason for the nation's drug problems. Alcohol abuse rises with income, with high earners the most likely to drive while drunk, according to the CDC. Those making over $75,000 also binge drink 50 percent more than those making less than $25,000.[3] Levels of illegal drug use stand at 11 percent in almost all income groups, except the poorest Americans (individuals earning less than $9,000 per year) among whom prevalence is 50 percent higher.[4]

Both illegal drug use and excessive drinking correlate strongly with mental health problems, with depression and anxiety among the leading factors.

Of course the problem is that the most reviled drugs—like heroin, morphine, and cocaine—are derivatives of pain medicines that affect *both* the mind and body. But many commonly used medicines like analgesics, antibiotics, fever-reducing agents, and hormone replacements also work in this dual fashion. The point to keep in mind is that the simple mind/body distinction is sloppy when it comes to drugs. But this dichotomy, like so many others, nevertheless maintains a powerful grip on the ways many think about medicines. The very idea of taking a psychopharmaceutical agent makes many people uneasy—and this anxiety about substances affecting the mind has both an irrational and rational basis. Few people realize that mind-altering medications like antidepressants and opioids are the second and third most commonly prescribed medications in the U.S.[5] Millions of people need these medicines to function without discomfort, especially when it comes to pain. But it's also true that certain people are vulnerable to becoming habitual users—as Rush Limbaugh's highly publicized oxycodone addiction made clear. The case not only accented Limbaugh's prior hypocrisy in excoriating American's "drug problem," but also helped to dramatize the accidental character of addiction.

The Narcotic Tower of Babel

In Plato's *Phaedrus*, an Egyptian god gives a special remedy ("pharmakon") to a forgetful king. The remedy is writing—the ability to put memories into words. But the wise king sees that the pharmakon isn't really a "remedy" for memory at all, but instead is a crutch—a kind of "poison" that will make his recall weaker. In this story—fascinatingly framed around the act of writing—the duality of the pharmakon was introduced, as Jacques Derrida would later discuss.[6] To Derrida, the idea of the pharmakon attaches to all sorts of related concepts (medicine, drug, recipe, charm, incantation) that produce oppositions: antidote/poison, truth/falsehood, good/evil, interior/exterior. And of course Derrida reveled over the notion of language itself being at the center of the dualistic metaphor. Writing both contains and remains separate from the ideas it conveys—much as an image both is and isn't the thing depicted. This is the essence of deconstruction, the deferral of the linkage between signifier and signified. What seems a remedy to the god, is seen as poison to the king—as the meaning of the pharmakon flickers between the two.

And of course Derrida also talked about the pharmakon *as drug,* in part because the idea has such philosophical resonance. In a 1990 interview Derrida explained the writing-as-drug connection:

> The *pharmakon* "writing" does not serve the good, authentic memory. It is rather the mnemotechnical auxiliary of a bad memory. It has more to do

> with forgetting, the simulacrum, and bad repetition than it does with anamnesis and truth. This pharmakon dulls the spirit and rather than aiding, it wastes the memory. Thus in the name of authentic, living memory and in the name of truth, power accuses this bad drug, writing, of being a drug that leads not only to forgetting, but also to irresponsibility.[7]

Derrida considered the ways medicines have been viewed over time as magical agents, gifts from god, technical wonders, addictive pleasures, health hazards, social threats, toxins, poisons, and evils. He noted the function of norms in thinking about drugs, pointing out that many natural substances can be either helpful or harmful, depending on the amounts used—and that modernity seemed to play a special role in the vilification of drug use and addiction. Especially since the 19th century, Western societies have equated the unsanctioned use of medicines with impropriety. "We do not object to the drug user's pleasure per se, but to a pleasure taken in an experience without truth." Derrida said.[8]

While this notion of "truth" can serve as a stand-in for many values, it also seems to capture popular worries and concerns over drugs—as well as rationales for their subversive use. After all, what societies see as truth varies over time and space, as Nietzsche pointed out. While truth often masquerades as a self-evident "fact," it is highly contingent on associated beliefs. Throughout history one sees a continual vacillation in views of the drug pharmakon as either a life-enhancing technology or a damaging artifice—with a bewildering array of in-between views, judgments, justifications, and worries—manifest in contesting philosophical arguments, reversals of public opinion, and ongoing changes in legal policy.

In historical terms, the contemporary usage of *addiction* as a drug-related term is just over 100 years old. Before that, the Latin term *addicto* referred to "an awarding, a devoting" of a slave after battle. In the 1600s the meaning of *addict* was generalized in English to mean an "inclination or proclivity" toward a behavior.[9] Eventually addiction would come to signify forms of compulsive attachment, with the word linked to opium use in the 1906 *Oxford English Dictionary*. The 19th century had witnessed the large-scale transformations of Western societies from religious oligarchies to state bureaucracies, with an emphasis on managing populations through institutions and laws. Alcohol and narcotics certainly had been ubiquitous in Western nations through the mid-1800s, but soon their regulation would become matters of public policy and social concern. Until the 1868 Pharmacy Act in England, opium use was rampant—with its addiction rationalized as "habitual" use. When Coca-Cola was introduced in 1886 by an American pharmacist, its energizing effects were powered by coca plants used in hundreds of drinks at the time.

In the U.S., the Pure Food and Drug Act of 1906 was the first piece of omnibus legislation to classify certain substances as "dangerous." Primarily intended to protect the public from "misbranded" or "adulterated" grocery items, the law also required the labeling of products containing alcohol, morphine, opium, cannabis, and caffeine, among other things. Also, the legislation regulated tobacco sales for the first time. However, not until the 1914 Harrison Act did the U.S. government actually restrict the sale or possession of such substances. Britain enacted similar laws in 1916 with the Defense of the Realm Act and the 1920 Dangerous Drug Act. Notably in this period, popular stereotypes linked drugs to new immigrant populations with figures such as the opium-smoking Chinese or marijuana-crazed Mexican. These views fed perceptions that laws were needed to sustain the imperial ambitions of Western nations, maintain order in growing cities, and guarantee the health of a burgeoning middle class. Hence, the image of the irrational, immoral, and drug-addled foreigner rose in the public imagination as a threat and contaminant. During the first decades of the 20th century American government bureaucrats, medical professionals, social reformers, criminologists, and academics began speaking in one voice against narcotic "risks" to the social order—framing drugs and their purveyors in the language of "anti-Americanism." As Janet Farrell Brodie and Marc Redfield explain in their anthology, *High Anxieties: Cultural Studies in Addiction*:

> Much can be made, then, of this sudden pathologization and criminalization of habit: it occurred as part of the emergence, on the one hand, of a disciplinary society in which typologies of deviance play a significant role in the operations of power, and, on the other hand, of a society of consumption in which identities and desires become attuned to the repetitive seriality of commodity production.[10]

From 1919 through 1933 the U.S. embarked on the disastrous social experiment known as Prohibition—when the Eighteenth Amendment of the Constitution criminalized the manufacture, sale, and transportation of alcohol. Public demand for booze during Prohibition led to massive violations of the law and a generalized resistance to legal authority. This fueled an underground economy and a huge increase in organized crime. In the interest of political compromise, a later amendment of the Constitution ceded the regulation of alcohol to state governments. Among other things, this gave states the ability to set age requirements, and also to impose their own taxes on alcohol sales. By the 1980s evidence of the effects of alcohol on automobile death rates became so overwhelming that Congress enacted the 1984 National Minimum Drinking Age Act, which linked disbursement of federal highway monies to the age of 21. Within four years all states had adopted this standard.

Tobacco products followed a similar path, beginning with their inclusion in the Pure Food and Drug Act. But throughout American history the economic power of the tobacco industry has been a force to be reckoned with. Keep in mind that tobacco growing and exports played an important role the American colonial economy. In the late 1800s tobacco taxes accounted for one-third of the internal revenue collected by the U.S. government.[11] Tobacco farming and its related industries remain fixtures of the American South, contributing to national political divides even today as tobacco sales by American companies increasingly focus on foreign markets, especially in the developing world. Nazi Germany established the first modern antismoking campaign in 1941, condemning tobacco use and banning public smoking as a national health hazard. The Nazis blamed Jews for bringing tobacco to Germany.

In the U.S., federal tobacco laws were held in abeyance until the passage of the 1965 Federal Cigarette Labeling and Advisory Act, following a U.S. Surgeon General's report linking smoking to cancer and other diseases. The Public Heath Cigarette Smoking Act of 1970 banned cigarette ads from radio and TV, while enhancing warning labels with the expression "dangerous to your health."[12] An attempt in 1996 to place tobacco under the supervision of the Food and Drug Administration was successfully blocked by multinationals like Philip Morris and A.J. Reynolds. It may surprise many to know that comprehensive regulation of the tobacco industry by the federal government did not occur until the 2009 passage of the Family Smoking Prevention and Tobacco Control Act, which now monitors the ingredients, labeling, and use of such terms as "mild" or "light" cigarette advertising.

Laws regulating the distribution of drugs and alcohol are crude indicators of public attitudes, inasmuch as they at best reflect the views of putative majorities at certain moments in time. But what if laws don't work? The premise of "harm reduction," as the term implies, is that problems can be averted or minimized by altering rather than eliminating behaviors. Needle exchange programs remain the most controversial examples of harm reduction—in which injection drug users are provided with clean syringes to prevent infections from shared needles, as well as accidental overdosing by users. In some instances, secure locations to self-administer drugs are provided, along with medical supervision, education programs, and social services as a part of needle exchange. Countries like Canada, Germany, the Netherlands, Norway, and Spain have had such places for the last decade, generally sponsored by nonprofit groups. Studies conducted by the European Monitoring Centre for Drugs and Drug Addiction (EMCDDA) have shown no increases in drug usage as a consequence of the programs—despite such worries in countries like the U.S.[13] As a legislative concept, harm reduction often parallels efforts to decriminalize drug use. Many in the substance abuse field argue that treatment is more effective than punishment, and far less expensive than prosecution and incarceration. Efforts to decriminalize or legalize recreational marijuana use in the U.S. are manifestations of these efforts, as are programs distributing condoms and other materials to promote "safer sex," especially with at-risk populations or young people.

Medical marijuana highlights the pharmakon in the public mind as perhaps no other issue in today's news. There is really no dispute that pot can negatively affect judgment, memory, and the respiratory system, can be psychologically addictive, and is a gateway drug to other more dangerous substances. Moreover, in most of the U.S. marijuana remains illegal, thus exposing purchasers to criminal elements. At the same time, the medical benefits of marijuana also are now a matter of scientific fact, especially its ability to reduce nausea, pain, and muscle spasms—which is particularly important in sustaining cancer patients undergoing chemotherapy and people with HIV-AIDS. Some strains of marijuana also help control anxiety and sleep orders of the kind experienced by millions of Americans. One of the most convincing recent studies on medical marijuana, published recently in the *Journal of the American Medical Association*, documents a 25 percent reduction in opioid painkiller overdose death rates over the last decade in states allowing medical marijuana dispensing.[14] As things stand now, 54 percent of Americans favor the decriminalization or legalization of pot and 25 states have done so.[15]

Models of Addiction

Given its costs to American society, it's no surprise that addiction has been analyzed endlessly in medicine, psychiatry, law, social work, philosophy, and sociology, and throughout mental health, social science, and the humanities more broadly. When addicts or alcoholics speak about their substance use, many describe a kind of absence or void that is filled by the drug or drink—an initial interest that evolves into an uncontrolled craving for "something." But how this something gets described varies wildly, as, for instance, a social enhancement, diversion from boredom, release from pain, consumer habit, cultural convention, act of rebellion, and so on. This variation in why substances get used frustrated intervention methodologies for much of the 19th century, even as drug use grew. Drinking problems have a history dating back to antiquity. Largely focused on alcoholism, homes and asylums for the "chronically inebriated" appeared throughout America in the 1800s to warehouse addicts as they dried out. But little coherent theory or research lay behind their efforts until recent decades. For much of the past century, four models have dominated addiction treatment discourse: *choice, disease, social construction*, and *integration*.

Dominant through the mid-20th century, the "choice" model hinges on Western notions of subjectivity in suggesting that individuals govern their own consumption of cigarettes, alcohol, or illegal drugs. Hence, choice maps neatly onto American ideals of personal autonomy. Choice defines addiction as spiritual weakness or logical failure, for which it prescribes various strategies for returning to goodness and truth. When rational "self-control" wavers, morality is brought in to fill the void. Premises of abstinence driven by willful substitution inform 12-step programs like Alcoholics Anonymous, which first appeared in America in the 1930s, in which a "higher" power replaces the drug. More recent iterations of choice entail reconditioning via Cognitive Behavioral Therapy (CBT) as a means of "recovery" (i.e., return to reason). Choice-oriented programs always have had trouble addressing the issue of physical dependence on substances.

The "disease" model emerged from the medical field in the 1950s in response to choice doctrine, by redefining addiction as a form of progressive illness. Initially put forth by the American Medical Association, the disease model remains the official view of the National Institute on Drug Abuse, which states in its current literature that:

> Addiction is defined as a chronic, relapsing brain disease that is characterized by compulsive drug seeking and use, despite harmful consequences. It is considered a brain disease because drugs change the brain—they change its structure and how it works. These brain changes can be long lasting, and can lead to the harmful behaviors seen in people who abuse drugs.[16]

Critics of the disease model fault it for going too far in discounting the agency of the afflicted person, especially when dishonesty, criminality, or violent behaviors occur.

"Social construction" emerged in the 1980s and 1990s to address the role of groups, discourses, and institutions in addiction. Constructionism implicitly questions the premise of a self that is separate from the world around it. As such, social construction examines the contexts through which views about substances and addiction emerge. Learned attitudes and peer behaviors are examples of social construction—as are cultures of drug use, the marketing of medicines, stigma toward addicts, regulatory measures, and law enforcement. Some have faulted social construction for overlooking the phenomenological experience of the addict.[17] Cravings or withdrawal symptoms cannot be defined in socially constructed terms, for example.

In recent years, "integrated" approaches have brought together the three models discussed above. This parallels a rising interdisciplinarity among the fields of general medicine, psychiatry, and social work. For example, an integrative approach to addiction simultaneously addresses the individual's physical condition, psychotherapeutic needs, and socioeconomic context. Integrative approaches to both medicine and addiction have had difficulties getting traction in the largely privatized and compartmentalized U.S. health-care system. The story is different in Europe, where progressive nations increasingly use a "whole person" approach.

Science seems to point in the direction of integration. Recent advances in brain imaging have begun to break down long-standing separations of medicine and mental health—with growing recognition of the brain as an organ system like others. Neuroscience and psychiatry have grown closer, for example, as Magnetic Resonance Imaging (MRI) and CAT scans have allowed scientists more accurately to assign discrete mental functions to brain regions, which hitherto were matters of empirical observation or theoretical speculation. Drugs and medicines affecting thought and feeling are now known to chemically interact with neurons and glial cells, as signals circulate throughout brain regions. Different substances affect certain regions in certain ways. For example, glucose from eating carbohydrates can make thinking clear or cloudy depending on the amount consumed. Research has shown that highly processed carbohydrates stimulate brain regions involved in the same reward and craving systems as certain addictive drugs.[18]

The nucleus accumbens (the so-called pleasure center) of the brain receives stimulating signals from all sorts of things people consume, including sugar, nicotine, alcohol, opiates, and amphetamines—and also from exercise, music, and sex. Unfortunately when stimulation occurs with increasing frequency the signal weakens. People develop a tolerance for certain substances or activities, requiring more to get the same effect. Tolerance also has a negative effect in triggering craving states when the activating substance is absent. In other words, the addiction process actually means that the brain is undergoing a change. This is why a person can make it through the discomfort of an initial withdrawal and "quit," only to struggle afterwards with a brain "wired" for the addictive agent.

Seen in this light, addiction and recovery are more than simple cause/effect phenomena involving certain "bad" drug behaviors and their "good" removal. All sorts of stimuli can activate the brain's pleasure center, cause its desensitization, and become habit forming. In *Models of Addiction*, Robert West describes an integrated program developed in Great Britain and now used in many European countries.[19] The so-called COM-B system broadly maps the intersection of "capability," "opportunity," and "motivation" in interdisciplinary terms—as vectors for both drug use and nonuse. *Capability* entails the cognitive knowledge (what substances do and how to use them), psychological regulation or non-regulation (desire, guilt, ambivalence), as well as the physical skills (self-injecting, driving to a tavern) involved. *Opportunity* includes environmental factors (availability of substances, money, or economic incentives, cues that prompt use) and social factors (social mores, cultural attitudes, group practices). *Motivation* can be conscious or intentional (belief in a drug's risks, benefits, legality or illegality) as well as automatic (learned or associative processes, feelings, impulses, or counter-impulses). As West points out, COM-B "is not a psychological, sociological, or environmental model" per se, but rather a way of viewing the simultaneous interactions of multiple elements in what is often viewed as a single-solution problem.[20]

Writing on Drugs

"Who will ever relate the whole history of narcotica? It is almost the history of 'culture,' of our so-called high culture," wrote Nietzsche.[21] Western literature is full of writing about drugs, praising or condemning drugs, books written by authors on drugs, or simply works referencing drugs as a path to something transcendent or unknowable. The narcotic pharmakon, in its many simultaneous remedy/poison connotations, seems to avoid easy depiction or analysis—rendering singular discussions of medication and drugs extremely difficult. "Drugs refuse to be pinned down—they slip away, incessantly, from law as well as language," writes Dennis Schep.[22] The interdisciplinarity of drugs as a concept and a social issue has made coherent discussion elusive. All of this is further confounded by the stigma of speaking about drugs too personally. While drug use is prevalent in American society, nevertheless it is a subject that many people want to avoid. "Few academics have dared to engage the topic—and those that did have more often than not felt it necessary to employ certain inoculative measures in their texts to protect their reputation, if not their income," Schep writes.[23] In contrast, the more socially accepted "drug" of alcohol has been a celebrated topic in American literature and a commonplace feature of movies and TV dramas.

These cultural contradictions reflect a society of divided sentiments about substance use. Drugs are a lot like sex in the ways they are covered over in a culture of repressed craving. Moderate drinking and normative sex are fine as long as they remain contained—even as people's licentious imaginations may lead them elsewhere. This is one reason why literary and cinematic representations of excess have been so popular. Narrative provides the gateway to satisfy what the spectator can only imagine—often located somewhere between desire and fear. Drugs blur this line and lots of other boundaries, too. This gets even messier when America's addictive thrills attach to compulsive drives for money and success. More than one researcher has found that material desires are really symptoms of deeper yearnings, which get sublimated or displaced onto external objects like a new car or a promotion at work. At the end of the day, most people admit that what really matters are the connections that bring them close to others—with family members, intimate partners, and friends—and the basic necessities of life. But especially in times of economic stress, worries grow that the outside world is going to threaten those things or otherwise diminish the way people see themselves in comparison to others.

As set forth in the above, drugs need to be seen as the complex matter that they are—often inflected by physical, psychological, social, and economic factors. In many ways, drugs constitute a boundary concept between mind and body, subject and object, known and unknown. Really getting at the matter of drugs requires thinking of them in intersectional terms, but also as agencements that are contextual, relational, and often in motion across time and space. Language and philosophy have struggled for centuries to try to get their arms around drugs. This is the paradox of the pharmakon, which Derrida pointed out when he spoke of the wildly varying assertions of truth and untruth posed toward drugs—which are always both and neither. There is no single "world" of drugs we can even speak about, Derrida once said.[24] The confusing contemporary rhetoric of drugs plays perfectly into a neoliberal culture of obfuscation. Society is addicted to things it cannot name, much less combat.

The good/bad binary still exerts a powerful historical pull—in large part because language makes it so. Beginning with the truth/untruth dichotomy, one finds in drug discourse nearly every similar pairing in the lexicon of Enlightenment thought: good/evil, mind/body, reason/unreason, knowledge/ignorance, and civilization/savagery. Conceptualizations of "drugs" are deeply embedded in Western histories of secularization, jurisprudence, and technology—figuring prominently in contemporary critiques of medical reason and the scientific management of populations. Even in today's seemingly innocuous vocabulary of nutritional supplements, vitamins, dieting, exercise, and "wellness," one enters the realm of technologized correction or prevention of some perceived threat or deficit.

Thomas De Quincy's *Confessions of an English Opium-Eater* is often cited as one of the earliest frankly pro-narcotics books, launching the tradition of addiction literature in Europe. De Quincy wrote about both the positive and negative effects of his addiction to opium and to laudanum (an alcohol and opium mixture). Like some of today's prescription-pill addicts, De Quincy began taking laudanum in 1813 for pain and later found that it lifted his spirits. He continued using it for the better part of 40 years. *Confessions* stands out as one of the first books directly to address the quite widespread drug use in Victorian culture, and, as De Quincy would note, the book flew in the face of cultural mores and values:

> Guilt, therefore, I do not acknowledge; and if I did, it is possible that I might still resolve on the present act of confession in consideration of the service that I may thereby render to the whole class of opium-eaters. But who are they? Reader, I am sorry to say a very numerous class indeed. Of this I became convinced some years ago by computing at that time the number of those in one small class of English society (the class of men distinguished for talents, or of eminent station) who were known to me, directly or indirectly, as opium-eaters.[25]

Confessions is often cited for its lucid descriptions of intoxication: De Quincy's delight in wandering the streets of London while stoned on a drug that "stealest away the purposes of wrath" and "givest back the hopes of youth … Thou hast the key of paradise, O just, subtle, and mighty opium!"[26] De Quincy's account of opium as a powerful agent typifies 18th-century views of substances as possessing their own agency.

Not surprisingly, negative depictions of alcohol and drug use became more prevalent in the 19th century, with the rise of public health programs and temperance movements. Émile Zola's *L'Assommoir* (1877) told the story of a working-class couple in Paris whose lives were ruined by progressive alcoholism.[27] With its title translated into English as *The Drunkard, The Drinking Den*, and *The Gin Palace*, Zola's book directly equated alcoholism with the new "masses" of low-income urban dwellers. The book was disseminated widely among bourgeois readers as a warning against the dangers of excessive drinking. It's worth noting that while addiction had not yet been classified as a disease, its long-term health damage typically brought addicts and alcoholics to physicians who either prescribed remedies or referred patients to facilities for the chronically infirm or mentally ill. At this time, the bulk of addiction and alcoholism treatment took place on what now would be termed an "outpatient" basis, meaning that patients recovered at home or under the care of family members.[28]

The 19th-century quasi-medicalization of addiction led to a theory known as "degeneration"—the view that biological and moral factors combined with toxic social influences could trigger a downward cascade within an individual, which would replicate in subsequent generations. Degeneration theory emerged as a parallel to Darwinian principles of evolution in suggesting that certain "character traits" were passed on to offspring. An omnibus list of behaviors found explanation in degenerative pathology—including learning disorders, impulsivity, alcoholism, homosexuality, dementia, and epilepsy. In its crude determinism, the concept framed addiction as an essential characteristic of people and their families. Such beliefs contributed significantly to early 20th-century temperance movements. Addiction was seen as a plague infecting certain populations—and the cure would lie in nationwide prohibition. But by the 1930s America discovered that this strategy wouldn't work. Part of the novelty of Alcoholics Anonymous, launched during this period, was the treatment of a predominantly invisible population cohort. From its earliest days, AA spoke to functioning alcoholics who had jobs and families, as well as those at rock bottom—as AA also recognized the incremental trajectories of addiction in people's lives.

This was also the time of the great American writer-alcoholic: F. Scott Fitzgerald, Ernest Hemingway, Tennessee Williams—all the way through Charles Bukowski, John Cheever, and Raymond Carver, among others. These men valorized their booze, blackouts, and bad behavior in a way that introduced an invigorated sense of agency in addiction. Without doubt, American attitudes toward alcohol received periodic license in times of war and economic stress as well. Substance use, and especially heavy drinking, has always played an important role in military culture as both a stress reliever and bonding ritual. All of this provided important forms of social sanction for heavy substance use, the normative aspects of which in 1950s America were so aptly depicted in the *Mad Men* (2007–2015) TV series. While substance use/abuse clearly became fused with competitive masculinity, the ethos of the hard-working alcoholic also complemented broader ideals of self-determination and even patriotism. American beer and liquor companies promoted their brands with nationalist zeal, as exports of many U.S. products continued to rise in the post–World War II years.

In 1953 *Junkie: Confessions of an Unredeemed Drug Addict*, by William Burroughs appeared in print as a mass-market paperback, in obvious homage to De Quincy. *Junkie* chronicled beat-era use of heroin and other drugs—and was one of the books condemned by Senator Joseph McCarthy for its "appeals to sensuality, immorality, filth, perversion, and degeneracy."[29] Burroughs's work drew on the author's life on the street, reading like a travel guide to the American underworld. The book didn't so much romanticize substance abuse as it detailed the stresses of supporting a drug habit, its daily discomforts, and the sickness of withdrawal. Owing to Burroughs's eloquence as a writer, *Junkie* was peppered with philosophical reflections on drugs, the most potent of which speak of the subjective transformations experienced in various states of intoxication. "Junk is not a kick. It is a way of life," Burroughs wrote.[30] In this Burroughs was not simply describing a "lifestyle." He would later elaborate upon the cycle of withdrawal and satiation through which addicts experience what seems like an approaching "death" and subsequent "rebirth" on a daily basis. But more deeply, Burroughs was also describing the long-term internalization of addiction as a form of self-knowledge and insight about the nature of being—as the junkie experiences these things.

Putting a somewhat different inflection on the notion of self-knowledge through drugs, Aldous Huxley published his *The Doors of Perception* in 1954, following his mescaline use in the American Southwest. Huxley cautiously framed his account as a limited and quasi-scientific experiment with the drug—which he said could create "temporary bypasses" to alternate realities of the kind "certain people seem to be born with." Huxley wrote that through these gateways flows "something more than, and above all something different from, the carefully selected utilitarian material from which our narrowed, individual minds regard as a complete, or at least sufficient, picture of reality."[31] In different ways and using different drugs, Burroughs and Huxley charted what would become an important dichotomy of drug use, which would play out in the following decades. As Burroughs painted a picture of substance use as a consuming identity and one-way street, Huxley was among the first to introduce the idea of touristic "experimentation" with drugs and their nonaddictive use.

In a post–World War II America infused with alcohol, the infamous 1960s drug culture was more of a continuation of substance use than a radical break. Of course the big difference had to do with legality—and the signature role of drug use as a symbol of anti-authoritarianism for the youth culture of the era, especially among demographics that could afford to pay. As drug cartels gained the upper hand on Mexican law enforcement, U.S. demand for marijuana grew steadily in the 1960s and 1970s. Columbia would become another leading exporter of marijuana and more lucrative drugs like cocaine. Southeast Asia produced most of the world's heroin during this time, with U.S. military personnel exposed to the drug while stationed there. With the rise of disease addiction models in the 1960s, terms like "epidemic" and "plague" would enter popular discourse in describing the spread of "hard" drugs like heroin and amphetamines, especially as they "infected" inner cities. This thinking was very much in keeping with "culture of poverty" beliefs in the 1960s that recast notions of degenerative defects with views that poverty was disseminated by community attitudes and social learning. Unfortunately this sometimes gave the drug problem racial connotations, especially when associated with urban populations. In this way, the disease discourse rekindled the nationalist health anxieties of the 19th century—with worries voiced about immigrants bringing the "sickness" of drugs across American borders, especially from the south.

Throughout the 1960s heroin was the most feared and romanticized drug in America—with an estimated 500,000 addicts by the decade's end.[32] During this period the heroin market expanded from big cities and jazz clubs to college campuses and music festivals, as 15–20 percent of military personnel returning from Vietnam addictively used the drug.[33] In the public imagination, the 1960s were the heyday of illegal drug taking. But historical data indicate this wasn't the case. Instead, surveys from the time show that drug abuse was relatively rare, as was reliable information about the effects of illegal drugs. In a 1969 Gallup poll, only 4 percent of American adults said they had tried marijuana and 34 percent said they didn't know what pot did.[34] Nevertheless, the decades of the 1960s and 1970s would be romanticized for the "Summer of Love," and remembered for the psychedelic writings of Carlos Castaneda and Timothy Leary, among others. If this writing shared a common theme, it lay in extending Huxley's philosophical approach to intoxicants as a form of inquiry as well as escape. The very language of psychedelic "tripping" or "experimentation" evoked a purposeful aura of drug use as a search for meaning. As Leary explained his famous mantra of "Turn on, tune in, drop out":

> "Turn on" meant go within to activate your neural and genetic equipment. Become sensitive to the many and various levels of consciousness and the specific triggers that engage them. Drugs were one way to accomplish this end. "Tune in" meant interact harmoniously with the world around you—externalize, materialize, express your new internal perspectives. "Drop out" suggested an active, selective, graceful process of detachment from involuntary or unconscious commitments.[35]

While Leary's expansive rhetoric would be critiqued as inherently solipsistic, it also spoke of the era's ethos of resistance—manifest in student activism, civil rights struggles, and in uprisings in cities around the world throughout the 1960s. Antiwar demonstrations were but one manifestation of growing antiauthoritarian sentiment. Violence had broken out throughout the U.S. in such cities as Baltimore, Chicago, Minneapolis, Philadelphia, and Rochester. Writing in "An Essay on Liberation," Herbert Marcuse would state: "Today's rebels want to see, hear, feel new things in a new way: they link liberation with the dissolution of ordinary and orderly perception," adding in reference to drugs as both metaphor and actuality that "the 'trip' involves the dissolution of the ego shaped by established society—an artificial and short-lived dissolution."[36] Marcuse saw drug use as a component of what he termed "the new sensibility" emerging in opposition to the "one-dimensional society" of consumer capitalism and media consolidation. As Marcuse's thinking evolved into a post-Marxist view, he would characterize one-dimensional society as a fusion of material and cultural hegemony that also was hijacking language itself. He even saw the hippy lexicon of "grass," "pot," and "acid" running parallel to African-American terms like "soul music" and "black is beautiful." But Marcuse also noticed that lots of college kids were simply getting high and forgetting politics, writing that:

> Awareness of the need for such a revolution of perception, for a new sensorium, is perhaps the kernel of truth in the psychedelic search. But it is vitiated when its narcotic character brings temporary release not only from the reason and rationality of the established system but also from that other rationality which is to change the established system, when sensibility is freed not only from the exigencies of the existing order but also from those of liberation.[37]

Notwithstanding this ambivalence, Marcuse sympathized with drug users seeking the alternative consciousness he saw as a prerequisite to social change. Marcuse would point out that his vision was less a matter of anticapitalism than it was a critique of Enlightenment positivism. Specifically, Marcuse argued that "revolutionary" movements of the past had tended to replicate dominance/submission paradigms. A new "consciousness" was needed and drug experience could leverage a new politics of knowledge. Marcuse described the need for an "aesthetic education" powered by art and artists, which would lead society beyond its current psychological state of "surplus repression." Eventually Marcuse would be pilloried by Marxists for romanticizing what they saw as bourgeois conceits.[38]

Themes of post-positivism percolated in much writing and media of this period, with critiques of establishment "reason" manifest in works valorizing the *unreason* of certain states of mind, ranging from intoxication, to spiritualism, and to psychiatric disorders. But nothing exemplified the assault on reason more than the rise of drugs—especially in assertions that drugs held the key to unconventional wisdom. This is what upset conservatives the most: the radical potential of drugs to subvert the civilizing project of Western epistemology. And in true Enlightenment fashion, a counterattack would soon be launched to villainize and expel the narcotic enemy. Derrida would write that the Enlightenment "is itself a declaration of war on drugs," especially in its public or "official" manifestations.[39]

Keep in mind that this was also a time when the very category of "normal" also was being mapped and critiqued by academics in psychology, sociology, and other disciplines—even as conventions of patriarchy, patriotism, heterosexuality, white privilege, and the nuclear family were coming under assault. It's no small irony that Ken Kesey wrote *One Flew Over the Cuckoo's Nest* (1962) while a subject in a CIA-sponsored LSD research program.[40] Kesey depicted patients in a psychiatric hospital as victims of a disciplinary institution whose pathologizing logic blinded it to the humanity of those consigned to its care. He would later recount that his role as a medical guinea pig, as well as his time spent working in a state veterans' hospital, informed his writing of the book. Popularized in a later film adaptation (1975), *One Flew Over the Cuckoo's Nest* invited readers/viewers to identify with patients as arbitrarily othered through medical technology, forcibly imposing on them ways of being that were anything but reasonable. The work urgently underscored the relative character of such ideals as "mental health" and normalcy in its depictions of institutional control and punishment manifest in forced medication, electroshock therapy, and lobotomy treatments. As the story unfolds, one rebellious "patient" introduces his fellows to such simple pleasures as televised baseball and a fishing trip—which trigger damaging reprisals from the hospital, even though they seem to help the patients a great deal. In effect, *One Flew Over the Cuckoo's Nest* turned the tables on institutional authority in depicting the hospital itself as the source of malevolent and "crazy" behavior, bent on perpetuating the illnesses of those confined. Tom Wolfe's *The Electric Kool-Aid Acid Test* (1968) would later make Kesey himself an American folk hero in its celebration of his exploits with his LSD-fueled band of "Merry Pranksters" as they cavorted with Allen Ginsberg, the Hell's Angels, and the Grateful Dead.[41] While seen at the time as a gospel work of the hippy generation, in stylistic terms, *The Electric Kool-Aid Acid Test* demonstrated an approach to reportage that openly blurred the lines between fiction and nonfiction—paralleling in its accounts of the Prankster's mission of tripping the spaces between imagination and reality.

Substance abuse problems are ubiquitous in American life, but until recently they were rarely addressed in movies and TV as matters affecting "ordinary" people. As such, alcoholism and drug addiction have been waiting for their moment on stage—until mainstream audiences could connect with them. The shift began about a decade ago in such TV shows as *Breaking Bad* (2008–2012), *Weeds* (2005–2012), *House* (2004–2012), *Shameless* (2011–), *The Killing* (2011–2012), *Nurse Jackie* (2009–) *Mad Men* (2007–2015), *True Blood* (2008–), *Orange Is the New Black* (2013–), *Elementary* (2012–), *Nashville* (2013–), and *Terriers* (2010–)—all featuring leading characters with substance abuse conditions. Significantly, many of these shows also depict recovery programs in a destigmatized manner, which marks a departure from the avoidance or outright mockery of drug treatment (especially 12-step programs) in the past.

Hollywood's own drug problems partly account for this shift. The cocaine epidemic of the 1990s and early 2000s took a heavy toll on the entertainment industry, with many celebrities succumbing to overdose or other health problems. And of course many in the industry simply drank. The combined death toll included Chris Farley, Corey Hiam, Phillip Seymour Hoffman, Margaux Hemingway, Whitney Houston, Michael Jackson, Heath Ledger, River Phoenix, Anna Nicole Smith, Ike Turner, and Amy Winehouse—although these are simply the more well-known figures. While the episodic character of news reporting has tended to treat these tragic deaths as isolated incidents, growing numbers of performers have come forward, sometimes after public embarrassments, to disclose their addictions. The list includes Tom Arnold, Drew Barrymore, Ed Begley, Jr., Lynda Carter, Susan Cheever, Judy Collins, Jamie Lee Curtis, Robert Downey, Jr., Edie Falco, Colin Farrell, Michael J. Fox, Lou Gosset, Jr., Melanie Griffith, Ed Harris, Richard Lewis, Lindsay Lohan, Kelly McGillis, Nick Nolte, Tatum O'Neal, Katey Sagal, and Martin Sheen.

The term "rehab chic" has become synonymous with celebrities who go into recovery—often at expensive boutique clinics—in a manner that leaves many wondering about the sincerity of the gesture. As National Institutes of Health Addictions Director Alexandre Laudet commented, "If you bring in millions at the box office or the runway, chances are that you get away with more than the average person can. After a binge of bad behavior, some flee to expensive clinics to convince the public—and the companies that hire them—that they're sorry."[42] The television series *Celebrity Rehab with Dr. Drew* (Pinsky), purportedly launched to bring "sensitivity" to the matter of high-profile addiction, ran for five years and featured such guests as Daniel Baldwin, Mary Carey, Jeff Conaway, Jaimee Foxworth, Brigitte Nielsen, Jessica Sierra, among others. The series went off the air amid criticisms that Pinsky's high-profile guests often relapsed. Rebranded as *Rehab with Dr. Drew*, the program went on to feature ordinary people living through some of the worst moments of their lives. But in this iteration the program relentlessly zeroed in on crisis, often exacerbating it for the camera with a brutally confrontational style. It made for entertaining television, but the show made treatment look like a living hell.

Before this recent visibility, substance abuse mostly appeared only in movie or TV crime dramas—whether this meant hard-drinking detectives, secret agents, or the drug-addled underworld. A notable early exception was Otto Preminger's *The Man with the Golden Arm* (1955), starring Frank Sinatra as a heroin addict, a film that historians cite as the first Hollywood feature to directly address illegal drug use—so notable, in fact, that *The Man with the Golden Arm* was rejected by the rating board of the Motion Picture Association of America. Within the film noir genre a few movies about alcoholism also appeared during this period—such as *The Lost Week End* (1945) and *The Days of Wine and Roses* (1954). But for the most part, depictions of drinking (and smoking) served to reify alcohol use.

If the entertainment industry was in denial about alcoholism and hard-core addiction, moderate social drinking would be treated in the media and the public mind as a pleasurable and disinhibiting social lubricant, sometimes cast as a quintessentially American (Joe Six-Pack) way of having a good time—often inflected with subversion, sophistication, sexual innuendo. Between 1965 and 1975, *The Dean Martin Show* aired 265 prime-time episodes featuring the visibly intoxicated Martin as the quintessential rascal drunk. Later series like "Cheers" (1982–1993), which was set in a Boston tavern, would similarly minimize the downside of excessive boozing in the character of the always-loveable Norm. The 50-year James Bond movie franchise (1962–2015) featured the hard-drinking, but never intoxicated, spy in a relentless pursuit of his signature martini ("shaken, not stirred") through 24 films. A key element in these and hundreds of other depictions was the uniform presentation of alcohol as a mostly positive, harmless, and above all, normal diversion.

In 1982 the phrase "Just Say No" entered the sobriety lexicon in a speech given by First Lady Nancy Reagan at an Oakland, California, elementary school.

The expression would soon become an emblem of Reagan administration admonitions against underage drinking, drug use, and premarital sex. Like the "War on Drugs," "Abstinence Education," and "Zero Tolerance" policies that emerged during this period, "Just Say No" appealed to the moral absolutism characteristic of the Reagan Revolution. The rigidity of "Just Say No" was its weakness, as manifest in the failure of its most visible program, D.A.R.E. (Drug Abuse Resistance Education) launched in 1983. Popular among teachers and parent groups, D.A.R.E. brought friendly police into schools to educate and warn young people about the consequences of substance abuse (car crashes, injuries, arrests, incarceration)—with the program eventually reaching 75 percent of the nation's schools. Owing to its scale, D.A.R.E is one of the few programs of its kind to have undergone empirical study by the mental health field. A ten-year analysis published in the *Journal of Consulting and Clinical Psychology* found that the massive program had no effect whatsoever on young people's subsequent cigarette, alcohol, marijuana, cocaine, or heroin use, and also did nothing to reduce the effects of peer pressure.[43] In fact, the studies found that D.A.R.E.'s message of saying no and its panic-laden message that "drug abuse is everywhere" made matters worse. Not only did kids ignore the scare tactics, but they also got the impression that drugs were more prevalent than they actually were—with one study conducted by the University of Illinois showing *increased* drug usage due to the D.A.R.E program. Other research revealed that students exposed to D.A.R.E scored lower on self-esteem measures for as long as a decade.

Then there is the Budweiser effect. By the end of the 1990s American alcohol companies were spending $596 million annually on televised sports advertising, with an additional $85 million on college game program guides and professional car-racing materials.[44] Total alcohol advertising now stands at approximately $4 billion a year. Generalized public health concerns notwithstanding, the big worry among policy makers has been the youth market. Currently, alcohol advertisements can only appear in public contexts where 70 percent of the audience is above the legal drinking age—and the style and content of messages may not appear to appeal to people under the age of 21. As with cigarette ads, using cartoon characters as spokespeople is discouraged. Research from numerous studies conducted in the 2000s has shown that advertising for beer and other drinks does not so much convince teenagers to drink a particular brand as it promotes a non-specified interest in alcohol. The Federal Trade Commission has linked alcohol advertising with persistent underage drinking, and claims that by regulating ads it has lowered youth alcohol use by 24 percent since the 1990s.[45]

The image of drugs and alcohol in television dramas has changed a lot in the past decade. As America was crashing into economic recession, *Breaking Bad* became a sensation for its nuanced portrayal of a kindly high school teacher driven by economic hardship to become a ruthless drug lord and killer. The show would become part of a growing trend on television to blur the line between good and evil through plots and characters that resisted pigeonholing. Morally ambiguous "TV shows and films of today are popular because they are touching upon issues that we, in the culture, are conflicted about," explains Richard Krevolin, a screenwriter and former professor at the University of Southern California Cinema/TV School. "In doing so, they allow us to work out these issues for ourselves."[46]

Not all TV drug and addiction narratives are created equal. While some recent shows depict the tragic downside of substance abuse (*Breaking Bad, Orange is the New Black*), others treat it as normative or transgressive (*Mad Men, Weeds*). More intriguing still are programs exploring the ambiguous middle zones of addiction. *Nurse Jackie* has made the philosophical quandary of addiction a central motif in depicting its central character as perpetually conflicted between abstinence and use, honesty and deception, and insight and denial. In episode after episode, viewers watch Jackie's pill habit wax and wane, wreaking havoc on her family life and putting her patients at risk. This sets *Nurse Jackie* apart from series that use addictive proclivities as sidebars. Relapse is a common theme in much of this programming, as it is in real life. Such is the case with *Elementary*, featuring a latter-day Sherlock Holmes (famous in literature as a druggie) still fresh from heroin rehab and living with a "sober companion" (Dr. Watson) hired by his family. Viewers watch Sherlock attend recovery meetings, as they also do in many of these new addiction shows—although the recovery groups are generally depicted as an episodic fix, rather than an ongoing part of the addict's of life.

Almost all of these programs depict a very particular kind of addict—one who is personable, highly functional, and attractive. This is very much in keeping with popular representations of alterity in general, as difference is both "shown" but also sanitized for prime-time audiences. *Nashville*'s Deacon Claybourne may be a recovering drunk, but he is also a multi-talented hunk of a guy, who has a heart of gold. Even when *Mad Men*'s Don Draper passes out from his daily diet of scotch, he wakes up the next morning even more brilliant and handsome than the night before. These images of addiction get a lot of credit from audiences and critics for introducing the topic of substance abuse into mainstream media. But they do so by showing only a palatable kind of addiction story. Of course none of this is new in Hollywood screen writing. Pick just about any category of social marginalization, and one finds a similar formula—from initial exclusion/demonization to later tokenization/sanitization—accenting one aspect of difference while flattening all others. This fits perfectly within a neoliberal agenda of "managing" alterity by containment.

For this and other reasons, *Shameless* holds a unique position in current broadcasting—both in its unvarnished portrayal of alcoholic psychology and its equally detailed depiction of a family living in poverty. In *Shameless*, Frank Gallagher is a single father of six children who spends his days drunk or stealing money (sometimes from his own children), and leaving his dependents to fend for themselves in the face of debt collectors, police, or the welfare system. The show's exploration of addiction's destructive effects on a family system sets it apart from others in this genre. When first proposing the series in 2010, John Wells said he had to fight efforts to place the drama in the South or in a trailer park. He explained, "We have a comedic tradition of making fun of the people in those worlds. The reality is that these people aren't 'the other'—they're people who live four blocks down from you and two blocks over."[47]

Big Pharma

To return to a point made earlier, almost everyone takes "drugs" or medications of some form or another, either on a short-term or long-term basis—and the line gets very messy with over-the-counter meds, natural remedies, and nutritional supplements. Seven in ten Americans currently receive at least one prescription of some kind.[48] Twenty percent take five or more medications regularly. The largest-selling drugs in the U.S. are Lipitor (cholesterol-lowering), Nexium (heartburn), and Plavix (blood thinner), Avdair (asthma), and Abilify (depression/anxiety).[49] But one-a-day vitamins also are a kind of "drug," and some argue an unhealthy one for many people. The point is that drugs constitute one of America's biggest industries. Even limiting the discussion to the "pharmaceutical industry" itself, expenditure on medicines account for over $1 trillion of the world economy, one-third of which is spent in the U.S.[50] And business for drug makers has been growing at an astronomical rate. By most recent accounts the number of prescriptions written in America has grown by 61 percent in the past decade to 4 billion per year.[51] The money spent by consumers has grown by 250 percent from $72 billion to $250 billion. And this isn't counting the nearly $500 billion spent each year on over-the-counter medications and the $100 billion spent on illegal drugs.[52] With the Affordable Care Act, the vast majority of prescriptions are paid by insurance of some kind—making drugs the third-largest cost in health care.

In the 2000s the circulation of prescription drugs noticeably began to leak medications into the nonprescription market. According to the National Institute for Drug Abuse (NIDA), prescription psychotherapeutic medications such as pain medicines, tranquilizers, stimulants, and sedatives are used illegally by approximately 2.7 percent of the population (seven million people).[53] Nearly 1 in 12 high school seniors reported nonmedical use of Vicodin and 1 in 20 said they had used OxyContin. Stimulants of the kind prescribed for Attention Deficit Disorder are also in wide circulation. NIDA reports that 70 percent of 12th graders said they received such pills from friends or relatives.

Much of the rise in prescription drug use is due to advertising and the recent increase in direct-to-consumer sales of medications via the Internet. Consumer drug advertising is banned in most of the world, except in the U.S. and New Zealand. And prior to the 1990s drug companies were required to list both the purpose of the drug and a complete list of side effects and potential risks, which often took pages of documentation with each ad. In 1997 FDA rules changed to require companies to list only the most significant potential side effects. Owing to this change, the number of ads has exploded in the past decade—to an average of 80 drug ads every hour on national television.[54]

Earlier in this book I discussed some of the realities of heath and sickness in America. Approximately 80 percent of the population see a doctor at least once per year, with four in ten failing to meet standards of relatively good health.[55] That translates into approximately 120 million people with some form of chronic or acute complaint—with high blood pressure, diabetes, depression, anxiety, and thyroid problems topping the list. Beyond this, it's no surprise that the massive amount of advertising carried out by the pharmaceutical industry has helped contribute to worries about nonserious illness, as well as issues that are undiagnosable or are simply imaginary. This isn't helped by the huge amount of misinformation circulated on the Internet, suggesting that headaches may mean brain cancer and so on.

But hype and misinformation aren't the whole problem, or even the worst concern. While advertising may influence the consumer, most critics of "big pharma" are more worried about the way the drug industry develops medications, secures their approval, and then manipulates doctors to prescribe them. In his recent book *Bad Pharma: How Drug Companies Mislead Doctors and Harm Patients*, physician Ben Goldacre details the role of pharmaceutical industry funded "trials" in testing the effectiveness of new drugs.[56] The industry's resources allow it to overwhelm federal studies with its purportedly "independent" research—returning positive findings at 20 times the rate of government studies. According to Goldacre, drug makers have become increasingly adept at designing studies and selecting patient cohorts to make results come out in their favor. Or they simply cancel or suppress studies that don't pan out. Everyone involved knows this is the case, but the political will to stop it seems to be lacking. A small cottage industry of books emerged in the early 2000s telling this story, with titles like *Selling Sickness: How the World's Biggest Pharmaceutical Companies Are Turning Us All into Patients* (2006), *Big Pharma: Exposing the Global Healthcare Agenda* (2006), *The Truth about Drug Companies: How They Deceive Us and What to Do About It* (2005), and *The Big Fix: How the Pharmaceutical Industry Rips Off American Consumers* (2003).[57]

Prescribing physicians provide a critical link in the drug supply chain, with pharmaceutical companies spending as much as $24 billion to secure the support and cooperation of doctors, according to the Pew Charitable Trusts.[58] In the past year 81,000 pharmaceutical representatives made visits to the nation's 830,000 prescribers to pitch drugs to doctors, buy them meals, and give them such gifts as medical textbooks—while dispensing huge quantities of drug samples that often get passed on to patients at no cost. Drug reps commonly call on doctors in two-to-three week cycles. The behavior of industry representatives was reigned in somewhat in 2009 with rules that free meals for doctors had to be "occasional" and "modest," and that other gifts had to have an educational rationale. But drug samples are an important perk for doctors, who can start patients on medications immediately by dispensing drugs themselves. From the consumer side, the samples provide an instant incentive to try an expensive product. Drug companies also pay doctors to speak about new products at professional meetings, with $220 million paid to physicians in this way last year. Following the 1997 FDA ruling that made drug advertising more widespread, print and online drug ads have become the wunderkind of the advertising world, returning a staggering $2.22–$6.86 for ever dollar spent.[59]

Drug companies often say they need large profits to offset the research and development cost of life-saving medicines, which run as high as $65 billion per year. Last year, 36 new medicines went on the market, including 10 for cancer and 17 for serious but rare diseases. The retail cost of some of these drugs to consumers can be staggering. According to *The Boston Globe*, "Drugs for rare genetic disorders cost $300,000 to $400,000 per year. Therapies for cancer, multiple sclerosis, rheumatoid arthritis, and HIV, which belong to a category called 'specialty medicines,' often cost north of $100,000 per year."[60] These medicines accounted for one-third of spending on drugs in the United States last year, even though they comprised only about 1 percent of all prescriptions. Prescription drug coverage was one of the major advances of the 2013 Affordable Care Act, although it got less press attention. Despite this added layer of support, the typical American household still pays 28 percent of the cost of medicines and other medical care—a big reduction from the 37 percent paid two decades ago, but still a sizeable amount.[61]

Since the vast majority of health complaints are minor, people tend to treat themselves. Thus, the over-the-counter "drug" industry has grown as quickly as the prescription market. Ubiquitous advertising (and scare tactics) feed an anxious culture predisposed to favoring self-repair as the primary way of fixing problems both small and large. Hence the population is perfectly set up for pharmaceutical industry solutions—in real or imaginary terms. Mental health experts have long known that psychosomatic illnesses often are signs of worry, depression, or other factors. Sometimes these are more-or-less imagined physical illnesses; other times they are quite real indeed. The term "somatic symptom disorder" recently entered the most recent iteration of the *Diagnostic and Statistical Manual of Mental Disorders (DSM-5)* to describe bodily aliments linked to something going on in the mind: digestive problems, numbness, paralysis, or even temporary blindness are on the list.[62] Pain is another leading symptom of this kind. New in recent years is the recognition that certain conditions can manifest without an identifiable physical cause. In fact, the new *DSM* even says that in such instances "It is not appropriate to give an individual a mental disorder diagnosis solely because a medical cause cannot be demonstrated."[63]

American attitudes toward drugs need to change for the simple reason that drugs are so ubiquitous in contemporary society. Clearly this is more than a matter of people taking an Advil every now and then. Most of the population takes prescription medications and many require psych meds of some kind. Add to this the millions of Americans who use or abuse unprescribed medicines and alcohol. Old stereotypes about drug dependence and addiction require rethinking at a time when America's "need" for medication is self-evident, even as it is denied. This not to minimize the very real problem of substance abuse. But it is to say that in many ways, America has no clear idea of what its problems really are or how to address them.

Everyone is implicated in America's "drug problem"—from the everyday consumer of prescription medications, to the pharmaceutical industry that pushes real and imagined ills, to the media system that promotes quick fixes to problems, to an economic system that keeps everyone on edge. Throughout this book I've discussed the general sense of "emptiness" that pervades U.S. culture, an absence often twinged with underlying anxiety.[64] In her book, *Crack Wars: Literature, Addiction, Mania*, the theorist Avital Ronell reflected on how contemporary society deals with its worries, often seeking out objects on which to project them.[65] Drugs are easy fear-objects, as are so many popular figures of threat: the terrorist, the mental patient, the illegal immigrant, the welfare mother, the sexual deviant, the homeless person, and so on. But because drugs are both ubiquitous and personal, Ronell suggests that they resonate in people's deepest thoughts about health and happiness, sickness and misery—and have done so, often without acknowledgment, throughout history:

> Drugs resist conceptual arrest. No one has thought to define them in their essence, which is not to say "they" do not exist. On the contrary. Everywhere dispensed, in one form or another, their strength lies in their virtual and fugitive patterns. They do not close forces with an external enemy (the easy way out) but have a secret communications network with the internalized demon. Something is beaming out signals, calling drugs home.[66]

Drugs and addiction go right to the metaphysical heart of American culture.[67] Heidegger wrote about this phenomenon when he said that addictive urges were rooted in the instability of human existence—what he termed the "thrownness" of being.[68] Heidegger asserted the inevitability of a certain degree of anxiety in life—especially in the face of the alienation human subjects experience in the face of the "world" of things different from itself. He wrote that this latent anxiety was a necessary driver of desire, motivation, and, ultimately, the source of freedom itself. One only ever perceives "freedom" in relation to an oppositional force, Heidegger pointed out—explaining that drugs (and other technologies) upset the necessary tension either by obfuscation or control. While this seems to suggest an antidrug attitude, Heidegger's framework, like that of many of the writers discussed in this chapter, suggests something primal to the human culture of drugs and medicine—so primal that it is almost unspeakable. As suggested in the figure of the pharmakon, the enigmatic confluence of remedy/poison can be traced to the very function of language in its awkward articulation of philosophy, especially as inherited from history's archive. Drugs and addiction speak of absence and presence, life and death, past and future—and the elusive craving for something that seems always just beyond reach.

Notes

1 Drew Desilver, "Who's Poor in America? 50 Years into the 'War on Poverty,' a Data Portrait," Pew Research Center (Jan. 13, 2014) http://www.pewresearch.org/fact-tank/2014/01/13/whos-poor-in-america-50-years-into-the-war-on-poverty-a-data-portrait/ (accessed Sept. 3, 2014).
2 "Drug Offenders in the Correctional System," Drugwarfacts.org (2013) http://www.drugwarfacts.org/cms/Prisons_and_Drugs#sthash.N03DRLic.dpbs (accessed Sept. 7, 2014).
3 Timothy Stenovec, "Binge Drinking More Common among Higher Income Households," *Huffington Post* (Jan. 11, 2012) http://www.huffingtonpost.com/2012/01/11/binge-drinking-household-income_n_1200230.html (accessed Sept. 3, 2014).
4 "National Survey on Drug Use and Health," U.S. Substance Abuse and Mental Health Services Administration (2007) http://www.samhsa.gov/data/nsduh/2k7nsduh/2k7results.pdf (accessed Sept. 4, 2014).
5 Roni Caryn Rabin, "A Glut of Antidepressants," *New York Times* (Aug. 12, 2013) http://well.blogs.nytimes.com/2013/08/12/a-glut-of-antidepressants/?_r=0 (accessed Feb. 9, 2015).
6 Jacques Derrida, *Dissemination*, trans. Barbara Johnson (London: Althone, 1981) p. 102.
7 Jacques Derrida and *Autrement*, "The Rhetoric of Drugs. An Interview," *Autrement* (1989) p. 106. www.clas.ufl.edu/users/burt/deconstructionandnewmediatheory/DerridaTheRhetoricofDrugs.doc (accessed Sept. 2, 2014).
8 Ibid.
9 "Addiction," *Oxford Dictionaries* (2014) http://www.oxforddictionaries.com/us/definition/american_english/addiction (accessed Sept. 3, 2014).
10 Janet Farrell Brodie and Marc Redfield, *High Anxieties: Cultural Studies in Addiction* (Berkeley, CA: University of California Press, 2002) p. 4.
11 Brian Roach, "History of Taxation in the United States," *Encyclopedia of Earth* (Nov. 1, 2001) http://www.eoearth.org/view/article/153529/ (accessed Feb. 9, 2015).
12 "Nixon Signs Legislation Banning Cigarette Ads on Radio and TV," *This Day in History* (n.d.) http://www.history.com/this-day-in-history/nixon-signs-legislation-banning-cigarette-ads-on-tv-and-radio (accessed Feb. 9, 2015).
13 "Needle and Syringe Programs," European Monitoring Centre for Drugs and Drug Addiction (EMCDDA) (2010) http://www.emcdda.europa.eu/stats07/HSR (accessed Sept. 2, 2014).
14 Marcus Bachhuber and Colleen Barry, "Of Pot and Percocet," *New York Times* (Aug. 31, 2014) www.nytimes.com/2014/08/31/opinion/sunday/of-pot-and-percocet.html?_r=0 (accessed Sept. 7, 2014).
15 "Marijuana in America: Shifting Attitudes, Events and Laws," Pew Research Center (Apr. 4, 2013) www.people-press.org/2013/04/04/marijuana-timeline/ (accessed Sept. 7, 2014).
16 "The Science of Drug Abuse and Addiction," National Institute on Drug Abuse and Addiction (2014) http://www.drugabuse.gov/publications/media-guide/science-drug-abuse-addiction (accessed Sept. 5, 2014).
17 Darin Weinberg, *Of Others Inside: Insanity, Addiction and Belonging in America* (Philadelphia, PA: Temple University Press, 2005).
18 Morten L. Kringelbach and Kent C. Berridge, "Towards a Functional Neuroanatomy of Pleasure and Happiness," *Trends in Cognitive Science*, 13, no. 11 (2009) pp. 479–487.
19 Robert West, *Models of Addiction* (Lisbon: EMCDDA, 2013) http://www.emcdda.europa.eu/publications/insights/models-addiction (accessed Jan. 23, 2015).

20 *Models of Addiction*, p. 90.
21 Friedrich Nietzsche, *The Gay Science: With a Prelude in Rhythm and an Appendix of Songs*, trans. Walter Kaufman (New York: Vintage, 1974) p. 142.
22 Dennis Schep, *Drugs: Rhetoric of Fantasy, Addiction to Truth* (New York: Atropos, 2011) p. 9.
23 *Drugs*, p. 10.
24 Jacques Derrida, "The Rhetoric of Drugs: An Interview," in Anna Alexander and Mark S. Roberts, *High Culture: Reflections on Addiction and Modernity* (Albany, NY: SUNY Press, 2003) p. 19.
25 Thomas De Quincy, *Confessions of an English Opium-Eater: Being and Extract from the Life of a Scholar* (1821), Project Gutenberg (2005) http://www.gutenberg.org/files/2040/2040-h/2040-h.htm (accessed Sept. 7, 2014) p. 1.
26 *Confessions of an English Opium-Eater*, p. 82.
27 Émile Zola, *L'Assommoir*, trans. Margaret Mauldon (Oxford: Oxford University Press, 1995).
28 Michel Foucault, *The Birth of the Clinic: An Archaeology of Medical Perception* (1973), trans. Alan Sheridan (New York: Vintage, 1994).
29 Nathaniel Rich, "American Dreams, 1953: 'Junky' by William S. Burroughs," *The Daily Beast* (June 23, 2103) http://www.thedailybeast.com/articles/2013/06/27/american-dreams-1953-junky-by-william-s-burroughs.html (accessed Sept. 8, 2014).
30 William S. Burroughs, *Junkie: Confessions of an Unredeemed Drug Addict* (New York: Ace, 1953) p. 43.
31 Aldous Huxley, *The Doors of Perception* (1954) https://www.erowid.org/psychoactives/writings/huxley_doors.shtml (accessed Sept. 10, 2014).
32 "The History of Drug Abuse and Addiction in America and the Origins of Drug Treatment," *Narconon News* (July 15, 2009) http://news.narconon.org/drug-abuse-treatment-origins-america/ (accessed Sept. 9. 2014).
33 Alix Spiegel, "What Vietnam Taught Us about Breaking Bad Habits," *NPR.org* (Jan. 2, 2012) http://www.npr.org/blogs/health/2012/01/02/144431794/what-vietnam-taught-us-about-breaking-bad-habits (accessed Sept. 8, 2014).
34 Jennifer Robinson, "Decades of Drug Use: Data from the '60s and '70s," *Gallup.com* (July 2, 2002) www.gallup.com/poll/6331/decades-drug-use-data-from-60s-70s.aspx (accessed Sept. 8, 2014).
35 Timothy Leary, *Flashbacks: A Personal and Cultural History of an Era* (Los Angeles, CA: Tarcher, 1983) p. 253.
36 Herbert Marcuse, "An Essay on Liberation" (1969) http://www.marxists.org/reference/archive/marcuse/works/1969/essay-liberation.htm#s2 (accessed Sept. 10, 2014).
37 Ibid.
38 Ralph Dumain, "Reactionary Philosophy and Ambiguous Aesthetics in the Revolutionary Politics of Herbert Marcuse: A Review Essay," *Nature, Society, and Thought* 16, no. 2 (2003) pp. 1–9.
39 Jacques Derrida, *Points … Interviews 1974–1994*, trans. Peggy Kampf (Stanford, CA: Stanford University Press, 1995) p. 275.
40 Ken Kesey, *One Flew Over the Cuckoo's Nest* (New York: Penguin, 1963).
41 Tom Wolfe's *The Electric Kool-Aid Acid Test* (New York: Farrar, Straus, and Giroux, 1968). The New Journalism also was practiced in the 1970s by Truman Capote, Joan Didion, Norman Mailer, and Hunter S. Thompson (whose drug-crazed "gonzo journalism" would establish its own notoriety in his 1971 book *Fear and Loathing in Las Vegas: A Savage Journey into the American Dream* (New York: Straight Arrow, 1971)).
42 Jessica Kowal, "Rehab Chic: Is It Helping Anyone?" (2007) http://www.glamour.com/health-fitness/2007/03/celebrites-in-rehab (accessed Sept. 11, 2014).
43 Jessica Reaves, "Just Say No to DARE," *Time Magazine* (Feb. 15, 2001) http://content.time.com/time/nation/article/0,8599,99564,00.html (accessed Sept. 11, 2014).

44 "Alcohol Advertising in Sports on TV," Campaign for Alcohol-Free Sports TV (2003) http://www.cspinet.org/booze/CAFST/QuickFacts.pdf (accessed Sept. 9, 2014).
45 "Answering Questions about Underage Drinking," Federal Trade Commission (2014) http://www.consumer.ftc.gov/articles/0390-answering-questions-about-underage-drinking (accessed Sept. 11, 2014).
46 Kandra Polatis, "Why Moral Ambiguity Is Popular on TV and the Big Screen," *Desert News* (June 9, 2014) http://national.deseretnews.com/article/1640/why-moral-ambiguity-is-popular-on-tv-and-the-big-screen.html (accessed Sept. 12, 2014).
47 Margy Rochlin, "The Family That Frays Together," *New York Times* (Dec. 31, 2010). http://www.nytimes.com/2011/01/02/arts/television/02shameless.html?pagewanted=all&_r=0 (accessed Sept. 12, 2014).
48 "Nearly 7 in 10 Americans Take Prescription Drugs," Mayo Clinic (Jan. 19, 2013) http://www.mayoclinic.org/news2013-rst/7543.html (accessed July 29, 2013); "Alcohol Use," U.S. Centers for Disease Control and Prevention (2014) http://www.cdc.gov/nchs/fastats/alcohol.htm (accessed Aug. 31, 2014).
49 "The 10 Most Prescribed Drugs," WebMD (2011) http://www.webmd.com/news/20110420/the-10-most-prescribed-drugs (accessed Sept. 13, 2014); "U.S. Pharmaceutical Sales—2013" Drugs.com (Feb. 2014) http://www.drugs.com/stats/top100/2013/sales (accessed Sept. 13, 2014).
50 "Total Unaudited and Audited Global Pharmaceutical Market by Region" (2012) *IMS Health* (May 2012) http://www.imshealth.com/deployedfiles/ims/Global/Content/Corporate/Press%20Room/Top-Line%20Market%20Data%20&%20Trends/2011%20Top-line%20Market%20Data/Regional_Pharma_Market_by_Spending_2011-2016.pdf (accessed Sept. 12, 2014).
51 "Nearly 7 in 10 Americans Take Prescription Drugs"; "Alcohol Use."
52 "Fact Sheet: The Use of Over-the-Counter Medicines," http://www.bemedwise.org/press_room/sep_2003_fact_otc.pdf (accessed July 30, 2013); "Through 2010, Spending on Illicit Drugs Held Steady, But Distribution Shifted" (2012) Rand Corporation, http://www.rand.org/pubs/research_reports/RR534.html (accessed Sept. 1, 2014): "Americans Spending More on Alcohol, Drinking Less," *Huffington Post* (Dec. 31, 2012) http://www.huffingtonpost.com/2012/12/31/americans-alcohol_n_2389375.html (accessed Sept. 1, 2014).
53 "Prescription Drug Abuse Remains a Significant Problem in the United States," NIDA (2014) http://www.dsm5.org/Documents/Somatic%20Symptom%20Disorder%20Fact%20Sheet.pdf (accessed Sept. 14, 2014).
54 "Selling Sickness: How Drug Ads Changed Health Care," *NPR.org* (Oct. 13, 2009) http://www.npr.org/templates/story/story.php?storyId=113675737 (accessed Sept. 12, 2014).
55 "Summary Health Statistics for US Adults, National Health Interview Survey, 2011," U.S. Centers for Disease Control and Prevention (Dec. 2012) http://www.cdc.gov/nchs/data/series/sr_10/sr10_256.pdf (accessed July 30, 2013).
56 Ben Goldacre, *Bad Pharma: How Drug Companies Mislead Doctors and Harm Patients* (New York: Faber and Faber, 2013) p. 4.
57 Jacky Law, *Big Pharma: Exposing the Global Healthcare Agenda* (New York: Carrol and Graf, 2006); John Abramson, *The Overdosed American: The Broken Promises of American Medicine* (New York: Harper, 2004); Marcia Angell, *The Truth about Drug Companies: How They Deceive Us and What to Do about It* (New York: Random House, 2005); Ray Moynihan *Selling Sickness: How the World's Biggest Pharmaceutical Companies Are Turning Us All into Patients* (New York: Nation Books, 2006); Katharine Greider, *The Big Fix: How the Pharmaceutical Industry Rips Off American Consumers* (New York: Public Affairs, 2003).
58 "Persuading the Prescribers: Pharmaceutical Industry Marketing and Its Influence on Physicians and Patients," Pew Charitable Trusts (Nov. 11, 2013). http://www.pew

trusts.org/en/research-and-analysis/fact-sheets/2013/11/11/persuading-the-prescribers-pharmaceutical-industry-marketing-and-its-influence-on-physicians-and-patients (accessed Sept. 14, 2014).

59 Ibid.

60 Sylvia Pagan Westphal, "Drug Pricing: A New Prescription," *Boston Globe* (Sept. 14, 2014) http://www.bostonglobe.com/opinion/2014/09/13/drug-pricing-new-prescription/IaZrB2asExUqWY5yZnqciN/story.html (accessed Sept. 14, 2014).

61 "Who Really Pays for Health Care Might Surprise You," *Kaiser Health News* (April 30, 2014) http://www.kaiserhealthnews.org/Stories/2014/April/30/five-misconceptions.aspx (accessed Sept. 14, 2014).

62 "Somatic Symptom Disorder Factsheet," American Psychiatric Association (2014) http://www.dsm5.org/Documents/Somatic%20Symptom%20Disorder%20Fact%20Sheet.pdf (accessed Sept. 14, 2014).

63 Ibid.

64 Gabor Maté, *In the Realm of Hungry Ghosts: Close Encounters with Addiction* (Berkeley, CA: North Atlantic Books, 2010) p. 272.

65 Avital Ronell, *Crack Wars: Literature, Addiction, Mania* (Urbana and Chicago: University of Illinois Press, 2004).

66 *Crack Wars*, p. 51.

67 *Crack Wars*, p. 13.

68 Martin Heidegger, *Being and Time* (1953), trans. Joan Stambaugh (Albany, NY: SUNY Press, 2010).

12

THE ONE AND THE MANY

The Ethics of Uncertainty

It's not always easy living up to one's ideals, either personally or as a nation. Americans like to think of the United States as a welcoming place where everyone has equal chance. But historical baggage and anxious times can make such generosity difficult. As the new millennium began, the U.S. was decades into a postindustrial, postcolonial, postmodern, post-American phase. Uncertain about its relatively shallow past, the nation has become increasingly vulnerable to a sound-bite culture of quick fixes, instant gratification, and fleeting attention—manifest most dramatically in the short-term profit-seeking that threw the world into recession. Pervasive historical amnesia creates a vacuum space in which old ways become contested, only to have their underlying structures replicated in new form. As America lumbers into the future, there is little coherent vision of what *after* it is moving toward. As any good post-theorist will tell you, this presents both a problem and an opportunity.

This final chapter of *Elsewhere in America* discusses the country's utopian aspirations and its difficulties in reaching them. The country's persistent faith in forward momentum and upward mobility frequently are frustrated with the recognition that history sometimes moves sideways and backwards, or doesn't move at all. In what follows, attention will turn to what can be done to overcome some of what seems to pit citizen against citizen and the country itself against the rest of the world. The point of this chapter is not so much to name "solutions" as it is to discuss America's crisis of belonging as a set of open questions. This is not as simple as it sounds, given the challenge of remaining receptive to new ways of seeing things in the face of familiar answers and "common sense" remedies. While certain types of questions respond to rational analysis, others might call for a leap of faith. And of course solving any problem for an "unknown" can leave one in a temporary state of uncertainty or frustration. This is where ethical sensibilities can come into play, especially in instances where one might need help in the search for answers. In such cases, working with one another can be vitally important, especially in the struggle of anticipating the future.

Be Here Now

Of course time travel is never innocent, as it so frequently is laden with projection and ideology. In popular discourse, futures lean heavily on coming generations as legatees of the now. Conservatives are especially fond of pandering to parental concerns about "the children," although liberals use such terminology as well. These days the U.S. worries about the future as never before. Current polling data show that seven in ten Americans, spanning all generations, say that young adults face more economic challenges than their elders did.[1] This raises the question of how possible it is to engage the "utopian imagination" without succumbing to the current juncture. Difficult moments have a tendency to pull people backward and forward between nostalgia and speculation—with both always value-laden reflections of the moment from which they are viewed. This is one of the reasons that this book has consistently sought to compare discussions of the past with their present interpretations, even as those views continue to shift. The same principle applies to talking about any *after*—and it may well explain why the futures depicted in so much popular media today seem based on disillusionment with the present. Or maybe it's simply that today's audiences are sick of happy endings.

So what about a utopian America? Fredric Jameson has noted that while utopias don't always appear achievable, they retain a certain pedagogical value.[2] In one way or another writers and philosophers throughout history, beginning well before Thomas More's *Utopia*, have described idealized states of existence or speculative imaginary worlds. This repetition gives evidence of the persistence of the idea. Utopian visions have taken many names: the Garden of Eden, Atlantis, Erewhon, Neverland, Shangri-La, Tao Hua Yuan, and Walden. It all boils down to the search for a better place. Some even say that utopia is an instinctual desire—a primal yearning for comfort, safety, and security. This may explain why so many religious traditions describe a perfect afterlife. But what about the idea of utopia in everyday experience? Is it possible to encourage utopian thinking in the here and now?

This was the spirit in which Ernst Bloch approached utopia in his classic work *The Principle of Hope*.[3] Bloch fully recognized that wishful thinking historically often had served to weaken revolutionary impulses. He also spoke at length about the temporary fix that a cheerful consumer culture can offer. But Bloch also described what he termed a "not yet consciousness" underlying all of this, beneath both the current moment and what has come before. Such longings for a state of "something else" inform many subtexts in philosophy, psychology, politics, scientific exploration, consumerism, media, and even schooling—all with legitimacy. Utopian consciousness is a truly interdisciplinary concept—and obviously tricky.

These days utopia commonly finds expression in speculative stories about future worlds. As a literary genre, science fiction can be dated back to 19th-century writings like Jules Verne's *From Earth to the Moon* (1865) and H.G. Wells's *The Time Machine* (1895).[4] Visions of unknown or futuristic worlds have now become a staple of popular entertainment, often dramatizing the negative effects of uncontrolled human enterprise. But the dystopian flip side of the utopian impulse was apparent even in More's famous 1516 book.[5] Conceived with full knowledge of the then-recent discovery of America, *Utopia* contrasted the European society of the day with what More imagined the "new world" might be. More detailed the poverty, extreme wealth, and aristocratic class divisions he saw around him—and thus envisioned an opposite universe, a "utopia," suggesting ideas that would take form in socialism centuries later. In More's words, "The only path to the welfare of the public is the equal allocation of goods; and I doubt whether such equality can be maintained where every individual has his own property."[6] More imagined a utopia in which "private property is utterly abolished" and citizens "contribute more to the common good than to themselves."[7]

When communism and socialism finally did appear in the 1800s and 1900s, they ended up giving utopia a bad name. At a national level people seemed willing to share—but only so much. Aggravated by disparate population needs and heavy pressure (not to mention covert subversion) from capitalist countries like the U.S., collective governments began to crumble. Many accounts date the collapse of European communism to 1989, with the fall of regimes in Poland, Hungary, East Germany, Bulgaria, Czechoslovakia, and Romania. Before long the world would be celebrating the "triumph of democracy" around the globe, even as inequities widened within purportedly free societies. Owing to widening gaps between rich and poor, America's free market ideals eventually fell into doubt. As its own utopian brand, U.S. capitalism had always made big promises to those equipped to play the game: the Protestant work ethic, the American dream, and all variety of Darwinian success stories. But the capitalistic game always favored insiders. And no amount of legislation, social engineering, or moral argument could alter the axiom that a system producing winners must also produce losers.

Given utopia's disappointing history, inversions of the idea now seem more on people's minds—especially in popular media. Distrust of government and institutions of all kinds now runs at an all-time high—driving the box office successes of hugely successful offerings like *The Hunger Games* (2012–present) and *Divergent* (2014–present) franchises. The genre first emerged from obscurity during the Cold War years, when nationalistic anxieties over communism and nuclear attack drew audiences to movies about alien invasion and global destruction in films like *Invasion of the Body Snatchers* (1956) and *On the Beach* (1959). Today's post-apocalypse craze was probably born in 1979 with *Mad Max*, casting Mel Gibson as a revenge-driven, motorcycle-riding, dystopian hero in an ecologically devastated Australia of the future. Soon to follow were dozens of films like *Blade Runner* (1982), *Waterworld* (1995), and *The Postman* (1997), to name but a few. Many of the most potent post-apocalypse films combined critiques of technology and capitalism run amok, most famously in the *Terminator* franchise (1984–present) and in films like *Avatar* (2009) by James Cameron. And it goes without saying that TV was supplying plenty of science fiction dystopia in such long-running series as *Doctor Who* (1963–1989), *Star Trek* (1966–1999), *Babylon 5* (1994–1998), *Farscape* (1999–2003), *Battlestar Galactica* (2004–2009), *Stargate* (2004–2011), *Revolution* (2012–2014) *Continuum* (2012–present), and *Nikita* (2013–present).

Could there be something more to this nihilistic fare? Might these stories speak to a deeper yearning in contemporary culture? It's not exactly a secret that a generalized despair lurks in the public mind of the Western world, especially in contemporary America. For decades the U.S. population lived through military misadventures, lackluster political leadership, revelations of corporate corruption, as well as a recent economic crisis triggered by greed and incompetence. Powerlessness and alienation have become palpable in a society smothered by a creeping authoritarianism, which seems to tell citizens that their only means of expression or choice lies in buying things.[8] What kind of worldview could this produce? Certainly for many people, "politics" has become simply another set of *Daily Show* gag lines that may (or may not) affect their actual lives. The philosopher Alain Badiou speaks of the public's widening disappointment with politics as represented in the media, which is the main way most citizens are made conscious of their political world. In Badiou's thinking, possibilities exist for finding new "political truths" beyond the confines of public opinion or consensus—in what he terms a "metapolitics."[9] But this metapolitics lies dormant and rarely addressed—waiting to be awakened.

In some reckoning, this free-floating disaffection might seem like a form of groundless ambivalence and uncertainty. But one can also view in this distancing a certain capacity for critical reasoning, a resistance to quick answers or convenient solutions to problems. Most Americans have long come to believe that life is complicated, truth is fleeting, and that much of what appears in the world of images isn't genuine. In other words, postmodern consciousness has gone mainstream. So where does this leave things? Maybe the time is ripe for a touch of utopian thinking. More than one contemporary philosopher has grappled with this possibility. In his book, *Cruising Utopia*, José Esteban Muñoz drew on work by dozens of recent writers and artists such as Giorgio Agamben, Judith Butler, Samuel Delaney, Lisa Duggan, LeRoi Jones, Yvonne Rainer, Jack Smith, and Andy Warhol in calling for a radical consciousness. In different ways, Muñoz saw these thinkers describing an ongoing struggle with dissatisfaction and discomfort—and an urge to find a way out of it. He famously wrote: "We must strive, in the face of the here and now's totalizing rendering of reality, to think and feel a *then and there*."[10] This is undoubtedly a multidimensional conversation—and an often-frustrating one at that—since many of those speaking would say that the conversation can never truly end.

Possession and Dispossession

Self-reliant, self-made, self-taught, self-service, self-help. From the time they are born, most Americans begin learning to regard their own personhood as the most prized of possessions. This takes a toll on broad-based understandings of relationality and mutual dependence. Attitudes toward belonging may change over time and circumstance, but a certain implication of ownership often remains operative. In social terms, belonging is to both give attention and receive it from a collectivity. While belonging may have a primal basis, the idea has a special relevance to American thought as a matter of individual "choice" and freedom. Notions of citizenship and patriotism connect to principles of personal autonomy in which an actively owned self is willingly given over to the nation. And recent "take back my country" rhetoric has clearly shown that certain groups feel the nation belongs to them. Even as active belonging attaches to free will, involuntary belonging happens all the time in the social construction of identities, often with rules and limitations attached. Some born in America may not see themselves as citizens, but they "belong" to the nation by default—as they are counted, governed, and taxed.

Principles of self-possession run deep in the national psyche, often creating a double bind when it comes to belonging. In the grand tradition of "American values," most people would conjure freedom and equality as utopian ideals. Both of these values derive from Enlightenment beliefs in the sovereignty of the individual. Seventeenth-century philosopher John Locke often receives credit for codifying these principles in formulating the notion of the subject unbound from the tyranny of authority or other people.[11] The purportedly "natural" ideals of freedom and equality were appealing antidotes to monarchical traditions, but they failed to account for the complexities of human difference and the mind. For example, further consideration of freedom reveals two valences: one negative (the absence of interference), and the other positive (the presence of unbridled possibility). Both kinds of freedom have a familiar feel, except (of course) in the relinquishment of little freedom to live with others. Many Americans have difficulty seeing the inseparability—or simultaneity—of freedom's two sides. One exists in any organized society as both a ruler and one who is ruled—but this dialectic creates a certain cognitive dissonance, especially in two-party political discourse.

The idea of equality has its own conceptual difficulties. Even taken at face value, the achievement of "equality" rarely happens without effort (or a fight). Besides these logical contradictions, equality often gets sidetracked into a presumed equivalence among people. The quaint 18th-century idea that all (men) were created equal presumed an unstratified society in which no one was born into advantage or disadvantage. But the great American experiment in democratic capitalism would soon reveal just how quickly opportunity ends up unevenly distributed. This is one reason the term "equity" (fairness) now is used to describe strategies for leveling the playing field—in recognition of the ways that the pathway to equality isn't the same for everyone.

If classical views of freedom and equality hinge on the idea of the individual as "owner" of the self, what happens when a person's "self" is simply ignored or eliminated from view? This kind of effacement informs the contemporary concept of "dispossession," in which personhood (recognition, rights) and material (property, benefits, etc.) no longer accrue to someone. Political theorists now speak of dispossession as a way of describing the netherworld created in the current neoliberal moment, which deprives certain populations of citizenship, livelihood, property, and of course land itself. If freedom and equality imply a reciprocal relationship to possession (citizens belong to a nation that belongs to them), the reverse can be said of dispossession. The person doesn't disappear in dispossession, but the relationship is mediated, deferred, or severed. This creates a situation in which certain objects retain a presence (the commodity, the institution, the government, etc.) but the human subject is rendered irrelevant.

Dispossession precludes the existence of civic belonging through which the very idea of equality can be considered. Take voting as one obvious example. Women and certain minorities not only lacked access to ballots for many years; their dispossession from the electoral process rendered them outside processes that would bestow this privilege. In this sense, questions of freedom and equality can't really apply to subjects not recognized as existing in the first place. Behind such grand ideals are forces that precede and exceed the very thing people think of as the self. Put another way, it is impossible to conceive of freedom or equality without giving up the idea of the "self" as the source of knowledge or understanding.[12]

This is more than a matter of economic disparity. Gender, age, race, health status, sexuality, locality, and educational opportunity are but some of the factors that place some people ahead of others. Regulations and policies make surface corrections, and give democracy its "liberal" inflection. But critics of neoliberalism point out that this invariably turns out to be a cat-and-mouse game. Every time one inequity seems fixed, another one pops up. And of course most attempts at correction are fraught with argument. This is one reason why efforts at change always result in partial measures.

Possession and dispossession can wreak havoc on the delicate tension between individual and community—a dynamic built into America from the start, premised on a certain reciprocity between competitive and cooperative impulses. Earlier in this book, I discussed Adam Smith's often-misconstrued notions of society. Like many of his contemporaries, Smith recognized the interplay of personal and collective interests, with each supporting and balancing out the other. This was the true meaning of the famous "invisible hand" principle.[13] Smith didn't exactly come up with this idea himself. The premise can be traced back as far as Socrates—in the idea that "self-care" (in the form of personal interest and deep knowledge) is the bedrock of any society. It's no small irony that American business would soon override Smith's idealistic interpretation of self-care. But remember that Smith was writing well before industrialism would change the game of capitalism, as Marx so cogently discussed—turning the free enterprise system into a technology with an expansive life of its own.

Things seem to worsen in times of threat or hardship (real or imagined), as both the nation and its citizens exhibit a troubling tendency to turn inward rather than to each other. This takes a toll on belonging in both general and specific terms. Whether acknowledged or not, anxiety factors heavily in national identity—with distress about scarcity, decline, and harm most commonly seen. Some of America's worries link to deeply entrenched habits of opposition, broadly writ, which externalize objects to be confronted or accommodated. In most citizenship debates, the idea of "nation" remains imperative as a marker of inside/outside, manifest in terms like "homeland" and "alien"—although this fundamental principle can be extended to other ways that alterity is named. The nation's fierce attachment to competition in daily life only makes matters worse. In foreign relations, this externalization plays out in U.S. State Department calculations of how other nations help or hinder America's "national interests." In either instance, this reductive view of human affairs doesn't work very well. For one thing, relationships often precede and exceed one's awareness of them. This means that relationality is but partially accessible to the conscious self.

In stressful times people often look for ways to explain their discomfort. Media sensationalists and opportunistic politicians often are quick to find someone to blame. Julia Kristeva took on the figure of the "stranger" in challenging beliefs that the only modern, acceptable, and clear definition of the foreigner is the one who does not "belong" to the state in which citizenship is bestowed. In *Nations without Nationalism*, Kristeva explored the particular ways that notions of home attach themselves to exclusionary practices that nationalize the members of given societies.[14] Why do so many people cling to autochthonic myths of origins in conceiving nationalistic belonging and non-belonging? Is it possible to be together in different ways? Evoking Freud, Kristeva proposed that "foreignness" is something that resides in the elementary constitution of human consciousness—in "uncanny" depths one can never fully grasp. In this sense, it is no surprise that many fearfully deny, repress, or otherwise seek to expunge the strangers within themselves. The alien being is not merely someone seen on the street. The alien lives inside the human subject. As Kristeva puts it, "We know that we are foreigners to ourselves, and it is with the help of that sole support that we can attempt to live with others."[15]

The One and the Many

Concerns about a "divided" America have been rising for decades, along with worries about political polarization and resentment within the public at large.

Certainly none of this augurs well for the sort of nondialectical thinking just discussed. Oppositionality seems more on people's minds. Researchers and theorists during the 20th century began to take a hard look at this issue, and especially the role of mass communications in shaping public opinion and its underlying ideologies. From initial studies of product advertising, such scholarship would soon consider the relationships among representation, subjectivity, and group identities. As movies and radio grew in the early 1900s, their effects on audiences were at first charted in systematic terms, as the new "science of signs" (semiotics) began setting forth broad principles about the structures of language. The effectiveness of political propaganda seemed to further confirm the seemingly irresistible power of media, in processes famously described and critiqued by Marxist scholars of the Austrian Frankfurt School from the 1920s through the 1940s.

Further scholarship in the decades following World War II began to raise doubts about such universalizing views, however. A rising recognition of cultural diversity was one contributing factor. And with this came the recognition that audiences "decode" messages and use them in quite varied ways. Communication theorists soon recognized that information was not simply "transmitted" or directly "reproduced" in the receiving subject. Instead, a kind of mental conversation took place between sender and receiver in which interpretation always played a role. The 1960s and 1970s saw the development of even more nuanced theories of reception, which took into consideration such factors as context, time, prior knowledge, and state of mind. Later this would be further developed in postmodern assertions about the relative character of knowledge and the frequent instability of meaning itself.

All of this has implications for belonging, especially if one thinks about communication as a reciprocal "dialogue" rather than a one-directional process. Degrees of sentient activity reside in all parties of an informational exchange. And a space of instability always remains between them. Putting this another way, Jean-Luc Nancy observed in his book, *Being Singular Plural*, that "There is no meaning if meaning is not shared, and not because there would be an alternate or first signification that all beings must have in common, but because *meaning is itself the sharing of Being*."[16] Here Nancy is making two important points: first, that people communicate through certain shared signifying practices; and second, that these ways of making meaning are not identical to each other. Decades of deconstruction and reception theory have shown that a vital element in the idea of difference-in-language lies in the infinite variability of encoding and decoding. But even so, relationships to language remain shared even if usage and contents are not the same. To some this might seem a sort of paradox, since intelligibility presumably resides in common understandings. But to a post-structuralist like Nancy, rock-solid denotations are mostly the stuff of fantasy. Rather than assuming a coherent catalogue of signs, one does better to focus on the process of negotiating meaning. "Everything, then, passes between us," Nancy explains:

> This "between," as its name implies, has neither a consistency nor continuity of its own. It does not lead from one to the other; it constitutes no connective tissue, no cement, no bridge ... It is neither connected nor unconnected; it falls short of both; even better, it is that which is at the heart of a connection, the inter*lacing* [l'entre*croisment*] of strands whose extremities remain separate even at the very center of the knot.[17]

This inflects on belonging by accenting tensions between presumably commonly understood words (like "democracy," "freedom," and "equality") and differing ways they play out. Time and again, notions of universal meaning are evoked in the name of shared sovereignty, even as they obscure partisan interests or the workings of power. This is how selected signifying practices of inclusion create the kinds of exclusion described above.

Extending the idea of the mutual construction of meaning between people, Bernard Stiegler recently adopted the term "transindividuation," (a neologism coined in the 1960s by philosopher Gilbert Simondon). Transindividuation reverses the notion of a "self" that defines an individual, instead casting subjectivity as an "effect" of individuation. As such, Stiegler describes a plural quality of the self that always generates both a solitary and collective subject. As he puts it, "the individuation of the psyche is always already an individuation of a group of psyches, because the psyche is never alone. It always operates in relation to another psyche."[18] This is more than a matter of communication or meaning, inasmuch as the "I" and the "we" are constantly formed and transformed by each other. Stiegler's use of the word "psyche" in describing this intersubjectivity is hardly incidental, since he sees the process extending beyond conscious thought into the field of desire. Hence, transindividuation is heavily implicated in active and passive processes, including political ideology, consumer culture, education, and even in efforts for social change. The very openness of the concept enables transindividuation to project simultaneous negative and positive valences, making it yet another form of the pharmakon.[19]

Let's put this concept to work on this issue of neoliberal capitalism. On the one hand, Stiegler sees ownership and production churning out a seemingly endless array of goods—driven, to put it bluntly, by insatiable greed. In supply-and-demand terms this production is met by the hunger of consumers, driven by libidinous desires for objects of possession. As noted earlier, this process is relatively transparent when one thinks of the way advertising works to substitute products like telephone rate plans, for example, for more deeply held things people want like "Friends and Family." Hence, "The *American way of life* invented the figure of the consumer whose libido is systematically put to work to counter the problems of excess production," Stiegler states.[20] Unfortunately there is a problem with this relationship, inasmuch as libidinous consumer drives are but momentarily satisfied by purchases. While this insatiability may feed an addictive hunger for products, it also reveals an excess of desire.

Today one sees this excess manifest in countless expressions of dissatisfaction, alternative culture, and outright activism—many of which are enabled by electronic networks and emerging social movements. In this a dynamic tension becomes manifest in the push and pull between "pluralist" and "unitarian" impulses.[21] While radical pluralism may be a noble ideal, it rarely manifests itself in any society, much less in neoliberal democracies. The task ahead seems to keep the field as open as possible for new forms of alliance, especially as the political system increasingly gets driven by big money. There exists a relationality between pluralism and unitarianism—as minoritized individuals and groups systematically contest the overpowering impulses of majorities. This is a major point of contention in contemporary American politics, given the consolidation of power in the hands of major parties, billionaire contributors, not to mention the collusion of corporate interests and the state. And the obvious question that arises is just how effective minority contestation can be. After all, the seemingly monolithic hold of majorities is subject to fluctuation—as periodic spaces of vulnerably open themselves to intervention, especially in times of crisis. Just as these openings can permit more aggressive forms of control, such ruptures also provide opportunities for intervention.[22]

Insurgent populism has a powerful potential that only occasionally is mobilized—but waits in the background as an untapped revolutionary force. Here again, one might see the enormous support for the OWS "We are the 99%" movement as a case in point, emerging as it did from the depths of the economic recession of the early 2000s. This is very much in keeping with the notions of "radical democracy" discussed earlier in this book as a theoretical model for integrating difference theory into contemporary politics. Most proponents of radical democracy see its implementation beginning at the grassroots level of day-to-day encounters. But keep in mind that OWS sputtered and collapsed rather quickly. More common than such direct activism is the anti-politics of alienation and nihilism, manifest in withdrawal from organized politics altogether. The trick is to turn this around somehow in the field of transindividuation.

How does this process get started? Where does agency reside in a land in which choice is defied by "one-click" shopping? Lots of factors influence political subjectivity. But in general terms, motivation usually gets traction from the frictions of power. Aristotle identified a balancing act in defining the citizen as caught between "the fact of ruling and the fact of being."[23] Simply put, this contradictory position puts each individual in a perpetual spot of instability—in a fluctuating field of struggle and possibility. On the one hand, struggle percolates in the gap between absolute freedom and total control. Possibility emerges from the capacity to simultaneously to guide and participate in a collectivity. This means seeing oneself always inside and outside these relationships, and in the same way, all such dualisms. The challenge lies in recognizing the simultaneity of freedom and control in negotiating the world.

Put another way, agency manifests from particular forms of knowledge about the world and its workings. At one level, this can manifest simply as a matter of pragmatics or an awareness of the way the political apparatus operates to satisfy rational ends. But beneath such instrumentality lies what might be described as ethics—or, the ideals that drive the project. What does one "care" about enough to take action? This needn't necessarily be an ethics based on the prescriptive rationality of gains and losses, or even the morality of "right" and "wrong." A growing number of contemporary theorists describe a form of ethics unbound by such partisan distinctions, even when they are knowable or discernable. This isn't so much a search for a particular "truth" or morality as it is a commitment to the search for such things. This Socratic form of ethics emerges from a sense of self-care as a form of self-knowledge—but one that can negotiate dialectical orthodoxies. In this sense, care of the self and care of others become fused. This means finding the courage to resist the seductions of certainties that divide people.

It's easier said than done. One often feels an internal struggle in unlearning familiar patterns—that is, in questioning what might feel like instinct. It's hard sometimes to recognize that the presumed rationality of readily visible answers can lead one astray, and that the old reliable self may not have all the answers. What is needed might not always be apparent, but instead requires a determined approach—perhaps even a seemingly impossible way of thinking. Finding this different path involves paying attention to alternative or devalued views—including an embrace of failure itself as an opportunity for insight. Finding the way blocked may be a frustrating experience, but it also opens new fields of engagement—both to that "other" entity and to the self. Rather than clinging to the tragic "stand-your-ground" posture that features so much in today's news, an encounter with resistance can be a cause for examining the ground itself. More than a matter of empathy or compromise, this is a willingness to become open to the unseen, unrecognized, or unknown. It entails an ethics in which the known self becomes mutable in relationship to another being. In contrast to the self that is owned and guarded, such a subject emanates capacities of shared meanings and actions. Admittedly, this isn't easy in a culture so predicated on certainty and competition at every turn. But ethics call out for such risks to be taken in the spirit of courage and generosity. Judith Butler put the matter this way:

> Ethics requires us to risk ourselves precisely at moments of unknowingness, when what forms us diverges from what lies before us, when our willingness to become undone in relation to others constitutes our chance of becoming human. To be undone by another is a primary necessity, an anguish, to be sure, but also a chance—to be addressed, claimed, bound to what is not me, but also to be moved, to be prompted to act, to address myself elsewhere, and so to vacate the self-sufficient 'I' as a kind of possession.[24]

Americans and people around the world are hungering for a new kind of belonging. This calls for new forms of affinity of the kind I have discussed in this book. Traditional political party structures hand power back and forth, as government and business maintain business as usual. Fantasies of a radical revolution or the undoing of neoliberalism are no longer sufficient. Something more fundamental and subtle is required. Forms of care are needed that restore new forms of belonging. A renewed democratic consciousness is needed to satisfy the desire for "something else" lingering in the minds of so many. How does this consciousness manifest itself? How is this yearning for a better future satisfied? Clearly, certain causes merit attention—arguments for transparent governance, the end of war, or the emancipation of the disenfranchised, for example. These are necessary and worthy causes. But underlying them there should also be a general grasp of the larger "metapolitics"—otherwise one worthy purpose can blind one to others. Important early feminist movements for a time failed to address race. And contemporary campaigns to stem global food emergencies can overlook the poverty a few blocks away.

Sometimes it's helpful to take a step back to see the entire picture. Across America inequities and injustices abound in everyday life. The answer resides less in a partisan program than in a frame of mind. The oppositional politics that runs society—mainstream electoral contests that repackage worn-out ideas—isn't going to change things very much. While it remains tempting to blame capitalism or xenophobia, these alone are not the source of what augers against belonging in America. Utopian futures emerge from utopian minds. Hence, change resides not in the toppling of any given regime, but in the recognition of possible subjectivities that exceed the limits of existing belonging. *Elsewhere in America* began with a discussion of this nation as an unfinished project. While such efforts are often advanced through design and planning, sometimes life's most vexing challenges present themselves without a roadmap. Even though the past can be useful in an experiential sense, there are instances that call for learning by doing. It's no secret that this can be a difficult process. Perhaps the best argument for "belonging in America" is that no one is alone on the journey to elsewhere.

Notes

1 "Millennials in Adulthood," Pew Research Center (March 7, 2014) http://www.pewsocialtrends.org/2014/03/07/millennials-in-adulthood/ (accessed Sept. 21, 2014).
2 Fredric Jameson, *Archaeologies of the Future: The Desire Called Utopia and Other Science Fictions* (London and New York: Verso, 2005).
3 Ernst Bloch, *The Principle of Hope*, trans. Neville Plaice, Stephen Plaice, and Paul Knight (Cambridge, MA: MIT Press, 1986).
4 Jules Verne, *From Earth to the Moon* (1865) (New York: Bantam Classics, 1993); H.G. Wells, *The Time Machine* (1895) (New York: Buccaneer, 1996).
5 Thomas More, "Utopia/1516," in Richard Noble, ed., *Utopias* (Cambridge, MA: MIT Press, 2009) p. 22.
6 Ibid.

7 Ibid.
8 Giorgio Agamben, *Homo Sacer: Sovereign Power and Bare Life*, trans. Daniel Heller-Roazen (Stanford, CA: Stanford University Press, 1998); Henry Giroux, *Against the New Authoritarianism: Politics after Abu Ghraib* (New York: Arbeiter Ring, 2005).
9 Alain Badiou, *Metapolitics*, trans. Jason Baker (London and New York: Verso, 2005).
10 José Esteban Muñoz, *Cruising Utopia: The Then and There of Queer Futurity* (New York and London: New York University Press, 2009) p. 1.
11 John Locke, *Two Treatises of Government* (1689) (Cambridge and New York: Cambridge University Press, 1988).
12 Judith Butler and Athena Athanasiou, *Dispossession: The Performative in the Political* (Cambridge: Polity, 2013) p. 4.
13 Adam Smith, *The Wealth of Nations* (1776) (New York: Penguin Books, 1982) p. 456.
14 Julia Kristeva, *Nations without Nationalism* (New York: Columbia University Press, 1993).
15 Julia Kristeva, *Strangers to Ourselves* (New York: Columbia University Press, 1991) p. 170.
16 Jean-Luc Nancy, *Being Singular Plural* (Stanford, CA: Stanford University Press, 2000) p. 2.
17 *Being Singular Plural*, p. 5.
18 Bernard Stiegler and Irit Rogoff, "Transindividuation" *e-flux journal* 14 (Feb. 2006) http://www.e-flux.com/journal/transindividuation/ (accessed Oct. 15, 2015).
19 Bernard Stiegler, *What Makes Life Worth Living: On Pharmacology* (Malden, MA: Polity, 2010) p. 18.
20 Bernard Stiegler, "Care within the Limits of Capitalism, Economizing Means Taking Care," in Tom Cohen, ed., *Telemorphosis: Theory in the Era of Climate Change*, Vol. 1. (Ann Arbor, MI: MPublishing, 2012) p. 110.
21 William E. Connolly, *Pluralism* (Durham, NC: Duke University Press, 2005).
22 Naomi Klein, *The Shock Doctrine: The Rise of Disaster Capitalism* (New York: Picador, 2008).
23 Jacques Rancière, "Ten Theses on Politics," *Theory and Event*, 5, no. 3 (2001). http://muse.jhu.edu. (accessed Aug. 10, 2014).
24 Judith Butler, *Giving an Account of Oneself* (New York: Fordham, 2005) p. 88.

INDEX